THE CAMBRIDGE COMPANION TO
GADAMER

Each volume of this series of companions to major philosophers contains specially commissioned essays by an international team of scholars, together with a substantial bibliography, and will serve as a reference work for students and nonspecialists. One aim of the series is to dispel the intimidation such readers often feel when faced with the work of a difficult and challenging thinker.

Hans-Georg Gadamer (b. 1900) is widely recognized as the leading exponent of philosophical hermeneutics. His work has exerted a profound impact on contemporary philosophical and theological discourse and has shaped new modes of interpretation in the social sciences. The essays in this collection examine Gadamer's biography, the core of hermeneutical theory, and the significance of his work for ethics, aesthetics, the social sciences, and theology. There is full consideration of Gadamer's appropriation of Hegel, Heidegger, and the Greeks, as well as his relation to modernity, critical theory, and poststructuralism.

New readers will find this the most convenient and accessible guide to Gadamer currently available. Advanced students and specialists will find a conspectus of recent developments in the interpretation of Gadamer.

CAMBRIDGE COMPANIONS TO PHILOSOPHY:

AQUINAS *Edited by* NORMAN KRETZMANN *and*
ELEONORE STUMP
HANNAH ARENDT *Edited by* DANA VILLA
ARISTOTLE *Edited by* JONATHAN BARNES
AUGUSTINE *Edited by* ELEONORE STUMP *and*
NORMAN KRETZMANN
BACON *Edited by* MARKKU PELTONEN
DESCARTES *Edited by* JOHN COTTINGHAM
EARLY GREEK PHILOSOPHY *Edited by* A. A. LONG
FEMINISM IN PHILOSOPHY *Edited by*
MIRANDA FRICKER *and* JENNIFER HORNSBY
FOUCAULT *Edited by* GARY GUTTING
FREUD *Edited by* JEROME NEU
GALILEO *Edited by* PETER MACHAMER
GERMAN IDEALISM *Edited by* KARL AMERIKS
HABERMAS *Edited by* STEPHEN K. WHITE
HEGEL *Edited by* FREDERICK BEISER
HEIDEGGER *Edited by* CHARLES GUIGNON
HOBBES *Edited by* TOM SORELL
HUME *Edited by* DAVID FATE NORTON
HUSSERL *Edited by* BARRY SMITH *and*
DAVID WOODRUFF SMITH
WILLIAM JAMES *Edited by* RUTH ANNA PUTNAM
KANT *Edited by* PAUL GUYER
KIERKEGAARD *Edited by* ALASTAIR HANNAY *and*
GORDON MARINO
LEIBNIZ *Edited by* NICHOLAS JOLLEY
LOCKE *Edited by* VERE CHAPPELL
MALEBRANCHE *Edited by* STEPHEN NADLER
MARX *Edited by* TERRELL CARVER
MILL *Edited by* JOHN SKORUPSKI
NIETZSCHE *Edited by* BERND MAGNUS *and*
KATHLEEN HIGGINS
OCKHAM *Edited by* PAUL VINCENT SPADE
PLATO *Edited by* RICHARD KRAUT
PLOTINUS *Edited by* LLOYD P. GERSON
ROUSSEAU *Edited by* PATRICK RILEY
SARTRE *Edited by* CHRISTINA HOWELLS
SCHOPENHAUER *Edited by* CHRISTOPHER JANAWAY
SPINOZA *Edited by* DON GARRETT
WITTGENSTEIN *Edited by* HANS SLUGA *and*
DAVID STERN

The Cambridge Companion to
GADAMER

Edited by

Robert J. Dostal
Bryn Mawr College

CAMBRIDGE
UNIVERSITY PRESS

PUBLISHED BY THE PRESS SYNDICATE OF THE UNIVERSITY OF CAMBRIDGE
The Pitt Building, Trumpington Street, Cambridge, United Kingdom

CAMBRIDGE UNIVERSITY PRESS
The Edinburgh Building, Cambridge CB2 2RU, UK
40 West 20th Street, New York, NY 10011-4211, USA
477 Williamstown Road, Port Melbourne, VIC 3207, Australia
Ruiz de Alarcón 13, 28014 Madrid, Spain
Dock House, The Waterfront, Cape Town 8001, South Africa

http://www.cambridge.org

First published 2002

Printed in the United States of America

Typeface 10/13 Trump Medieval   *System* LaTeX 2$_\varepsilon$ [TB]

A catalog record for this book is available from the British Library.

Library of Congress Cataloging in Publication Data
The Cambridge companion to Gadamer / edited by Robert J. Dostal.
     p.   cm. – (Cambridge companions to philosophy)
     Includes bibliographical references and index.
     ISBN 0-521-80193-1 – ISBN 0-521-00041-6 (pbk.)
     1. Gadamer, Hans Georg, 1900–   I. Dostal, Robert J.   II. Series.
   B3248.G34 C35   2002   2001037367

ISBN 0 521 80193 1 hardback
ISBN 0 521 00041 6 paperback

CONTENTS

List of Contributors   *page* ix

Abbreviations   xiii

Introduction
ROBERT J. DOSTAL   I

1   Gadamer: The Man and His Work
    ROBERT J. DOSTAL   13

2   Gadamer's Basic Understanding
    of Understanding
    JEAN GRONDIN   36

3   Getting it Right: Relativism, Realism, and Truth
    BRICE WACHTERHAUSER   52

4   Hermeneutics, Ethics, and Politics
    GEORGIA WARNKE   79

5   The Doing of the Thing Itself: Gadamer's
    Hermeneutic Ontology of Language
    GÜNTER FIGAL   102

6   Gadamer on the Human Sciences
    CHARLES TAYLOR   126

7   Lyric as Paradigm: Hegel and the Speculative
    Instance of Poetry in Gadamer's Hermeneutics
    J. M. BAKER, JR.   143

vii

viii   CONTENTS

8   Gadamer, the Hermeneutic Revolution,
    and Theology
    FRED LAWRENCE   167

9   Hermeneutics in Practice: Gadamer
    on Ancient Philosophy
    CATHERINE H. ZUCKERT   201

10 Gadamer's Hegel
    ROBERT B. PIPPIN   225

11 Gadamer's Relation to Heidegger
    and Phenomenology
    ROBERT J. DOSTAL   247

12 The Constellation of Hermeneutics, Critical
    Theory, and Deconstruction
    RICHARD J. BERNSTEIN   267

    Bibliography   283
    Index   313

CONTRIBUTORS

J. M. BAKER teaches in the Liberal Arts division at the University of the Arts in Philadelphia. He has previously written on the romantic literature of England and Europe, with special attention to the intersection of poetic discourse with the kind of long-standing philosophical issues addressed in the present essay. He is in the process of revising a book-length study of Hölderlin: *Recursive Poetics: Hölderlin and the Tradition*.

RICHARD J. BERNSTEIN is Vera List professor of philosophy and chair, New School for Social Research. His books include the following: *Beyond Objectivism and Relativism; The New Constellation; Hannah Arendt and the Jewish Question;* and *Freud and the Legacy of Moses*. He is currently working on a book dealing with conception of evil in modern thought.

ROBERT J. DOSTAL is the Rufus M. Jones professor of philosophy and provost at Bryn Mawr College. He is co-editor of *Phenomenology on Kant, German Idealism, Hermeneutics and Logic*. He has published numerous articles on the German philosophical tradition including essays on Kant, Heidegger, Arendt, and Gadamer.

GÜNTER FIGAL is professor of philosophy at the University of Tübingen. He is the author of *Theodor W. Adorno: Das Naturschöne als spekulative Gedankenfigur* (1977); *Martin Heidegger: Phänomenologie der Freiheit* (1988/1991); *Das Untier und die Liebe: Sieben platonische Essays* (1991); *Martin Heidegger zur Einführung* (1992); *Für eine Philosophie von Freiheit und Streit* (1994); *Der Sinn des Verstehens,* (1996); and *Nietzsche* (1999).

ix

JEAN GRONDIN is professor of philosophy at the Université de Montréal. His books include: *Hermeneutische Wahrheit? Zum Wahrheitsbegriff Hans-Georg Gadamers* (1982; 2nd ed. 1994); *Le tournant dans la pensée de Martin Heidegger* (1987); *Kant et le problem de la philosophie: l'a priori* (1989); *Introduction to Philosophical Hermeneutics* (1994); *Sources of Hermeneutics* (1995); *Hans-Georg Gadamer Eine Biographie* (1999); *Einführung zu Gadamer* (2000).

FRED LAWRENCE is an associate professor in the theology department at Boston College. He did his doctoral thesis at the University of Basel on *Believing to Understand: The Hermeneutic Circle in Gadamer and Lonergan*. For twenty-eight years he has directed the Lonergan Workshop at BC. He has been active in founding and teaching in the Perspectives Program at BC, taught at the law school, and been involved in the education of judges. He has published in a variety of philosophical and theological journals. Besides teaching the systematic theology of the Trinity, his areas of expertise and interest include theology as hermeneutical, method in theology, and theology in a political mode.

ROBERT PIPPIN is the Raymond W. and Martha Hilpert Gruner Distinguished Service Professor in the Committee on Social Thought, the department of philosophy, and the College, and he is the chair of the Committee on Social Thought at the University of Chicago. He writes about the German philosophical tradition, and is the author of several books on Kant and Hegel, on the nature of European modernity, and articles and reviews on similar topics. His most recent book is about literature, *Henry James and Modern Moral Life*. In addition to his work on the philosophies of Kant, Hegel, and Nietzsche, Professor Pippin has published work on theories of self-consciousness, the nature of conceptual change, and the problem of freedom.

CHARLES TAYLOR is professor emeritus of philosophy at McGill University. His books include *Sources of the Self, the Malaise of Modernity, and Philosophical Arguments*.

GEORGIA WARNKE is professor of philosophy at the University of California, Riverside. She is the author of *Gadamer: Hermeneutics, Tradition and Reason; Justice and Interpretation; and Legitimate Differences: Interpretation in the Abortion Controversy and other Public Debates*.

BRICE WACHTERHAUSER is Professor of Philosophy and Associate Dean of the College of Arts and Sciences at Saint Joseph's University in Philadelphia. He is the author of *Beyond Being: Gadamer's Post-Platonic Hermeneutical Ontology* (1999) and editor of *Hermeneutics and Truth* (1994), *Phenomenology and Skepticism* (1996), and *Hermeneutics and Modern Philosophy* (1986).

CATHERINE H. ZUCKERT is Nancy Reeves Dreux professor of government and international studies at the University of Notre Dame. Author of *Postmodern Platos: Nietzsche, Heidegger, Gadamer, Strauss, Derrida* (1996), she is currently working on a book on Plato's philosophers.

ABBREVIATIONS

Abbreviation for Gadamer's *Gesammelte Werke*: GW
Abbreviations for Gadamer's English works:

DD   *Dialogue and Dialectic*
EH   *The Enigma of Health*
EPH   *Gadamer on Education, Poetry, and History*
GDE   *Dialogue and Deconstruction: The Gadamer-Derrida Encounter*
HD   *Hegel's Dialectic*
IG   *The Idea of the Good in Platonic-Aristotelian Philosophy*
HW   *Heidegger's Ways*
LPD   *Literature and Philosophy in Dialogue*
PA   *Philosophical Apprenticeships*
PDE   *Plato's Dialectical Ethics*
PG   "Reflections on my Philosophical Journey"
PH   *Philosophical Hermeneutics*
PL   "Philosophy and Literature"
RAS   *Reason in the Age of Science*
RB   *The Relevance of the Beautiful*
TM   *Truth and Method*

Introduction

GADAMER'S PHILOSOPHICAL HERMENEUTICS

In 1960 Hans-Georg Gadamer, then a sixty-year-old German philosophy professor at Heidelberg, published *Truth and Method* (*Wahrheit und Methode*). Although he authored many essays, articles, and reviews, to this point Gadamer had published only one other book, his habilitation on Plato in 1931: *Plato's Dialectical Ethics*. As a title for this work on a theory of interpretation, he first proposed to his publisher, Mohr Siebeck, "Philosophical Hermeneutics." The publisher responded that "hermeneutics" was too obscure a term. Gadamer then proposed "Truth and Method" for a work that found, over time, great resonance and made "hermeneutics" and Gadamer's name commonplace in intellectual circles worldwide. *Truth and Method* has been translated into ten languages thus far – including Chinese and Japanese. It found and still finds a receptive readership, in part, because, as the title suggests, it addresses large and central philosophical issues in the attempt to find a way between or beyond objectivism and relativism, and scientism and irrationalism. He accomplishes this by developing an account of what he takes to be the universal hermeneutic experience of understanding. Understanding, for Gadamer, is itself always a matter of interpretation. Understanding is also always a matter of language. "Being that can be understood is language," writes Gadamer in the culminating section of the work in which he proposes a "hermeneutical ontology" (TM 432). For his concept of the understanding and the task of ontology, Gadamer relies importantly on Martin Heidegger's treatment of these concepts in *Being and Time* (1927). He follows the later Heidegger's turn to language with the centrality of language and linguisticality (*Sprachlichkeit*). At the same time, he develops these notions in original ways, free of Heideggerian jargon and, arguably, in ways that depart significantly from Heidegger's thought.

Hermeneutics has a long history with roots in Greek and Hellenistic philosophy as well as in the Church fathers. Until Heidegger in the 1920s characterized his project of fundamental ontology as hermeneutical, hermeneutics had, for the most part, been considered narrowly as pertaining to the interpretation of texts. In the nineteenth century in Germany hermeneutics was taken out of what had been a largely theological context and developed as a methodology for interpreting texts generally, especially those texts at some historical distance. August Boeckh importantly contributed to this development and to the systematization of hermeneutics as the basis for a scientific philology that, in turn, was central to the historical sciences (*Geisteswissenschaften*) and their claim on the title, "science." Wilhelm Dilthey in his masterful attempt to establish a critique of historical reason provided a hermeneutics in the context of his life-philosophy (*Lebensphilosophie*). Gadamer, whose training was in classical philosophy and philology and who took refuge in philology in the Nazi period of the 1930s, explains that in the late 1950s he wrote *Truth and Method* to present in writing to his students what he had been doing throughout his life in the lecture and seminar room, that is, the careful reading and interpretation of texts.[1] In spite of this overmodest understatement of the project of *Truth and Method*, this characterization is in one aspect fitting, because the work affirms the primacy of the spoken over the written, the primacy of *Rede* over *Schriftlichkeit*. This characterization might be considered misleading inasmuch as the work does not directly address how Gadamer or anyone ought to approach and read a text; that is, the work is not at all a "how to" treatment of reading texts. In fact, Gadamer attacks the narrow reliance on methodology in approaches such as that of Boeckh. Gadamer sees the methodologism of "scientific" hermeneutics to be a version of scientism. The word 'method' in the title of the volume is ambiguous and ironic, for Gadamer would have us give up the notion that truth is to be understood primarily as the function of rigorous method. The *wissen* (knowing) in *Wissenschaft* (science) is, on his account, not simply a function of methodology. As he famously writes in the second foreword to *Truth and Method*:

My revival of the expression 'hermeneutics,' with its long tradition, has apparently led to some misunderstandings. I did not intend to produce an art or technique of understanding, in the manner of earlier hermeneutics. I did not wish to elaborate a system of rules to describe, let alone direct, the methodical procedure of the human sciences (*Geisteswissenschaften*). Nor was it my aim to investigate the theoretical foundation of work in these fields in order to put my findings to practical ends. If there is any practical consequence of the present investigation, it certainly has nothing to do with an unscientific 'commitment'; instead, it is concerned with the 'scientific' integrity of acknowledging the commitment involved in all understanding. My real concern was and is philosophic: not what we do or what we ought to do, but what happens to us over and above our wanting and doing.

Hence the methods of the human sciences are not at issue here (TM xxviii).

Accordingly, *Truth and Method* is a descriptive or "phenomenological" account of "all understanding" (*Verstehen*). This phenomenological effort is, at the same time, ontological inasmuch as the work attempts to answer the question, "What is understanding?" As we have already noted, on this account all understanding is interpretive, hermeneutical. To show this Gadamer importantly utilizes Edmund Husserl's phenomenological concept of the "horizon." And he relies on Heidegger's account of the radical historicity of the human situation and the human understanding. Understanding is, according to Gadamer, linguistic and dialogical. He characterizes the dialogic event of understanding as a "fusion of horizons," which is led by a concern for whatever is at stake, the matter of concern, *die Sache selbst*. To show how the individual's understanding occurs in a larger historical and hermeneutical context, Gadamer develops the notion, difficult to translate, of "effective historical consciousness" (*Wirkungsgeschichtliches Bewusstsein*) and accords great importance to the role of tradition and prejudice (*Vorurteil*) in any interpretation. What one understands makes a difference in what one does. The practical application of knowledge is inherent in the very understanding of something. Practical application is not, on Gadamer's account, an external, after the fact, use of understanding that is somehow independent of the understanding. All understanding is practical.

THE RECEPTION OF *TRUTH AND METHOD*

The response to *Truth and Method* has been extensive, rich, and varied. The reception in the English speaking world was slowed and complicated by the fact that the work was first published in English translation in 1975 and that this first English edition was marred by numerous errors and omissions. At the risk of oversimplification, one can identify three waves of critique and discussion of this work. The first wave of criticism and discussion concerned charges that Gadamer's hermeneutical theory is historicist (Leo Strauss), relativist (E. D. Hirsch, Emilio Betti), and linguistically idealist (Thomas Seebohm).[2] The seeming identification of Being and language leads to the idealist charge. The seeming reliance on Heidegger's thought, which gives priority to the futural aspect of the understanding together with Gadamer's insistence on the importance of the historical situation of the interpreter and the applied character of any understanding, are important aspects of the debate about historicism and relativism. Gadamer's attempt to undermine the traditional hermeneutic distinction between meaning (*Sinn*) and significance (*Bedeutung*) plays an important role in this discussion. The second wave follows from the appropriation and critique of Gadamer's hermeneutics by a young and then relatively unknown philosopher, Jürgen Habermas. In his inaugural lecture, "Knowledge and Human Interests," of 1965 (published as an appendix to the book of the same title), Habermas explicitly adopts Gadamer's hermeneutics for what he called the "historical–hermeneutical sciences," but he, at the same time, criticizes Gadamer's thought for being insufficiently "critical" and too reliant upon and subordinate to tradition; that is, it is inadequate for a critique of ideology and, hence, for critical theory. This set off an exchange with Gadamer that received much attention and comment.[3] Not only is the relation of Gadamer's hermeneutical theory to phenomenology (Husserl, Heidegger) and to critical theory (Adorno, Horkheimer, Habermas) controverted, but also there has been consideration of the relation of Gadamer's interpretive theory to the recent modes of interpreting texts and the philosophical tradition that has been developed particularly in France and has been identified as poststructuralist, postmodern, and deconstructionist (Derrida, Foucault, and Lyotard among others). The third wave follows from the first direct meeting and exchange between Gadamer and Derrida in Paris in 1981 under the auspices of the Goethe Institute. The papers of this meeting ("exchange" overstates what actually transpired), which eventually appeared in French, German, and English, elicited much response from the philosophical community.[4] Relevant for situating Gadamer in the landscape of the contemporary philosophical scene, especially in relation to Habermas and Derrida, is the consideration of his views on modernity and the Enlightenment. It is worth noting that Habermas, who criticizes Gadamer as a traditionalist, embraces the Enlightenment project and modernity more closely than Gadamer, who keeps a critical distance. This aspect might seem to place Gadamer in proximity with the postmodernists, but the very definition of his project as an ontology of the universal experience of understanding distinguishes his project from postmodernism and deconstructionism. A specifically American aspect of this third wave was Richard Rorty's somewhat misdirected appeal to Gadamer as an existentialist and edifying philosopher in the conclusion of his much discussed *Philosophy and the Mirror of Nature* (1979) and his later consideration of Gadamer in *The Consequences of Pragmatism* (1982) as a "weak textualist" – this, by way of contrast, to the strong textualism of Derrida and Rorty. Most recently (2000) Rorty casts Gadamer as a nominalist whose lead would end the "epistemic wars."[5]

Gadamer's hermeneutics has had a much broader impact than these significant debates in philosophical circles about truth, interpretive method, tradition, and modernity. "Hermeneutics," resulting largely but not solely from Gadamer's work, became a commonplace part of titles or subtitles especially in literary theory, sociology, and social theory, as well as in theology and biblical commentary. In literary theory, Gadamer's work was particularly invoked in the development of reception and "reader-response" theory, for example in the work of Hans-Robert Jauss. His work importantly assisted social theory in taking the "interpretive turn." In 1979, Paul Rabinow and William Sullivan published *Interpretive Social Science*, which announces this "turn" and makes a case against either naively realistic or positivistic human science. Gadamer has been a frequently invoked figure in the debates about the human sciences and the philosophy of social science.

Though Gadamer is not a religious thinker, his work has found enormous resonance in theology and biblical criticism. This area, to be sure, has had a stronger and livelier hermeneutic tradition than other areas of inquiry. In the twentieth century, among others, Rudolf Bultmann, with whom Gadamer studied in Marburg in the 1920s, made hermeneutics a central theme for theology. In the late 1950s, just prior to the publication of *Truth and Method*, Ernst Fuchs and Hans Ebeling published important work on the significance of hermeneutics for theology.[6] The appearance of *Truth and Method* importantly shaped the ensuing and wide-ranging discussion of hermeneutics in religious and theological thought. An example of the practical impact of Gadamer's thought in this area is the publication (December 1999) of a theological study commissioned by the Vatican on the faults of the Roman Catholic Church in the past: *Memory and Reconciliation: The Church and the Faults of the Past*. To establish a theoretical basis for its work, the study asks, "What are the conditions for a correct interpretation of the past from the point of view of historical knowledge?" Its answer relies explicitly and almost entirely on *Truth and Method*.[7] This document provided the theoretical and theological background for Pope John Paul II's pronouncements in 2000 about the faults and sins of the Church, especially with regard to the Jewish people.

Finally, it should be observed that Gadamer's work importantly contributed to a hermeneutic turn in philosophy and the human sciences that goes beyond the direct influence of his work. Other philosophers, especially in Europe and more or less independent of Gadamer, have attempted their hand at developing a philosophical hermeneutics. Work in France by Paul Ricouer, in Italy by Emilio Betti and Gianni Vattimo, and in Germany by Hans Albert, Manfred Frank, and Thomas Seebohm, among others, come to mind. We find, in addition, many scholars in other fields invoking hermeneutics with little or no explicit invocation of the work of Gadamer. This is particularly so in America where an intellectual divide between Anglo-American and so-called Continental thought has played a decisive role in philosophy and in the human sciences. Thomas Kuhn, the historian and philosopher of science, whose book *The Structure of Scientific Revolutions* (1962) has had such a profound impact on the history and philosophy of science and beyond, came to understand his own efforts as hermeneutical and articulates well the situation of many American intellectuals in this regard:

What I as a physicist had to discover for myself, most historians learn by example in the course of professional training. Consciously or not, they are all practitioners of the hermeneutic method. In my case, however, the discovery of hermeneutics did more than make history seem consequential. Its most immediate and decisive effect was instead on my view of science . . . . The early models of the sort of history that has influenced me and my *historical* colleagues is the product of a post-Kantian European tradition which I and my *philosophical* colleagues continue to find opaque. In my own case, for example, even the term "hermeneutic," to which I resorted briefly above, was no part of my vocabulary as recently as five years ago. Increasingly, I suspect that anyone who believes that history may have deep philosophical import will have to learn to bridge the longstanding divide between the Continental and English-language philosophical traditions.[8]

The translation of Gadamer's work into English and his teaching and lecturing presence in North America for over twenty years has surely contributed to building this bridge.

GADAMER'S OTHER WORK

As suggested above, Gadamer not only developed a theory of hermeneutics but he practiced it in his teaching and his writing. He spent his scholarly life engaged with philosophical and literary texts. Gadamer understands his own particular strengths to be in the lecture hall or seminar room and in the written essay. As Gadamer himself notes, he has written only three books in his lifetime, even though a recent published bibliography of his work is over 300 pages.[9] With the exception of *Plato's Dialectical Ethics* (his habilitation), *Truth and Method*, and *The Idea of the Good in Platonic-Aristotelian Philosophy*, each of his many published books is either a collection of essays, the reworking of a lecture series, or an extended essay published as a small monograph. On the literary side, he writes primarily about poetry, especially Goethe, Hölderlin, Immerman, George, Rilke, Celan, and Domin. In a small number of essays, he has given attention to painting. On the philosophical side he writes about classical Greek thinkers like Democritus, Parmenides, Heraclitus, Aristotle, and Plotinus as well as modern philosophers such as Herder, Schleiermacher, and Dilthey. Most importantly, however, he writes about Plato, Hegel, and Heidegger. These three thinkers provide for Gadamer more than a number of interesting and important philosophical issues; they are the grindstone on which Gadamer sharpens his own interpretive theory. Gadamer opens the second volume of his collected works, a volume that collects numerous essays that develop or explain aspects of *Truth and Method*, with a 1985 retrospective essay that was written as the introduction to the volume and is entitled "Between Phenomenology and Dialectic – An Attempt at a Self-Critique." As the title suggests, Gadamer locates his hermeneutical theory between phenomenology and dialectic. The phenomenology here is primarily, though not solely, that of Martin Heidegger. The dialectic is the dialectic of Hegel and, even more importantly, the dialectic of Plato.

Gadamer's dissertation and habilitation both concerned Plato. Most of Gadamer's teaching and writing in the 1930s and 1940s was devoted to Greek philosophy (the pre-Socratics, Plato, and Aristotle). He continued to give classical Greek philosophy much of his attention throughout his scholarly career. Three of the ten volumes of his collected works are dedicated to classical philosophy; this represents as much space in the collection as the three volumes dedicated to hermeneutics. He is particularly interested in the concept of the good in Plato and Aristotle, in the relation of theory and practice, and in the relation of the philosophy of Plato and Aristotle more generally. He provides a reading of Plato and Aristotle that shows a deep proximity of their thought. Although Gadamer's work on classical philosophy stands in its own right and has had an important impact in this field, his reading of the Greeks is not unrelated to his hermeneutical theory. The Aristotelian concept of *phronesis* (practical reasoning) is central to his development of hermeneutical understanding in *Truth and Method*. In Plato he finds a paradigm of the logic of question and answer that underlies his account of dialogue in the hermeneutic experience. The concluding section of *Truth and Method* relies importantly on Plato, especially the Plato of the *Phaedrus* and the *Seventh Letter* for establishing the priority of speech to writing and for treatment of truth in relation to beauty. Gadamer explicitly, if somewhat ambiguously, ties his own effort in hermeneutics to the Platonic tradition:

The fact that we have been able to refer several times to Plato, despite the fact that Greek logos philosophy revealed the ground of the hermeneutical experience only in a very fragmentary way, is due to this feature of the Platonic view of beauty, which is like an undercurrent in the history of Aristotelian and scholastic metaphysics, sometimes rising to the surface, as in neoplatonic and christian mysticism and theological and philosophical spiritualism. It was in this tradition of Platonism that the conceptual vocabulary required for thought about the finiteness of human life was developed. The continuity of this Platonic tradition is attested by the affinity between the Platonic theory of beauty and the idea of a universal hermeneutics (TM 486–7).

Truth and Method begins importantly with a critique of the subjectification of aesthetic consciousness in Kantian aesthetics and much of subsequent philosophical aesthetics. It concludes with a discussion that relies importantly on Plato and that argues for the proximity of truth and beauty.

Beauty, then, is a central consideration for Gadamer. We have already noted his attention to poetry and painting, interests that have spanned his career. It is only after the publication of *Truth and Method*, however, that Gadamer begins to write extensively about philosophical aesthetics. The short monograph, *The Relevance of the Beautiful*, and eleven essays are available in English translation (1986) under the title of the monograph. In these essays Gadamer continues his critique of idealist aesthetics, engages contemporary discussions (especially in Germany) of philosophical aesthetics, and attempts to show that art is a "unique manifestation of truth whose particularity cannot be surpassed" (RB 37). The concepts of representation, *mimesis*, and the festival are important to Gadamer's considerations. Art's proximity to and distance from philosophy is another significant theme. Gadamer's voice in contemporary aesthetics is singular in its call for us to find truth in beauty.

Two other themes that Gadamer has taken up particularly in the last two decades are Europe and health. He published two collections of essays on Europe in the 1980s and has published a collection of essays on health, which has been translated into English under the title *The Enigma of Health: The Art of Healing in a Scientific Age* (1996). These two concerns are related. It is the modern Europe with which Gadamer is concerned – the Europe of the Enlightenment, of science and technology. And it is the question of health in a scientific age that Gadamer considers. As the subtitle of *The Enigma of Health* indicates, Gadamer continues to consider the relation of theory to practice and continues, in the context of specifically "scientific" and technological era, to return to a Platonic and Aristotelian understanding of this complex relationship. Healing is not so much a science or technique, Gadamer argues, but it is an "art." "Art" is a possible translation of the Greek *techne*, which sometimes finds itself translated as "technique." "Practice," Gadamer tells the assembled psychiatrists of the United States in their annual convention in 1989, "is more than merely the application of knowledge." Gadamer would have us recover this classical understanding of practice in relation to theory whether it is in the context of medicine or reading texts. This classical understanding of practice importantly underlies Gadamer's project of philosophical hermeneutics. This is provocatively displayed in the concluding statement of *Truth and Method*: "Rather, what the tool of method does not achieve must – and effectively can – be achieved by a discipline of questioning and research, a discipline that guarantees truth" (TM 447). More fundamental than the methods of hermeneutics (for method there must be) is the hermeneutic discipline or the art. Elsewhere he defines hermeneutics simply as "the art of agreement."[10]

THIS VOLUME

The essays in this volume present and assess Gadamer's philosophical achievement from a wide variety of perspectives. They consider the implications of Gadamer's philosophical contributions for metaphysics and epistemology, the philosophy of language, ethics and politics, aesthetics, theology, and the philosophy of the social sciences. Three papers address quite directly Gadamer's theory of interpretation. Jean Grondin considers Gadamer's account of understanding. Brice Wachterhauser discusses Gadamer's concept of truth and the issues of realism/idealism and relativism. Günther Figal examines Gadamer's philosophy of language. Two papers consider themes, which, though important to Gadamer's hermeneutics, have philosophical interest independent of their relevance to hermeneutics. Georgia Warnke takes up the ethics and politics of Gadamer's thought, and Jay Baker considers the significance of lyric poetry for Gadamer's aesthetics. Two papers focus on the relevance of Gadamer's thought to areas outside philosophy narrowly construed.

Charles Taylor discusses the implications of Gadamer's philosophical hermeneutics for the human sciences, and Frederick Lawrence writes of the significance of Gadamer's work for theology and religious thought. Three papers attend to the three figures from the history of philosophy most significant for Gadamer's thought: Catherine Zuckert on Plato, Robert Pippin on Hegel, and Robert Dostal on Heidegger. Richard Bernstein considers the question of Gadamer's understanding of modernity and places this consideration in relation to Gadamer's philosophical encounters with Jürgen Habermas and Jacques Derrida. The volume concludes with an extensive English language bibliography of both primary and secondary work. We begin with a short biography of Gadamer by Robert Dostal.

NOTES

1 *Hans-Georg Gadamer on Education, Poetry, and History: Applied Hermeneutics*, edited by Dieter Misgeld and Graeme Nicholson, translated by Lawrence Schmidt and Monica Reuss (Albany: SUNY Press, 1992), p. 63.

2 Gadamer responds to these criticisms in Supplement I to *Truth and Method*, entitled, "Hermeneutics and Historicism" (TM 460–91). Emilio Betti's critique of Gadamer's hermeneutics has not been translated into English: *Die Hermeneutik als allgemeine Methodik der Geisteswissenschaften* (Tübingen: J. C. B. Mohr, 1962). For Leo Strauss's critique, see his correspondence with Gadamer: "Correspondence concerning *Wahrheit und Methode*," *The Independent Journal of Philosophy* 2 (1978), 5–12. E. D. Hirsch focused on the distinction of meaning and significance: "Truth and Method in Interpretation," *The Review of Metaphysics* 18 (1965), 488–507. See also his *Validity in Interpretation* (New Haven: Yale University Press, 1967). Hirsch significantly takes back some of his criticism in "Meaning and Significance Re-interpreted," *Critical Inquiry* 11 (1984), 202–25. See also Thomas Seebohm, *Kritik der hermeneutischen Vernunft* (Bonn: Bouvier, 1972) and "The New Hermeneutics," in *Continental Philosophy in America*, edited by Hugh Silverman, John Sallis, and Thomas Seebohm (Pittsburgh: Duquesne University Press, 1983), pp. 64–89.

3 Jürgen Habermas, *Knowledge and Human Interests*, translated by Jeremy Shapiro (Boston: Beacon, 1968). In the Appendix Habermas writes: "Thus the rules of hermeneutics determine the possible meaning of the validity of statements of the cultural sciences" (p. 309). The footnote to

the sentence reads: "I concur with the analysis in Part 2 of Hans-Georg Gadamer, *Wahrheit und Methode*" (p. 348). Habermas' review of *Truth and Method* can be found in English translation in *The Hermeneutic Tradition*, edited by Gayle Ormiston and Alan Schrift (Albany: SUNY Press, 1990), pp. 213–45. Other contributions to this discussion can be found in this collection. For Gadamer's response to Habermas see "Reply to My Critics" in this same volume. See also Gadamer's "On the Scope and Function of Hermeneutical Reflection, " in *Philosophical Hermeneutics*, edited and translated by David E. Linge (Berkeley: University of California Press, 1976), pp. 18–43; also reprinted in *Hermeneutics and Modern Philosophy*, edited by Brice Wachterhauser (Albany: SUNY Press, 1986), pp. 277–99.

4 *Dialogue and Deconstruction: The Gadamer-Derrida Encounter*, edited and translated by Diane F. Michelfelder and Richard E. Palmer (Albany: SUNY Press, 1989).

5 Richard Rorty, *Philosophy and the Mirror of Nature* (Princeton: Princeton University Press, 1979); *The Consequences of Pragmatism* (Minneapolis: University of Minnesota Press, 1982), pp. 139–59; "On Gadamer and the Philosophical Conversation," *The London Review of Books* 22, no. 6 (March 16, 2000), pp. 23–25.

6 Ernst Fuchs, *Zum Hermeneutischen Problem in der Theologie* (Tübingen: J. C. B. Mohr, 1959); Hans Ebeling, "Wort Gottes und Hermeneutik," *Zeitschrift für Theologie und Kirche* (1959), pp. 224–51. See also Rudolf Bultmann, *Essays: Philosophical and Theological*, translated by James Greig (London: S. C. M. Press, 1955), and *Existence and Faith: Shorter Writings of Rudolf Bultmann*, translated by Schubert Ogden (London: Hodder and Stoughton, 1961). Wolfhart Pannenberg contributed an important essay to the discussion, "Hermeneutics and Universal History," in *Hermeneutics and Modern Philosophy*, pp. 111–46.

7 *Memory and Reconciliation: The Church and the Faults of the Past*, see especially footnote #65. This document can be found at www. vatican.va/ roman_curia/congregations/cfaith/documents/rc_con_cfaith_ doc_ 20000307_memory-reconc-itc_en.html.

8 Thomas Kuhn, *The Essential Tension* (Chicago: University of Chicago Press, 1977), pp. xiii–xiv.

9 Etsuro Makita, *Gadamer-Bibliographie: 1922–1944* (New York: Peter Lang, 1994).

10 "Reply to My Critics," in *The Hermeneutic Tradition*, p. 273.

1 Gadamer: The Man and His Work

In many respects the philosopher Hans-Georg Gadamer has led an unremarkable life. Born into a well-to-do middle class, academic, German family, he enjoyed a *Gymnasium* (a secondary school preparatory to the university) and a university education that led to a career as a philosophy professor. He retired from the university at age 68 and continues to lecture and write. What distinguishes Gadamer's life is his work. With the publication of *Truth and Method* in 1960, he helped inaugurate, in philosophy and human studies, an interpretive turn with a worldwide impact. We also note that Gadamer has led a very long life. Born in 1900, his life spans the entire twentieth century. It goes without saying, that Gadamer has led a German life – a German life in a century that might well have been a German century on the world stage but instead was an unmitigated disaster for Germany and for the world. Gadamer's life is closely bound to Germany and its intellectual life, though in his retirement he lectured around the world and spent extensive time teaching and lecturing in North America. A look at his life can illuminate Germany's century as well as the context for his philosophical work. The work, however, is not to be understood merely within this context, for, as Gadamer himself has often argued, a philosophical or literary work always surpasses what the author understands. In addition, this German philosopher found himself with audiences and a readership worldwide.

YOUTH, FAMILY, AND EDUCATION

Hans-Georg Gadamer was born on February 11, 1900, in the small university town of Marburg, in the Germany of the second empire.

13

His family was from Silesia (now Poland) and they soon moved back to its principal city, Breslau (now Wroclaw), then one of the largest cities in Germany, where Gadamer grew up. His father, Johannes, was a prominent chemistry professor. At the time of Gadamer's birth, his father was on the faculty at Marburg University, and in 1902 followed the call to the chair of pharmaceutical chemistry in Breslau. His mother died when he was four and his father soon remarried. Gadamer had one sibling, an older brother who suffered from epilepsy and was institutionalized when Gadamer was in his teens.

Although the family was nominally Protestant, religion played little role in their family life – unless one counts as religious the deep respect and awe in which reason and science were held. His family and the milieu in which he grew up were very much participants in what has been called a religion of reason, *Vernunftreligion,* for which the professoriate, especially those in natural science, was the priesthood. It is difficult for us, at the turn of the twenty-first century, to appreciate the progressive hopefulness with regard to science and technology and the loyalty to the nation and its emperor that imbued the professional class, all university trained, of Wilhelmine, especially Prussian, Germany. Gadamer remembers Breslau as being "more Prussian than Prussia" (PA 3). The two domains, science (*Wissenschaft*) and culture (*Kultur*), sometimes in conflict and sometimes in harmony, often took the place that elsewhere was occupied by religion and politics. This milieu, though progressive and modernizing in spirit, was at the same time authoritarian, antidemocratic, and nonegalitarian.

All of this characterized Gadamer's father, who was a very strict disciplinarian. Gadamer writes of his father: "My father was ... a significant researcher, a self-conscious, accomplished, energetic, and capable personality – a man who drastically embodied authoritarian pedagogy in the worst way but with the best of intentions"(PA 3). Although his father was cultivated, he had little respect in the university context for the disciplines that concerned themselves more with culture than science. For him the humanities professors were the "chattering professors" (*Schwatzprofessoren*). He did his best to interest the young Hans-Georg in natural science but to no avail. Already, in his secondary school years, Hans-Georg was clearly interested in the humanities – especially in "Shakespeare, ancient Greek and classical German writers" (PA 3). In 1918, Gadamer enrolled at the University of Breslau where he studied literature, the history of art, psychology, and philosophy. In 1919, Johannes accepted a call back to Marburg, and Hans-Georg followed him. There the young Gadamer settled on philosophy and classical philology, and in 1922 wrote a dissertation with the preeminent neo-Kantian Paul Natorp on Plato. His father, who became the rector of the university in 1922, never reconciled himself to philosophy as a career path for his son. When he was dying of cancer in 1928, Johannes, out of concern for his son's life prospects, sent for Martin Heidegger with whom Gadamer was studying and writing his habilitation. Heidegger assured him that his son was a good philosopher and would find a position and a career.[1] Although Johannes was a strong admirer of Bismarck, he was not interested in politics. As a scientist and university professor he was above politics. He appears not to have shared with his fellow academics their great enthusiasm for the war when it broke out in 1914. Gadamer remembers his own childish enthusiasm for the war when it was announced in the late summer – and his father's stern rebuke.[2] The war and its aftermath brought dramatic changes to Europe, to Germany, and to Gadamer. The German empire had collapsed. Revolution was in the air. Gadamer succinctly reminds us of the time, when he writes:

This was the end of an age: the age of liberalism, the unlimited belief in progress, and the unquestioned leadership of science within cultural life. All of this perished in the War's battles of materiel.[3]

Although there were surely many influences on the development of Gadamer's thought at this time including Kierkegaard and Dostoyevsky, Gadamer accords his "awakening" and intellectual liberation from his parents and from Prussian Germany to reading Theodor Lessing's *Europa und Asien*, "a spirited and sarcastic work of cultural criticism that bowled me over. At last I had found something else in the world beside Prussian efficiency, performance, and discipline" (PA 4).[4]

HEIDEGGER AND MARBURG

The 1920s were tumultuous times in Germany and tumultuous times for Gadamer in Marburg. He attended lectures in a wide variety of fields, including those of the leftist art historian Richard Hamann who declared the end of European culture. He associated with the politically conservative Stephan George circle; with Ernst Curtius, the literary historian; and he became friends (as a student might with a professor) with the philosopher Nicolai Hartmann. Later in Marburg he became acquainted with the visiting Max Scheler and worked closely with the theologian Rudolf Bultmann. At Hartmann's suggestion he chose for his dissertation advisor Paul Natorp, the leading neo-Kantian philosopher in Germany. He finished the work for the doctorate relatively early in 1922.[5] Shortly thereafter, in April 1923, he married – "too young," he says (PA 35). Between the completion of his doctorate and his marriage, he became ill with polio and convalesced. The polio affected the way he walked for the rest of his life, but it did not keep him from tennis and hiking. His treatment included quarantine for several months, during which time he read intensively, among other things, the phenomenologist Edmund Husserl's multivolume *Logical Investigations*, much of the writing of the romantic Jean Paul, and an unpublished essay on Aristotle by a young assistant to Husserl in Freiburg, Martin Heidegger. This unpublished work came to Gadamer by way of Natorp, who had solicited the essay via Husserl with the expectation that it would soon be published and that Heidegger might then qualify for a position at Marburg. The essay, which announces a major work on Aristotle from a phenomenological perspective, was not then published and the project was not carried out. Gadamer writes that the essay "affected me like an electric shock" (PA 47). The essay stirred Gadamer to write Heidegger directly and express his intention to come to Freiburg.

The encounter with Heidegger was a fateful one: a relationship that was difficult, complicated, and decisive from the very beginning. Gadamer spent the spring semester of 1923 in Freiburg, where he attended Husserl's lectures and all the courses Heidegger was teaching. Among these were two different classes on Aristotle, a seminar on Husserl's *Logical Investigations*, and a lecture series titled "Ontology," which soon found a more exact title: "The Hermeneutics of Facticity." Heidegger invited Gadamer and his wife up to his hut in Todtnauberg for several weeks during the summer break where they read Aristotle and Melanchthon together. This helped lay the groundwork for Gadamer's appreciation of the importance of religious and theological thought for the philosophical tradition and provided the basis for his later studies with the theologian Rudolf Bultmann. A position for Heidegger materialized in Marburg beginning in the winter semester of 1923–4. Gadamer recalls vividly a farewell celebration Heidegger held for his students up in the Black Forest mountains near his hut. A large bonfire was built and Heidegger spoke, encouraging his students to remain "awake" (*Wachsein*, an injunction from Paul's epistle to the Thessalonians), reminding them of the task of humanity to stand between the revelation and withdrawal of Being, and invoking the Greeks.

The year 1923 was also the time of the great inflation in Germany. Gadamer, at this point, for reasons that he never makes clear in his autobiographical writing, was trying to help support his father. Earlier, Gadamer had inherited a trust fund from his father that bore one condition – that it not be used to purchase books. The inflation reduced the fund's value to nothing. Although Gadamer had grown up in Breslau in affluence, the Great War and its aftermath took away much, if not all, of the family's resources. Money would remain a worry for Gadamer, the head of a family and a household, until he finally secured the position of professor in the late 1930s.

Gadamer returned from Freiburg to Marburg that fall (1923), assisted Heidegger in his new surroundings, and immediately became part of the circle around Heidegger. Student friends in this circle included Karl Löwith, Gerhard Krüger, Jakob Klein, and Leo Strauss. Gadamer did not know well Hannah Arendt or Hans Jonas, two others who studied at this time with Heidegger and who, like Klein and Strauss, emigrated to the United States in the 1930s and 1940s and had an important impact on philosophy in post-World War II America. Each of these students/philosophers has attested to Heidegger's powerful presence in the classroom.

Gadamer hoped to write under Heidegger's guidance his habilitation – a second work after the doctorate required in the German university system in order to qualify for an academic position. Yet after a year Heidegger expressed disappointment in Gadamer's work. His confidence shaken, Gadamer decided to concentrate on the study of classical Greek (classical philology) with Paul Friedländer. To borrow a phrase from Gadamer's biographer, Jean Grondin, Gadamer took "refuge in the Greeks."[6] This could have led to a university or a secondary school career. In these years, while concentrating on classical philology, he continued to attend Heidegger's lectures. In the summer of 1927, Gadamer successfully passed the state examinations to qualify as a teacher of classics. Heidegger was one of his examiners. Friedländer spoke to Heidegger about inviting Gadamer to write a habilitation with him, and Heidegger, to the great surprise of Gadamer, immediately wrote Gadamer inviting him to habilitate with him. In addition, Heidegger expressed concern that it be done quickly because Heidegger knew he had only one more year in Marburg. The appearance of *Being and Time* in 1927 paved the way for Heidegger to assume Husserl's chair in Freiburg, because Husserl was retiring.

Gadamer was up to the task and submitted, in the summer of 1928, his habilitation: a reading of Plato's *Philebus*. The work was clearly hurried. It had only a few footnotes, a very small bibliography, and only two chapters: (1) a treatment of Plato's dialectic and the way we come to an understanding (*Verständigung*) and (2) a reading of the *Philebus*. With some correction, the work was published in 1931 under the title: *Plato's Dialectical Ethics: Phenomenological Interpretations Relating to the Philebus*. He had thought of a habilitation on Aristotle and saw Aristotle as responding to Plato, but he settled for the preliminary work on Plato. With the habilitation completed, Gadamer became a "privatdozent" and received the right to lecture at the university. There was no position for him and no salary, but he could lecture and receive tuition from his students. He received a two-year stipendium from the German government to prepare his habilitation for publication. From 1929 to 1934 he offered lectures on ethics, aesthetics, Aristotle's ethics and physics, and Plato's *Republic* and treatment of the immortality of the soul, among others. In 1932 and 1933, he lectured on the idea of the university and on Karl Jasper's current assessment of the situation in Germany and Europe, "On the Spiritual Situation of the Age."[7]

EARLY CAREER AND NAZI GERMANY

Like so many of his friends and colleagues, Gadamer was surprised and shocked by the Nazi seizure of power (*Machtergreifung*) in 1933. In an interview in 1986 he recalls that

My belief was that it was absolutely impossible that Hitler could prove to be a figure of significance. This was the general conviction of liberal intellectuals in Germany.... And you must grasp ... the confinements and restrictions of the experience of a young student undertaking academic work under life conditions which were often threatened by hunger. You must grasp that it was only very, very slowly that I began to see the fatal possibility that lay before us (EPH 142).

Gadamer and his circle of friends in Marburg were also surprised and horrified by the news that Heidegger in Freiburg had joined the party and taken on the leadership of Freiburg University as rector with the express purpose of reshaping the liberal and cosmopolitan milieu of the university into a willing participant in the Nazi revolution. The universities were to submit to the will of the *Führer*, and clearly Heidegger had aspirations, quite ungrounded, to provide intellectual leadership to the nation's leader.[8] Heidegger sent Gadamer a copy of his famed Rectoral Address and signed his letter "With German greetings." Gadamer reports: "From that moment on I gave him up" and "this was the time that something false came into our relationship" (EPH 10). Gadamer broke off all contact with Heidegger until 1937, years after Heidegger had given up his active political engagement with Nazism.

In the Nazi period, Gadamer avoided politics and never became a party member. His career moved ahead, but slowly. He found a temporary position as a replacement for a year in Kiel in 1934–5. He returned to Marburg in 1935, again as a replacement. In 1938, he finally found a regular position as professor in Leipzig, as the successor of Arnold Gehlen, where he taught through the war years. He published little during this period. In fact, he comments later that he succeeded, in part, because he published so little and because he stayed, for the most part, within the realm of Greek philosophy.[9] His published efforts included work on classical Greek atom theory, on Plato on the poets and on education, on Hegel and historical spirit (*Geist*), and on "People (*Volk*) and History in the Thought of Herder." Gadamer's lectures in this period were almost exclusively on Greek philosophy or German idealism (Schelling, Hegel). Gadamer's critics question the compromises Gadamer had to make to further his career in Nazi Germany.[10] In the fall of 1933, German academics were asked to sign a document supporting Hitler and the Nazi regime, and Gadamer's name appears. In interviews and statements in the 1980s and 1990s Gadamer does not recall exactly the circumstances of this event, acknowledges the "compromise," claims he never saw the statement under which his name appeared, and explains that in the circumstance the choice was clear – agree or pack your bags.[11] Critics have also pointed out that the professors in Kiel and Marburg whom Gadamer replaced temporarily were Jews who were forced out of the university. In both cases, Gadamer was a friend of the philosopher he was to replace (Richard Kroner in Kiel and Erich Frank in Marburg) and, according to Gadamer, was encouraged personally by each of them to assume the temporary position. In addition, in the summer of 1935, after the University of Marburg rejected Gadamer's request for a position for reasons that appear to be his lack of enthusiasm for Nazism, Gadamer freely signed up for a "rehabilitation camp" for academics outside Danzig. He reports that he was lucky in that the leadership of the camp was tolerant and that he made a number of friends including the leader of the camp, a jurist, Graf Wenzel Gleispach. Gadamer credits his call to the professoriate at Leipzig in 1938, in part, to Graf Wenzel Gleispach's intervention. The two main competitors for the position in Leipzig were ardent Nazis. Werner Heisenberg, a prominent physicist on the Leipzig faculty, was impressed with Gadamer's work on Greek classical atomic theory and was another advocate for Gadamer's appointment.

With regard to his research and writing in this period, Gadamer informs us that, following his habilitation's consideration of Plato's ethics, he began in the early 1930s to plan for a work on Plato's politics. Because of the political developments in Germany he dropped this project, even though the two published essays in the Nazi period on Plato were pieces of what would have been this work: "Plato and the Poets," (1934) and "Plato's Education State" (1942). Gadamer, in many respects, appears to have been keeping a low profile during this very difficult time. Yet both of these essays consider political topics and both can be read as critiques of the politics of the time, critiques of the role of the humanities in the German academy and intellectual life, and, even, self-critique.[12] In the first essay in which Gadamer considered Plato's banishment of the poets from the city in the *Republic*, he wrote:

The real object of Plato's criticism is not the degenerate forms of contemporary *art* and the perception of the older, classical poetry which the contemporary taste in art had defined. Rather it is the contemporary *morality and moral education* which had established itself upon the basis of the poetic formulations of the older morality and which, in adhering to aging moral forms, found itself defenseless against arbitrary perversions of those forms brought on by the spirit of sophism (DD 61).

The essay begins with a reference to the reliance of the German classical and romantic periods on ancient models of art. Most importantly, the essay reads Plato as providing a critique of "aesthetic consciousness." It is with this very critique that Gadamer begins *Truth and Method*. The romanticism and aestheticism that pervaded so much of German humanism and the human sciences (*Geisteswissenschaften*) in the universities helped, usually inadvertently, prepare the way for National Socialism. One cannot help but think, for example, of the significant influence that the poet Stefan George and his circle exerted on intellectual life in Germany in the 1920s – and on Gadamer. This circle, contemptuous of modern mass society, held that the poets should rule and explicitly awaited a *Führer*. But when Hitler came to power and the Nazis offered Stefan George a position in the academy of poets, he refused and left Germany (and died shortly thereafter).

LEIPZIG, THE WAR, AND THE RECTORATE

In his memoirs, Gadamer writes about the welcome shift from the repressiveness and "moral terror" of Marburg to the freer atmosphere of the university in Leipzig "where the Nazi party hardly put in an appearance" (PA 33). Hitler started the war in the year after Gadamer's appointment as professor. The war years were a terrible time. Leipzig was heavily bombed. In these years Gadamer received his first international invitations to speak – in Florence, Paris, Lisbon, and Prague. Gadamer acknowledges in his memoirs that he, "a political innocent" (PA 99), was used for propaganda purposes. His lecture in Paris in 1941 was before French officers from a prisoner of war camp; it was published as a monograph (26 pages), *Volk and History in Herder's Thought* (1942). This lecture was republished in 1967 under a different title ("Herder and the Historical World") with a different introduction and a new very brief conclusion. The body of the essay saw few changes.[13]

In Leipzig, Gadamer socialized with Carl Goedeler, the former mayor of Leipzig, and became a fringe member of a group that met

regularly at his home. Gadamer never participated in this group's po-
litical activities, although he was aware that they were active against
Hitler. He became worried for his own safety in the aftermath of
the failed attempt on Hitler's life in 1944, because Goedeler and his
group participated in the plot against the Nazi-regime and because
Goedeler had spoken positively, though vaguely, about the role that
Gadamer might play in the time to come. Goedeler and several of
Gadamer's other friends and associates were arrested and executed.

At the time of the end of his stay in Marburg and his move to
Leipzig, his marriage began to unravel. His wife, Frida, had a dal-
liance with a romance language professor in Marburg, Werner Krauss.
Krauss, a committed Marxist, was later associated with the "White
Rose" movement in Germany, and in 1943 Gadamer intervened with
the authorities on his behalf. Gadamer was instrumental in getting
Krauss a position in Leipzig after the war. Gadamer met his second
wife in Leipzig. Katie Lekebusch was a philosophy student who became Gadamer's assistant. In the spring of 1945, she was denounced
for a statement she made against Hitler. She barely escaped immediate execution for treason and was imprisoned in Berlin where she was
scheduled to be sent to Ravensbruck, a concentration camp. However, she was freed with other prisoners during the final battle for
Berlin. They were married in 1950.

When the war ended, Gadamer was called upon to lead the reconstruction of the University of Leipzig as its rector. One of the
reasons given for the call was that Gadamer helped alienate students
in the human and social sciences from Nazism. His rectoral address
was titled " On the Primordiality of Science," and is an interesting
contrast to the rectoral address of Heidegger in Freiburg in 1933.[14]
Both addresses identified *Wissenschaft* (science in a broad sense) as
the essence and mission of the university. Both underscored the important educational role of the university in the larger context of
the nation and the world. Historically, both pointed to the significant role of ancient Greece in the development of science. Gadamer
spoke of science as the foundation of modern European culture, while
Heidegger sneered at the "pseudocivilization" of the West and saw
Germany as the successor to Greece. Both understandably saw the
university and Germany in a significantly new situation – in 1933,
the beginning of the Nazi Third Reich and in 1947 the beginning of

the communist Democratic Republic of East Germany. In the name of science, Gadamer silently resisted the new regime, while Heidegger embraced the new regime in his attempt to redefine science as being one with the *Führer* and *das Volk*. Both were interested not so much in science's results, but in the life of science. Both asserted that a questioning stance is the central characteristic of this life. Yet Heidegger presented this questioning life as the life of the will and its fate and asked that this life identify itself with the new regime. Gadamer argued that a life of science has three primary characteristics: absent-mindedness (objectivity), doubt, and humility. Had the scientists (human, social, and natural scientists) showed these characteristics, he argued, they would not have accommodated themselves so readily to Nazism and, implicitly, to the new Marxist–Leninist ideology. At approximately the same time as Gadamer's rectoral address, which concluded with a call to the revival of humane culture in Germany, Heidegger published his *Letter on Humanism*, which decried what humanism has wrought.

In an effort to rebuild the university, Gadamer spent approximately two years working with the Russians and the rising leaders of what would become East Germany, including Walter Ulbricht. Gadamer characterizes himself as resisting many of the Marxist–Leninist reforms of the university, yet "when I did not get my way with them, and that was of course most of the time, the Russians could at least be certain that I would carry through their directives exactly, even against my own convictions" (PA 107). Some of the difficulties had little to do with ideology but with the fact that the Russians had a differing view of universities. For them research was for research academies and institutes, and university teachers were not so different from high school teachers. The German Humboldtian university with its mission to combine teaching and research was foreign to them. After a year of doing administrative work night and day and constantly struggling with the authorities, Gadamer began to look elsewhere and in 1947 accepted an offer at Frankfurt in the West. At one point during his travels back and forth from Leipzig to Frankfurt, he was arrested upon his return to Leipzig and imprisoned for several days and interrogated at length. When he was released, he was all the more happy to be making the move to the West.

HEIDELBERG

Gadamer was eager to return to teaching and research, yet he did not find Frankfurt – the city, the university, or the philosophy department – welcoming. In 1949 he accepted a call from Heidelberg to assume the chair which had been Karl Jaspers'. Jaspers had moved to Basel, Switzerland, after the war. Heidelberg became Gadamer's home for the rest of his life. Noteworthy events of the time in Frankfurt were a radio broadcast on the significance of Nietzsche with Max Horkheimer and Theodor Adorno and an invited public discussion at Marburg with Paul Tillich about Heidegger's newly published "Letter on Humanism."

In Frankfurt he began an active professional philosophical career of participating in and organizing philosophical conferences and editing, publishing, and reviewing philosophical work. He translated, edited, and commented on Book XII of Aristotle's *Metaphysics* (1948) and he edited Wilhelm Dilthey's *Sketch of a General History of Philosophy* (1949). In 1953 with Helmut Kuhn he founded a journal, *Philosophische Rundschau* (Philosophical Review [literally, "Panorama"]), which became and remains an important publication. His list of book reviews and review discussions is very extensive. He served as president of the General German Society for Philosophy. He actively participated with the Heidelberg Academy of Sciences. He had many students and he devoted much of his energy to his teaching. For a while he accepted the administrative responsibilities of a dean. The list of professional activities goes on, and yet he published little. He felt pressure from his students, colleagues, publishers, and, indirectly, from Heidegger to publish something. In the mid-1950s he began to plan the project that was to become *Truth and Method*, but it was very difficult for him. Years after the publication of his major work he reported that "I always had the damn feeling that Heidegger was looking over my shoulder."[15]

In the late 1930s Gadamer had renewed his relationship with Heidegger. While in Frankfurt Gadamer put together a Festschrift in honor of Heidegger's sixtieth birthday. It was a delicate matter, inasmuch as Heidegger was a very controversial figure. At that time, he was forbidden to teach because of his engagement on behalf of National Socialism. At the same time there was enormous enthusiasm among students and in intellectual circles for Heidegger. Gadamer succeeded in putting together a volume that included critics of Heidegger's work and avoided what Gadamer refers to as "Heidegger scholasticism." Both Gerhard Krüger and Karl Löwith, who had habilitated under Heidegger at the same time that Gadamer had and were close friends of Gadamer, had published or were about to publish sharply negative critical essays on Heidegger's philosophy. Both contributed to the volume, which, for complicated reasons, appeared a year late and without Gadamer's name as editor. It should be added that in 1953 Gadamer persuaded Löwith to return to Germany and to a position at Heidelberg. Over the years Gadamer regularly invited Heidegger to visit his classes. Gadamer recalls that there was too much enthusiasm for Heidegger in the 1950s and, from his perspective, too little interest in the 1960s and beyond.

In 1957, Gadamer accepted an invitation to give a series of lectures, the Cardinal Mercier lectures, at the University of Louvain in Belgium. The lectures, entitled "The Problem of Historical Consciousness," were published as a small book in French. These lectures articulated the central theses of *Truth and Method*. He requested and received the first sabbatical of his career in the winter semester of 1958–9. In this fall and winter he finally completed the manuscript. As mentioned in the introduction of this volume, Gadamer initially proposed "Philosophical Hermeneutics" as a title for the work, but the publisher rejected it. "Fundamental Characteristics of a Philosophical Hermeneutics" became the subtitle for *Truth and Method*, which appeared in 1960.

Initially, the book did not elicit a large response. Emilio Betti published a critical review in which he charges Gadamer's hermeneutics with historicism and relativism.[16] In part as a response to Betti, Gadamer wrote an essay, "Hermeneutics and Historicism," for the *Philosophische Rundschau* in 1961.[17] In this essay he places his effort in *Truth and Method* in the larger context of developments in interpretation theory, addresses Betti's charges, takes issue with Leo Strauss, and relates his work to considerable work being done at the time in theological hermeneutics. This essay became an appendix to the second edition of *Truth and Method*, which appeared in 1965. Gadamer was not interested in continuing to concentrate on hermeneutics. He did not see himself as developing a system or a school of thought. He turned to other work, especially work on

Plato and Hegel, and he continued to be very active in the profession. Among other things, he helped found an international Hegel society. As the response to *Truth and Method* grew, however, Gadamer was consistently called upon to present and to defend his philosophical hermeneutics. Books on Hegel, Plato, and the poet Celan were completed in the 1970s after his retirement in 1968.

RETIREMENT AND LIFE AS A WORLD PHILOSOPHER

The year 1968 was an opportune time for Gadamer to retire. His health remained good. Retirement enabled him to escape the ugly confrontation with the student movement, which, from Gadamer's perspective, was attempting for the third time in his lifetime to submit the university and its teaching and research to ideology. At this time Gadamer was spared some of the bitter attacks by the student movement because he and his work were perceived to be somewhat sympathetic with the work of Jürgen Habermas who was popular with the left. Gadamer's retirement also enabled him to accept the many invitations to speak and lecture abroad. In particular, it allowed him to begin a regular pattern of spending the fall semester as a guest professor in the United States and Canada, first at Catholic University, then at McMaster University in Canada, and finally, for many years, at Boston College. In addition, the conditions of retirement at that point in Germany were such that Gadamer could continue to lecture at the university. Through the 1970s, almost every "summer" semester (April to July) Gadamer offered lectures in Heidelberg.

In this decade Gadamer became a world philosopher. *Truth and Method* was translated into Italian (1972), English (1975), French (1976), Spanish (1977), and Serbo-Croatian (1978). It was later translated into Japanese, Chinese, Russian, Hungarian, and Polish. Four more editions appeared in German. Intellectual developments worldwide in philosophy, literary studies, theology, and the social sciences took an interpretive turn and Gadamer's work was much discussed. He received countless invitations to lecture; he accepted many and lectured throughout Europe, North and South America, and Africa. Many awards and honorary degrees began to make their way to him. His extended stays in North America enabled him to perfect his English and to acquaint himself with English poetry and

Anglo-American philosophy. He enjoyed the more relaxed contact with Canadian and American students. In his memoirs he calls this period his "second youth" (PA 158).

A controversy that developed at the end of the 1960s and into the early 1970s that helped boost his prominence and the interest in his work was an exchange with Jürgen Habermas. Although Habermas in the appendix to his *Knowledge and Human Interests* (1968) explicitly endorsed Gadamerian hermeneutics as the appropriate method for what he calls the "historical–hermeneutical sciences," he criticized Gadamer's hermeneutics for taking a too uncritical posture with regard to tradition.[18] Gadamer's rehabilitation of the concepts of "prejudice" and "tradition," for Habermas made Gadamer's hermeneutics inadequate to the highest level of critical thinking, which should provide a "critique of ideology." Such a critique would be liberating and emancipating, on Habermas' account. He appealed to psychoanalysis as a model. Gadamer responded, in part by criticizing the appropriateness of the psychoanalytic model under which the therapist knows better than the disturbed patient. Gadamer's hermeneutics calls instead for a dialogue between the text and the interpreter. In 1971 much of this discussion was collected in a volume entitled *Hermeneutik und Ideologiekritik* which concludes with a "Reply" by Gadamer to Habermas and to the larger discussion.[19] Habermas later, in an award ceremony for Gadamer in Stuttgart, praises Gadamer for "urbanizing the Heideggerian province."[20]

Ten years later in 1981 an encounter of quite a different sort drew worldwide philosophical attention. Gadamer was invited to Paris to discuss with Jacques Derrida, the deconstructor of texts, their differing views of interpretation and textuality. Derrida and Gadamer shared much by way of their intellectual background and interests. Like Gadamer, Derrida cut his philosophical teeth on the phenomenology of Husserl and the philosophy of the later Heidegger. Hegel is an extremely important thinker for both of them. To be sure, French existentialism and, especially, structuralism were very important for Derrida's early development – movements unattended to by Gadamer. Gadamer prepared a paper, "Text and Interpretation," in which he tried to locate the basis for their differences. Historically he did this by criticizing Nietzsche. Gadamer, in an earlier exchange with Leo Strauss, acknowledged that he had never been interested in Nietzsche's thought. He agreed with Strauss that this represented an important difference between himself and Heidegger.[21] Gadamer's hermeneutics developed, in large part, in response to Dilthey; Heidegger, in his later work, was responding to Nietzsche. Gadamer clearly identifies Derrida's deconstructive thought as developing from Nietzsche and the later Heidegger. In this paper Gadamer asked the central question, "What is linguisticality?" And he followed this question with the rhetorical question, "Is it a bridge or a barrier?" For Gadamer it was a bridge of understanding, and he implied that it was a barrier for Derrida. Gadamer criticized privileging the psychopathological in the consideration of a paradigm case for interpretation. Such privileging led to a hermeneutics of suspicion. He insisted that understanding is to be understood as a discovery of meaning and not an insertion. Finally, he suggested that the task of the interpreter is to disappear in the face of the text: "The interpreter, who gives his reasons, disappears and the text speaks." Derrida responded briefly with three questions about the "good will" and with the assertion that he was not convinced that we ever really have the experience that Gadamer referred to as "the experience that we all recognize," i.e., the experience of understanding. Derrida's paper for the conference challenged Heidegger's reading of Nietzsche but did not address Gadamer. Gadamer was disappointed in the exchange, which together with a number of commentaries was eventually published in French, German, and English.[22] There were several other later encounters with Derrida, of which we have, to date, a single publication.[23]

The retirement years have been productive years for Gadamer. In the 1970s he completed a small book on Hegel, *Hegel's Dialectic*; a commentary on Paul Celan's "Atemkristall," *Who am I?*; and a book on Plato and Aristotle, *The Idea of the Good in Platonic-Aristotelian Philosophy*. He also wrote his memoirs, *Philosophical Apprenticeships*, which focused more on the philosophers he had known well personally – Natorp, Scheler, Heidegger, Bultmann, Krüger, Kroner, Lipps, Reinhardt, Jaspers, Löwith – than on himself. He chose as a motto for the volume, *De nobis ipsis silemus*, ("about ourselves we should be silent"), which fits well the tone and voice of the memoirs and which has a long and distinguished career as a motto. It was the motto for Natorp's memoirs and, before that, the motto for Kant's *Critique of Pure Reason* who borrowed it from Francis Bacon.

In these later years, he produced a number of autobiographical writings. Many were occasioned by special events, e.g., the death of a colleague, a celebration at Heidelberg University, an invitation back to Breslau, or the publication of a volume that memorialized an individual, such as an historical volume on Husserl. He contributed an extensive set of "Reflections on My Philosophical Journey" for the volume in the Library of Living Philosophers series that is dedicated to his work (1997). He agreed to many interviews that have appeared in newspapers, news journals, and philosophy journals in many languages. He also made a number of radio and television appearances in which he gave lectures, was interviewed, or was the subject of a media production. Most recently, on the occasion of his 100th birthday, an interview appeared in the *Frankfurter Rundschau*, in which Gadamer says that what he meant by the famous proposition of *Truth and Method*, that "Being that can be understood is language," is that "Being that can be understood begins to speak to us."[24]

Among these writings that consider his long life in German philosophy, the most notable are those that deal with Heidegger.[25] They are memorials, intellectual history, and philosophy. In these writings Gadamer assesses Heidegger's importance for the development of philosophical thought – not the least, for his significance for Gadamer's own development. Here he comes to terms with his powerful mentor. Although he had occasionally lectured on Heidegger's work, Gadamer did not publish any essays about Heidegger's thought until 1960, the year of the publication of *Truth and Method*, when Heidegger invited him to add an introduction to the second edition of Heidegger's *Origin of the Artwork*. In the late 1960s and 1970s, he published a number of essays on Heidegger in which Gadamer acknowledged his great debt to Heidegger, clarified what he takes to be Heidegger's extraordinary contributions to philosophy and thought, and yet, at the same time, exhibited a critical distance from Heidegger. He proudly pointed out that he learned to read poetry, especially Rilke and Hölderlin, without the help of Heidegger. The fact that Heidegger had never expressed much enthusiasm for Gadamer's philosophical hermeneutics was a large disappointment to Gadamer. But *Truth and Method*'s attempt at ontology and its appeal to the Platonic dialectic were not digestible for Heidegger, who was attempting to leave metaphysics and ontology behind and for whom Plato was the figure most responsible for the Western tradition's forgetfulness about Being.

Although in his own work and thought Gadamer had followed Heidegger's later turn to language, Gadamer did not and does not think that the language of the philosophical tradition is constraining in the way that Heidegger did. Heidegger's attempt to leave philosophy and its metaphysical language behind is a failed and unnecessary attempt, according to Gadamer. In an answer to a 1986 interview question as to why he does not use Heideggerian language, Gadamer responded that "the poeticizing mode of speech used by the later Heidegger ... bothered me. It made it easy to raise the charge of mythological thinking against him." He went on to say that

I am opposed to creating a special language and want to make the language which we normally use say what Heidegger speaks about. Yes, Heidegger knew this to some extent, knew of this danger; therefore he once interrupted himself when reading one of his essays to us and got quite impatient and said: "All of this is Chinese." And he was right. It is (EPH 128).

Fundamental to Gadamer's resistance to Heidegger's later views about the metaphysical tradition and metaphysical language is Gadamer's reading of Plato. Gadamer rejected Heidegger's view, which identified Plato and Platonism with metaphysics and the blindness of the philosophical tradition with regard to Being. Gadamer proudly suggested that his work on Plato was instrumental in persuading Heidegger at the end of his life of the inappropriateness of his reading and use of Plato. In a talk in 1983 at Castel Gandolfo to a small group of distinguished intellectuals invited by Pope John Paul II, Gadamer suggested that in the contemporary era of science and technology we can

learn something especially from the Greek heritage of our thought, which has indeed left us "science," but a science which remains integrated in the conditions of the human life world and in the guiding concept of its thinking, *physis*. Here it appears to me that Plato's dialectic achieves a new exemplary status. Plato had understood the task of philosophy to be the awakening of our thought of what in truth already lies in our life world experience and its sedimentation in language ....

And further,

it appears to me that the important presuppositions for solving the modern world's problems are none other than the ones formulated in the Greek experience of thought. In any case the progress of science and its rational application to social life will not create so totally different a situation that "friendship" would not be required, that is a sustaining solidarity which alone makes possible the organized structure of human coexistence (EPH 216–219).

In the 1980s and 1990s, as the above citation shows, Gadamer became increasingly interested in the relation of hermeneutics to practical philosophy. Aristotelian *phronesis* had provided a certain sort of model for his hermeneutics, and Gadamer returned to this relation and considered the relevance for contemporary issues in ethics and politics. This is given a particular development in his collection of essays on health and medical care, *On the Enigma of Health* (1993). The themes of theory and practice, science, and technology are prominent here as well as in essays on the fate of Europe and the role of reason in the contemporary world.

But most important to Gadamer among his most recent works is the work in aesthetics. In his later taking stock of the accomplishment of *Truth and Method*, Gadamer suggested that the book has appeared to some to be a response to issues in the *Geisteswissenschaften* (the human and social sciences), and that although this is true, the basis for the book's phenomenology of the hermeneutic experience of understanding is as much the experience of a work of art.[26] *Truth and Method* begins with a critique of aesthetic consciousness, both in its subjectivism and its idealism. This beginning echoes the critique of aesthetic consciousness he developed in his 1934 essay, "Plato and the Poets." Further, *Truth and Method* concludes with a treatment of a hermeneutic ontology that relies heavily on the treatment of language in Plato, especially in Plato's *Phaedrus* in which Socrates suggests that it is through beauty that the recollection of truth is awakened (*Phaedrus* 250).[27] For Gadamer, poetry is a paradigm of the artwork's beauty and the awakening of the experience of the truth of the other. The artwork exemplifies the dialectic of distance and closeness in its claim upon us, for in spite of its alien character, Gadamer argues, it can speak to us. Gadamer places the artwork in a social context when he considers its place in the festival, "which represents community in its most perfect form" (RB 39). With the analysis of the festival, Gadamer establishes the practical, social, and historical context of the work of art.

Not only is beauty importantly related to the true for Plato and Gadamer, it is also closely related to the good. Although Gadamer never attempted to develop an ethics or a politics, his hermeneutics is both ethical and political. The basic posture of anyone in the hermeneutical situation has profound implications for ethics and politics, inasmuch as this posture requires that one always be prepared that the other may be right. The ethic of this hermeneutic is an ethic of respect and trust that calls for solidarity. Gadamer himself embodies this ethic, not only in his work, but also in his life. All those who have encountered him, whether they find themselves in agreement with him or not, have found him, like the Socrates he so much admired, always ready for conversation.[28]

NOTES

1 Gadamer first learned of this episode from Mrs. Heidegger in 1976. See the biography of Gadamer by Jean Grondin, *Hans-Georg Gadamer: Eine Biographie* (Tübingen: Mohr Siebeck, 1999), p. 31.

2 *Das Erbe Europas* (Frankfurt: Suhrkamp, 1989), p. 8.

3 "Gadamer on Gadamer," in *Gadamer and Hermeneutics,* edited by Hugh J. Silverman (London: Routledge, 1991), p. 14.

4 See the interview, "The 1920's, 1930's, and the Present," in *Hans-Georg Gadamer on Education, Poetry, and History* (EPH), edited by Dieter Misgeld and Graeme Nicholson, translated by Lawrence Schmidt and Monica Reuss (Albany: SUNY Press, 1992), p. 136; see also "Reflections on My Philosophical Journey," where Gadamer calls the book "second-rate," in *The Philosophy of Hans-Georg Gadamer*, Library of Living Philosophers, edited by Lewis Hahn (Chicago and LaSalle: Open Court, 1997), p. 4.

5 "Too early of course; it was no good," he comments in an interview in 1995 with Alfons Greider, "A Conversation with Hans-Georg Gadamer," *Journal of the British Society for Phenomenology* 26 (1995), p. 116.

6 Grondin, pp. 131–51.

7 For a complete list of all of Gadamer's announced lectures at German universities, see the second appendix to Grondin's biography, pp. 390–99.

8 See Hugo Ott, *Martin Heidegger: A Political Life*, translated by Allan Blunden (New York: Basic Books, 1993), especially p. 252; and Otto

Pöggeler, "Den Führer führen? Heidegger und kein Ende," *Philosophische Rundschau* 32 (1985), pp. 26–67.

9 EPH 66: "I tried to have a career, and I succeeded by publishing little."

10 See Teresa Orozco, *Platonische Gewalt: Gadamers politische Hermeneutik der NS-Zeit* (Hamburg: Argument, 1995) and "The Art of Allusion: Hans-Georg Gadamer's Philosophical Interventions Under National Socialism," *Radical Philosophy* 78 (1996), pp. 17–26; also, Robin May Schott, "Gender, Nazism, and Hermeneutics," in *The Philosophy of Hans-Georg Gadamer*, edited by Lewis Hahn, vol. XXIV of The Library of Living Philosophers (Chicago and LaSalle, Illinois: Open Court, 1997), pp. 499–507 (Gadamer's reply p. 508). Robert Sullivan has also written about the politics of the young Gadamer. He acknowledges the compromises but is much more sympathetic to Gadamer than Orozco and Schott. See his *Political Hermeneutics: The Early Thinking of Hans-Georg Gadamer* (University Park: Pennsylvania State University Press, 1980). Most recently Richard Wolin has addressed this question in a review: "Untruth and Method," *The New Republic* 4, 432 (May 15, 2000), pp. 36–45. Wolin finds Gadamer's thought (quite unfairly, I think) in the 1930s and 1940s and even now to be "essentially immune to the lessons and the virtues of a democratic political culture" (p. 45), contrary to Gadamer's self-characterization as a liberal. For Wolin this follows from Gadamer's critique of the Enlightenment and his rehabilitation of prejudice and tradition. According to Wolin, though Gadamer was no Nazi, his "conservative" thought with its support for "authority" fit well the circumstances. It is not clear from Wolin's account whether he considers any critique of the Enlightenment to be fascist. Further, Wolin does not attend to Gadamer's nuanced treatment of prejudice, tradition, and authority.

11 The document was the *Bekenntnis der Professoren an die deutschen Universitäten und Hochschulen zu Adolf Hitler und dem nationalsozialistischen Staat* (A Declaration of Belief in Adolf Hitler and the National Socialist State by the Professors of the German Universities), November 11, 1933. For a discussion of this see Grondin's biography, p. 184.

12 Orozco in *Platonische Gewalt* does not find these two Plato essays critical of, but rather in collusion with, his political and historical context. There is some ambiguity in the texts – quite intentional, it would seem. Orozco points out how a number of philosophers who were active Nazis appealed to Plato to support Nazi politics, and she considers Gadamer's consideration of Plato on politics to be a less explicit version of the same. She cannot look past Plato's critique of democracy in the *Republic* and has no ear for Plato's irony.

13 The essay is untranslated and can be found in GW 4, pp. 318–35. The bibliographical comment (GW 4, p. 487) neglects to mention the 1942 publication: *Volk und Geschichte im Denken Herders* (Frankfurt: Klostermann, 1942). The 1967 version was first published as an afterword to an edition of Herder's *Auch eine Philosophie der Geschichte zur Bildung der Menschheit* (Frankfurt, 1967). Gadamer critic Richard Wolin finds this lecture and its circumstances indicative of Gadamer's complicity with Nazism ("Untruth and Method," pp. 43–4). Gadamer writes that the essay avoided "any relevance to the present" and that it offended the Nazis because he referred to Herder's discussion of the Slavs. Gadamer adds that he was proud of the occasion because in the discussion he commented that "an empire that extends itself beyond measure is ... near its fall" – a comment clearly understood and appreciated by the French prisoners. ("Reflections on My Philosophical Journey," p. 14)

My own careful comparison of the 1942 and 1967 versions of the essay shows that Wolin's claims that "the concept of *das Volk*, which was the intellectual focal point of the original text, has been excised virtually without a trace" is clearly unfounded in both its assertions. The focal point of the essay in 1942 as well as of the substantially unchanged 1967 essay is the concept of history, not the concept of *das Volk*. Further, the 1967 version does not excise the language of *das Volk*. The introduction to the 1942 essay scarcely mentions *das Volk*. Of the changes in the body of text there is only one sentence removed that speaks of *das Volk*. The several paragraph conclusion of the 1942 essay, which is replaced by a single paragraph in 1967, does speak of the particularity of the self-consciousness of the German *Volk* but concludes by referring to Herder's contribution in this regard as restoring a recognition of the "value and honor" of the German Middle Ages – not exactly the model of *das Volk* that the Nazis were promoting.

14 For Gadamer's rectoral address, see EPH, pp. 15–21. For Heidegger's rectoral address, see "The Self-Assertion of the German University," *The Review of Metaphysics* 38 (1985), pp. 467–81 (translation by Karsten Harries). Another translation by William Lewis can be found in *The Heidegger Controversy: A Critical Reader*, edited by Richard Wolin (New York: Columbia University Press, 1991), pp. 29–39.

15 My translation, GW 2, p. 491; in English in "Reflections on My Philosophical Journey," p. 15.

16 Emilio Betti, *Die Hermeneutik als allgemeine Methodik der Geisteswissenschaften* (Tübingen: J. C. B. Mohr, 1962).

17 *Philosophische Rundschau* 9 (1961), pp. 241–76; this is available in English as Supplement I to *Truth and Method*, pp. 460–91.

18 For his qualified endorsement, see *Knowledge and Human Interests*, pp. 309 and 348. For his critical review of *Truth and Method*, see *The Hermeneutic Tradition*, edited by Gayle Ormiston and Alan Schrift (Albany: SUNY Press, 1990), pp. 213–45.

19 *Hermeneutik und Ideologiekritik* (Frankfurt: Suhrkamp, 1970). Much of this is to be found in English in *The Hermeneutic Tradition*.

20 The occasion was the bestowal of the Hegel Prize by the city of Stuttgart in 1979. For the English translation see "Hans-Georg Gadamer: Urbanizing the Heideggerian Province," in *Philosophical-Political Profiles*, translated by Frederick Lawrence (Cambridge: MIT Press, 1983), pp. 189–97.

21 "Correspondence concerning *Wahrheit und Methode*: Leo Strauss and Hans-Georg Gadamer," *Independent Journal of Philosophy* 2 (1978), pp. 5–12. See also "Gadamer on Strauss – An Interview," *Interpretation* 12 (1984), pp. 1–13.

22 For the English see *Dialogue and Deconstruction: The Gadamer-Derrida Encounter*, edited by Diane P. Michelfelder and Richard E. Palmer (Albany, N.Y.: SUNY Press, 1989).

23 The proceedings of a conference in Capri on religion, which includes papers by Derrida, Vattimo, and others, have been published. Gadamer contributes a brief concluding summary statement. See "Dialogues in Capri," in *Religion*, translated by Jason Geiger and edited by Jacques Derrida and Gianni Vattimo (Stanford: Stanford University Press, 1998), pp. 200–11.

24 "Die Muttersprache kommt vor dem Internet," an interview with Hans-Dieter Jürger, *Frankfurter Rundschau*, February 11, 2000. For a list of a number of these interviews, published and broadcast, see the bibliography compiled by Richard Palmer in *The Philosophy of Hans-Georg Gadamer*, pp. 588–99.

25 Many, but not all, of these writings are collected and translated in *Heidegger's Ways*, translated by John W. Stanley (Albany: SUNY Press, 1994)

26 "Selbstdarstellung Hans-Georg Gadamer," GW 2, pp. 479–508, especially p. 495.

27 In 1983 Gadamer wrote that two things always stood and continue to stand in the foreground of his work: Plato and art. See *Das Erbe Europas* (Frankfurt: Suhrkamp, 1989), p. 171. Gadamer's reliance on Plato's *Phaedrus* for the culminating analysis of hermeneutical ontology in *Truth and Method* is testimony to the significance of these two "things" for Gadamer's work.

28 See *Begegnungen mit Hans-Georg Gadamer*, edited by Günter Figal (Stuttgart: Reclam, 2000), especially Richard Rorty's and Dennis Schmidt's accounts of their experiences with Gadamer.

2   Gadamer's Basic Understanding of Understanding

When presenting his own ideas or analyzing concepts, Hans-Georg Gadamer likes to follow the lead of language. The fact that the basic notions he is unfolding often have many very different meanings does not bother him. Quite on the contrary, he sees in this plurality of meaning an indication that language, long before thinking, is perhaps up to something essential. So it is with Gadamer's basic notion of understanding. This notion carries many different meanings, which nonetheless all point to one central phenomenon, i.e., the understanding that he characterizes, following Heidegger, is "the original form of the realization of our existence."[1] Because this is a rather vague formula, I will single out, in what follows, three different, yet very prominent connotations this notion has in *Truth and Method*, which all refer back to a particular origin of the hermeneutical problem of understanding, but that according to Gadamer all pertain to a central phenomenon that has to be comprehended in its unity.[2]

UNDERSTANDING AS AN INTELLECTUAL GRASP

First, one can quite naturally associate understanding with an epistemological or cognitive process. To understand (*verstehen*) is, in general, to grasp something ("I get it"), to see things more clearly (say, when an obscure or ambiguous passage becomes clear), to be able to integrate a particular meaning into a larger frame. This basic notion of understanding was certainly dominant in the hermeneutical theories of the nineteenth century. Wilhelm Dilthey saw in this *Verstehen* the elementary cognitive process at the root of all social and human sciences. In understanding, an expression (*Ausdruck*) is

36

understood as the manifestation of a life experience (*Erlebnis*), which our understanding actually strives to reenact (*nacherleben*) or to reconstruct. If the human sciences are to be strict and rigorous, Dilthey concluded, they will have to rest on a methodology or a hermeneutics of understanding. This notion of understanding stands in the continuity of the Latin notion of *intelligere* (to comprehend, have insight) in the older theories of hermeneutics. Ernesti and Morus spoke of a *subtilitas intelligendi* and Schleiermacher of hermeneutics as a *Kunstlehre des Verstehens*, a doctrine of understanding. Understanding in this tradition is the process by which an ambiguous or obscure passage (of Scripture, for instance) is made intelligible. How one construes this notion of understanding more precisely is of secondary importance here and does not concern Gadamer directly either. Nevertheless, it is clear that his notion of understanding also stems from this tradition, when he seeks to clarify what understanding means in the human sciences and asks whether a methodology is all that makes up the cogency of our understanding.

UNDERSTANDING AS PRACTICAL KNOW-HOW

This epistemological understanding of understanding as an intellectual grasp was certainly shaken up, if not undermined, by Martin Heidegger, whom Gadamer follows in this regard. In what can be termed a more "practical" notion of understanding, Heidegger argued in *Being and Time* (1927) that understanding designates less a cognitive (and thus methodological) process than a know-how, an ability, a capacity, a possibility of our existence. He follows the lead of language here. The German locution "*sich auf etwas verstehen,*" means "to be capable of something." In this regard, one who "understands" something is not so much someone endowed with a specific knowledge, but someone who can exercise a practical skill. A good cook, a good teacher, a good soccer player is not necessarily an apt theoretician of his trade, but he "knows" his trade, as the English locution puts it. This "knowing" is, of course, less cognitive than practical, as one "knows" how to swim. So it is with the basic understanding on which we thrive and by way of which we sort our way through life. The German locution Heidegger draws on is also reflective in German: "*sich*" *verstehen.* To understand always implies an element of self-understanding, self-implication, in the sense that it is always a possibility of my own self that is played out in understanding. It is I who understands Plato, who knows French, in the sense that "I can do it," I am capable of it, up to the task (but always only to a certain extent).[3] Why this notion is of so paramount a consequence for Heidegger (and Gadamer) is clear enough. As a being that is always concerned by its own being, human existence is always concerned and in search of orientation. This basic orientation is acted out in some sort of attuned "understanding," in my abilities, my capacities that make up "the entire realization" of my existence. Heidegger, to be sure, writes of the understanding more dramatically than Gadamer, who may seem basically concerned with the problem of understanding in the human sciences in the main sections of *Truth and Method*. According to Heidegger, every understanding presupposes an interpretation of Being or of what it is "to be there," that must be cleared up, sorted out by a being (*Dasein*) that, as a being of understanding, can also understand its own self and its own possibilities of understanding. This sorting out of understanding (*Verstehen*), Heidegger terms "interpretation" (*Auslegung*), so that his "hermeneutics" (derived from the term *Auslegung*) will be a sorting out of the possibilities of human understanding. It is a hermeneutics of this concerned existence and understanding that Heidegger hopes to develop in order to clear up the preconceptions of being that silently govern our understanding. Gadamer presupposes all of this, of course, but he shies away from the idea of such a direct hermeneutics of existence. Instead, he uses this "practical" notion of understanding to shake up the epistemological notion that prevailed in the tradition of Dilthey and the methodology of the human sciences. To understand, even in these sciences, he claims, is to be concerned, repeated, that is, to be able to apply a certain meaning to my situation. To understand is thus to apply, Gadamer strongly argues, following Heideggerian premises. It is always a possibility of my understanding that is played out when I understand a text.

A very important source for this Gadamerian notion of practical or applicative understanding, perhaps more so than for Heidegger, was Aristotle's notion of practical understanding (*phronesis*, often rendered by prudence, following the Latin translation). As early as 1930, thirty years before *Truth and Method*, Gadamer devoted a short essay to this notion of practical knowledge ("Praktisches Wissen,"

GW 5, 230–48, first published in 1985). In this type of understanding, application is indeed crucial. Because practice is all about action, it is of no use to have an abstract notion of the good (as in Plato's idea of the good, Aristotle polemically argued). What counts is to be able to do the good in human affairs. It would be a misunderstanding and an anachronism to see in this the seeds of a situative or relativistic ethics.[4] According to Gadamer, Aristotle only recognizes that the point of practical wisdom lies in its actualization, which always entails an element of self-knowledge, since it is always a possibility of myself that is involved in the situation of practice and where distance from this practice can induce a distortion. Perhaps more importantly, Aristotle saw that this presence of the "knower," this proximity or attentiveness to what is at stake is a mode of "knowledge," one, Gadamer contends, that can be fruitfully applied to the "interested" knowledge displayed in the human and social sciences. In short, if Gadamer's practical understanding appears less linked to Heidegger's project of a hermeneutics of preoccupied existence, he does retain its notion of reflectivity and application in order to *understand better* what understanding is all about.

UNDERSTANDING AS AGREEMENT

As if to complicate matters, but in order *to grasp better* the phenomenon, Gadamer single-handedly draws on yet another meaning of understanding, a third source for our purposes, after (1) the epistemological understanding of the tradition and (2) the practical understanding of Heidegger. "To understand" (*sich verstehen*), he points out, can also mean in German "to agree," "to come to an agreement," "to concur." *Sich verstehen* (to understand one another) is thus pulled in the direction of the notion of *Verständigung*, or agreement, accord. This connotation can also be heard in the English locution "we understand each other," meaning that the partners in a conversation find themselves in a basic agreement, generally on this or that matter. Yet, how does this relate to the basic notion of understanding that concerns Gadamer with? Is it the same thing to try to understand a text (epistemological *Verstehen*), to know one's way around (practical *Verstehen*), and to agree on something (*sich verstehen*)? The least one can say is that the similarity is less than striking. How does Gadamer manage to fit them all into one coherent notion of understanding? One can hardly say his texts shed full clarity on this notion of understanding qua agreement. The notion of agreement is certainly less evident than the conflation of epistemological and practical understanding (because to understand a text can also mean that one knows one way around the text). I believe Gadamer draws on this notion of agreement for two reasons.

First, he wishes to take issue with the notion that to understand is to reconstruct, in a disinterested fashion, the meaning of the text according to its author (*mens auctoris*). This notion prevailed in Dilthey and the epistemological tradition. Gadamer deems it too "aesthetic" or too "contemplative" in the sense that it does not do justice to the fact that the interpreter is also very much concerned by the matter at hand. The notion of *Verständigung* (agreement) here underscores the fact that the reader or interpreter of a text shares a basic "agreement" or "understanding" (hence the important relation) about what the text is about. When I read a text of Plato on justice, for instance, I do not merely want to record Plato's opinions on the subject. I also share (and put into play, Gadamer will say) a certain understanding of justice, in the sense that I know or sense what Plato is talking about. According to Gadamer, such a basic understanding of what he emphatically calls the *Sache*, the matter at hand or the subject matter, is inherent in every understanding (it also applies in conversation where the discussion partners share a common ground). If Gadamer insists on this element of agreement, it is to underline the point that understanding is primarily related to the issue at hand and not to the author's intention as such. This is polemically directed against the nineteenth-century notion according to which the primordial task of interpretation is to reconstruct the author's (original) meaning. Following Gadamer, this attention to the author's meaning is at best a secondary direction of understanding. It only arises – as a kind of detour – when the basic agreement on the subject matter is disturbed. Let us take, for example, the extreme case of one who seeks to understand the book *Mein Kampf*. It is obvious enough that one can and must "understand" it without agreeing with it. This is why the book can only be read, by a person in her sound mind, as a document of Hitler's perverse ideas; that is, one can only understand it historically or psychologically. But this is so because basic agreement has been completely shattered. One will read a poem of Rilke, a tragedy of Sophocles, or the *Elements* of Euclid very differently, i.e., by relating to the subject matter, by being concerned by what is said, not by who says it. Of course, one can also inquire about the personal opinions of Rilke, Sophocles, or Euclid, and there is a vast literature on these subjects. However, Gadamer believes this is a secondary direction of understanding, one that aims at reconstructing an expression as the opinion of a subject and thus by suspending the basic relation to the truth of what is being said. It is thus a misunderstanding to see in Gadamer's applicative model of understanding a complete rejection of the notion of the *mens auctoris* (the author's intention). Gadamer never says that there is no such thing or that it can never be the goal of any interpretation (which would be preposterous); he only says – aiming polemically at its exacerbation in nineteenth-century hermeneutics – that it is never the primary focus of understanding, which is always first and foremost guided by the subject matter. Furthermore, it is obvious that I can only hope to reconstruct the author's intention if I also have an idea of what he is talking about. There is thus a precedence of the understanding (or the "agreement," though this might sound awkward in English, but it is also not all that evident in German either) of the *Sache*, the thing at stake, over the *mens auctoris*.

A second reason helps explain why Gadamer emphasizes this notion that understanding implies a form of agreement. Agreement, namely, is something that occurs mostly through language, dialogue or conversation. This notion bestows specific weight on the linguistic element of understanding. To understand is to put something into words or, to put it more prudently, to couch understanding in a potentially linguistic element (the meaning of this restriction will become apparent shortly). This linguisticality of understanding was not crucial to Heidegger's practical understanding in *Being and Time*, nor for that matter to the epistemological notion that understanding is the reconstruction of a process of creation (for Dilthey). But it is for Gadamer, even if it only stressed at the end of *Truth and Method* – to the point of supporting the universality of hermeneutic experience altogether. To understand, in Gadamer's sense, is to articulate (a meaning, a thing, an event) into words, words that are always mine, but at the same time those of what I strive to understand. The application that is at the core of every understanding process thus grounds in language.

One could raise here the important objection that not everything that I understand can be put into words. I can understand a signal, a piece of art, or music. I can also be confronted with the unsayable that cannot be put into words. In *Truth and Method*, Gadamer evokes in this regard the very revealing example of the painter, the sculptor, or the musician who would claim that any linguistic rendition or explanation of his work would be beside the point (TM 399; GW 1, 403). The artist can only discard such a linguistic interpretation, Gadamer contends, in light of some other "interpretation" that would be more to the point. But this interpretation, as an accomplishment or realization of meaning (*Vollzug*), is still geared to a possible language, even if it espouses the form of a dance or a mere contemplation. The important idea for Gadamer's notion of interpretation and its inherent linguisticality is that the listener be taken up by what he seeks to understand, that he responds, interprets, searches for words or articulation and thus understands. It is in this response that Gadamer sees the applicative, self-implying nature of understanding at work. Of course, understanding often fails. But it then fails to say what would need to be said. The failure of words can only be measured by what they fail to say. The unsayable is only the unsayable in light of what one would like to say, but cannot. The limits of language thus confirm – and very eloquently – the universality of language as the medium of understanding, as Gadamer sees it. Thus, it is the idea of agreement (*Verständigung*) that enabled Gadamer to introduce language into the scope of his hermeneutic conception.

UNDERSTANDING AS APPLICATION AND TRANSLATION

To recapitulate the three connotations and philosophical origins of Gadamer's notion of understanding, one can say that it displays a cognitive, a practical, and a linguistic element. The three elements are summed up in the notion of application, one of the most original of *Truth and Method*. It has widely been misunderstood, however, in a subjectivistic sense, one that would open the door to relativism. It was assumed here that "application" meant something like an appropriation, an interested adaptation to our situation, or some form of modernization. This would lead to a cheap form of subjectivism indeed. It is not what Gadamer intended. He distinctly rejected such a "hermeneutic nihilism," as he strongly put it and that he associated with Valéry's seeming blank check to interpretation: "My verses have whatever meaning is given them" (TM 95, GW 1, 100). Indeed, interpretations that are too subjectively biased or modernizing are easily recognized as such and, whatever their intrinsic creative merits, are mostly viewed as doing violence to the work they are "over-interpreting." What was forgotten here, is that Gadamer's notion of application is much more akin to that of "translation," which plays a prominent part in his hermeneutics (TM 384; GW 1, 387, where it ushers in the linguistic thematic of the third and concluding section of the volume). The meaning (event, person, monument) that is to be understood is always one that needs to be translated, so that understanding, application, and translation become almost equivalent terms for Gadamer. What I seek to translate (understand, apply) is always something that is at first foreign to me, but that is in some way binding for my interpretation. I seek to understand Plato, Schubert, a scientific theory, and so forth. I cannot say whatever I want, but I can only unfold my understanding in terms that I can follow and hope to communicate. Understanding, as an application, is thus always a challenge, but I can only raise up to it if I succeed in finding words for what needs and cries to be understood. I can only understand Plato by using language that is familiar to me, even if what I am striving to comprehended is a thinking that was formulated in the ancient Greece of the fourth century B.C. Even the sheer otherness of the foreign meaning I am striving to understand – for instance, a Greek word for which there is seemingly no modern equivalent – must be rendered in terms that are present and give me a sense of this otherness. Application is here required, and always involved, because it is a *Sache*, a vaguely common subject matter that hopes to be understood. Of course, this understanding can only be tentative. It is an attempt on my part to come to grips with what needs to be understood, but which can never be absolutely final. One can always find better words for what needs to be understood, more suited "applications."

The words we use are such applications. The example of a Plato interpretation is a good case in point. If a student asks a teacher about a good introduction to Plato, one rarely recommends a book from the eighteenth or nineteenth century. One will generally think of a more recent one, because it will better convey for us today the thought developed by Plato (the same is obvious in history). This does not necessarily imply that we understand Plato "better" than other epochs. It simply means that these recent interpretations articulate an understanding (i.e., a translation) of Plato and his subject matter to which we can relate and that has an appeal worthy of the title of objectivity because it gives us a better idea of Plato. Further, this does not entail a historical relativism (although most construed it in that way – a charge Gadamer always rejected) because it only means that interpretations must be articulated in a language that is to the point because it reaches its public and thus conveys what strives to be understood.

What leads to the suspicion of historical relativism was certainly Gadamer's stress on the prejudices of interpretation at the very outset of his systematic analysis of understanding. His point seemed to be – because it was after all the title of an important section – that our prejudices are "conditions of understanding." Nothing would seem closer to relativism. But what Gadamer actually showed in this section was that our understanding is always subject to revision when confronted with more convincing evidence and interpretations (which can only be articulated in words we can understand and follow). The entire point of his analysis of the hermeneutical circle concerned indeed this tentative nature of understanding. We start off with vague anticipations of the whole, which are, however, revised the more we engage the text and the subject matter itself. The basic hermeneutic experience (in the strong sense of *Erfahrung*), Gadamer will argue, is the experience that our anticipations of understanding have been shattered. Most experience, true experience that is, that delivers insight, is negative, he insists. In the masterful, conclusive, and undoubtedly very personal chapter on this nature of hermeneutic experience at the end of the second section of *Truth and Method*, Gadamer draws from this the conclusion that true experience must thus lead to an openness to ever newer experience. Someone with experience, he argues, will also be ready to leave things open, to even tolerate a plurality of possible interpretations, because no single one can really be exhaustive. Gadamer's Socratic wisdom clearly finds expression in this hope that the insight in the prejudiced character and negativity of hermeneutic understanding can only lead to further openness. But a shrewd critic of Gadamer, Claus von Bormann, drew a very different consequence from Gadamer's analysis of the finite and prejudiced character of every human understanding. Is it not the case that this finitude, more often than not, leads less to the openness to new experience than to the stubborn reaffirmation of one's own prejudices? He thus spoke of the *Zweideutigkeit*, the equivocal nature of the hermeneutical experience.[5] But the very fact that Gadamer had stressed openness rather than closure (which, of course, can never be excluded as long as we are finite beings) shows in what direction he wished his hermeneutics would lead. We can never transcend the realm of prejudices (because we are always implied in our understanding), but we can transcend those that have proven inept or fruitless. So, Gadamer never disputes that one must distinguish between "the true prejudices, by which we understand, from the false ones, by which we misunderstand" (TM 298–99; GW 1, 304). How does one go about this? Gadamer's short answer is that there is no quick fix. This would only be a delusion fostered by the modern technological age. As finite beings, we must learn and work through this distinction by ourselves, through experience, and Gadamer warns it is mostly negative. But we can learn, and that is not nothing. How we learn, Gadamer cannot specify, because his hermeneutics does not aim to offer a methodology or technology, but an account of what understanding is and how it involves our very being. Yet he alludes to the help of dialogue and temporal distance in sorting out the crucial difference between the true prejudices and the false ones. Often, it is through experience and time that we come to recognize what is appropriate and what is not. Again, there might be some optimism in this conviction of Gadamer, but who can deny that through time (and better insight) we learn to depart from some of our prejudices? Gadamer's prime example for the distinction between true and false prejudices was the experience of art, because it is only through time that we come to recognize what is of value in art and what is only passing. So he defended in 1960 the strong thesis that "it is only temporal distance that can solve the critical question of hermeneutics," i.e., the distinction to be made between true and false prejudices. That was perhaps too optimistic, even if it was not totally incorrect. But temporal distance can also serve to cement false prejudices and to repress innovative, better ideas, and it is of no effect when one has to adjudicate the value of contemporary works. It is interesting to note that Gadamer himself came to recognize the one-sidedness of his strong thesis of 1960. In what amounts to a nonnegligible revision of one of its central tenets, Gadamer modified the text of *Truth and Method* when it was published in his Complete Works edition in 1986 and, instead of "it is only temporal distance," he now prudently writes: "Often temporal distance can solve the critical question of hermeneutics" (TM 298; GW I, 304). This is a very minor change linguistically, but it highlights Gadamer's own willingness to revise interpretations that have proven untenable or too restrictive. He was thus faithful to his own understanding of understanding. For Gadamer, understanding is essentially open, but also a risk. This tentative nature of our understanding might be unsettling to more methodologically attuned hermeneutical theories, which will settle for nothing less than methodical certainty. But, in so doing, they will perhaps also do away with the basic openness of understanding.

THE HERMENEUTICAL CIRCLE

From Gadamer's threefold notion of understanding, which is summed up in the notion of understanding as application, one can also better understand his famous thesis on the circularity of interpretation. Here again, he followed the lead of Heidegger's insight in the positive, i.e., ontological or constitutive nature of this circularity. Heidegger's point was that every interpretation (*Auslegung*) presupposes understanding (*Verstehen*), because every interpretation is guided by (comprehensive) anticipations. One should note however that Heidegger had strong reservations about the notion of circle in this regard. He found it too geometrical, because it was modeled on spatial being and therefore unsuited to express the preoccupied mobility of human understanding. This is why he warns – and even does so twice in *Being and Time* – that one should avoid describing *Dasein* using the circle metaphor.[6] If he did so himself, one has to see that it was only to respond to the suspicion of logical circularity or *petitio principii* that his basic thesis (namely that interpretation always presupposes understanding) seemed to entail. According to the elementary rules of logic, Heidegger writes, this circle can only be *vitiosus*, utterly vicious! Thus, the provoking irony of Heidegger, paraphrasing him: well, if you insist on talking about a circle, then perhaps the important thing is not to run away from it, but to just jump into it.[7] With full sarcasm, Heidegger obviously wanted to turn the tables on the logical criticisms he anticipated.

In order to clarify what is at stake and to emphasize Gadamer's own position on the issue, one should distinguish an *epistemological* from a more *phenomenological* reading of this circularity. From a logical – epistemological perspective, the circle can only be a "vice" because it consists, in a proof for instance, in presupposing what needs to be established. It is a tautology to speak here of a circle or a *petitio principii*. But Heidegger and Gadamer are interested by something else, namely the phenomenological insight that every interpretation draws on anticipations of understanding. In this perspective, it is the proclamation that an interpretation is free from any anticipations that must appear naive and uncritical.

Despite this basic agreement, there are some important differences between Heidegger's and Gadamer's account of the hermeneutic circle. First of all, it is striking to observe that Heidegger *never* speaks of the circle of the whole and its parts, but always of the circle between understanding (*Verstehen*) and its unfolding in the interpretative process (*Auslegung*). It is precisely this argument that raises the suspicion of logical circularity. Is interpretation then nothing but the confirmation of a preestablished understanding? Gadamer, for his part, clearly associates the idea of circularity with the idea of the coherence of the whole and the parts. He usefully points out that this rule (*hermeneutische Regel!*) stems from ancient rhetoric (TM 291; GW 1, 296; a reference absent in Heidegger's account), where it was intended as a general principle of composition, according to which a text must articulate the parts with the intent of the whole (a requirement already found in Plato's *Phaedrus* 264c). Through authors such as Melanchthon, it passed from rhetoric to hermeneutics where it originally had a purely phenomenological meaning. It was used to describe the to-and-fro motion of any attempt at understanding, from the parts to the whole and from the whole back to the parts. The circle for Gadamer does not describe a logical vice, but, and indeed quite on the contrary, the constant process that consists of the revision of the anticipations of understanding in light of a better and more cogent understanding of the whole. Gadamer will justly see in this coherence of the whole and the parts a "criterion of correct understanding" (TM 291; GW 1, 296).

This coherence of the whole and parts is guided by what Gadamer calls the "anticipation of perfection" of what is to be understood. According to this tacit anticipation, understanding presupposes that the meaning to be understood builds a perfectly coherent whole... until all else fails. Gadamer luminously underlines that this anticipation is a consequence of the notion of the hermeneutical circle (TM 293–4; GW 1, 299). For it is the coherence that is assumed of the *interpretandum* that brings me to a revision of my earlier anticipations if they are proven untenable. The adequation between my anticipations and the meaning to be understood thus continues to function as the teleological goal of interpretation for Gadamer. What receives confirmation in this is Gadamer's notion that understanding always implies an agreement concerning the issue at hand. If this agreement fails, one will have to risk the detour of a psychological or historicist interpretation, alluded to above.

From all this, one sees that Gadamer's account of the circle is in one sense *less* epistemological than Heidegger's, because it doesn't start off from the suspicion of logical circularity raised by the idea that interpretation always presupposes (pre-)understanding. But in another sense, Gadamer's analysis turns out to be *more* epistemological because it is far more concerned with the notion that the hypotheses of interpretation are only provisional and constantly need to be rectified. This slight difference can be explained by the fact that Heidegger and Gadamer have different applications of understanding in mind. Whereas Heidegger is primarily concerned with the anticipation of existence that is involved in every understanding and that his hermeneutics of existence is interrogating, Gadamer seems to concentrate more on the certainly more limited problem of text interpretation in the human sciences. One could say that Gadamer "philologizes" or rather "re-philologizes" what was for Heidegger primarily an existential circularity. This shift has led Odo Marquard to claim, humoristically, that Gadamer thus replaced Heidegger's "Being-towards-death" with a "Being-towards-the-text."[8] This is obviously in part a caricature, because who could deny that one's Being-toward-death always remains in play when one is reading a text? Nevertheless, Gadamer's main focus seems to be indeed different than that of Heidegger, whose hermeneutics of existence ultimately aims at sorting out an "authentic" mode of understanding (an aspect that is, if not entirely absent, certainly less predominant in Gadamer's presentation).

Closely related to this difference of focus is Heidegger's insistence on the fact that understanding is oriented toward the future, to future existence and the resoluteness it calls for, whereas Gadamer prefers to insist on the determination of understanding by the past. Gadamer himself alluded to this difference in his answer to Karl-Otto Apel in the Library of Living Philosophers volume, but which can also be read as an answer to his master Heidegger as well:

Apel describes what disturbs him in my thought, namely, the 'strange primacy of the past over the future.' This, however, must astonish me. The future which we do not know is supposed to take primacy over the past? Is it not the past which has stamped us permanently through its effective history? If we seek to illuminate this history we may be able to make ourselves conscious of and overcome some of the prejudices which have determined us.[9]

It might be useful to put these differences between Heidegger's and Gadamer's account of the hermeneutical circle in the following table:

	Heidegger	*Gadamer*
Terms of the circle	Circle of understanding (*Auslegung*) and the interpretation (*Verstehen*) that guides it	Circle of the whole and the parts
Logical value	The circle stems from the appearance of a vicious circle (*circulus vitiosus*) or a *petitio principii* –thus an ⟨⟨epistemological⟩⟩ circle (but only from the point of view of some logicist critics)	The circle renders a ⟨⟨hermeneutical rule⟩⟩ (which stems from ancient rhetoric) –phenomenological circle (that describes a process)
Limit of the circle metaphor	A spatial, geometrical figure that is unsuited to the preoccupied mobility of existence because it was modeled on the paradigm of substantial being or *Vorhandenheit*	There is not really a circle, because it only expresses a requirement of coherence that calls for a constant revision of the hypotheses of interpretation (following the anticipation perfection) – in this regard Gadamer appears far more epistemological than Heidegger
Main application focus	Hermeneutics of existence	Hermeneutics of text interpretation

	Heidegger	*Gadamer*
Understanding is mainly	To know one's way around, to be up to a task	To agree on the thing itself
The prestructure of understanding consists of	An anticipation of existence in fore-sight (*Vorsicht*), pre-acquisition (*Vorhabe*) and pre-conceptuality (*Vorgriff*)	Prejudices (*Vorurteile*)
Source of the anticipations	Primacy of the future	Primacy of the past and effective history

The basic agreement between Gadamer and Heidegger pertains, of course, to the "ontological" nature of the circle, i.e., the recognition that the circle is not some flaw that can be wished away, but rather a constitutive element of understanding. Nevertheless, it would be erroneous to assume that Gadamer simply repeats or takes over Heidegger's own notion of understanding. Although he certainly builds on it, it is his merit to have applied it to the field of the hermeneutical disciplines and the linguistic nature of our experience.

NOTES

1 TM 259; GW 1, 264. See also Gadamer's explanation of this formula in his "debate" with Paul Ricoeur, published under the title "The Conflict of Interpretations," in *Phenomenology: Dialogues and Bridges*, edited by R. Bruzina and B. Wilshire (Albany: SUNY Press, 1982), p. 302: "On this basis, Heidegger developed his hermeneutics of facticity. He interpreted the temporal structure of *Dasein* as the movement of interpretation such that interpretation doesn't *occur* as an activity in the course of life, but *is* the *form* of human life. Thus, we are interpreting by the very energy of our life, which means 'projecting' in and through our desires, wishes, hopes, expectations, as well as in our life-experience; and this process culminates in its expression by means of speech. The interpretation of another speaker and his speech, of a writer and his text, is just a special aspect of the process of human life as a whole."

2 According to Gadamer, and this could also be seen as one of the basic insights of his philosophy, "every specialization is associated with a certain narrowing of horizon." See "Die Philosophie und ihre Geschichte,"

in *Grundriss der Geschichte der Philosophie,* begründet von Friedrich Ueberweg, *Die Philosophie der Antike* (Basel: Schwabe, 1998), p. V: "Es gibt keine Methodik des Fragens und alle Spezialisierung ist mit Horizontverengung verknüpft."

3 According to Heidegger, this 'ability' or 'familiarity' of existence is only the reverse expression of the sheer unfamiliarity or uncanniness of our being in this world. Any successful understanding appears as a kind of respite, but also, in a way, as a covering-up of our basic failure to understand, as if there would be an inherent delusion to every attempt at understanding. See *Being and Time* (BT), translated by John Macquarrie and Edward Robinson (New York: Harper & Row, 1962), p. 234. For the German see *Sein und Zeit* (SZ) (Tübingen: Niemeyer, 1967), p. 189.

4 For a discussion of this misunderstanding see my *Introduction à Hans-Georg Gadamer* (Paris, Cerf, 1999), p. 156.

5 See Claus von Bormann, "Die Zweideutigkeit der hermeneutischen Erfahrung," in *Hermeneutik und Ideologiekritik* (Frankfurt, Suhrkamp, 1971), pp. 83–119. Gadamer appears to acknowledge the legitimacy of von Bormann's observation in GW 2, 256.

6 BT 195, 362; SZ 153, 314.

7 BT 194-195, SZ 152-3.

8 See O. Marquard, *Abschied vom Prinzipiellen* (Stuttgart: Reclam, 1981), p. 130 et passim.

9 *The Philosophy of Hans-Georg Gadamer,* The Library of Living Philosophers, vol. XXI, edited by L. E. Hahn (Chicago and LaSalle: Open Court, 1997), p. 95.

3 Getting it Right: Relativism, Realism and Truth

Is there a conception of reality that can be rationally justified independently of the standpoint of the persons whose conception it is? Such a conception has sometimes been referred to as an "objective" or "absolute" conception of reality, and philosophers such as Bernard Williams and Thomas Nagel think we can find it among the most advanced and secure truth-claims of the natural sciences.[1]

Nowadays, however, it seems more common to hear philosophers deny that there are any absolute conceptions of reality, even in the natural sciences. Every theoretical advance, they point out, has a "history" that conditions and thus "relativizes" the truth of the position advanced. Traces of such histories can be seen in the contingent changes in the conceptual languages in which truth-claims are put forth. For example, Hilary Putnam recently reminded us that even terms such as "electron" can have a conceptual history that changes with the historically shifting context of research.[2] What makes this fact problematic for traditional notions of objectivity is that such notions usually insist that the objects of research or the referents of terms such as "electron" or "genes" are what they are independent of our conceptual vocabulary. This creates the expectation that we ought somehow to be able to compare the adequacy or accuracy of any conceptual vocabulary against the object itself. But if we have no way to locate such referents independently of those same vocabularies and, moreover, if those vocabularies are subject to change (even seemingly random and unpredictable change), then where, it is often asked, are we to find the fixed, concept-independent object?

Even more troubling, perhaps, for traditional notions of objectivity is a fact that many sociologists of science are fond of pointing out, namely, that every truth-claim comes somehow laced with the values and interests of the researchers and the research community. This creates a similar problem for traditional notions of the object of research. Not only should the object be cognitively accessible to us independent of any contingent conceptual language, but also its cognitive availability should not depend on anything so seemingly subjective as our "values" and "interests." If we take into account that such values and interests are not purely "theoretical" values such as the "value" of simplicity or an "interest" in truth or in the lawful prediction of future events, but are also always inextricably linked to the normative notions of human flourishing, then it becomes even more difficult to deny that all truth-claims are in some important sense "relative" to the point of view or "interpretation" of the researchers. Putnam points out that research in the natural sciences is not devoid of practical or normative conceptions of what it means to function well in this sphere.[3] For example, contributions to all fields of research are framed with an eye to conceptions of what counts as "worthwhile knowledge," a conception that cannot be separated from a conception of either the research community's needs or, for that matter, from the normative notions of what counts as a "rational," "defensible," or "successful" contribution. In other words, all such "successful" contributions presuppose a normative understanding of what theoretical and practical needs ought to be addressed, as well as an understanding of what it means to succeed relative to those needs and thereby flourish in this area of human endeavor. Thus, it seems that so-called "pure" theory is not so pure, if being "pure" means being conceptually independent of implicit normative notions of intellectual success.

Taken together, such considerations seem to justify the claim that there are no "value-free" or "conceptually neutral" facts to which our "interpretations" might simply "correspond." Accordingly, we seem to be in the uneasy position of having to admit that interpretation goes, as it were, "all the way down." There simply is no value-free, context-independent ground on which to stand and in terms of which we can hope to adjudicate our disagreements. If "relativism" or "interpretation" is simply our intractable condition as knowers, then the only hope we have for dealing with our disagreements in a rational way is to develop yet another interpretation or relative standpoint from which (we hope) the dispute can be resolved (or at least softened). Of course, those new interpretations will, in all likelihood, generate further conflicts and the need for still more relative interpretation. There seems no way out of this endless cycle of interpretation; like it or not, we all exist as knowers within a kind of "hermeneutical circle."[4]

The position I just outlined is broadly shared by philosophers who consider themselves "hermeneutical" philosophers. Philosophers such as Hans-Georg Gadamer and Richard Rorty, who invoke the term "hermeneutics" to categorize their own positions, should be able to recognize themselves in it. Even philosophers such as Hilary Putnam or Thomas Kuhn, who never or rarely have used the term "hermeneutics" in their self-descriptions could find a great deal with which to agree.

But if this general agreement points to an emerging consensus among certain philosophers, it also threatens to hide some very important divisions within the hermeneutical movement. Almost every claim in my opening paragraph lends itself to at least two different interpretations regarding its actual meaning and import. While this is not in the least surprising, it is important to be aware of these ambiguities. Unfortunately, there is a tendency both inside and outside hermeneutically oriented philosophies to ignore these differences and assume simply that all those who insist on the inescapable nature of interpretation have the same thing in mind. But just like any other group of philosophers, hermeneutical philosophers sometimes talk past each other and even when they do not misunderstand each other, they often do not see eye to eye on many key issues.

To ignore this fact of real difference not only tends to oversimplify the field, but also it has even led to misunderstandings of Gadamer's position by some who consider themselves his followers. The mistake is to assume that "hermeneutics" points to essentially one position (such as the one with which Rorty identifies himself, for example) and then to insist that Gadamer must conform to this picture because he is, after all, a preeminent hermeneutical philosopher. This is particularly easy to do for those of us for whom the philosophical idioms of the German tradition are not our first philosophical language. Nevertheless, faulty assumptions such as this lead not only to misrepresentations of Gadamer, but they also sometimes encourage a dismissive arrogance toward hermeneutics in general by those outside the tradition because they mistakenly assume that they know what the term "hermeneutics" stands for and they simply want nothing to do with it. Needless to say, if we hope to avoid such hasty conclusions and genuinely assess both Gadamer's position and its possible significance for the larger philosophical community, then these differences need to be carefully articulated.

The most fundamental difference between hermeneutical philosophers can be characterized as the "hermeneutical fork." I call it the "hermeneutical fork" because it is so fundamental that it divides hermeneutical thinkers into two broad camps. This is not to say that all other differences pale to insignificance in its light, nor is it to imply that no real common ground exists between those on either side of this divide, but it is to say that we have here a profound difference of philosophical program. Simply put, it is a disagreement about whether the "hermeneutical circle" is, in some important sense, vicious or not. Stated in the most general terms possible, the hermeneutical fork divides those within the hermeneutical movement who think that hermeneutics, properly understood, implies the demise of traditional philosophy and those who do not. It is a difference between an essentially destructive, debunking program and a critical, constructive program. Of course, philosophy has always made room for both types of programs within its discourse. Neither is in principle less philosophical, even those who across the centuries have tried to end philosophy have sometimes ended up making key philosophical contributions. This may be the truth in Gilson's perceptive remark that "philosophy always buries its undertakers," but this is not the place to explore philosophy's phoenix-like character, however tempting that might be.[5] What I am pointing to here is a division in the hermeneutical or "relativist" camp between those who think that it no longer makes sense to try to clarify such philosophically or rationally normative terms as truth, reason, reality, fact, object, value, good, right, correct, and so forth, and those who think this task is still worth pursuing. One side says that hermeneutics, properly understood, has brought this whole philosophical endeavor to a grinding halt. It is simply a conversation we should cut off, perhaps consigning it at best, like alchemy, to the great historical trash heap of cognitive *cul-de-sacs*. On this view, traditional philosophy presents a history of failure, interesting perhaps, but not central to the realization of an important aspect of our humanity.[6] The other side, however, argues that hermeneutics, properly understood, is simply an important corrective within this conversation and that the conversation itself can and should continue, but now sobered by the lessons of hermeneutics itself. Even our failures can shed an indispensable light on our condition. It is a question of whether hermeneutics marks the end of philosophy or the end of a phase of philosophy. Both sides think hermeneutics has important lessons to teach, but which lessons and their proper import deeply divide the community.

Gadamer clearly sees himself on one side of this hermeneutical fork. He sides with those who see hermeneutics as a critical corrective to much recent philosophy. I find myself agreeing with him that hermeneutics has important things to say, but these things do not license us to leave philosophy behind. Instead, hermeneutics warns us about certain pitfalls in the paths philosophy has recently taken. Unlike hermeneutical thinkers such as Nietzsche, the later Heidegger, Derrida, or Rorty, all of whom try in their own way to bring philosophy to some kind of definitive closure, Gadamer does not understand his position to signal the end of philosophy, but a new beginning of sorts.

But what kind of "new beginning" does Gadamer have in mind? Obviously, if he understands himself as inviting us to a new phase of philosophical reflection, rather than to some type of thinking that is outside of philosophy altogether, he cannot be advocating some kind of radical rupture with our philosophical past. But something has also obviously changed with the growing use of the term "interpretation" as shorthand to describe our new self-understanding as knowers. What changes then does Gadamer think his hermeneutical reflections impose on us and what differences do these make for our understanding of human knowing?

The simplest, quickest way to say what Gadamer's hermeneutics hopes to teach us is that all human understanding is "finite."[7] By calling all human knowing "finite," Gadamer is not pointing out that no one knows everything nor could anyone ever hope to know everything. While this is certainly true, it is not his point. Gadamer's concern goes deeper in that the "finitude" of human knowledge is meant to point to conditions of human knowledge that our knowledge itself cannot hope to survey in order to predict how they will operate in any given situation. "Finitude" points to a dependency of knowledge on conditions that the human knower can never fully know. And if these conditions cannot be fully known, then this challenges us to revise our understanding of the type of autonomous control we can hope to exercise over our own cognitive endeavors. Gadamer's concept of finitude is meant to force us to rethink our self-understanding of what it means to be a free agent in the realm of knowing.

History and language are the two conditions of knowledge that Gadamer thinks make our knowing "finite." History and language are what Habermas has called "transitory a priori" conditions of knowledge in that they condition all knowledge, but the extent of their conditioning is elusive for two key reasons.[8] On the one hand, these conditions stretch back into a past we cannot retrieve. Thus, we cannot be exactly sure what they contain or how they will manifest themselves. On the other hand, history and language are permanently fluid in that they always operate, at least in part, within human freedom and are therefore subject to a seemingly infinite extendability. In other words, their application is never entirely rule-governed, but subject to unpredictable variations in different contents. If this is the case, then we can know, at least to some extent, the operations of such conditioning factors contingently, but we cannot specify necessary and sufficient conditions for the way they condition our knowledge-claims in all cases.

Before we further explore these claims, however, it is important to avoid a potential misunderstanding about what Gadamer is saying. Notice that Gadamer is *not* saying that we cannot in any sense know these conditions. That would be to argue that we know that knowledge is dependent on factors we simply cannot know. How could this be known? If this is not a contradiction, it is of little or no value for understanding our position as knowers. If something is beyond our ken, like a Kantian *Ding-an-sich*, it is questionable what part it can play in our self-understanding as knowers. If history and language were such conditions they would be at best an "I-know-not-what" that can function as a limit of our knowledge, but they could not function as cognitively accessible conditions. What Gadamer is saying is that history and language function as conditions of our knowledge that outstrip our ability to identify and justify fully our dependence on them. They are known partially, but our knowledge cannot encompass all the possible ways these factors function as conditions of knowledge. If we cannot survey these conditions exhaustively, making them transparent to our reason, we cannot hope

to be absolutely certain about how, in any given instance of knowing, they will exercise their influence. If this is so, then there is a
certain ineluctable inarticulacy and inescapable opacity in all our
knowing.

One important consequence of this claim is that the skeptic cannot be silenced once and for all. If the desire to refute skepticism
fires the epistemological dream of specifying conditions of knowledge that are both necessary and sufficient, then Gadamer's claim
about the "finite" nature of all human knowledge shows us that
this particular epistemological dream is one from which we should
awaken as soon as possible. In other words, if Gadamer is right, then
traditional transcendental philosophy cannot hope to complete its
program of making the conditions of knowledge transparent to the
knower. Neither the knower as such, nor the conditions of her
knowledge can be completely known.

But is Gadamer right about these far-reaching claims? Must we
surrender as much ground to the skeptic? And if we must, is it the
case that such a surrender spells a loss for us in our struggle to understand our own condition as knowers? We can explore Gadamer's
insistence on the "finitude" of knowledge in greater depth by looking
at history or the "historicity" of human knowledge, as hermeneutical philosophers usually call it.

According to Gadamer, all truth-claims are historical in the sense
that they are all framed in some "tradition" of inquiry. This tradition might function in many complex ways from conditioning the
conceptual language of inquiry to the protocols that govern the gathering and reporting of data, but we can say that one salient feature
of the way tradition functions in Gadamer's account of knowing is
that tradition sets the *normative* context of inquiry for a community of learners. In this sense, "tradition" determines things such as
which questions are most important, which have priority for a particular research community at a particular time, and it sets at least
prima facie boundaries of what conceptual tools are acceptable in attempting to answer these questions. In short, a normative tradition
not only determines the questions in some sense, but also it plays
a substantive role in determining what counts as a good answer to
these questions. Such traditions are normative in that they guide
communities of inquiry toward an epistemic ideal, an ideal that is
historically conditioned.

Following Wilfred Sellars' lead, philosophers such as John McDowell have argued quite convincingly that whenever we offer a justification for a belief we bring it within a normative "space of reasons."[9] This "space of reasons" is the logical or epistemic framework in terms of which such a belief is seen to be justified. For example, we might explain how the belief that nicotine is not a carcinogen is related to canons of empirical testing or experimentation that provide repeated and repeatable corroboration for nicotine's noncancer-causing effects. In other words, we offer a "justification" for nicotine's noncarcinogenic character that is inseparable from normative claims about such things as the nature and reliability of empirical evidence.

In pointing out that notions such as "empirical," "experiment," "corroboration," "repeatability," and even "cause" are normative notions, McDowell wishes to highlight the claim that we cannot explain the inescapability of our reliance on such notions in causal terms. For example, the inescapability of certain perceptions, such as color perceptions, can and must be explained in causal terms involving the interaction of light and the neurophysiology of our eyes, but when we arrive at an epistemic claim, such as the one mentioned above about the noncarcinogenic nature of nicotine, we are not simply being pushed and pulled by the causal network of the natural world, but we are making a normative judgment. To understand how it is possible for us to arrive at these judgments it is not sufficient to appeal to causal relationships in nature because such judgments are not caused in us in the way, say, that our color perceptions are caused by certain physical factors such as the physical effects of light on our nervous system.

If we hope to understand better how it is that we are capable of such judgments we must look to both tradition and to human freedom. On the side of freedom, McDowell points out that the space of reasons within which we offer justification for our beliefs is intentional in nature, i.e., it cannot be adequately understood as a product of physical laws. Instead, it can only be understood as a product of extended rational reflection on experience, which presupposes that we can disengage from the push and pull of nature, and freely survey at least a part of that same causal network. For example, we can draw distinctions within the skein of nature between events that are merely correlated and those that are connected by the stronger connection of causation itself. We say that such distinctions require insight or understanding, which is another way of saying that they occur within the space of freedom and are not simply churned out by the causal mechanics of nature itself. Such insights, we sometimes say, are derived, not produced; they are a function of free beings, who are always more than moments of a closed system governed solely by causal law.

But McDowell also points out that such reflection is engaged in by humans over generations of inquirers and passed on explicitly and implicitly as the norms of a community of inquiry. But to say that reflection takes place across time and among participants in a community of inquiry is to say that it takes place in history and within an ongoing tradition of discourse. Such a claim invokes something very much like Gadamer's notion of tradition. Our understanding of such norms evolves historically within communities into which we are socialized and shaped through a matrix of language, practice, and individual and corporate experience. This process forms in us, over time, a "second nature," a space of reasons, as McDowell and Sellars call it, in which we understand and debate the value of our various knowledge-claims. However, such a "second nature" is not simply caused in us through a process of social conditioning. To say this second nature is "intentional" is to deny that it is simply caused, even if the causes are "social" in nature. This would be simply exchanging physical or natural causes for social causes. While social conditioning occurs, we can say with good justification that it occurs within human freedom, so to speak. For example, while there are always internal and external sanctions that may be imposed on those who ignore these norms, it is important to point out that these standards are "recommended" to us; we are encouraged to appropriate "freely" them, to make them our own, by demonstrating that that we can "apply" them intelligently.[10] "Intelligently" means that we do not ape them blindly, but apply them in new ways, which, despite their novelty, attain readily recognizable "family resemblances" to the previous applications of such norms. Such norms are "intentional" because they are products of the reflective conscious experience of a community of researchers. When we are encouraged to learn and apply such norms, we are being appealed to as free agents, capable of exercising our own insight. Our reliance on such norms cannot be understood as the result of a causal process that simply implanted in us norms, which then continue to exercise their effects independently of our conscious reflection on them. Instead, it must be stressed that whatever causal imposition of these norms may have occurred in the course of our social formation as members of a community of inquiry, these same norms evolve in the space of free reflexivity that is generated whenever we think about our own thinking,

I have already argued that there is a link between McDowell's notion of a normative "second nature" and what Gadamer has in mind by a "tradition." This is not an incidental connection. Both authors recognize a common Aristotelian source for these ideas, and McDowell even recognizes Gadamer's influence on his own position as well. But Gadamer has used the term "tradition" in a way that has caused some controversy. Gadamer provocatively says such traditions or frameworks exercise "authority" (TM 277f.). While this has raised the hackles of some of Gadamer's readers, McDowell's gloss on some central Gadamerian ideas sheds important light on Gadamer's meaning. If we bring Gadamer's claim regarding the "authority" of tradition in proximity to McDowell's understanding of a normative "space of reasons," which is essential for all acts of knowing, then Gadamer's claim that the traditions that govern inquiry exercise "authority" over us should not be surprising. Normative claims by their very nature impose themselves on us; they make "authoritative" demands on us or address us as if they had a right to be heard. What this "authority" means, however, needs to be carefully spelled out. Gadamer is quick to point out that "authority," in his sense of the term, is rational in principle. "Authority" for Gadamer is something a tradition earns by demonstrating its value in the pursuit of knowledge. In McDowell's terms, we can say that such authority is normative because it has the capacity to operate within our freedom and should not be conceived as simply imposed on us from a point beyond our freedom.

I emphasize this point because it rightly reinforces the claim that Gadamer is not an enemy of human freedom. Gadamer's notion of "authority" is not "authoritarian." Nevertheless, what many people still find troubling about his notion of tradition and its concomitant notion of the "finitude" of our understanding is that it does challenge a certain view of rational autonomy. Gadamer opposes a view of our freedom as rational agents that has its roots in the Cartesian and Enlightenment tradition. What such a view of rational freedom requires of us is that we be able to judge the full nature and extent of any norms that govern our knowledge. If we are to submit to the authority of such norms, we can only be justified in doing so if we can make these norms transparent to our own reason and thus control the conditions of our own submission to them. This model of rational autonomy is very clear in Descartes' refusal to accept anything that his own intellect or "natural light" cannot fully justify with its own powers. Such a model demands the full command or transparency of these norms. In a sense, this dominant view of rational or epistemic autonomy requires that we become "second authors" of these norms. In other words, although it doesn't literally require that we invent our own norms, it demands that our insight into these norms be so transparent and self-evident that we would be in a position that is as good as their first mythical authors, whoever they may have been. Such "second authorship" would enable us, when challenged to justify our reliance on such norms, to reconstruct the full weight of their authority out of our own insight, without any recourse to our *de facto* reliance on the tradition as such. Not only Descartes operates with such a model of autonomy, but Kant does so as well when he recommends the "categorical imperative" to us as the only possible means to justify our *de facto* reliance on any moral norm. Once a moral norm has passed this test, its *de jure* status suddenly becomes evident and fully justifiable by reason alone. Whatever contingencies may have attended its inception become irrelevant to the inherent rational grounding of the norm. History is suddenly transcended in reason.

Such a notion of autonomy is precisely what Gadamer wishes to deny when he insists on the "finitude" of our knowledge. To put it in my terms, Gadamer would argue that autonomy does not require us to place ourselves in the fictional position of the first authors of the tradition somehow; autonomy neither requires that we know exhaustively the grounding of such norms, nor that we be able to see in advance all the implications of such norms. One merely has to state this ideal as baldly as I have attempted in order to see its deeply problematic nature. Gadamer would insist that autonomy can coexist with an element of *de facto* reliance upon tradition. It is enough that we can move with some freedom *within* a historical tradition, even when we cannot make its grounding or logical trajectory plain and clear in all respects. Gadamer's account of "finitude" insists that there will always be certain level of contingent opacity and inescapable inarticulacy in our reliance on tradition. Nevertheless, such factors do not preclude freedom, but instead situate it within an ongoing dialogue, which is the driving force of any historical tradition.

The claim that our freedom is always a situated, i.e., finite, freedom can be illustrated by pointing out a well-known relationship between how we are formed by such traditions and how we contribute to their development. Only if we are deeply formed by a tradition are we capable of modifying those traditions in meaningful ways. There is a sense in which anyone who wishes to make a contribution to some sphere of human understanding must have already been formed by that tradition of inquiry. Even before such a desire can arise there is a sense in which this tradition has appropriated us. We belong to history (or tradition) long before it belongs to us, says Gadamer.[11] Such traditions of inquiry form and shape us as epistemic agents long before we can even begin to turn around and shape them and we never cease to belong to them more than they belong to us, to paraphrase Gadamer once again.

Nevertheless, when we do "turn around" and begin to act on the traditions that have formed us, this is still a significant act of freedom. One way to illustrate both this dependence on tradition and our freedom within it is to remind ourselves that one of the most common ways in which a tradition evolves is by the *ad hoc* revision of the norms that constitute the tradition itself. Such revisions show us how better to capture the goal of the norm itself in the particular epistemic context in which we happen to find ourselves. Thus, even in critically revising the norm, its authority is acknowledged, even though we have freely modified it to fit the context of inquiry. The need to "tweak" the norm is not necessarily evidence for its inadequacy, but may in fact provide evidence for its normative strength in the sense that such a norm demonstrates its normativity by its flexible applicability to diverse situations. While such normative conditions bind us and form us, they do not deny us all freedom of movement. We are not just "made" by them, but we can freely appropriate them and shape them responsibly, albeit in a limited fashion.

We might say that such frameworks are open, but binding conditions of inquiry. They are "open, but binding" in that even anyone

who wishes to challenge them in a meaningful way must demon-
strate a deep understanding of them and argue for changing them in
terms that always maintain at least some significant contact with
them. In other words, we are bound to argue from within such norms
and not from some imagined gods-eye-view outside them. Simply
put, one can change such norms only by demonstrating a deeper
grasp of them. Otherwise, we simply opt out of this conversation,
which of course we can attempt, although it is not clear what space
there is completely outside these norms. Be that as it may, if we seek
the required, deeper grasp of these norms, we tacitly admit their normative authority over us; they have, as it were, a "grip" on us and
their grip exceeds our grasp.

This is so in the sense that any tradition of inquiry we investigate stretches back into the far recesses of time. Its final grounding
permanently eludes us. It is as if we suddenly become conscious of
standing on an iceberg; we can see that there is something below the
surface, but exactly what it is and how far it goes down we cannot
be sure. And this holds true whether the tradition of inquiry is our
own and it holds *a fortiori* for a tradition that is much more distant
from us either chronologically or in its substantive normative commitments. We cannot survey, in an all-encompassing vision, either
our own roots or the roots of others in the past and thus make them
transparent to the light of reason. For these reasons, our knowledge is
"finite" because of its history. Gadamer claims that all inquiry presupposes participation in a normative tradition whose foundations
can never be completely unearthed.

But what are the epistemic consequences of our implication in
normative tradition or "second nature"? Does such involvement necessarily imply that we are shut off from others or the truth claims
of others in other normative traditions by an unbridgeable gulf of
radical incommensurability? In other words, could our normative
concepts be so radically different from each other that no points
of significant contact between traditions are possible? Gadamer rejects this extreme skeptical interpretation of our finitude as knowers. Even to be aware of others as occupying a different normative
space of inquiry requires that their space and ours not be completely
sealed off from each other. How else could we recognize the problem
as a problem having to do with *normativity* if there was not some
common ground between these traditions in terms of which the

problem itself is identified. In this sense, such disagreements presuppose deeper agreements of a more general kind. In other words, radical incommensurability is a myth, a skeptic's dream, the intelligibility of which cannot be accounted for. For Gadamer, diverse normative traditions exist but they must necessarily overlap at points, although their points of divergence and convergence are contingently governed. This implies a rejection of a priori incommensurability, but not necessarily a rejection of contingent incommensurabilities. This would not imply that communication between traditions is always easy – quite the contrary – but it does imply that there is no reason in principle why inquirers from one tradition cannot find meaningful points of contact between their own traditions of inquiry and those of others. There is a sense in which all traditions occupy the same normative ground, but they may very well occupy different pieces of it at different points in time. In this sense, the historicity of our traditions places a real limit on the completeness of our knowledge, but it does not preclude knowledge as such. The grip of tradition is not a stranglehold; it places a real limit on the completeness of our knowledge, but it allows for real knowledge of ourselves, of others, and of the world.

An equally fundamental truth about our finitude, according to Gadamer, is that it is linguistically constituted. All traditions of inquiry understand themselves in terms of a particular conceptual language, which has its own contingent history. This is true of the strictly normative terms of a tradition, which we briefly discussed above, but it also may well extend beyond such terms to include other elements of language such as rhetorical elements of style, as well as the models, the analogies, and the metaphors that exercise a substantial influence over our imaginations. "We are always already biased in our thinking and our knowing by our linguistic interpretation of the world. To grow into this linguistic interpretation means to grow up in the world. To this extent, language is the real mark of our finitude. It is always out beyond us" (PH 64). Language is always out beyond us in the sense that its influence over us far extends the limits of our awareness of its influence. This is a defining mark of our finitude. Language is the primary vehicle (although not the only vehicle) by which history exercises a series of effects on us. Gadamer calls these effects a *Wirkungsgeschichte* or a "history of effects" to point out the aspect of causal conditioning in our relation to history

(TM 300f.). But these effects are taken up into human intentionality in that any historical influences, even those of physical, economic, or political domination and oppression, are refracted through language. Their effects, while not reducible to language or to "mere words" as it were, are partially constituted by the linguistic frameworks in which they are comprehended with more or less perspicacity. All such historical effects are refracted through language, even if they are not reducible to language. This is a fundamental point that Gadamer makes in his famous exchange with Habermas (PH 18–43).

There are no contexts of human understanding that are not constituted in terms of some linguistic framework and when we understand the world, ourselves, or others, we do so in terms of that framework. "We never find ourselves," Gadamer writes, "as consciousness over against the world and, as it were, grasp after a goal of understanding in a wordless condition. Rather in all our knowledge of ourselves and in all knowledge of the world, we are always already encompassed by the language that is our own" (PH 62). But although Gadamer says that we always understand the world in a language that is our own, it's important to emphasize that what we understand is not simply our own world, but *the* world, the one world we all have in common. Gadamer is an uncompromising realist. I will discuss some of the implications of Gadamer's realism below, but it is important to point out that Gadamer does not think that our words produce the intelligibility of reality in some strong sense. It's not as if our words project an intelligibility onto reality, which would then stand between us and the real world like a shroud. No, Gadamer says that growing into a linguistic interpretation means "grow[ing] up in *the* world" (my emphasis). It's only within this realist framework that we can begin to understand Gadamer's much misunderstood remark that "being that can be understood is language" (TM 474). Gadamer is not saying that all reality or "being" is literally "just words." What he is saying is better comprehended by saying that all intelligible reality is "enhanced" or "increased" by the words we find to comprehend it. "[T]he word is that in which knowledge is consummated, i.e., that in which the species is fully thought. Thomas points out that in this respect the word resembles light, which is what makes color visible" (TM 426). Words are not mere signs conventionally assigned to concepts that we otherwise have complete access to apart from words. Words are not neutral with respect to the intelligibility of the world. Gadamer claims that they actually make the world more intelligible than it would otherwise be. In this sense, words "enhance" or "increase" the intelligibility of reality; they make the world more manifest to us than it would otherwise be. There is a sense for Gadamer in which words "complete" and "complement" the intelligibility of the world. Words do not create the intelligibility of the world, but they do more than simply mirror it in a representation. Words make the world more intelligible and accessible than it would be without words.

Gadamer's position can be further illuminated by focusing on his claim that language is a "medium" through which the world is disclosed to us. According to Gadamer, "language is not only an object in our hands, it is the reservoir of tradition and the medium in and through which we exist and perceive our world" (PH 29). But as a medium, words mediate the world to us; they are the vehicle by which the intelligibility of the world is delivered to us, as it were. These are strong claims, but they are not saying that language is the ontological ground of the world's intelligibility. They are claiming that because we always grasp the world through some historically particular language that our grasp of the world is always limited, "finite," subject to possible revision, emendation, and so forth. Nevertheless, Gadamer is also saying that without words our understanding of the world would be considerably poorer than it is. The "languages" we speak provide a window onto the world that otherwise would remain shut. Such "languages" are therefore not a hindrance to our comprehension of the world, but a condition of its possibility.

Once again, we can say that our freedom is situated within these linguistic traditions. In fact, such languages seem infinitely extendable, but exactly how we can extend them is no more readily explicable than our ability to explain the peculiar aptness of a new metaphor that suddenly takes hold of our minds. Language develops and is extended and contracted in many ways, but this process does not seem to follow a complete set of rules. Linguistic development seems to be an even more complicated example of doing something such as making a move in complex game like chess. Of course, chess has its rules that require or preclude certain moves under certain conditions and it even has famous strategies or tactics, within these rules, that can be learned and applied. If we hope to become proficient at chess we must submit ourselves to these normative standards. But it is also important to point out that none of this explains why a particular game unfolds, move by move, in just the pattern that it does. Such explanations would remain necessarily incomplete at crucial junctures because there are an unspecifiable number of possible ways these very rules and strategies can be applied. The seemingly infinite ways a particular move can count as intelligent or stupid is part of the very "rationality" of chess. In a similar way, Gadamer argues that the development of our linguistic heritage involves "application" in that the seemingly infinite variability with which we can project and extend the use of a word is part of the reason inherent in language itself. Language is not fixed by or reducible to a set of rules. Of course, there are rules of language, but like the rules of chess they allow for and even seem to require an open variability that cannot be delimited a priori on all fronts. Our intelligence as speakers is not reducible to these rules. Because intelligent use of language requires a kind of unconscious creation, I am tempted to speak here of linguistic "genius," but the point is that such creativity is a regular occurrence that transpires every time we extend or "apply" a familiar term in a new way. Such ability is something every competent speaker possesses at least to some degree. Hence, Gadamer insists that "application" is a kind of interpretation that presupposes the *authority* of a linguistic tradition and a *freedom* to extend that tradition, neither of which can be surveyed and made transparently available to us. These features of language make us conscious of our finitude as knowers. Here again, we become conscious that our knowing can never master its own conditions. Although we can know these linguistic conditions up to a point, we cannot know them completely. We remain beholden to them and neither the extent of the debt nor the freedom with which we appropriate it can be definitively measured. When it comes to language, "the last word" belongs to no one.

One implication of our limits as knowers, which philosophers on either prong of the so-called hermeneutical fork can agree on, is that the epistemological program of "foundationalism" is naïve. Although there are different forms of foundationalism that will not be discussed, one aspect they all have in common is the aspiration to discover the conditions of possibility of all forms of knowledge, including both first- and second-order knowledge-claims. In other words, what all foundationalisms share in common is the belief that any adequate account of human knowledge must not only explain how our knowledge-claims about "the world" can be justified beyond all doubt, but also how we arrived at such an account of justification itself. Foundationalism in all its forms is an epistemological program unified by its desire to defeat skepticism. If Gadamer is right, however, "history" and "language" are not the kind of conditions that can be known in such a way that we can answer all doubts about our *de facto* reliance on them. The foundations of historically mediated normativity, as well as those of our contingent linguistic resources, stretch into an irretrievable past that puts them beyond our full grasp. Moreover, their *de facto* application, in any given case of knowledge, takes place within a context of freedom and is unpredictable in principle. If these are indeed conditions of all cognitive activity, then we can never make them transparent enough to secure them from all possible doubt. In short, the skeptic cannot be answered, at least not on her own terms, because the full extent of our reliance on historically mediated normativity and the contingencies of language cannot be surveyed sufficiently to rule out the possibility of error that might result from being the unconscious dupes of our own indebtedness. The same must be said, *mutatis mutandis*, for the freedom with which we are able to move within language and history. The range of our freedom to apply these resources cannot be strictly delimited any more than the scope of our indebtedness to language and history can be. In short, "finitude" makes it impossible to carry through any version of foudationalism and thereby defeat the skeptic by the rules of her own game.

Does this mean that skepticism has won the day? Is the complex relativity of all our knowledge-claims, which hermeneutical philosophers insist upon, just the most recent version of skepticism? Some philosophers within the hermeneutical tradition (and some outside it, as well) think that this is indeed the case. In their eyes, hermeneutics is just skepticism dressed up in German and French clothes. But I would argue that this is just another version of the "hermeneutical fork" I alluded to above. Gadamer does not think that hermeneutics amounts to skepticism. Hermeneutics would imply skepticism if skepticism and the foundationalist program, which is designed to answer it, represent the only viable model of knowledge available to us. But this is precisely what Gadamer contends. His insistence on the "finitude" of knowledge contests the feasibility of a view of knowledge that has, admittedly, a deep grip on our imaginations. So much so that if this model of knowledge turns out to be wrong-headed, we are tempted to conclude that the entire enterprise of knowing is deeply wrong-headed as well. But to conclude that the demise of such a powerful epistemic model is anything more than the demise of that particular *model* of knowledge would be premature at best. In other words, it is simply a *non sequitur* to conclude that if foundationalist programs of knowledge have failed, then the whole enterprise of human knowledge, including the knowledge of knowledge we call "epistemology," collapses like a house of cards. If the foundationalist game has run its course, it does not follow that it is the only game in town.

From Gadamer's side of the hermeneutical divide, the collapse of foundationalism does not imply a victory for skepticism, but a more nuanced commitment to fallibilism. If the conditions of history, language, and rational creativity or freedom preclude the kind of transparent certainty the foundationalists thought was necessary to refute the skeptic, it does not follow that we are no longer justified in attributing knowledge to ourselves about a whole array of subjects. From the fact that we cannot attain certainty, it does not follow that we cannot attain knowledge. This would follow only if knowledge was synonymous with certainty and Gadamer explicitly denies the equation of knowledge with certainty.[12] In fact, "certainty" is not one normative, epistemic concept, but instead refers to a family of such concepts whose scope of meaning ranges over well-known analytical domains such as logic and math and also to some even more narrowly circumscribed empirical situations. For example, "It's as certain as death" is a phrase whose truth we cannot ignore, even when we are aware that such a proposition is not true in just the same way that some propositions in logic or math are. What does follow from the fact that many of our knowledge-claims enjoy no such certainty is that they might just turn out to be wrong. In other words, fallibilism follows from the demise of foundationalism and this commits us to the near ever-present possibility of having to change our minds when the weight of evidence against us makes it preposterous to stick to some belief or set of beliefs we once thought true.

But from the possibility that we may be wrong, it certainly does not follow that we cannot be right. Not only may we be right, but we can provide sufficient warrant, humanly speaking, to justify our self-confidence. We are not like the deaf, dumb, and blind person, traveling alone, who just happens to strike out on the right road. Our epistemic self-confidence is not a matter of luck and the truth of probability, that in any case where we must choose between two conflicting knowledge-claims we have a 50 percent chance of guessing the right one. Even this would provide a rational warrant of sorts, albeit a very thin one. But in fact our epistemic warrants stand on much firmer ground than luck and the law of noncontradiction. While our best justifications are qualified by the fallibilistic awareness that we may be wrong, they are far from arbitrary and even further from an "anything goes" relativism. We can develop, apply, and retest criteria of knowledge that can give us enough reliable evidence or rational assurance to claim in multiple cases that we in fact know something and do not just surmise or opine that it is the case. In some cases of perceptual knowledge, for example, it is often enough that what I am seeing is seen under normal lighting conditions, seen by multiple others in similar circumstances, consistent with my memory of other similar perceptual circumstances, and so forth, to assure ourselves that we have in this case reliable perceptual knowledge. Could we be wrong in such cases? Of course, but our assurances to the contrary are anything but arbitrary or blind. As John Austin once remarked, "Enough is enough, enough isn't everything."[13] And we often find ourselves in epistemic situations where we know that enough is enough even though we also know that we do not have, epistemically speaking, everything we might imagine. In other words, "enough" does not mean "enough to convince the skeptic" but it means something like "enough to convince other analogously-placed epistemic agents." Such "finite" rational assurances are not just available in situations of perceptual knowledge, but are available, *mutatis mutandis*, across the whole range of what is humanly knowable. If the skeptic cannot be definitively refuted by means of these rational assurances of epistemic warrant, they can be shown just how far they stand from the standpoints of epistemic agents who do not operate under their model of human knowledge, which, if Gadamer is right, is most human beings most of the time across all cultures. This should shift the burden of proof unto the skeptic herself to show that her model is indeed binding on all of us at all times and places. That she can succeed at this challenge is something that hermeneutical philosophers such as Gadamer doubt sufficiently to deny her the right to dictate the terms of what will and will not count as human knowledge. There is simply not sufficient reason to stand frozen in the headlights of her demand for "complete justification."

One important consequence of neutralizing the skeptic's demand for absolute certainty is that relativism, understood as a version of skepticism, is also neutralized. Skeptical relativism, on Gadamer's account, becomes a philosophical red herring. This is so in as much as the fact that all knowledge is relative to some historical and normative linguistic context ceases to undermine knowledge. Once the criterion of absolute certainty is seen as irrational and surrendered as the mark of all legitimate knowledge, then the fact that many or all spheres of human knowledge fail to live up to this standard ceases to be alarming. The fact that knowledge is always dependent on historical, linguistic, and normative conditions, which constitute a relative standpoint, is not an inherent danger to knowledge, but a condition of its possibility.

One way to say this more clearly is to point out that historical, linguistic, and normative conditions are only a threat to knowledge if they are inherently irrational, but in many cases such conditions, or "prejudices" as Gadamer provocatively calls them sometimes, are rational and conducive to knowledge. Such "prejudices" (*Vorurteile*) are not necessarily irrational biases, but prejudgements (*Vor-urteile*) that constitute a standpoint in terms of which the objects of our knowing are approached (TM 277f.). The fact that we almost always occupy a standpoint (perhaps even multiple standpoints) from which the world discloses itself to us in a great variety of ways needs not be imagined as a situation where our vision is blocked by our perspective, but rather made possible by it. A "standpoint" is in principle a point from we see something, but, of course, not necessarily everything. What needs to be emphasized here is that a standpoint is precisely a point from which we *see* and not a point from which we are necessarily blinded. Gadamer makes this point by saying that the linguistic preconditions of knowledge are not barriers between us and the world, but they encompass everything that is humanly knowable. As such language is like light; it is a "medium" in which the world discloses itself to us; it is the vehicle that delivers the intelligible world to us. "[T]he verbal world, in which we live, is not a barrier that prevents knowledge of being in itself, but fundamentally embraces everything in which our insight can be enlarged and deepened" (TM 447). As a fallibilist, who is acutely aware of our finitude, Gadamer recognizes that such a vehicle can sometimes carry us into error, but it need not do so, and we have the critical resources within language to exercise a real but "finite" epistemic responsibility for its effects on us.

We have already noted that Gadamer is not worried that a relative standpoint is something that must cut us off from the world. So little does this possibility preoccupy him that he does not hesitate to affirm an epistemic realism of a particularly bold kind. What we know is "the world" in all its complex variety. Not just natural objects and their law-like relations make up the world, but other people, other cultures, traditions, languages, norms, texts, institutions, practices, and so on make up "the world" as the meaningful and knowable reality that it is. Moreover, our world has an "inherent" intelligibility that is, in a certain sense, "independent" of the languages, traditions, and standpoints through which the world is mediated to us. "[B]ehind all the relativities of language and convention there is a common trait which is no longer language, but which looks to ever possible verbalization, and for which the well-tried word 'reason' is, perhaps, not the worst" (TM 547). When we know at all, what we know is this inherently intelligible world as it is in itself independent from our mutifaceted "standpoints." Both the word "inherent" and the word "independent," however, need careful explication. The world's intelligibility is "independent" from the standpoints from which it is known only in the sense that its intelligibility is not a product of language or human projection of those linguistic standpoints. To say, as Gadamer does, that these standpoints constitute means of access to the world is not the same as saying they constitute human projections onto a determinate, but inherently unknowable world. One could say that the reality of the world's intelligibility is not dependent on our standpoints, but the way in which we are able to access that intelligibility is always dependent on such standpoints to some degree. Were it necessarily the case that the world's intelligibility is ontologically constituted by our linguistically constituted epistemic endeavors, then what we would know in principle would not be an "independent" world, but something like an image of ourselves or a self-projection mirrored back to us by something like a Kantian *Ding-an-sich*. This is not the picture Gadamer wishes to convey.

In principle, what a "standpoint" is capable of delivering to us is a "piece" of *the* world, a "view" of *the* world, a "perspective" on *the* world. In principle, a standpoint renders the world accessible, not inaccessible. If the situation were by necessity otherwise, it would render the world's ability to reject or confirm our projections or hypotheses utterly mysterious and unintelligible. That the world has its own intelligibility is a thesis Gadamer affirms. In this sense, intelligibility is "inherent" in the world and ontologically "independent" of our standpoints.

As a necessary corollary to the thesis that the world is inherently intelligible, Gadamer rejects the thesis that this intelligibility could be utterly foreign to our languages and concepts with which we analyze or carve it up, as it were. As a realist, Gadamer thinks the world has "real joints" that can be discovered and probed by our linguistic resources. As the medium that gives us access to the world, language enhances and increases our ability to carve reality at its own joints. So impressive in fact is even our very fallible ability to do this with the limited cognitive resources that we have that Gadamer claims that we must not think of the intelligibility of language and the intelligibility of the world as completely autonomous domains separated by a chasm of unbridgeable ignorance, but, instead, we should think of both intelligible realities as "belonging together."[14] This is Gadamer's way of saying that concepts and objects, or language and the world, constitute spaces of overlapping or interpenetrating intelligibility or meaning. Neither side is reducible to the other; neither side is the product of the other. The world or the object has its own intelligibility that can resist or confirm our ways of thinking and speaking about it, but language has a creative power to elicit or evoke the intelligibility of the object. We are dealing with relatively autonomous realms, which means we are dealing with relatively interdependent realms. It is as if word and world are in "dialogue," where each side has enough intelligible meaning in common with the other to make a meaningful exchange possible and enough independence to give it a critical edge. Our choice of words has something to do with the way the world shows itself to us, but it is also the case that how the world comes back at us is often a function of what we try to make it say. There is a very real sense in which the world answers our questions; we are involved in a dialogue with the world, not a soliloquy before a deaf and dumb world. Such a "dialogue" is possible because both the world and the languages we speak to comprehend it share a common inherent meaning.

Of course, this talk of being in dialogue with the world should not be taken literally. This should not be dismissed as a weird metaphysics; the world is not conscious, nor is it a free linguistic agent who can deliberate about how it should respond to a query. There are in fact some metaphysical commitments involved in Gadamer's view (and I will try to touch on them further below) but for now I want to emphasize that what Gadamer is saying is that we cannot account for responsible human belief formation outside a realist picture. Gadamer would disagree with Donald Davidson's remark that "nothing can count as a reason for holding a belief except another belief."[15] This is supposedly so because we can never get outside our beliefs. Intelligibility, on this view, is a strictly "intra-doxic" affair. The way the world is has nothing to say to us because it says nothing or if it does, it simply does not speak our language. Thus, Davidson leaves us with a coherentist account of responsible belief formation. Gadamer would find this view deeply unsatisfying. It simply cannot account for the normative experience of being challenged or confirmed by the way things are. Davidson's view is, in the words of John McDowell, a view of our beliefs as a "frictionless spinning in the void."[16] As such "our beliefs can make no contact with the world. The only contact our beliefs can make is with other beliefs." Davidson's view in fact makes it impossible to account for experience as a corrective or confirmation of the private conversation we have with ourselves or the public conversation we have with each other. If our experience of the world is not, at least in part, an experience of the world's independent, inherent intelligibility, it cannot mediate between our beliefs and the world. Gadamer's view about a common intelligibility being shared jointly by language and the world does not make him a "linguistic idealist" in the sense of someone who argues that intelligibility is a projection of the languages we speak, although it may still allow him to be legitimately called an idealist in a certain realist (and, we might add, Hegelian) sense.

The fact that Davidson's "frictionless coherentism" has sometimes been equated with Gadamer's account of human knowledge is understandable, but mistaken in my view. It's understandable because to take Gadamer's claim seriously that language and world present complimentary, if not identical, intelligible realities, seems to imply a metaphysical claim that there is between these two spheres a kind of "preestablished harmony" as it were. Since Hume, however, we have become increasingly comfortable with thinking that the connections between things can only be deeply contingent ones. Consequently, any views like Gadamer's that seem to suggest otherwise are dismissed as throwbacks to an earlier "Platonic" metaphysics. Surely, Gadamer must not be advocating the metaphysical views about the inherent intelligibility of world and language that I ascribe to him? I think he does and for good reason. We simply cannot make sense of human knowledge in all of its relativity to historically conditioned, linguistically constituted, value-laden standpoints, if we do not see these standpoints as in principle compatible with and in contact with the intelligibility of the world. Of course, we cannot know a priori that this "harmony" obtains, but neither is this a dogmatic assertion that it simply must obtain. In fact, it is the Humean/Davidsonian picture that is dogmatic in its insistence that such a relationship cannot exist. Gadamer's metaphysical picture is, like all metaphysical pictures, a kind of "inference to the best explanation." It is a sober account of what we must assume is the case given our experience as knowers. This experience simply cannot be described without gross distortion unless it includes in it the experiences of both being called up short and being validated as knowers by the world. To render these fundamental epistemic experiences intelligible, we must assume that word and world "belong together."

John McDowell has recently made a similar "metaphysical turn" within his hermeneutically informed epistemological reflections. This is not the place to discuss McDowell at any length. His views are, in my opinion, very interesting and worth separate treatment. Nevertheless, McDowell's "relaxed naturalism" or "naturalized platonism" as he sometimes refers to it, is markedly like Gadamer, not only in its defense of a realist account of knowledge, but also in his suggestion that the category of "nature" not be confined to the realm of law but include the realm of meaning as well. "Meaning is not a mysterious gift from outside nature," writes McDowell.[17] But if this is the case, then McDowell is right to claim that "there is no ontological gap between the sort of thing one can mean, or generally the sort of thing one can think, and the sort of thing that can be the case".[18] If we add to this the explicitly Gadamerian thesis that all understanding is in terms of some language, situated in a normatively charged history, we come within the same metaphysical space that Gadamer points to when he claims that "being that can be understood is language." This is not the vision of a skeptical relativist who sees us as trapped inside language, but it is the vision of a metaphysical realist, who has incorporated Hegel's insight into the historically mediated nature of human knowing with Hegel's (and Plato's) conviction that the world is inherently intelligible.

Our beliefs are answerable to the world, even though they are formed through "interpretation." Any interpretation in part or in whole, may correspond, or, as the case may be, fail to correspond to the world. When it does correspond, it is true insofar and only insofar as it corresponds to the way things are. But Gadamer's position enables us to see that when we make such judgments about correspondence, we do not somehow miraculously stand outside the relationship between language and the world; we stand within a common space of intelligibility and meaning, a common intelligible space that penetrates the world, our experience, and our languages. From this space, judgments of correspondence between word and world are possible because we don't need to stand outside of language to make them. Instead our experience can mediate between language and the world because all three are in principle "intelligible." If this is so, we can speak again about "getting it right" even though "getting it right" is relative to an interpretation. This makes sense on Gadamer's account because interpretation is not necessarily a projection of a "human, all too human" perspective, but a finite participation in an intelligible world where intelligibility and meaning "go all the way down."[19]

NOTES

1 Thomas Nagel, *The View from Nowhere* (Oxford: Oxford University Press, 1986), p. 15; and Bernard Williams, *Descartes: The Project of Pure Enquiry* (Hormandsworth: Penguin, 1979), pp. 64–8.

2 Hilary Putnam, *Realism with a Human Face* (Cambridge: Harvard University Press, 1990), p. 33. Hereafter cited as *Realism*.

3 *Realism*, p. 21.

4 The "hermeneutical circle" originally referred to the problem of interpreting any text where it seems we can only interpret the "whole" text in light of the meaning of its "parts" but the meaning of its parts can't be determined apart from the meaning of the whole text. Thus, interpreters

are forced to move in a "circle" between parts and whole, and whole and parts when interpreting a text. I am obviously using the term more loosely to refer to the situation in which all human understanding takes place within and between interpretations and never between interpretations and something that is not an interpretation.

5 Quoted in *Realism*, p. 19.

6 The principle view I am thinking of here is, of course, Richard Rorty's.

7 Hans-Georg Gadamer, *Truth and Method*, translation by Joel Weinsheimer and Donald G. Marshall (New York: Crossroad, 1990), pp. 232–5; see also pp. 276, 357, and 457. All references to this text will be to this edition. Hereafter, it will simply be cited in the text as TM.

8 Jürgen Habermas, *Towards A Rational Society*, translation by Jeremy J. Shapiro (Boston: Beacon, 1970), p. 84.

9 John McDowell, *Mind and World* (Cambridge: Harvard University Press, 1996). Hereafter cited as *Mind and World*.

10 Speaking of this same limited space of freedom Gadamer uses the term "application." He insists that all interpretation takes place with an eye to "applying" or developing the interpretation in light of the interests that in part constitute the standpoint of interpretation. See TM 307f.

11 TM 276: "In fact history does not belong to us; we belong to it."

12 Hans-Georg Gadamer, "What is Truth?" in Brice R. Wachterhauser, ed., *Hermeneutics and Truth* (Evanston: Northwestern University Press, 1994).

13 Quoted in *Realism*, p. 121

14 TM 474. See also Brice R. Wachterhauser, "Gadamer's Realism: The 'Belongingness' of Word and Reality" in *Hermeneutics and Truth*.

15 Quoted in *Mind and World*, p. 14.

16 *Mind and World*, p. 11.

17 *Mind and World*, p. 88

18 *Mind and World*, p. 22

19 For an account of Gadamer's "Platonic" roots, see Brice R. Wachterhauser, *Beyond Being: Gadamer's Post-Platonic Hermeneutical Ontology* (Evanston: Northwestern University Press, 1999).

4 Hermeneutics, Ethics, and Politics

It is a familiar thought about Gadamer's hermeneutics that its political and ethical implications lead in too conservative a direction. Gadamer locates the conditions of understanding meaning, whether textual, aesthetic, or historical, in the traditions to which interpreters belong and in the authority of those traditions (TM 277–85). That authority takes the form of expectations and assumptions that Gadamer calls prejudices, and he suggests that we can test these prejudices only in limited ways. Hence, some theorists have questioned whether his hermeneutics can be sufficiently critical of unwarranted prejudices and whether it can give sufficient recognition to the force of reason in undercutting them.[1] In this essay, I want to cast doubt on this analysis of Gadamer's hermeneutics by suggesting that it leads in a more democratic and less authoritarian direction and that the form of criticism it allows is an interpretive form of democratic deliberation. I shall begin by exploring what Gadamer calls the hermeneutic situation in which ethical and political action takes place and then turn to the Aristotelian form of ethics and politics that he suggests follows from it.

For Gadamer, following Heidegger, the hermeneutic situation signals the way in which, as human beings, we are "thrown" into a history or set of stories that we did not start and cannot finish, but which we must continue in one way or another.[2] We must always act in one way or another, because not acting or acting to end the necessity of continuing to act is itself a form of action. Yet, in order to determine how to act, we must also understand ourselves and the set of stories in which we find ourselves. If we have to act, we have to understand, in some better or worse way, who and where we are and who and where we want to be. From the beginning then, we are involved in the practical task of deciphering the story or stories of which we are a part so that we know how to go on.

The actions we take also react back upon our action-orienting understanding. They become part of what we understand when we understand our past and ourselves as well as part of how we anticipate our future. Hence, not only are we always deciphering the story or stories of which we are a part so that we know how to go on, but also we are always already in the process of going on. To this extent, our understanding of these stories is an understanding from the middle of an ongoing narrative. We have to reflect on and understand ourselves in the middle of continuing to live and act as we have already understood ourselves. Put otherwise, we live or write our lives according to the meanings we think they have possessed and understand those meanings according to the ways we continue to live and write our lives.

The circular character of this form of understanding leads Gadamer to modify the strictly methodological account of the hermeneutic circle that issues from F. D. E. Schleiermacher's work. For Schleiermacher, at least as Gadamer reads him, the circle indicates a method for avoiding textual misunderstanding (TM 185). The interpreter projects an interpretation of the meaning of a text on the basis of an initial hypothesis about it. In reading more of the text he or she then checks and revises this initial hypothesis in light of further evidence, or he or she rejects the hypothesis for another if the remainder of the text or different parts of it do not confirm the initial projection.

Yet, for Gadamer, the importance of the image of a hermeneutic circle lies in its characterization of our "historicity." The texts we most fundamentally need to understand, in one way or another, are the narratives in which we find ourselves. The interpretations we project onto these texts are not our own autonomous creations, however, but are rather bequeathed to us as part of the narratives themselves. These already possess specific vocabularies, plots, and sets of issues and insofar as we are "thrown" into the narratives, their languages and trajectories necessarily provide the contours for our understanding of them. The range of our possible understandings of the texts that constitute our historical lives is thus conditioned in advance by our implication what Gadamer refers to as effective history (*Wirkungsgeschichte*) (TM 300). As historical beings, we find ourselves in historical and cultural traditions that hand down to us the projections or hypotheses, the prejudices, in Gadamer's terminology, in terms of which we approach them. The hermeneutic circle is a historical one in which our understanding is oriented by the effective history or history of influences of that which we are trying to understand.

Of course, this description makes the hermeneutic circle sound less historical than simply "vicious."[3] If we project understandings on the narratives in which we are involved that are themselves a product of those narratives, how is new knowledge or understanding possible? Indeed, why is it necessary? The image of the hermeneutic circle captures not only the circular character of understanding, in Gadamer's view, but also its temporality. When we try to understand ourselves, our past and our future, we do so from a constantly changing temporal position. Moreover, we do so from a temporal position effected by a history that reflects understandings other than our own. The narratives in which we are involved and which we have to understand in one way or another not only continue even as we try to understand them, but also they continue as a confluence and even conflict of different interpretations of different narratives. History, Gadamer makes clear in a criticism of Hegel, does not progress as the movement of a monolithic Spirit becoming transparent to itself. It continues, instead, as the scripts of a myriad of screenwriters who are involved in writing different plots for the same film. The confluence and interaction of these plots determines what the final "take" will be and this take then becomes the film the writers need to understand and continue in what they write in succeeding days.

In this way, texts, or what might be called text analogues, acquire relations to different and new texts and text analogues. The history of World War I becomes part of the more recent history and wars of the Balkans. Questions change and become part of different questions. How are genocide and ethnic cleansing still possible after the holocaust? Can psychology and sociology really replace a theory of evil? How do we think of evil once we inhabit what some have called a postmetaphysical world? We inherit an understanding of the meaning of our history and traditions from them and we re-project that understanding back onto them. Still, because our history and traditions continue and because they continue in ways over which we do not exercise ultimate control and in ways that reflect (better or worse) understandings other than our own, our understanding must continually encompass more, sift through events differently, and continually reform or modify itself. We project our prejudices back on our history from the point of view of how that history has developed and how we anticipate that it will continue to unfold. Hence, what and how we understand changes.

Gadamer takes this account of the hermeneutic predicament to have important consequences for ethical and political knowledge. If our attempts to understand ourselves and to consider how we ought to act proceed only on the constantly shifting ground of an ongoing history, we cannot hope to transcend that history. Moreover, if what and how we understand changes, it is not clear that we can appeal to an unchanging human nature or human reason for our moral foundations. Instead, Gadamer thinks we require an ethics that can accommodate a human nature and reason that is also historical or, as Gadamer puts it, a form of "reason and ... knowledge, not detached from a being that is becoming, but determined by it and determinative of it" (TM 312). Hence, he turns to Aristotle's ethics and to the distinction it makes between a theoretical reason that grasps universals and a practical reason concerned with human action. In this regard, "What we find to be good in the theoretical sense – 'good' here meaning immutable being – is something quite different from the right thing to do ... at which the practical rationality of human beings aims" (IG 160).

For Gadamer, ethical "theory" is a kind of "ethical pragmatics" (IG 161) that assumes a relation between theory and practice that is not part at least of a more contemporary account of theory. The ethical knowledge of the individual ethical actor, for Aristotle, according to Gadamer, is the knowledge he or she has of how to act appropriately in a specific situation. It is not the objective knowledge that observers have of necessary or constant relations between objects. Rather, the situations to which the actor must respond in an ethical way vary; they are multifaceted and substantially unique. This variation is thus one sense in which ethical knowledge must remain connected to a "being that is becoming." Ethical knowledge is not knowledge that a specialist or theoretician can discover for others once and for all; it is not the same as a theory of the good or an account of a separate and unchanging universal, a charge Aristotle sometimes levels at Plato. Rather, a theory of the good has a tentative status in Aristotle's schema. It may refer to a list of virtues but it does so only as a kind of guide for action. Its task is the primarily practical one of providing an outline or sketch and "by means of this sketch" giving "some help to moral consciousness." As Gadamer continues:

This asks a lot of the person who is to receive this help, namely the person listening to Aristotle's lecture. He must be mature enough not to ask that his instruction provide anything other than it can and may give. To put it positively, through education and practice he must himself already have developed a demeanor that he is constantly concerned to preserve in the concrete situations of his life and through right behavior. (TM 313)

What prior education and practice are involved here? If ethical knowledge is not an objective knowledge of, for example, what a thing is, but marks instead the ability to behave correctly in specific situations, how does one acquire this ability? If ethical knowledge is not a form of theoretical knowledge, it would appear to be closer to a type of technical knowledge – a knowing how to act well or a kind of ethical skill rather than a knowing only what the good is. Indeed, Gadamer notes that Plato and Socrates use craftsman images in their attempts to get clear on the nature of ethical and political knowledge (TM 315). The moral actor or skilled craftsman takes a set of instructions, whether moral or technical, and applies them to the case at hand. The capacity to memorize or repeat the instructions does not in itself count as knowledge. Instead, one has to be able to use the instructions one has memorized or repeated to perform the skill or action at issue and that ability requires a knowledge or skill learned through prior education and practice, whether moral or vocational. Neither moral nor technical instructions can be given to an untrained person; rather, they make sense only to someone who has the ability and skill to use them.

Still, Gadamer is adamant that for neither Socrates, Plato, nor Aristotle can ethical knowledge be taught or disseminated in the way that technical knowledge can. Socrates finds his own craftsman images ultimately unsatisfying and in Gadamer's view, Aristotle's advance over both Plato and Socrates is to have successfully clarified important differences between skill and action or between a craftsman's technical knowledge of how to do or make something and the ethical person's practical knowledge of how to do something good. According to Gadamer, for Aristotle the latter is a form of self-knowledge; moreover, "man is not at his own disposal in the same way that the craftsman's material is at his disposal . . . he cannot make himself in the same way that he can make something else" (TM 316). Gadamer takes three differences between technical and ethical knowledge to be particularly significant.[4]

First, for Aristotle, the instructions one has for acting ethically constitute a list of virtues. These are sketches or images to which one refers in the situation in which one has to act, just as one refers to the image of a piece of furniture that one wants to make or to the understanding one has of how to perform a particular surgical operation. However, the latter cases point to a discretionary use or application of knowledge that Aristotle and Gadamer suggest is irrelevant to the case of moral action. One can decide whether to make a certain piece of furniture or whether to perform a certain surgery. One can also decide whether or not one is ready or skilled enough to perform the carpentry or surgery in question. One cannot decide whether to act, however. Ethical knowledge is therefore not knowledge that we possess in the sense that we can decide whether to apply it or even decide whether we are ethically skilled enough to apply it. Rather, Gadamer suggests that Aristotle teaches us that we are always applying our ethical knowledge, whether adequate or not, in acting as we do. This nondiscretionary element of ethical knowledge thus constitutes a second sense in which ethical knowledge is "not detached from a being that is becoming, but is determined by it and determinative of it." Our application of the ethical knowledge we possess occurs within a history that is unceasing in its demand that we apply it, however much or little of it we may possess.

The second distinction between ethical and technical knowledge that Gadamer attributes to Aristotle pertains to the character of a nondiscretionary form of application. Creating a piece of furniture or performing surgery allows for a relatively straightforward application of skills and knowledge. One learns how to drive a car or build a house and applies this knowledge in a consistent manner. Particular circumstances may be beyond one's level of expertise at a certain time; one may improve one's skills through practice and experience and particular circumstances may require particular accommodations or lead to less than perfect results. Still, the ideal of a good driver or of a good builder remains unchanged and what one learns through practice is to perform the practices at issue more skillfully. The application of ethical knowledge, however, is never straightforward, Gadamer suggests, because the ideal to which one looks in acting is never independent of the action itself. It is not possible to separate means and end in the same way that one can separate a skill from its ideal result. Rather, the application of ethical knowledge involves both means and end. In other words, what the virtue or end in question is, is partially determined by the action meant to enact it, as is our understanding of ourselves as virtuous beings.

Gadamer emphasizes two aspects of the connection Aristotle establishes between means and end. In the first place, he notes the elements of habituation and character molding that is part of Aristotle's ethics. "Man is not at his own disposal in the same way that the craftsman's material is at his disposal" because I become a certain sort of person in the course of my actions. If my character is the end at issue, then the means I take to realize that end are not irrelevant to but rather "determinative" of the person I become. Second, what a virtue is, is not independent of the actions taken to realize it. What the virtue of courage is and who courageous people are, for example, cannot be understood independently of those acts that are taken to realize the virtue: if both fighting a war and going to jail rather than fighting it are to count as courageous acts, then courage itself becomes a different virtue than if only fighting counts as an application of it. Consequently, there is yet a third sense in which ethical knowledge is for Gadamer "not detached from a being that is becoming, but determined by it and determinative of it." Not only must ethical knowledge deal with a constantly changing set of circumstances and not only is its application determined by a history that is, in the course of its becoming, unceasing in its demands on us. In addition, we make and remake our ethical knowledge and ourselves in these changing circumstances, in the actions we take to apply the ethical knowledge we already possess.

The third aspect of Aristotle's ethics that Gadamer thinks clarifies the difference between ethical and technical knowledge involves *syneses*, the relationship, in giving ethical advice, between advisor and advisee. One need have no relationship to someone from whom one asks or to whom one gives technical advice. Where ethical advice is involved, however, one needs to rely on those one understands to be involved with one, to be concerned for one, and sympathetic to one. As Gadamer puts this point:

Both the person asking for advice and the person giving it assume that they are bound together in friendship. Only friends can advise each other or, to put it another way, only a piece of advice that is meant in a friendly way has meaning for the person advised... we discover that the person who is understanding does not know and judge as one who stands apart and unaffected but rather he thinks along with the other from the perspective of a specific bond of belonging as if he too were affected (TM 323).

Gadamer's point here is that ethical advice involves the same level of participation as one's involvement in one's own life. It is not possible to give sound advice unless one takes the situation to be one that affects one's own life and self-understanding. Hence, sound advice possesses the same structure that Gadamer takes Aristotle to impart to ethical knowledge in general. Our understanding of what we ought to do in any particular situation is not the objective knowledge of an observer but the engaged understanding of someone who must act. Both ethical action and ethical advice to others involve applying the ethical knowledge one already possesses because of practice, upbringing, and education to new and different situations in which that application changes the ethical knowledge and the ethical character or being that one has and takes forward into future situations of action, themselves partially determined by present actions. The same holds for ethical–political understanding of communities. They must apply the norms and values they possess because of their histories and traditions to the new historical circumstances in which they find themselves in which this application modifies and revises the ethical–political understanding they take into a changed future. Questions of what we should do as either individuals or communities are not, Gadamer suggests, questions to be answered by appealing to fixed foundations. They are rather questions that require us to consider who we already are and who we want to become, where the decisions we make will affect and modify the considerations we can make in the future.

Still, it is not clear that this circular or, better, spiraling structure of ethical and ethical–political knowledge allows for a sufficiently critical stance toward the history or tradition of which one is a part. Indeed, despite Gadamer's criticism of the objectivity of ethical theory, it would seem that some degree of distance and objectivity are necessary to overcome the effects of entrenched assumptions and illegitimate expectations. If our sole resources for action are the set of norms and values handed down to us in the course of our upbringing within the ongoing histories and traditions to which we belong, can we simply assume that these histories and traditions allow for ethical action? Suppose, in Aristotle's terms, we are simply barbarians and have been brought up to participate in barbarian traditions? In this case, the reworking that our traditions undergo in the course of being handed down and applied to new and different situations may not be enough. Otherwise put, what ensures that the circle or spiral of ethical and political knowledge does not simply surround a disastrous core?

This question is similar to one that Jürgen Habermas raises in distinguishing between an Aristotelian–Gadamerian form of ethics and what he calls morality. Ethics, as he conceives of it, concerns individual or collective ideas of who we are and who we would like to be, where such ideas go beyond merely superficial preferences to include our ideals and conceptions of the good.[5] Like Gadamer, Habermas connects such ideals and conceptions of the good to cultural values and to the shared traditions in which individuals participate. Individuals do not create their ideals and conceptions of the good in a vacuum but rather do so as members of traditions who have grown up with specific conceptions, values, and ethical orientations. Hence, the way they understand themselves, their community, and their goods is bound up with their heritage and culture. Still, Habermas denies that this self-understanding can ground the morality as opposed to the ethical character of actions. Justifying a particular course of action requires more than asking whether it reflects either an individual conception of who I am and want to be or a collective conception of who we are or what our values mean for a particular situation. Rather, it includes a consideration of whether the action is just, and issues of justice involve a consideration of whether the interests embodied in contested norms are unreservedly universalizable:

In moral discourse the ethnocentric perspective of a particular collectivity expands into the comprehensive perspective of an unlimited communication community, all of whose members put themselves in each individual's situation, worldview, and self-understanding, and together practice an ideal role-taking.[6]

The deficiency of a merely ethical standpoint, from Habermas's point of view, then, is that it cannot free itself from a particular tradition and its "ethnocentric" values and self-understanding. He acknowledges that "A hermeneutics that critically appropriates traditions . . . thereby assists in the intersubjective reassurance or renovation of authentic life orientations and deeply held values."[7] Still, as long as reflection is limited to reassurance and renovation, actors cannot "work themselves free of the form of life in which they *de facto* find themselves."[8] A process of ethical self-reflection within a Christian fundamentalist community, then, could reflect on what fundamentalism is and requires of its practitioners and who they should want to become without ever addressing questions of the equal rights of women or to the equal right of individuals to pursue their own alternative conception of the good.[9] Hence, Habermas concludes that "the making of norms is primarily a justice issue, subject to principles that state what is equally good for all. Unlike ethical questions, questions of justice are not inherently related to a specific collectivity and its form of life."[10]

Michael Walzer makes a distinction similar to the one Habermas makes between morality and ethics in distinguishing thin or minimal moralities from thick or maximal ones.[11] Still, he comes to opposite conclusions that serve to support the thrust of a Gadamerian ethics and politics. Minimal moralities point to universal principles such as truth or justice to which everyone can adhere, at least in their outlines. Thus, Westerners can understand the struggles against oppressive regimes that marked the downfall of communism in the late 1980s although they may never have suffered under the specific oppression that characterized those regimes. More importantly, they can understand the justice of these struggles although they might disagree with those struggling about the specific form justice might plausibly take within their different communities. Justice in its more specific form is a thick conception. It refers to specific institutions and practices that are laden with particular values and sets of historical resonances and that are imbued with the specific character of particular communities.

Habermas argues that morality is primarily thin: it relates to what is equally good for all rather than what is "inherently related to a specific collectivity and its form of life." In contrast, Walzer argues that morality is primarily thick and that we come to thin ideals through a kind of hollowing out of our initially thick ethical conceptions, those more intimately bound up with our collectivity and form of life. We understand the struggles of others against tyranny because of our own thick conceptions of freedom and oppression: the struggles of outcasts in our society to achieve the rights and privileges of equal citizens gives us a purchase on the struggles of others who seem at least somewhat similarly situated. Still, the mistake of minimal moralities, as Walzer understands it, is to suppose that thinness precedes thickness, that a set of universal principles is to be adapted to different ethical cultures. Rather, morality is thick from the beginning and what are expressed in thin moralities are simply the common or overlapping aspects of a reiterated set of thick values.

The procedural morality that Habermas distinguishes from the thick ethical conceptions of a community serves Walzer as a case in point. For Habermas, only those norms are morally justified to which all those affected can agree under certain ideal conditions of symmetry and reciprocity: all speakers must have the same chances to raise and challenge claims to the validity of a norm; all intrusions of internal or external force must be eliminated and only the force of the better argument may hold sway.[12] Walzer remarks that Habermas's theory is particularly "ingenious"[13] because the moral procedures it specifies allow for different ethical conceptions of the good as long as they do not violate the universal moral principles justified by the procedure. Nonetheless, he argues that Habermas's minimalism, like any minimalism, "turns out to be rather more than minimal" and, instead, possesses "an entirely decent liberal or social democratic thickness."[14] The rules of discourse, which are meant to ensure that "the speakers are free and equal, to liberate them from domination, subordination, servility, fear and deference," derive from a thick way of life; they instantiate social democratic or liberal ideas of how people ought to be situated with regard to one another, and they anticipate the specifically thick goods of freedom and equality. As Walzer continues,

Men and women who acknowledge each other's equality, claim the rights of free speech, and practice the virtues or tolerance and mutual respect, don't leap from the philosopher's mind like Athena from the head of Zeus. They are creatures of history; they have been worked on, so to speak, from many generations; and they inhabit a society that "fits" their qualities and so supports, reinforces and reproduces people very much like themselves. They are maximalists even before they begin their rule-governed discussions.[15]

To this extent, a minimal morality based on a theory of discursive reason is merely a hollowed out form of a thick democratic culture. Yet, this conclusion means that the distinction Habermas draws between ethics and morality might rather be reversed. A minimal procedural morality does not provide for the boundaries between which ethical cultures can vary nor does it provide for a neutral process for adjudicating the compatibility with justice of the values of particular ethical cultures. It is rather itself the abstracted or thinned out form of a specific and thick ethical culture. Indeed, Walzer insists that "when full-grown democrats imagine that the rules of discursive engagement are the generative rules of morality in all its kinds, they are very much like an oak tree that...solemnly declares the acorn to be the seed and source of the entire forest."[16]

To be sure, this analysis of Habermas's discourse theory neglects Habermas's own acknowledgment of the historical roots of discourse theory. Appealing to a Weberian account of rationalization, Habermas relies on the historical development of a reason differentiated into theoretical, practical, and aesthetic domains. Nevertheless, Walzer argues that minimal theories such as Habermas' do not only suppose that the historically developed domains of Western reason are the source of morality in general. They also suppose that no morality that does not trace back to this source can be a morality at all. It is as if, Walzer claims, an oak tree "acknowledged the full range of arboreal difference and then argued for the cutting down of all those trees, now called illegitimate, that did not begin as acorns."[17] But if minimal moralities serve this function only at the costs of ignoring their own thick roots and denying the legitimacy of any thick morality or ethical culture incompatible with their own, how is criticism of an ethical culture possible? What is illegitimate in a fundamentalist ethical self-understanding that insists on its own thick values and ideals and their consistency with its practices despite their possible violation of the freedom and equality of others? Does our participation in particular, thick ethical traditions not entail the kind of restriction on our moral imagination that Habermas's attacks? Are forms of ethical reflection sufficient if actors ultimately cannot "work themselves free of the form of life in which they *de facto* find themselves"?

One response to these sorts of question that Gadamer's work suggests re-emphasizes the force of ethical traditions, on the one hand, and, on the other, points to the modifications and revisions they undergo as a consequence of their participation in an ongoing history. If ethical cultures or forms of life and self-understanding are thick, they are not static for Gadamer. Instead, in a historicized hermeneutic circle we apply the norms and values our traditions hand down to us in a way that changes who we are and what we, in turn, hand down to our children. Gadamer contrasts this circular form of participation in continuing traditions to the self-understanding of what he calls the objectivistic sciences insofar as they assume that they can explain traditions and the thick conceptions they involve from a disconnected observer, and therefore neutral standpoint. The norms and values of a tradition, however, are not orientations from which we can disentangle ourselves, no matter how thin we attempt to make them. Indeed, to the extent that we assume that we can disentangle ourselves, we simply allow our own orientations and the expectations they establish to operate unnoticed, as Walzer also suggests. Objectivistic sciences proceed as Walzer's oak trees do. They suppose not only that acorns are the seed and source for the forest but also that they are not themselves partial to acorns.

Still, Gadamer also suggests another dimension to answering the question of the adequacy of ethical reflection, one that goes beyond simply indicating the deficiencies of an objectivistic or thin approach. His suggestion is clearest in the move he makes from Aristotle to Kant and to what he calls the moral experience of the "thou." In what follows I want to examine his account of three possible relations to the thou or other people, all of which have their counterparts in our relation to the traditions to which we belong. I want to suggest that what Gadamer sees as a moral experience of the thou and a genuine experience of tradition provides for a thick but critical form of ethical reflection.

The first experience of the thou to which Gadamer turns is an experience of a kind of generalized human nature, directed toward the capacity ultimately to predict the behavior of others. Gadamer calls this attitude purely "self-regarding." Its point is not as much to understand others as to predict their behavior so that we can more easily effect the ends of our own or of our society. Nevertheless, if, following Kant, "the other should never be used as a means but always as an end in himself," then this behavioristically oriented experience of others is a contradiction of the "moral definition of man" (TM 358). For Gadamer, the counterpart of this relation to others in our relation to our own traditions is "a naïve faith in method and in the objectivity that can be attained through it" (TM 358). Here the target of his criticism is an objectivistic form of social science that looks to general sociological laws and methodological ideas to explain and predict social action and behavior. But such a naïve faith in method ignores the thickness at its source or, in other words, the extent to which its explanations and predictions can ignore the specificity of the "other" and overgeneralize from particular practices and behaviors that are always elements of particular cultures with particular traditions. The criticism thus seems to pertain to minimalist moralities as well, insofar as they ignore the thickness of their principles and procedures.

A second way of experiencing the thou is also self-regarding, Gadamer claims, although it does not bend others to our ends, but rather tries simply to absorb them into ourselves. This experience of the thou claims an empathy with others that presumes to understand them better than they understand themselves. In this way they are "co-opted and presumed reflectively from the standpoint of the other person" (TM 359). What the other says or does has no autonomy or legitimacy of its own but can be acknowledged only in its identity with oneself.

The equivalent to this experience of the thou in our relation to tradition, Gadamer calls historical consciousness. One assumes that one can understand the past in the same way that the original participants understood it. In making this presumption, however, one simply substitutes one's present understanding for that original understanding. That is, one simply ignores temporality and the historical distance that separates one from the past, and more importantly from Gadamer's point of view, one ignores the wealth of historical events, associations, and relationships that have affected its meaning. The result is that once again, one allows one's own prejudices to prevail unchecked – in this instance, not because one remains wedded to one's own projects and ideas without recognizing their thickness or historicity but rather because one simply takes one's thick prejudices for the original meaning of the text itself.

Both self-regarding ways of experiencing the thou differ, according to Gadamer, from the ability to experience the thou "truly as a thou." In this case, one does not "overlook his claim but [lets] him really say something to us" (TM 361). This moral relationship to the thou is based on openness. We neither instrumentalize the other nor claim to speak for him or her but are rather open to the other, as someone who has his or her own autonomous autonomous position and claims. Gadamer sees this relationship as a dialogic one. At work is a conversation in which I seek to understand and address the independent claims of the thou and am, in turn, addressed by them. As Gadamer writes, "When two people understand each other, this does not mean that one person "understands" the other... Openness to the other... involves recognizing that I myself must accept some things that are against me, even though no one else forces me to do so" (TM 361).

Again, this third experience of the thou corresponds to a way of approaching tradition. What Gadamer sees as a genuine understanding of the past requires a similar dialogic openness to it, an openness that he says requires approaching it "in such a way that it has something to say to me" (TM 361). Historical consciousness assumes that what the past has to say to us, we already know better. The point of a genuinely hermeneutic relation to the past is our openness to its difference or autonomy from what we already believe and our willingness to be addressed by it.

The condition of a "true" experience of the thou or of our own past is thus the presumption that the other or our past has something to say to us, or something, in other words, to teach us. In avoiding a reduction of others or our traditions to either instruments or ourselves, we respect their autonomy and presume them to possess an independence and voice we must address and by which we ourselves are addressed. To a certain extent, this analysis simply elaborates on the idea of the hermeneutic circle. If the application of ethical knowledge changes what we know and who we are, the quality of this change depends upon an openness or sensitivity to difference. We must presume that we can always discover in our traditions dimensions that may undermine or complicate what we thought we already knew about them and ourselves. Part of testing or monitoring our ethical traditions will therefore involve checking them and reflecting on who we are or take ourselves to be by being open to new possibilities and new dimensions in our understanding of ourselves. If we have always accepted a national myth involving the American ideal of the independent individual, ready to defend himself with a rifle guaranteed him by the Second Amendment, we can confront this image with greater attention to the small place of militias in early American life, to the exorbitant expense of guns that kept them out of reach for most citizens and so on. Such historical work depends upon an openness to finding in our own history challenges to our inherited preconceptions.

But if we adopt this open, dialogic relation to the past, it seems to hold as well for our relation to thick ethical cultures other than our own and to alternative contemporary understandings of our own thick conceptions. Our openness to how they may address us provides an external, yet thick foil against which to evaluate our own ethical traditions as well as our own understanding of them. At work is a dialogue of ethical cultures and understandings in which each addresses and is addressed by the claims of the other and in which each provides for the other the check on ethical knowledge, the apparent absence of which motivates Habermas's critique of Gadamer. We possess this check not through recourse to thin moralities, however, but through an openness to thick ethical cultures other than our own and to interpretations of our own thick conceptions that differ from our interpretations of them.

If this ethical dialogue is Gadamer's answer to Habermas, how might we acquire or guarantee the openness to difference on which it depends? We are situated in particular histories, cultures, and ethical traditions, which provide our orientation toward that which we are trying to understand. We can understand a certain text as a novel, for example, because we belong to a history and culture that knows what a novel is. We have a particular anxiety about and understanding of war in the Balkans because of the history of the twentieth century of which we are a part. If, however, we understand only in terms of the pre-orientations and knowledge we already possess, how do we first create the space for our past, another ethical interpreter, or an alternative ethical culture to assert an autonomous voice? How do we hear fresh voices in a way, if not unconditioned by our pre-orientation toward them, at least able to hear their claims for or on us?

Gadamer addresses this question with reference specifically to textual understanding by insisting that an openness or sensitivity to texts involves neither neutrality with respect to content nor the extinction of one's self, but the foregrounding and appropriation of one's own fore-meanings and prejudices. "The important thing is to be aware of one's own bias, so that the text can present itself in all its otherness and thus assert its own truth against one's own fore-meanings" (TM 269). The condition of an openness to the difference or autonomy of a text from our own preconceptions about it is an awareness that we have preconceptions about it, that we are participants in an on-going history and tradition which already bequeaths to us assumptions and expectations about that which we are trying to understand. If we are to be open to an alternative understanding of a text, we must acknowledge that we possess a pre-understanding, that, indeed, we are part of thick traditions and conditioned by the inevitably parochial character of our historical situation. The significance of this acknowledgment with regard to our ethical knowledge is that if we are to recognize otherness in ethical cultures and alternative ethical understandings as well as in texts, then we must acknowledge our lack of neutrality, our pre-conceptions and our biases. At stake is a form of self-understanding that Gadamer, following Plato's account of Socrates, calls dialectic. "Wherever the concern is knowledge that cannot be acquired by any learning, but instead only through examination of oneself and of the knowledge one believes one has, we are dealing with dialectic. Only in dialogue – with oneself or with others can one get beyond the mere prejudices of prevailing conventions" (IG 43).

Gadamer also appeals to what he calls Socrates' *docta ignorantia*, the wisdom of knowing that one does not know (TM 362). If we are to acknowledge our embeddedness in thick cultures and if we want nonetheless to monitor the ethical trajectory on which they seem to place us, then we must assume that other thick cultures and other understandings of our own trajectory can speak to us and teach us about ourselves. We assume that our own ethical knowledge is prejudiced, historically conditioned, and incomplete and that the ethical knowledge of others is at least potentially capable of expanding our ethical understanding. We monitor and check on the adequacy of our ethical knowledge and culture not by thinning either into a procedure for validating norms that can hold for anyone but rather by comparing the norms and values that hold for us against other thick possibilities of what we might believe and be.

Current public debates in the United States offer numerous examples of the thick ethical dialogue that Gadamer's work seems to anticipate. In debates over legal access to abortion, the virtues of a euthanasia policy and the ethics of research on the uses of discarded fetuses or embryos, an ethical culture that bases itself on a particular conception of the sanctity and integrity of human life competes with one that bases itself on another. Those that argue against legal access to abortion or to physician-assisted suicide and oppose research on fetal tissue hold a particular idea of what gives human life its inviolable character. As Ronald Dworkin has shown, this position is indebted less to an argument, derived from a minimal morality, that fetuses have rights than it is to the idea that human life is sacrosanct just because it is human life. Here life is understood as a gift of God or as a result of natural and evolutionary processes that are miraculous and not be undone by human hands. On the other side, those that argue for legal access to abortion, physician-assisted suicide, and research on fetal tissue hold a different idea of inviolability. This position thinks of the sacrosanct character of human life in terms of its human investment, in terms of a human creativity that makes a particular life what it is. To sacrifice this life to an embryo or fetus is to undo it in a way that is itself blasphemous.[18]

One might argue that what impedes resolution of debates over euthanasia, abortion, and the like is a lack of hermeneutic sensitivity and openness. Conversely, if we recognize that our understanding of the inviolable character of human life is an interpretive understanding and that the meanings in question admit of different understandings, then we can acknowledge the legitimacy of interpretations other than our own and even try to see in them insights we may have missed. The upshot is an interpretive form of deliberative democracy in which participants in interpretive exchanges with others try to learn from the interpretive understandings of others and do so because they recognize the interpretive status of their own. Rather than holding dogmatically to their own interpretations, participants are open to developing them through the interpretations of others and even to integrating alternative interpretations and compromising on the policies to which they lead.

Struggles for recognition on the part of women and minority groups are amenable to the same hermeneutic approach. Such issues address the question of whether equal participation in the practices and institutions of a liberal democratic society is compatible with the preservation of cultural, ethnic, racial, or gender identities. Struggles for recognition claim that women and members of minority groups should be accorded equal rights and opportunities as who they are, that that they ought not to be compelled to cut and prune their identities to fit a standard modeled on the majority culture or white men. Instead, their difference is to be recognized and respected as part of their participation in the institutions and practices of the society to which they belong. Women may demand special pregnancy and child care leaves, for example, in order to maintain their identity as mothers while pursuing the same fulfilling careers that men can pursue.

But struggles for recognition may also imprison those for whom they struggle in essentialist or quasi-essentialist conceptions of identity. The same regulations that might allow women to be effective working mothers may also confine them to that mothering identity and thereby relegate them to mommy tracks and low-paying, dead-end positions. Thus, K. Anthony Appiah asks that we recognize the contingency of the identities that we currently possess, while feminists such as Judith Butler suggest that we actively subvert those tied to gender.[19] Rather than being the women or mothers that we are meant essentially or socially to be, we can perform identities that involve cross-dressing, drag, and butch/femme relations.

Martha Nussbaum has criticized Butler's response to questions of gender identity for lacking a normative dimension. Why should we subvert gender identities in particular? Why not subvert the identities of taxpayer or open-minded liberal?[20] Yet, perhaps missing from ideas of gender, racial, sexual, and ethnic identity is not only a normative dimension but also an interpretive one. For if we understand identity as interpretive, we can acknowledge a plurality of interpretive horizons from which we can understand both who we are and what the relevant meanings of gender, race, and ethnicity might be for us. From a medical perspective, for example, women, African Americans, or Jews might legitimately exist, if understanding individuals according to these categories allows for important sorts of genetic screening and diagnoses. Still, this medical perspective can neither claim to exhaust all the possibilities of identity nor to grasp that which is most fundamental or essential to who we are or what gender, race, and ethnicity are. But if we are no more women or men than we are black, white, gay, heterosexual, or lazy or workaholic, then current assumptions about social, ethnic, and gender identity will need to be modified. We might, for example, no longer concentrate on how the working world can accommodate women with children but whether we should take seriously certain values such as those involved in the care of future generations. Further, we might consider how, as a society, we might realize such values. Democratic deliberations of this kind include not only deliberation over norms but also interpretive deliberation over meanings and values and, moreover, through deliberation, a process of reciprocal education.

To be sure, the prospect of reciprocal education may seem too cheerily sanguine. From whom should we try to learn? Anyone? When do openness and hermeneutic sensitivity become a relativistic lack of standards or even a deference to any interpretive understanding different from our own? Does Nussbaum's question not remain? Suppose we learn to subvert our taxpayer identities as opposed to our gender ones? Suppose Americans had maintained an openness and sensitivity to racist interpretations of the meaning of principles of freedom and equality? Suppose we had continued to try to learn from and compromise with a set of values and self-understandings that denied to certain groups access to democratic representation, education, and professional careers? Are Americans simply lucky that its white-identified population eventually learned to listen to its black-identified one and to those identified as minorities and women instead of vice versa? Are we simply lucky to move toward gender variability rather than gender rigidification?

Thus far, we have examined two features of a Gadamerian ethics and politics: an Aristotelian dimension emphasizes the circular temporality of ethical action and understanding. We consider and decide how to act from a participatory perspective, as agents who must apply the ethical knowledge they already possess in a way that modifies both the knowledge and the ethical character they take forward to apply in the future. This analysis raises the worry that certain traditions might be so seriously barbarian that even a spiral of application, revision, and reform cannot work itself free of the barbarian forms of life in which it operates. The Kantian dimension of Gadamer's hermeneutics thus looks to a respect for difference and otherness as a foil against which to check our own form of life and its trajectory. This respect for difference is rooted in an awareness of the limitations and partialities of that form of life, in a recognition that our ethical knowledge rests on interpretive understandings of human life and of values, norms, and actions that others can understand differently. But if the worry posed by Gadamer's Aristotelianism is the inbred character of the application of traditional knowledge, the worry posed by his Kantianism is that, without Kant's recourse to a nonethnocentric moral principle, Gadamer's respect for difference becomes a relativistic deference to all otherness. This worry, I think, may be mitigated by yet another feature of Gadamer's hermeneutics, one that leads to pluralism but not relativism. I shall end this essay with a brief account of a remark that seems to signal this feature.

Now, the fact is that meanings represent a fluid multiplicity of possibilities ... but within this multiplicity of what can be thought ... not everything is possible; and if a person fails to hear what the other person is really saying, he will not be able to fit what he has misunderstood into the range of his own various expectations of meaning ... *The hermeneutical task becomes itself a questioning of things* and is always in part so defined. This places hermeneutical work on a firm basis. (TM 268–9)

The history of racialized segregation in the United States seems to provide an illustration of Gadamer's point here. If the question is whether the United States was simply the beneficiary of moral luck in its belated decision to end state-supported segregation, then Gadamer's answer would seem to be that it could not make sense out of its own principle of equality without doing so. To be sure, its history might be understood as the history of trying mightily to ignore what others were "really saying" from the Constitutional Convention on. Indeed, the doctrine of separate but equal was upheld in countless cases before the Supreme Court's decision in *Brown v. Board of Education* effectively overturned it.[21] Still, even if one insists on the distinction between social and political equality on which this doctrine seems to rely, the multiplicity of possible meanings of the principle of equality cannot include support for and enforcement of social segregation by political institutions. Were it to do so, we would "not be able to fit what [we] had misunderstood into the range of [our] own various expectations of meaning." And, in fact, we were not able to fit segregationist policies with the claim of the Declaration of Independence that all men are created equal, with the Fourteenth Amendment's guarantee of an equal protection of the laws, or with other parts of the Constitution. At issue here is the most basic element of the hermeneutic circle, even under its Schleiermacherian interpretation: the part must fit the whole and the whole the parts. If the part and whole at issue encompass American ideals and principles in general, then the enforced separation of different groups simply destroys any possibility for understanding their coherence. Meanings, including the meaning of the American principle of equality, "represent a fluid multiplicity of possibilities" but this multiplicity does not mean that "everything is possible." In the struggle against racial segregation, the principle of equality becomes articulated and defined so that it explicitly includes the conception of neutrality: the idea that no one should be discriminated against on the basis of race, gender or the like. It arguably comes to include the idea of inclusion as well: the idea that all Americans should be able to participate in its political institutions and social practices. Still, this multiplicity of meanings excludes racist and sexist possibilities. If we can now admit this exclusion in a way our predecessors chose not to, for Gadamer this circumstance supports his reliance not only on Aristotle and Kant but also on Hegel: "Is it so perverse," he asks, "to think that in reality," he writes, "the irrational cannot hold out in the long run?" (RAS 36).

NOTES

1 See, for example, Habermas's critique of Gadamer's hermeneutics in *On the Logic of the Social Sciences*, translated by Shierry Weber Nicholson and Jerry A. Stark (Cambridge: MIT Press, 1988).

2 See Martin Heidegger, *Being and Time*, trans. John Macquarrie and Edward Robinson, (New york: Harper and Row, 1962), section 29.

3 See TM 266 where Gadamer refers to Heidegger's worry about viciousness.

4 I have looked at these three differences elsewhere and characterized them slightly differently. See Georgia Warnke, *Gadamer: Hermeneutics, Tradition and Reason* (Cambridge: Polity Press and Stanford: Stanford University Press, 1986), pp. 92–4. Gadamer's use of Aristotle is particularly rich and open to different emphases and interpretations.

5 See Jürgen Habermas, "On the Pragmatic, the Ethical, and the Moral Employments of Practical Reason" in *Justification and Application: Remarks on Discourse Ethics*, trans. Ciaran P. Cronin (Cambridge: MIT Press, 1993), p. 4.

6 Jürgen Habermas, *Between Facts and Norms: Contributions to a Discourse Theory of Law*, trans. Willian Rehg (Cambridge: MIT Press, 1996), p. 162.

7 *Ibid.*, p. 160.

8 *Ibid.*, p. 163.

9 *Ibid.*, p. 167.

10 *Ibid.*, p. 282.

11 Michael Walzer. *Thick and Thin: Moral Argument at Home and Abroad* (Notre Dame: Notre Dame University Press, 1994).

12 See Jürgen Habermas, "Discourse Ethics: Notes on a Program of Philosophical Justification" in Habermas, *Moral Consciousness and Communicative Action*, translated by Christian Lenhardt and Shierry Weber Nicholson (Cambridge: MIT Press, 1990), pp. 88–9.

13 *Thick and Thin*, p. 12.

14 *Ibid.*, p. 12.

15 *Ibid.*, pp. 12–13

16 *Ibid.*, p. 13.

17 *Ibid.*, p. 13.

18 See Ronald Dworkin, *Life's Dominion: An Argument about Abortion, Euthanasia, and Individual Freedom* (New York: Alfred A. Knopf, 1993). I explore these and other interpretive differences involved in the debate over abortion further in *Legitimate Differences: Interpretation in the Abortion Controversy and other Public Debates* (Berkeley: University of California Press, 1999), Chapter 4.

19 See K. Anthony Appiah, "Identity, Authenticity, Survival" in Charles Taylor (et al.): *Multiculturalism: Examining the Politics of Recognition*, edited and introduced by Amy Gutmann (Princeton: Princeton University Press, 1994). See also Judith Butler, *Gender Trouble: Feminism and the Subversion of Identity* (New York, Routledge, 1990).

20 See "The Professor of Parody: The Hip Defeatist Feminism of Judith Butler" in *The New Republic*, February 22, 1999.

21 See Richard Kluger, *Simple Justice: The History of Brown v. Board of Education and Black America's Struggle for Equality* (New York: Vintage Books, Random House, 1977).

5   The Doing of the Thing Itself: Gadamer's Hermeneutic Ontology of Language

Translated by Robert J. Dostal

I

No one would disagree that the consideration of language stands at the center of Gadamer's philosophical hermeneutics. *Truth and Method* makes this obvious. Whoever follows the discussions and descriptions in the first two parts of the book can only affirm the logical development that leads to the consideration of language. As the work develops, we find again and again the principal theme to be the understanding: "the phenomena of understanding and of the correct interpretation of what has been understood" (TM 1). The historically effective consciousness, for which the "historicity of the understanding" is to be shown as a hermeneutical principle, is above all the history of transmitted texts. The relationship of the text and the interpreter is always a "conversation"; the logic of which is the "logic of question and answer." All these concepts, central to Gadamer's hermeneutics, point to forms of language, which can only be satisfactorily clarified in a treatment of its linguisticality.

But just there, where this clarification of language is undertaken, comes something additional that does not follow from the prior discussions. At the point at which language becomes the theme, the work takes "an ontological turn" (TM 343). This turn, considered from the analyses that Gadamer provides in the first two parts of the book, is amazing enough. In the introduction, Gadamer expresses the aim of his philosophical project much more carefully and reservedly. The "conscientiousness" of thought requires that we become aware of its "anterior influences" (*Voreingenommenheiten*) and, correspondingly, "it is a new critical consciousness, that now has to accompany all responsible philosophizing" (TM xv). Philosophical thinking itself belongs to the very tradition whose structure it attempts to clarify hermeneutically. It should make transparent the accomplishment of tradition, of historical life, but neither of these claims independent insight. Thus, Gadamer could conceive of practical philosophy in the sense of Aristotle as a model for philosophical hermeneutics. Just as Aristotle's practical philosophy "by outlining phenomena, helps moral consciousness to attain clarity concerning itself" (TM 279), so too should philosophical hermeneutics contribute to the transparency of "historically effective consciousness." Philosophical hermeneutics is subordinate to historical consciousness, just as practical philosophy is subordinate to action and to the "practical knowledge" that leads it.[1]

From this analogy we can begin to see the significance of the "ontological turn" in Gadamer's hermeneutics. If such a turn were impossible within the horizon of practical philosophy, then it should not be taken within the horizon of a Gadamerian philosophical hermeneutics. It is the case that Aristotle, around whom Gadamer orients his project, utilizes basic concepts that are ontological, although these are not expressly clarified and developed. These concepts depend on ontological presuppositions but do not constitute an ontology. It is particularly instructive to notice how Aristotle treats the basic question of practical philosophy. In order to be able to answer the question about the good life, i.e., the question about the highest goal of human activity, he considers first the actuality proper to the human (*ergon tou anthropou*) and establishes it as the activity of living according to reason that articulates itself in speech (*psyches energeia kata logon*, 1098a7).[2] The key concept in this formulation is *energeia*, and it remains completely vague, though this is appropriate since the goal of an ethic is not pure insight but orientation in action (1095a5–6). Clarifications that do not contribute to orienting activity have no place in ethics. On the other hand, an ethics without concepts that are developed with theoretical intent is not philosophical; and theoretical philosophy provides for Aristotle the measure for philosophy. As soon as one expressly seeks clarifications that are not directed to the question of the good or correct action, one has then taken a theoretical turn. And this turn is "ontological," if the theory is concentrated on the question of the Being of beings.

The ontological turn, however, is not only determined by its goal but also by its starting point. Because the work is carried out from an ethical perspective, it does not lead simply to the general question of the Being of beings, but rather to a determination of the human life in its Being. Because an ethics concerns itself with how one leads one's life and with the fulfillment of life in activity, the theoretical consideration must still concern itself with life in its activity, but not under the aspect as to how a life is "experienced" and fulfilled. It concerns rather the very structure of the activity itself and the question as to how far its constitutes the Being of life.

This may be related to Gadamer's project. According to this sketched turn from praxis to theory, an investigation of the Being of historical life comes out of a clarification of historical living in its fullness, i.e., the activity that it is. This activity, however, turns out to be linguistic, such that language shows itself to be the Being of historical life. Following the analogy with practical philosophy: out of a philosophical hermeneutic comes a hermeneutical philosophy.

Gadamer prepares for the ontological turn of hermeneutics in many ways. Already with his account of "play" in Part One of *Truth and Method* Gadamer emphasizes that he means neither "the attitude" nor "the state of mind of the creator or of those enjoying the work," and that he especially does not mean "the freedom of a subjectivity expressed in play," but rather he means the "mode of being of the work of art itself" (TM 91). Because play finds its fulfillment in a work of art, it is the work of art that best makes it clear that play cannot be understood simply from the activity of the players. Understood from the perspective of its fulfillment, playing is, in truth, a "being-played" (*Gespieltwerden*, TM 95) – a happening, therefore, which constitutes the Being of playing. Similarly, in his discussion of the "historicity of the understanding" Gadamer emphasizes that the "self-awareness of the individual," the reflectively complete grasp of meaning, is "only a flickering in the closed circuits of historical life" (TM 245). "To exist historically," writes Gadamer, means "that knowledge of oneself can never be complete," because "all knowledge of oneself" proceeds from "what is historically pre-given," out of a "substance" that is the basis for "every subjective meaning and attitude." Thus, philosophical hermeneutics must "move back along the path of Hegel's phenomenology until we discover in all that is subjective the substantiality that determines it" (TM 269). This is just what the "ontological turn" to language should accomplish. With it the "substantiality" of historical life should find its validity.

It is easy to misunderstand formulations such as this. It might appear that Gadamer would dispute the fact that, for a game to take place, players are required and that historical life is lived by persons. This impression comes from a confusion of "subject" with "person." When Gadamer takes issue with the subjectivity of a game and its historical life, he does not mean that there are no persons participating, but rather that the game and its historical life do not find their *basis* in the fulfillment of a knowing and self-conscious life. The concept of subjectivity indicates an understanding of life as a principle. Life would be taken as something from which everything else is to be conceived. With his reference to the "substantiality" of historical life, Gadamer articulates his doubt about the foundational strategy going back to Kant, which was radicalized by Fichte, and which was brought to its completion in Hegel's philosophy of absolute spirit. What happens, as Gadamer sees it, cannot be conceptualized from knowing and self-knowledge but rather knowing and self-knowledge stand in a connection with a happening that includes them. This happening itself, however, is to be determined as language.

This does not exclude the fact that language can only be grasped in the context of the experience that persons have in speaking. This is, as Gadamer says, the only possible way to approach the phenomenon of language. Language itself belongs "among the most mysterious questions for human reflection." And this is so, because the very pondering or thinking about language transpires in language. This thinking is "uncannily near" language: "When it functions it is so little an object that it seems to conceal its own being from us" (TM 340). Language is not an *object* (*Gegenstand*) of thought, which one can set before oneself as something both determinate and limited and which one can describe from a distance. Any attempt to distance oneself from language can only take place in language and, accordingly, either contradicts itself or must be limited to very elementary and isolated linguistic phenomena. One can scarcely clarify satisfactorily what language is by clarifying the structure of an assertion or some other isolated kind of sentence. Therefore, the only possibility for bringing into the open language's "own being" is to take the perspective of a speaker. Just as Heidegger in *Being and Time* attempted to work out the question of Being through an analysis of the understanding of Being, which lies in human existence, so too Gadamer takes the path to the being of language through the experience of speaking. Or, more precisely, Gadamer takes the path to that Being that language is through the experience of conversation: "In other words we are seeking to approach the mystery of language from the conversation that we ourselves are" (TM 340).

II

This formulation – "the conversation that we ourselves are" – which derives from Hölderlin, allows us to see immediately and clearly that Gadamer's understanding of conversation has a particular accent. If we examine this more closely, we see that we do not "lead" a conversation, but we "are" a conversation. Dialogical comportment is shown to belong in a linguistic context, i.e., in a conversation. It is therefore in conversations that one experiences what it is to be in language. Under two presuppositions this has an important consequence. Presupposing (1) that conversations do not take place only between persons, but that every experience of being addressed to which one can reply is an experience of conversation, e.g., the experience of a text; and (2) that there is no linguistic experience that is not dialogical, then it follows that we may consider the structure of conversation in general as the structure of linguistic human existence. This generalization, however, does not exclude the fact that we might best work out the structure of linguistic human existence by considering a conversation between two people. This is Gadamer's conviction, and, accordingly, the conversation between persons is for him the model and decisive example for the linguisticality of human life in general.

Gadamer's consideration of this phenomenon shows first the *nonwillfulness* (*Unwillkürlichkeit*) of the conversation. The more "authentic" the conversation, the less "its conduct lies within the will of either partner" (TM 345). An authentic conversation is "never one that we want to conduct" (TM 345). If the intentions of one of the participants in a conversation dominate it, the conversation quickly becomes monological or degenerates into a power struggle. In a power struggle each participant speaks only for herself and concerns herself only with articulating her convictions; the only thing that matters is to convince the other such that one tries not to let the other speak. Here, either the convictions stand isolated and untouched next to one another, or one of them shows that it alone is valid and is thereby victorious. One talks past one another or at one another and shows that one is not capable of conversing. One is prepared for a conversation only when one is prepared to listen, that is, when one is prepared to let the other say something. And one shows that one is capable of a conversation by talking in a way that corresponds to the preparedness for conversation of the other and not by using it as an opportunity to carry on a monologue. Listening to one another (*Zuhören*) and addressing one another (*Ansprechen*) are essential aspects of a conversation. These provide an openness that simultaneously renders a conversation both unpredictable and fruitful.

The fact that "authentic conversations" cannot be willfully controlled does not mean that they are determined by chance. Conversations that are arbitrary and without direction lead only to disappointment and fatigue. A conversation that succeeds must be about *something determinate* of which, as that which it is, we do not lose sight. Every agreement concerns "a matter that is placed before one" (TM 341). And it is the matter at hand (*die Sache selbst*) that leads the conversation. In so far as the matter at hand determines the conversation, as Gadamer says, "the people conversing are far less the leaders of it than the led" (TM 345), because whether a conversation is productive or not does not lie in their power: "Understanding or its failure is like a process which happens to us. Thus we can say that something was a good conversation or that it was a poor one" (TM 345).

This happening, this "coming to language of the matter at hand" (TM 341), does not occur, however, without the assistance of the participants in the conversation. What is most important is that one acts such that one does not hinder the conversation. This requires the readiness to place one's own convictions in question and to take seriously what the other says. Only in this way can one let something be said at all. In addition, one should not take what the other says as an expression of his feelings and opinions, his intentions and hidden motives, but rather as a contribution to the matter at hand. That the understanding that we seek in a conversation is not normally about the other's person is, for Gadamer, the most important objection against romantic hermeneutics that are fixated on the persons involved (TM 162–73).[3] What is done in an "authentic conversation" is therefore more an allowance (*Zulassen*), a letting it happen, for which attention, mental concentration, and linguistic skill are required. To participate in and contribute to a conversation, one must advance the meaning of the matter at hand that comes up for discussion. The doing in conversation consists, as Gadamer says, "in not interfering arbitrarily – reaching with one's own fancies for this or that notion that happens to be to at hand – with the immanent necessity of thought." And, laconically, he adds, "since the Greeks we have called this 'dialectic'" (TM 421). Dialectic, so understood, is not a philosophical method, but rather a skill in conversation; it is, therefore, not a technique (*techne*) in the usual sense. There are no masters of conversation from their own power.

The refraining from "one's own fancies" or "notions that happen to be at hand," the refraining from the moveable set pieces of everyday conversation and its schemata and cliches, is clearly only possible where the matter at hand, which is to come to language, already stands in view. As long as it is worthwhile to carry on the conversation, the matter at hand has not yet come sufficiently into clear view. It is therefore present in the conversation without one having it in an expected or wished for determinateness. In order that one can carry on a conversation about it, the determinate thing, which it is, is to be grasped as yet undetermined and nonetheless as this determinant thing.

However paradoxical it may sound, this is nothing other than the determination of the essence of the *question*.[4] By questioning, one "leads" a conversation. One gives the "meaning" a direction, "in which alone the answer can be given if it is to be meaningful" (TM 326). By questioning one holds on to the matter at hand of the conversation, and by questioning one keeps the conversation open, so that it can dialectically come to completion. Questioning provides the possibility "of avoiding the pressure of opinion" (TM 330), which is the freedom of conversation.

What Gadamer, oriented on the example of the Socratic dialogue, develops here is nothing more than the presupposition under which a thing can be experienced such that it comes to language. Through questioning the possibility is opened up – no more, no less. It is not the case that for the actualization of this possibility the thing under discussion is brought to speech, such that the area opened by the question is filled out by giving the correct answers. Answers only can *show themselves* inasmuch as they are *served* to us by the language in which one dwells as possibilities of articulation in the course and context of the conversation. There, where the conversation has removed the assumed actuality of strong convictions and modes of talking, is where the existence in language (*Dasein in der Sprache*) becomes the possibility of being. One is then open for language to happen. Gadamer in this case creates a variation of Heidegger's proposition that "language speaks" (*die Sprache spricht*).[5] Gadamer writes: "It would be literally more correct to say that a language speaks us than to say that we speak a language." It is first then, when the thing is held open through questioning, that it comes into its own. What happens in conversation is "not our action on the thing," ("*Tun an der Sache,*" GW 1, 467) but rather as Gadamer says with Hegel, "the doing of the thing itself" ("*Tun der Sache selbst,*" TM 421).[6] If we can work out what is meant here, we will be clear about what Gadamer understands by language.

III

With this in mind, let us return to the phenomenon of the question. From the point of view of the speaker it appears as if questions are *raised*. Something comes to the attention that is unclear and indeterminate, and one holds on to this in order to clarify it. What is required is an irritation or a collision (*Anstoss*); after this one can direct one's attention to something and to articulate the irritation in a determinate question. The articulation, however, arises out of the collision. Various dispositions may accompany the irritation – wonder or dread, surprise or disappointment – and constitute the experience of questionableness. The question, says Gadamer in beautiful ambiguity, is a sudden idea (*Einfall*) that occurs to one in a moment. It invades one's convictions as a foreign army invades a country. Thus, a question is "more a passion than an action" (*mehr ein Erleiden als ein Tun*). It "presses itself on us; we can no longer avoid it and persist in our accustomed opinion" (TM 366). What suddenly occurs to us in this way can be the strange or astonishing expression of another person. In this case a question back and a satisfactory clarification is possible. A text that is a fixed speech is more challenging because it cannot explain itself and requires an interpretation: "Thus interpretation always involves a relation to the question that is asked of the interpreter" (TM 370).

From the fact that texts can put accustomed opinions in question, Gadamer infers that "the hermeneutical phenomenon" of the interpretation of texts has "the primacy of conversation" (TM 370). This is revealing inasmuch as a text, which raises questions for the reader and motivates him to pause, challenges the interpreter to let the Being in the language come into dialogue. If the interpretation of a text is to be successful, it must be determined through the same openness that characterizes a successful conversation between persons. Yet something additional is decisive in the experience of a text, because texts always already have been. For the spoken or silent speech of reading, there is always another speech that precedes it and that makes it possible. The interpretation, says Gadamer, must "start somewhere" (TM 472). An interpretation is always tied to a situation to which the text speaks. Similarly, how the text is interpreted is determined by its situation. The interpretation must be appropriate to it and thereby is its "application" (TM 307–11). Yet as an answer to the provocation or challenge of the text, the interpretation is no beginning. It does not develop simply from its situation but goes to work as it joins in, as joining in a song that has already begun.

Through the ineluctability of this joining into the belonging together of question and answer is "the understanding determined as an event" (TM 472). It is an event that always already was what it is, and which in that moment comes into itself. Just as when one sees, one has already seen and when one thinks, one has already thought; every saying is preceded by a said. Language is an activity without a beginning, *energeia* in the sense of Aristotle.[7]

One only understands the decisive point of these thoughts when one understands the lack of a beginning of speaking, not in the sense of a retrospectively infinite succession of expressions, and not in the sense of something always already spoken, but in the sense that every linguistic expression stands in a linguistic context that makes it possible. Because every saying is to be conceived as an answer, whatever is brought to speech must already have been linguistically disclosed, and, at the same time, it must be said again. In this "dialectic of question and answer" (TM 472), the question refers to the possible answer and the answer refers back to the question.

In saying something, that which is disclosed in the question and is conceived as the sayable may perhaps be brought from the possible to the actual. From the perspective of the interpreter or whoever in a conversation between persons feels provoked to provide an answer, an answer is like a move in a game – from a set of possible moves, one chooses one and makes it actual. And the linguisticality that is to be conceived as the scope of possibilities within which the answerer already finds himself and that he confirms as a player confirms the possible moves in a game with a move.

Yet just as we have said, for Gadamer's understanding of language it is characteristic that he considers the question of the preceding linguisticality and the answer to it as an event. What already has been, for example a text, is as an event, because it addresses one with a question. And the interpretation happens as the saying again and the further saying of the said. The interpretation presents a possibility for the said to confirm its effect, which already has been. The structure of an event finds its validity in the dialectic of question and answer, and this happens from the question that is thought from the already said. However, inasmuch as the answer is a confirmation of that which has already happened, both the question and the answer in their belonging together is to be grasped as an event. Every accomplishment of understanding and interpretation *is* only in this event. The event is the movement (*Bewegtheit*) of language. Language, insofar as it is not only to be understood from the particular speaking, is this movement. It is the being of understanding and interpretation, which brings itself always new to language as just this particular existence in language and which brings itself to understanding as that which is its being.

Yet the event of language is thereby not sufficiently determined. In the example of the text, it is clear that the text and the interpretation belong together. Both are bound together in the dialectic of question and answer. Yet what is meant by this connection must be more precisely stated. The interpretation does not refer to the text as something that stands outside itself; and it is also not a mere repetition. How a text and its interpretation belong to one another is not to be understood by considering each separately and then seeking to determine the relation that holds between the two independent entities. Rather one should grasp what is common to them in order to show how what is in common can be differently developed, differentiated, or modified.

Now it is the case that Gadamer occasionally emphasizes that there is no important distinction between the interpretation of a text and its performance, i.e., in a performative interpretation such as in music and drama (TM 310, 399). On this account it is valid to claim of any interpretation of a text what might be claimed of a performance, i.e., that the medium is superseded such that "the work presents itself through it and in it" (TM 120).[8] Yet it is clear that what is meant by this presentness of the text or the work in the interpretation is the presentness of *meaning*. Accordingly, Gadamer once comments that the "miracle of understanding" is the "sharing in a common meaning" (TM 292). And later in *Truth and Method*, in the consideration of the logic of question and answer, Gadamer writes that whoever "wants to understand must question what lies behind what is said" (TM 370). "We understand the meaning of a text only by acquiring the horizon of the question – a horizon that, as such, necessarily includes other possible answers" (TM 370). The interpreter, however, takes up the challenge of the fixed and foreign text that stands over against him only if he questions the text, i.e., questions back "behind the said." That the text as such stands out is then only the *occasion* for the interpretation and the task is to dissolve its status as an object. The written character of the text in an intensive way allows the experience that something said stands over against oneself. This is the "self-alienation" of language (TM 390). The task of the interpreter in the face of this phenomenon of self-alienation in writing, according to Gadamer, is the "transformation back" of these written signs "into speech and meaning" (TM 393). The supersession or sublation (*Aufhebung*) of the interpretation (*Auslegung*) is accorded to this "transformation back" and not to the presentness of the text or the work. "The interpretive concepts," Gadamer writes, "are not, as such, thematic in understanding" (TM 398). If attention is drawn to these concepts, it is a sign that the interpretation is in difficulty and threatens to fail. In principle, it is "their nature to disappear behind what they bring to speech.... Paradoxically an interpretation is right when it is capable of disappearing in this way" (TM 398). In a successful interpretation the meaning is alive and "exists purely for itself" (TM 392).

It is thereby now clear how we are to consider more precisely the speech event, i.e., as an event of meaning. Speech is meaning that occurs in speaking and that is to be grasped as the possibility of this meaning, which is to be grasped in its occasion, place, and situation. Every speech enacts a meaning that is always already corresponding to it, and every written or reported speech fulfills itself when its written or reported character recedes so that the speech can take place, i.e., come to word.

IV

Language, as Gadamer understands it, is therefore something nonobjective and intangible, whose objectification in a text is always the occasion that confirms its nonobjectivity. Language is therefore difficult to grasp, all the more so when its various aspects – structures, words, sounds, or written signs – do not stand out. If one looks at the written signs and attempts to focus on their visibleness, they immediately lose their meaning. This is also the case with the reported word, which is all the more a "word" the less its sound is perceived. It is thus that a mispronunciation in speaking disturbs the understanding, and the dominating beautiful sound of the poem approaches the language of music such that the meaning tends to be superseded by sound and to disappear.

In spite of the nonobjectivity of the meaning that language is, it would be wrong, to set it as something spiritual over against the "material" of the written and reported word and then to ask what is the relation between the two. Meaning is not "beyond" the words, but rather just what happens when speaking in words is performed. Meaning, however, is not thereby simply equivalent to the word, for a meaning can be expressed variously in words. Although meaning and word must be distinguished, they must be considered to belong together such that neither can be thought without the other.

Gadamer has attempted to explain this belonging together of meaning and word in a way somewhat unusual for philosophy, i.e., by way of the theological conception of the incarnation. Gadamer is well aware of the unusualness of this attempt and shows an understanding for the concern "whether we are not here using the unintelligible to explain the unintelligible" (TM 421). Yet Gadamer obviously does not share this concern. He finds the theological model to be enlightening and full of implications. With this example, the motive of Gadamer's conception of language becomes particularly clear, both historically and thematically. Gadamer uses the theological model in order to distance his view from another problematic conception of language that has shown itself to be disastrous for the philosophical tradition. The theological model is subordinate to the interest of a contrasting clarification. With this model we can see the advantages and the weaknesses of Gadamer's conception of language.

In his attempt to clarify the nature of language by way of the incarnation Gadamer takes up John's Gospel. In this Gospel, God Himself is presented as word, as *logos* (John 1, 14). On the basis of the identification of God with the word something is said, as Gadamer will show, in the talk about the miracle of becoming human about the "speaking of the word" (TM 419). In both cases, the act of becoming is not the kind of becoming in which something turns into something else. Neither does it consist in separating one thing from the other ... , nor in lessening the inner word by its emergence into exteriority, nor in becoming something different, so that the inner word is used up" (TM 420). Just as God does not turn himself into man but rather becomes man while nonetheless remaining God, so also in speaking, nothing is exteriorized that as "inner" was completely different – such as a thought without speech. What comes to the fore is therefore no external shape (*Gestalt*), no mere appearance, which must be traced back to that which stands "behind" it. What appears has always already been that which is essential, and it brings its essence (*Wesen*) with it in the appearance. The "interior" is neither hidden behind some "external" appearance nor is it veiled or clouded, but rather it reveals itself.

Gadamer's explanation of language by analogy with the incarnation and by means of the distinction of "inner" and "outer," which he takes over from Augustine,[9] may be easily misunderstood. With this distinction Augustine wants to distinguish "the word of the Spirit (*Geist*)" (TM 421, translated as "the inner mental word") from the merely conventional "outer" language, which, as Gadamer recognizes, "was explicitly devalued by Augustine" (TM 420). Gadamer is not interested in this devaluation. What the model of the incarnation is to make clear is that in giving voice to speech nothing nonlinguistic is brought into linguistic form. Speaking is not a matter of something internal being translated into a medium so that it can be communicated but yet remaining in the process unchanged such that as internal it remains hidden. It is rather the case that what comes to word is understandable in the spoken word as itself. It is nothing other than "the intended thing" – this, not the mental or spiritual, finds expression in the word (TM 426).

Now we have to see how Gadamer can explain his conception of language as an event of meaning with the model of the incarnation. That something is communicated in a word requires, first of all, a distinction between the word and a mere sound or noise. The word has a meaning as an articulation and a communication of something. With the word comes at the same time the experience of meaning and, for Gadamer, only with the word. Something is understandable insofar as it can come to word. There is accordingly no understanding without language, which might be brought to language as something secondary. Even there, where "there is immediate understanding and no explicit interpretation is undertaken," does it "enter into the content of what is understood," because "interpretation is contained potentially within the understanding process" (TM 398). What is spoken about can come explicitly to word and is always already in language. One experiences it as always already under the point of view of a meaning, which makes possible the linguistic articulation and which find expression in it. Thus, meaning is what word and thing have in common – the being of the understandable just as much as the being of the understanding which comes to word: "Being, which can be understood, is language" (TM 474). This is Gadamer's formulation for this.

Gadamer's thought that anything that can be said is understandable in language should exclude therefore the thought of an interior that is fundamentally different from the spoken word. It belongs to the nature of language that it relates to nothing external. The very talk of "relationship" is not appropriate to the peculiar matter of factness (Sachlichkeit) of language. What comes into language is not simply an object or state of affairs in the "external" world, but something in its understandableness, in its meaning. Therefore, it follows that Gadamer does not understand language as a "mere sign system denoting the totality of objects" (TM 416). The word is "not a sign that one selects, nor is it a sign that one makes or gives to another; it is not an existent thing that one picks up and gives an ideality of meaning in order to make another being visible through it" (TM 417).

For Gadamer the view that language relates to objects and may itself become an object for objectivizing consideration displays a forgetfulness of language that began with Plato. Plato's attempt in the *Cratylus* to explain the nature of language by orienting on names (*onoma*) is tied to the view that the truthful access to beings should be sought independent of language and that the word is related merely as a clue to the understood thing. With the assumption of a language-free access to the meaning of beings, which Gadamer finds in the Platonic doctrine of ideas (*Ideenlehre*), Plato "conceals the true nature of language even more than the theories of the Sophists" (TM 408). One may well add that the Sophists disputed whether language allowed one to know something as that which it is. According to the saying of Protagoras (*Theatetus* 151e–151a) anything "is" only according to the measure of its appearing, and, insofar as this appearing is linguistic, it becomes completely absorbed into its factical coming-into-language (*Zur-Sprache-kommen*). This, in fact, is closer to the proposition that "Being, which can be understood, is language," than the view of language as a representation of a true and nonlinguistic knowledge.

Though the sophistic view is closer to this view than the Platonic, it is not equivalent to it. Gadamer allows there to be no doubt that he just as much mistrusts the view of the Sophists with regard to language. The Sophists also have covered over the nature of language – especially because they did not distinguish between word and thing. If every word were to present its own thing, it would be impossible in the exchange of a conversation to stay with the meaning of a thing as one seeks new formulations, and just as little could one understand from the thing that which is said and consider it to be insufficient. Both presuppose a difference between the speeches and the thing. Because this distinction is important to Gadamer, Gadamer emphasizes the priority of the question. The question brings something into speech, such that its further determination or explication is left open. The question grasps the thing so firmly that it indicates which direction the further conversation will take. The question shows the "only direction from which the answer can be given if it is to make sense" (TM 362).

This is said from the perspective of those who, in a conversation, first attempt to determine something. It is easy to forget that, already with the question which they follow, they are with the thing. If, however, one takes seriously the experience of questioning and seeking, Gadamer's thought about the event of meaning appears in another light. It obviously belongs to the event of meaning in a conversation that a thing that comes to word at the same time *withdraws*. Thus, the difference of word and thing belongs to the meaning of the conversation. One could not think this meaning at all without the difference, if one does not wish to absolutize the said in a sophistical way. Something that is questioned shows itself as it is inasmuch as it comes to word and not to "itself." It shows itself rather only as something to which one refers. The question merely indicates (*zeigt an*) that which we are interrogating.

If we consider this aspect, we see that Gadamer's conception of the philosophy of language stands much closer to the philosophy of language of the *Cratylus* than his critique might lead us to think. Plato too was not concerned with the objectification of the word but rather only with the difference between word and thing. Even here in the *Cratylus* (430A–433b) he considers their relation to be one of presentation (*mimesis*). The linguistic presentation (*eikon*) is to be understood from that which is presented, if one is not satisfied with the experience alone according to the measure of the presentation (439a–b). Only then can the presentational activity be understood and subordinated to the claim of a thing. The question as to how this might be possible is not answered in the *Cratylus*. Yet a look at other dialogues, such as the *Phaedo* and the *Sophist*, shows us that Plato thought less about a language-free grasp of things than about an appropriate presentation in language, i.e., about a discussion in which something is not immediately addressed but rather is developed in its structured unity such that the accord of its determinations stands as a proof of its matter of factness (*Sachlichkeit*). Knowledge that is presented as the attempt at an appropriate presentation is not something that happens beyond language but only beyond the orientation on "names." The attempt at knowledge comes from the difference between things and language and is made good only on the basis of the matter of factness (*Sachlichkeit*) of language.

If we were to understand the passages from the *Cratylus*, which Gadamer so critically considers as a clue to the dialectic, the objection to Platonic thought of the forgetfulness of language would not stand. On the contrary, Gadamer could have called upon the difference between word and thing, which Plato emphasizes in order to make understandable his conception of the important limited and provisional character of any speech. Nonetheless, it would not well fit with the central ideas of his ontology. If there is something that may be articulated linguistically but that nonetheless resists linguistic articulation, it is not the case that it address something that occurs to one as questionable and that wants to find linguistic expression. The language is in this case simply not the doing of the thing itself.

V

If we judge the matter from the text of *Truth and Method*, Gadamer clearly saw this difficulty and responded to it. He extended or replaced the model of the incarnation with which he had wished to explain the "doing of the thing itself." We will return later to the question as to whether the extension is consistent with the model of the incarnation. With this response the meaning is no longer equivalent to the linguistic self-showing of the thing, but rather is determined as the horizon of speaking. Thus, every word, writes Gadamer, "carries with it the unsaid"; every speech "brings a totality of meaning into play without being able to express it totally," and thereby shows its "living virtuality" (TM 458). Speaking is not understood because it displays something, but rather that in speaking "the said" is held together "with an infinity of what is not said in one unified meaning." Thus, every speech means more than it explicitly says. Not only does the thing under discussion and its state of affairs find expression in language but, at the same time, "a relation to the whole of being" finds expression (TM 469).

Gadamer explains what he means by this claim when he traces the "unique factualness" (*eigentümliche Sachlichkeit*) of language back to its "relation to the world" (*Weltverhältnis*). The determination of a state of affairs is always tied to "the recognition of its independent otherness," i.e., something in its determination is understood from what it is not: "To be this and not that constitutes the determinacy of all beings." Thus, in every determination "there is always a negative aspect as well" (TM 445). Therefore the meaning of the said is within the range of the possible. It is meaningful in that it relates to its place in this range of possibilities and thus has a place value.

Gadamer himself accentuated the relation of the said to the unsaid somewhat differently. It is less relevant for him that the said belongs in the context of the unsaid than that the presentness of the unsaid belongs to the said. This presentness he determines to be the "speculative" character of language for the explication of which he refers us to "the mirror relation," which "is like a duplication that is still only the one thing. The real mystery of a reflection is the intangibility of the image, the sheer reproduction hovering before the mind's eye" (TM 466). The mirror image, so understood, is a presentation without the shortening and the accentuating that otherwise every presentation has. In a mirror image, there is almost no difference between the presented and the presentation.

What is meant here is best understood if we consider again the hermeneutical experience in the narrow sense, i.e., the interpretation (*Interpretation*) of a work. In the performance of a piece of music or the recitation of a text not only is present that which is immediately played or spoken but also the whole to which the played and spoken belongs. One understands the whole and with it what is immediately presented and present; and yet one "has" the whole only from that which is momentarily presented. Thus, it is the case with anything said which is understood, if we follow Gadamer, that it brings with it a context to which it belongs, its "horizon of meaning," and lets it be present as "the purest reproduction" (TM 469).

It is unmistakable that here the speculative relation between meaning and the act of speaking is to be compared to the model of the incarnation. The difference of the unsaid and the said and the withdrawal of meaning is ignored in order that the meaning can appear in the understandableness of the said as in a mirror. But how would it be possible, if "an infinity of the unsaid" is in play, and if "someone repeats what is said," that "he does not need to distort consciously and yet he will change the meaning of what is said"? Is it actually here "in the most everyday speech" in which "there appears an element of speculative reflection" that "the intangibility of that which is still the purest reproduction of meaning" (TM 469) is experienced? Or is it not rather that we experience the intangibility of the context, in which something spoken stands and which it cannot secure? The "purest reproduction of meaning" is only possible, if the context of that which is said, in spite of all the openness that belongs to it, is determinate and unified.

One point of reference for the way in which such a "unity," a "whole" of meaning, might be understood, is the concept which we cited above, of the "horizon of meaning." A horizon is a "range of vision that includes everything that can be seen from a particular vantage point" (TM 302). The horizon is a limited openness, therefore, which changes as soon as one changes one's vantage point. A horizon of meaning, which is a continually changing range of linguistic existence, is a whole insofar as it can give itself together with the infinity of the unsaid. In this infinity the horizon of meaning is infinitely changeable, infinitely diverse, without losing its continually shifting determinateness.

Gadamer wants to understand the "speculative" character of language not only as the presentness of a limited range of meaning in what is said. Every individual horizon of linguistic existence is, according to Gadamer, itself circumscribed in a single horizon, i.e., in the speculative character of language is present the "whole of being." Gadamer's answer to the question of the identity (Selbigkeit) of the linguistic meaning event arises from his considerations of the history of philosophy in the second part of Truth and Method and his following up on them in the third part. The account of language in Part Three is based on that which should be accounted for in the account of language, which is to say that Part Three presumes what is to be shown. After it has been shown that the event of tradition is a meaning event and that the "historically effective consciousness" belongs to it and is an existence in language, then the unity or wholeness of meaning is grounded with a reference to its traditional character: "The content of the tradition itself is the sole criterion and it expresses itself in language" (TM 472–3). Tradition is distinguished by the fact that it is always concerned with "the same thing," (dasselbe) i.e., from the horizon of "historical consciousness" it bears a circumscribed set of "contents," which carries in its unity the infinite manifold of a possible interpretation and keeps it together.

This leaves the question as to how such an horizon, encompassing all tradition, may be experienced. As soon as "historical consciousness" is addressed through a traditional content, it is determined by this in its experience as to how its meaning can be present. The present (Das Gegenwärtige) is always only an "image," which the historically effective consciousness "presents" (TM 431). Meaning is presented in the understanding and interpretation according to this criterion of the historically effective consciousness – not willfully but simply in the fact that it is determined as this. Through this limitation of the horizon of meaning is the "speculative" in linguistic existence shaped. The "infinity of the unsaid" goes beyond any horizon. As the beautifully coined expression, "direction of meaning" (*Richtungssinn*) suggests, the infinity of the unsaid can at best be indicated in the openness of linguistic existence. Whoever points in a direction, always points beyond the horizon.

If these considerations are illuminating, the event of meaning, which Gadamer understands as language, can scarcely still be understood as an always already fulfilled actuality in the sense of Aristotle's *energeia*. The actuality of meaning should rather be considered as a presentation of a possibility, which is never fully realized. It possesses determinateness only inasmuch as it is a text or a work or appears from the limited perspective of the interpreter as determinate. Such a limited possibility can be experienced as the range of further possibilities of presentation and, at the same time, this very presentation can come forward in its individuality and uniqueness. An interpretation wins one over and persuades insofar as it stands freely within its parameter and strives to be convincing as an individual interpretation while avoiding turning into the interpreted matter. Thus, it is not so important for an interpretation to sublate itself in order to enable "the doing of the thing itself," but rather to hold itself within the uniqueness of the individual thing so that the parameter remains open for other possibilities.

It should be clear how the development of thought in *Truth and Method* makes possible considerations such as these. This allows the ambivalence of Gadamer's principal work to stand out clearly. *Truth and Method* brings two quite different things together: first, openness, which we find in the priority of the question, in the understanding of meaning as "direction of meaning," (*Richtungsinn*), and in the emphasis on the finitude of every interpretation; and, secondly, the closedness (*Geschlossenheit*) of the event of meaning, which finds expression above all in the thought of a continuous tradition that is always already completed, and in the image of a "unified stream of historical life." Gadamer wants both, and it is not easy to see how both can be convincingly brought together.

VI

This critical estimation may consider itself confirmed by Gadamer's later work. The perspective from the history of philosophy, which dominates in *Truth and Method*, scarcely continues to play a role, while the consideration of language as an event of meaning as explicated with the model of the incarnation is revoked. Indicative of this turn is the way in which Gadamer, in his essay "Text and Interpretation," which first appeared in 1984, interprets the central proposition of his ontology of language: "Being that can be understood is language." Here he writes that this also means that "that which is can never be completely understood" (GDE 35). Relying on Heidegger's concept of "facticity," Gadamer now explicates "Being" as that which is questionable and cannot be gotten behind (*das unhintergehbare Fragliche*) but which, at the same time, requires understanding and an understandable answer. It is, as Gadamer says in his 1989 work, "Hermeneutics and the Ontological Difference," that which challenges and provokes "the efforts of our understanding" such that "it constantly withdraws itself and thereby is always there."[10]

However, what is there *only* as withdrawing itself, does not allow itself to be grasped as the meaning of existence in language, as the range and context of the spoken word in which it is understandable. Nor does it allow itself to be grasped as that direction of meaning, in which one is referred to other possibilities of interpretation. Rather, it is, as Gadamer says with reference to Schelling, that prior to which one cannot think (*das Unvordenkliche*). One cannot understand oneself by referring to the inexplicable being whose origin cannot be thought. This being does not guarentee any continuity, because it allows that to be that always already has been. This being is simply impossible to remember and is the withdrawal of pastness (having-been-ness, *Gewesenheit*), the refutation of a reality that is and always already has been. Because Gadamer makes these thoughts his own, he acknowledges that Schelling and Heidegger are right at the cost of Aristotle and Hegel (GDE 35).

It follows that Gadamer now hesitates to determine ontologically the meaning context of existence in language and considers it a given only "ontically." This occurs in two ways. Although Gadamer never questions the priority of the spoken word over the written, he now develops a conception of the "eminent" text, usually a poetic text, which clearly goes beyond the relevant determinations of *Truth and Method*. The eminent text is more than merely "a phase in the execution of the communicative event" (GDE 35). It is not a self-alienation of spoken language, because instead of pointing back to "an original expression of something," it "prescribes all repetitions and acts of speaking," without the written being dissolved into a prescription: "No speaking can ever completely fulfill the prescription given in the poetic text" (GDE 42).

Gadamer's conviction about the priority of the spoken word requires that he not give up the thought of the continual event of language, which is so important for *Truth and Method*. Yet now he takes it back with a description of life–world comportment that reminds us of Wittgenstein. Language's founding of continuity, taken together with the founding of continuity by action, is "ritual." By "ritual" is meant any form of behavior in which there are "arrangements and understandings (*Übereinkunft und Übereinkommen*).[11] In ritual there is a complex of behavior patterns to which one must become accustomed to be able to say and do "the right thing," that is, to say that which has meaning in the context of customary behavior. It is a thoroughly human meaning, carried out in a fragile and ephemeral way – and yet an answer, perhaps a reply to the inexplicability of being (*das Unvordenkliche*). It is, as Gadamer interprets a statement of Heraclitus, the "light" that man infects himself with "in the silent night."[12] Like the texts, according to whose prescription one can act, rituals preserve something such as an ability to be in the abyss of that prior to which we cannot think (*Unvordenkliche*) – something that we have to doubt whether it still should be named "Being" at all. In this context, Gadamer's later renunciation of an ontology of language is probably to be understood as an answer. But then the question of the being of an existence illuminated by language would remain open. It would be a type of being that is connected to the abyss of that prior to which we cannot think (*das Unvordenkliche*), which is no longer defined ontologically, but would have to be defined philosophically, if philosophy does not wish to retreat in the face of the uncanny nearness of language.

NOTES

1 "Praktisches Wissen" (practical knowledge) is Gadamer's translation of *phronesis* and also the title of an early essay (1930) which was first published in Gadamer's *Collected Works* (5, pp. 230–48). [This has not appeared in English translation.] See also *Truth and Method*, Section II.2.b., "The hermeneutic relevance of Aristotle," pp. 278–89, as well as my essays "Verstehen als geschichtliche Phronesis," in *Internationale Zeitschrift für Philosophie* 1 (1992), pp. 24–37, and "Philosophische Hermeneutik–hermeneutische Philosophie. Ein Problemaufriss," in *Hermeneutische Wege: Hans-Georg Gadamer zum Hundersten*, ed. Günter Figal, Jean Grondin, Dennis J. Schmidt (Tübingen: Mohr Siebeck, 2000), pp. 335–44.

2 All citations of the *Nicomachean Ethics* are from the edition edited by I. Bywater (Oxford University Press, 1894).

3 The notion that it is the exception and not the rule when the interest of the understanding is directed to the person is an objection that Gadamer validly makes against the attempt of Jürgen Habermas to question the "claim to universality of hermeneutics," through raising the value of psychoanalytic understanding. See "Reply to My Critics," in *The Hermeneutic Tradition*, edited by Gayle L. Ormiston and A. D. Schrift (Albany: Suny Press, 1990), pp. 273–97.

4 For a treatment of the semantics of the question that connects hermeneutical and analytical considerations, see Thomas Schwarz Wentzer, *Das Diskrimen der Frage* in *Hermeneutische Wege*, pp. 219–40.

5 Martin Heidegger, "Language," in *Poetry, Language, Thought*, translated by Albert Hofstadter (New York: Harper & Row, 1971), p. 193. See also the collection of essays in *On the Way to Language*, translated by Peter Hertz (New York: Harper & Row, 1971), especially "The Nature of Language."

6 "Es ist der Tun der Sache..." In English translation, "It is the fact's own act..." See G. W. F. Hegel, *The Science of Logic*, translated by A. V. Miller (New York: Humanities Press, 1969), p. 474. This is the section on the "Absolutely Unconditioned" (*Das Absolute Unbedingte*) in the chapter on "Ground" (*Grund*).

7 See Aristotle, *Metaphysics* 6, 1048b22–26. Gadamer uses the concept of *energeia* in *Truth and Method* only once, but in a prominent place – in his account of play (TM 110), which "serves as the clue to the ontological explication." His exposition of play presents a structure that is later developed in the ontology of language.

8 "Interpretation" here is the more general concept that includes both *Auslegung* and *Aufführung*.

9 For a consideration of the "inner word," see the work of Jean Grondin,

Introduction to Philosophical Hermeneutics. New Haven: Yale University Press, 1994; and "Gadamer and Augustine: On the Origin of the Hermeneutical Claim to Universality," in *Hermeneutics and Truth,* edited by Brice Wachterhauser, Evanston: Northwestern University Press, 1994, pp. 137–47; and, finally, *Introduction a Hans-Georg Gadamer,* Paris, 1999, pp. 191–201. See also the self-critical remark of Grondin that he has "stretched too far the significance of the "inner word" for Gadamer (although not for hermeneutics itself)," in *Hermeneutische Wege* (Endnote 1), p. 212.

10 GA 10, 64 (untranslated).

11 See "Toward a Phenomenology of Ritual and Language," translated by Lawrence Schmidt and Monika Reuss, in *Language and Linguisticality in Gadamer's Hermeneutics,* edited by Lawrence Schmidt (Boston: Lexington, 2000), pp. 19–50, especially p. 27.

12 *Ibid.,* p. 50.

6 Gadamer on the Human Sciences

I

The great challenge of the coming century, both for politics and for social science, is that of understanding the other. The days are long gone when Europeans and other "Westerners" could consider their experience and culture as the norm toward which the whole of humanity was headed, so that the other could be understood as an earlier stage on the same road that we had trodden. Now we sense the full presumption involved in the idea that we already possess the key to understanding other cultures and times.

But the recovery of the necessary modesty here seems always to threaten to veer into relativism, or a questioning of the very ideal of truth in human affairs. The very ideas of objectivity, which underpinned our social science, seemed hard to combine with that of fundamental conceptual differences between cultures, so that real cultural openness seemed to threaten the very norms of validity on which social science rested. What often does not occur to those working in these fields is the thought that their whole model of science is wrong and inappropriate. It is here where Gadamer has made a tremendous contribution to twentieth century thought, for he has proposed a new and different model, which is much more fruitful, and shows promise of carrying us beyond the dilemma of ethnocentrism and relativism.

In fact, in *Truth and Method*, Gadamer shows how understanding a text or event, which comes to us out of our history, has to be construed, not on the model of the "scientific" grasp of an object, but rather on that of speech-partners who come to an understanding (*Verständigung*). If we follow Gadamer's argument here, we come to see that this is probably true of human science as such. That is, it is not simply knowledge of our own past that needs to be understood on the "conversation" model, but knowledge of the other as such, including disciplines such as anthropology, where student and studied often belong to quite different civilizations.

This view has come to be widely accepted today, and it is one of the great contributions that Gadamer has made to the philosophy of this and succeeding centuries. I would like to try to lay out here why this is so.

First, I want to contrast the two kinds of operation: knowing an object, and coming to an understanding with an interlocutor. Some differences are obvious. The first is unilateral, the second bilateral. I know the rock, the solar system; I don't have to deal with its view of me, or of my knowing activity.

But beyond this, the goal is different. I conceive the goal of knowledge as attaining some finally adequate explanatory language, which can make sense of the object, and will exclude all future surprises. However much this may elude us in practice, it is what we often seek in science; e.g., we look for the ultimate theory in microphysics, where we will finally have charted all the particles and forces, and don't have to face future revisions.

But coming to an understanding can never have this finality. For one thing, we come to understandings with certain definite interlocutors. These will not necessarily serve when we come to deal with others. Understandings are party-dependent. And then, frequently more worrying, even our present partners may not remain the same. Their life situation or goals may change, and the understanding may be put in question. True, we try to control for this by binding agreements, contracts, but this is precisely because we see that what constitutes perfect and unconstrained mutual understanding at one time may no longer hold good later.

Third, the unilateral nature of knowing emerges in the fact that my goal is to attain a full intellectual control over the object, such that it can no longer "talk back" and surprise me. Now this may require that I make some quite considerable changes in my outlook. My whole conceptual scheme may be very inadequate when I begin my enquiry. I may have to undergo the destruction and remaking of my framework of understanding in order to attain the knowledge that I seek. But all this serves the aim of full intellectual control. What does not alter in this process is my goal. I define my aims throughout in the same way.

By contrast, coming to an understanding may require that I give some ground in my objectives. The end of the operation is not control, or else I am engaging in a sham, designed to manipulate my partner while pretending to negotiate. The end is being able in some way to function together with the partner, and this means listening as well as talking, and hence may require that I redefine what I am aiming at.

So there are three features of understanding: they are bilateral, they are party-dependent, and they involve revising goals, which do not fit our classical model of knowing an object. To which our "normal" philosophical reaction is: quite so. These are features unsuited to knowledge, real "science." The content of knowledge shouldn't vary with the person who is seeking it; it can't be party-dependent. And the true seeker of knowledge never varies in her goal; there is no question of compromise here. Party-dependence and altered goals are appropriate to understandings precisely because they represent something quite different from knowledge; deal-cutting and learning the truth are quite distinct enterprises, and one should never mix the two, on pain of degrading the scientific enterprise.

How does Gadamer answer these "obvious" objections? In fact, his answer contains many rich and complex strands. I just want to mention two here, leaving aside others that are equally, perhaps even more important (such as the whole issue of "linguisticality," which is another of Gadamer's crucial contributions to the thought of our time).

The first is a negative point. Gadamer does not believe that the kind of knowledge that yields complete intellectual control over the object is attainable, even in principle, in human affairs. It may make sense to dream of this in particle physics, even to set this as one's goal, but not when it comes to understanding human beings.

He expresses this, for instance, in his discussion of experience. Following Hegel, he sees experience, in the full sense of the term, as the "experience of negation" (*Nichtigkeit*, TM 354). Experience is that wherein our previous sense of reality is undone, refuted, and shows itself as needing to be reconstituted. It occurs precisely in those moments where the object "talks back". The aim of science, following the model above, is thus to take us beyond experience.

This latter is merely the path to science, whose successful completion would take it beyond this vulnerability to further such refutation: "For experience itself can never be science. Experience stands in an ineluctable opposition to knowledge and to the kind of instruction that follows from general theoretical or technical knowledge" (TM 355).

Now Gadamer sees it as part of the finitude of the human condition that this kind of transcending of experience is in principle impossible in human affairs. To explain fully why would involve talking a great deal about linguisticality, for which I do not have the space here. But perhaps the main point can be made very tersely in terms of the place of culture in human life. Whatever we might identify as a fundamental common human nature, the possible object of an ultimate experience-transcending science, is always and everywhere mediated in human life through culture, self-understanding, and language. These not only show an extraordinary variety in human history, but they are clearly fields of potentially endless innovation.

Here we see a big watershed in our intellectual world. There are those who hope to anchor an account of human nature below the level of culture, such that cultural variation, where it is not trivial and negligible, can be explained from this more basic account. Various modes of sociobiology, and accounts of human motivation based on the (conjectured) conditions in which human beings evolved, share this ambition. They have the necessary consequence that most cultural variation is placed in the first category, and seen as merely epiphenomenal, a surface play of appearances. And then there are those who find this account of human life unconvincing, who see it as an evasion of the most important explananda in human life, which are to be found at this level of cultural difference.

Suffice it to say that Gadamer is one of the major theorists in the second camp, and that hence he sees the model of science, which I opposed above to understanding, as inapplicable to human affairs.

This may help explain why he refuses this model, but not the adoption of his alternative, based on interpersonal understanding. How does he justify party-dependence, and what analogue can he find to revising goals?

The first can be explained partly from the fact of irreducible cultural variation. From this, we can see how the language we might devise to understand the people of one society and time would fail to carry over to another. Human science could never consist exclusively of species-wide laws. In that sense, it would always be at least in part "idiographic," as against "nomothetic." But for Gadamer, party-dependence is more radical than that. The terms of our best account will vary not only with the people studied, but also with the students. Our account of the decline of the Roman Empire will not and cannot be the same as that put forward in eighteenth century England, or those that will be offered in twenty-fifth century China, or twenty-second century Brazil.

It is this bit of Gadamer's argument that often strikes philosophers and social sciences as scandalous, and "relativist", abandoning all allegiance to truth. This interpretation is then supported by those among Gadamer's defenders who are in a "postmodern" frame of mind.

But this grievously misunderstands the argument. Gadamer is anything but a "relativist" in the usual sense of today's polemics. But to see this, we have to bring out another way in which Gadamer breaks with the ordinary understanding of "science."

As we often have been led to understand it in the past, scientific explanation deploys a language that is entirely clear and explicit. It is grounded in no unthought-out presuppositions, which may make those who speak it incapable of framing certain questions, and entertaining certain possibilities. This false view has been very largely dispelled in our time by the work of such thinkers as Kuhn and Bachelard. We now understand the fact that the practices of natural science have become universal in our world as the result of certain languages, with their associated practices and norms, having spread and being adopted by all societies in our time.

But what has been less remarked is that these languages became thus universally diffusable precisely because they were insulated from the languages of human understanding. The great achievement of the seventeenth century scientific revolution was to develop a language for nature that was purged of human meanings. This was a revolution, because the earlier scientific languages, largely influenced by Plato and Aristotle, were saturated with purpose- and value-terms. These could only have traveled along with a good part of the way of life of the civilizations that nourished them. But the new austere languages could be adopted elsewhere more easily.

We can see how different the situation is with the languages of "social science." These too have traveled, but very much as a result of the cultural influence of and cultural alignment on the "West." Moreover, they seem incapable of achieving the kind of universality we find with natural sciences. The study of human beings remains in a preparadigmatic condition, where a host of theories and approaches continue to compete, and there is no generally recognized "normal" science.

This difference in the fate of the two kinds of "science" is connected to the fact that the languages of human science always draw for their intelligibility on our ordinary understanding of what it is to be a human agent, live in society, have moral convictions, aspire to happiness, and so forth. No matter how much our ordinary everyday views on these issues may be questioned by a theory, we cannot but draw on certain very basic features of our understanding of human life, those that seem so obvious and fundamental as not to need formulation. But it is precisely these that may make it difficult to understand people of another time or place.

Thus, we can innocently speak of people in other ages holding opinions or subscribing to values, without noticing that in our society there is a generalized understanding that everyone has, or ought to have, their own personal opinion on certain subjects – say, politics or religion; or without being aware of how much the term *value* carries with it the sense of something chosen. But these background understandings may be completely absent in other societies. We stumble into ethnocentrism, not in virtue so much of the theses that we formulate, but of the whole context of understanding that we unwittingly carry over unchallenged.

Now this is not a danger that we can conjure once and for all by adopting a certain attitude. That is because the context that will give its sense to any theoretical account of human life we are entertaining will be the whole, tacit, background understanding of what it is to be a human being. But this is so wide and deep that there can be no question of simply suspending it, and operating outside of it. To suspend it altogether would be to understand nothing about human beings at all. Here is where the striking contrast with the languages of natural science emerges. There it was possible to develop languages for the objects of science that bracketed out human meanings, and still think effectively, indeed, more effectively, about the target domain.

But bracketing out human meanings from human science means understanding nothing at all; it would mean betting on a science that bypassed understanding altogether, and tried to grasp its domain in neutral terms, in the language of neurophysiology, for instance.

If our own tacit sense of the human condition can block our understanding of others, and yet we cannot just neutralize it at the outset, then how can we come to know others? Are we utterly imprisoned in our own unreflecting outlook? Gadamer thinks not. The road to understanding others passes through the patient identification and undoing of those facets of our implicit understanding that distort the reality of the other.

At a certain point, we may come to see that "opinions" have a different place in our life-form than in theirs, and we will then be able to grasp the place of beliefs in their life; we will be ready to allow this to be in its difference, undistorted by the assimilation to "opinions."

This will happen when we allow ourselves to be challenged, interpellated by what is different in their lives, and this challenge will bring about two connected changes: we will see our peculiarity for the first time, as a formulated fact about us, and not simply a taken-for-granted feature of the human condition as such; and at the same time, we will perceive the corresponding feature of their life-form undistorted. These two changes are indissolubly linked; you cannot have one without the other.

Our understanding of them will now be improved, through this correction of a previous distortion. But it is unlikely to be perfect. The possible ways in which we, our background, could enframe them distortively cannot be enumerated. We may still have a long way to go. But we will have made a step toward a true understanding, and further progress along this road will consist of such painfully achieved, particular steps. There is no leap to a disengaged standpoint which can spare us this long march.

If a prejudice becomes questionable in view of what another person or text says to us, this does not mean that it is simply set aside and the text of person accepted as valid in its place. Rather, historical objectivism shows its naivete in accepting this disregarding of ourselves as what actually happens. In fact our own prejudice is properly brought into play by being put at risk. Only by being given full play is it able to experience the other's claim to truth and make it possible for him to have full play himself. (TM 299)

We can now see how our grasp of the other, construed on the model of coming to an understanding, is doubly party-dependent, varying not only with the object studied but also with the student: with the object studied, because our grasp will have to be true to them in their particular culture, language, and way of being. But it will also vary with the student, because the particular language we hammer out in order to achieve our understanding of them will reflect our own march toward this goal. It will reflect the various distortions that we have had to climb out of, the kinds of questions and challenges that they, in their difference, pose to us. It will not be the same language in which members of that culture understand themselves; but it will also be different from the way members of a distinct third culture will understand them, coming as they will to this goal through a quite different route, through the identification and overcoming of a rather different background understanding.

That is why the historiography of the Roman Empire, carried out in twenty-fifth century China or twenty-second century Brazil is bound to be different from ours. They will have to overcome different blocks to understanding; they will find the people of that time puzzling in ways that we do not; they will need to make them comprehensible through a different set of terms.

The coming-to-an-understanding model fits here, with its corollary of party-dependence, because the language of an adequate science of the Ys for the Xs reflects both Xs and Ys. It is not, as with the knowledge-of-object model, a simple function of the object, the scientific theory that is perfectly adequate to this reality. It is a language that bridges those of both knower and known. That is why Gadamer speaks of it as a "fusion of horizons." The "horizons" here are at first distinct, they are the way that each has of understanding the human condition in their non-identity. The "fusion" comes about when one (or both) undergo a shift; the horizon is extended, so as to make room for the object that before did not fit within it.

For instance, we become aware that there are different ways of believing things, one of which is holding them as a "personal opinion." This was all that we allowed for before, but now we have space for other ways, and can therefore accommodate the beliefs of a quite different culture. Our horizon is extended to take in this possibility, which was beyond its limit before.

But this is better seen as a fusion, rather than just as an extension of horizons, because at the same time, we are introducing a language to talk about their beliefs, which represents an extension in relation to their language. Presumably, they had no idea of what we speak of a "personal opinions," at least in such areas as religion, for instance. They would have had to see these as rejection, rebellion, or heresy. So the new language we're using, which places "opinions" alongside other modes of believing, as possible alternative ways of holding things true, opens a broader horizon, extending beyond both the original ones, and in a sense combining them.

Here we see the full force of the Gadamerian image of the "conversation." The kind of operation we are describing here can be carried out unilaterally, and must be when we are trying to write the history of the Roman Empire, for instance. But it borrows its force from comparison with another predicament, in which live interlocutors strive to come to an understanding, to overcome the obstacles to mutual comprehension, and to find a language in which both can agree to talk undistortively of each. The hermeneutical understanding of tradition limps after this paradigm operation; we have to maintain a kind of openness to the text, allow ourselves to be interpellated by it, take seriously the way its formulations differ from ours – all things that a live interlocutor in a situation of equal power would force us to do.

Horizons are thus often initially distinct. They divide us. But they are not unmovable; they can be changed, extended. I will discuss this notion of horizon below, but first a word about why this picture of a language for science, which varies with both knower and known, is quite different from the common idea of "relativism," and why this picture has a clear place for the concepts of correctness and truth.

Relativism is usually the notion that affirmations can be judged valid not unconditionally, but only from different points of view or perspectives. Proposition p could be true from perspective A, false from perspective B, indeterminate from C, and so forth, but there would be no such thing as its being true or false unconditionally.

It does not seem to me that Gadamer is in this position at all. If the historiography of the Roman Empire in twenty-fifth century China is different from our own, this will not be because what we can identify as the same propositions will have different truth values.

The difference will be rather that different questions will be asked, different issues raised, different features will stand out as remarkable, and so forth.

Moreover, within each of these enterprises of studying Rome from these different vantage points, there will be such a thing as better or worse historiography. Some accounts will be more ethnocoentric and distortive than others, still others will be more superficial. Accounts can be ranked for accuracy, comprehensiveness, nondistortion, and so on. In short, some will be more right than others and will approach closer to the truth.

But beyond this, we can also see a possible ranking between accounts from different starting points. Let us say that our twenty-fifth century Chinese historians take account of the work of Gibbon, Symes, Jones, Peter Brown, and so forth. They will be trying, in other words, not just to fuse horizons with the Romans, but also with us as we try to do the same thing. The fusion will not only be bipolar, but triangular, or if we see Gibbon as a distinct standpoint, quadrangular.

We can see now that there is another virtue here of accounts. They can be more or less comprehensive in a new sense; not depending on how much detail and coverage they offer of the object studied, but rather on their taking in and making mutually comprehensible a wider band of perspectives. In other words, the more comprehensive account in this sense fuses more horizons.

The ideal of the most comprehensive account possible ought in a sense to take the place of the old goal of a point-of-view-less nomothetical science, which grasps all humanity under one set of explanatory laws. Instead, we substitute the ideal of languages, which allows for the maximum mutual comprehension between different languages and cultures across history. Of course, this is a goal that can, in the nature of things, never be integrally realized. Even if, *per impossibile*, we might have achieved an understanding to which all cultures to date might sign on, this could not possibly preempt future cultural change, which would require the process of fusion to start over again.

But it is, nevertheless, an important ideal both epistemically and humanly: epistemically, because the more comprehensive account would tell us more about human beings and their possibilities; humanly, because the language would allow more human beings to understand each other, and to come to undistorted understandings.

II

And so, for human affairs, the model of scientific theory, which is adequate to an object, is replaced by that of understanding, seen as a fusion of horizons: "Understanding is always the fusion of these horizons supposedly existing by themselves" (TM 306).

Gadamer's concept "horizon" has an inner complexity that is essential to it. On the one hand, horizons can be identified and distinguished; it is through such distinctions that we can come to grasp what is distorting understanding and impeding communication. But on the other hand, horizons evolve and change. There is no such thing as a fixed horizon. "The horizon is, rather, something into which we move and which moves with us. Horizons change for a person who is moving" (TM 304). A horizon with unchanging contours is an abstraction. Horizons identified by the agents whose worlds they circumscribe are always in movement. The horizons of A and B may thus be distinct at time t, and their mutual understanding very imperfect. But A and B by living together may come to have a single common horizon at t + n.

In this way, "horizon" functions somewhat like "language." We can talk about the "language of modern liberalism," or the "language of nationalism," and point out the things they cannot comprehend. But these are abstractions, freeze frames of a continuing film. If we talk about the language of Americans or the French, we can no longer draw their limits a priori; for the language is identified by the agents, who can evolve.

This way of understanding difference and its overcoming through the complex concept of an horizon is to be contrasted with two others. On one hand, we have the classic model that comes from the epistemological tradition, whereby our grasp of the world is mediated by the inner representations we make of it, or the conceptual grid through which we take it in. This way of construing knowledge easily generates the conjecture that there may be unbridgeable differences. What if our inner representations diverge, even as we stand before the same external objects? What if our conceptual grids are differently constructed, through which all the information we receive is filtered? How will we ever be able to convince each other, even understand each other? Any consideration that one may adduce in argument will already be represented or enframed by the other in a systematically different way. All reasoning stops at the borders of conceptual schemes, which pose insurmountable limits to our understanding.

In reaction to this, there is the attempt to establish the possibility of universal communication through an outright rejection of the idea of a conceptual scheme, as famously proposed by Donald Davidson. Davidson means his argument to be taken as a repudiation of the whole representational epistemology. "In giving up the dualism of scheme and world, we do not give up the world, but reestablish unmediated touch with the familiar objects whose antics make our sentences and opinions true and false."[1]

As a rejection of the old epistemology (or at least attempted rejection; I am not sure that Davidson really does shake off the shackles of the representational view), this is obviously welcome. Further, Davidson's argument against the idea that we could be imprisoned in utterly incongruent schemes, invoking the "principle of charity," is obviously a powerful one. Davidson's principle of charity requires that I, the observer/theorist, must make sense of him, the subject studied, in the sense of finding most of what he does, thinks, and says intelligible, or else I cannot be treating him as a rational agent, and there is nothing to understand, in the relevant sense, at all.

What this argument shows is that total unintelligibility of another culture is not an option. For to experience another group as unintelligible over some range of their practices, we have to find them quite understandable over other (very substantial) ranges. We have to be able to understand them as framing intentions, carrying out actions and trying to communicate orders, truths, and so forth. If we imagine even this away, then we no longer have the basis that allows us to recognize them as agents. But then there is nothing left to be puzzled about. Concerning nonagents, there is no question about what they are up to, and hence no possibility of being baffled on this score.

The problem with this argument is that it is in a sense too powerful. It slays the terrifying mythical beast of total and irremediable incomprehensibility. But what we suffer from in our real encounters between peoples are the jackals and vultures of partial and (we hope) surmountable noncommunication.

In this real-life situation, Davidson's theory is less useful, mainly because it seems to discredit the idea of "conceptual schemes" altogether – this in spite of the fact that the argument only rules out our meeting a totally unintelligible one. But in dealing with the real, partial barriers to understanding, we need to be able to identify what is blocking us. And for this we need some way of picking out the systematic differences in construal between two different cultures, without either reifying them or branding them as ineradicable. This is what Gadamer does with his image of the horizon. Horizons can be different, but at the same time they can travel, change, extend – as you climb a mountain, for instance. It is what Davidson's position as yet lacks.

Without this, Davidson's principle of charity is vulnerable to being abused to ethnocentric ends. The principle tells me to make the best sense of the other's words and deeds as I can. In translating his words into my language, I should render him so that as much as possible he speaks the truth, makes valid inferences, and so on. But the issue is to know what counts as "my language" here. It can mean the language I speak at the moment of encounter. Or it can mean the extended language, the one that emerges from my attempts to understand him, to fuse horizons with him. If we take it in the first way, it is almost certain that I will ethnocentrically distort him.

For the problem is that the standing ethnocentric temptation is to make too quick sense of the stranger, i.e., sense in one's own terms. The lesser breeds are without the law, because they have nothing we recognize as law. The step to branding them as lawless and outlaw is as easy as it is invalid and fateful. So the Conquistadores had an easy way of understanding the strange and disturbing practices of the Aztecs, including human sacrifice. While we worship God, these people worship the Devil.

Of course, this totally violates Davidson's intent. But the problem is that we need to understand how we move from our language at the time of encounter, which can only distort them, to a richer language that has place for them; from making the "best sense" in our initial terms, which will usually be an alien imposition, to making the best sense within a fused horizon. I cannot see how we can conceive of or carry out this process without allowing into our ontology something like alternative horizons or conceptual schemes. This I think marks the superiority of Gadamer's view over Davidson's.

But Davidson's argument is nonetheless very valuable, in pointing out the dangers, even the paradoxes involved in using any such terms. We can see this when we ask the question, what does the concept "scheme" contrast with? The term "content" is certainly very bad – as though there were stuff already lying there, to be framed in different schemes. There is certainly a deep problem here.

It belongs to the very idea of a scheme, in the sense that one is tempted to use it in intercultural studies, that it indicates some systematic way in which people interpret or understand their world. Different schemes are incombinable ways of understanding the same things.

But "what things?" runs the objection. How can you point to the things in question? If you use the language of the target society to get at them, then all distinction between scheme and content disappears. But what else can you use? Well, let us say you can use our language, that of us, the observer/scientists, about this target area. But then we still would not have got at the "content" we share in common, which would have to be somehow identifiable independently of both schemes.

The point is well taken. It needs to be kept in mind in order to avoid certain easy pitfalls, such as thinking that one has a neutral, universal categorization of the structures or functions of all societies, e.g., political system, family, religion, which provide the ultimately correct description for what all the different fumbling, cultural languages are aiming at; as it were, the noumena to their phenomenal tongues. But the notion of two schemes, one target area, remains valid and indeed, indispensable.

Let's go back to the case of the Conquistadores and the Aztecs. We might say that one thing the Conquistadores had right was that they recognized that all that ripping out of hearts in some way corresponded in Spanish society to the Church and the mass, and that sort of thing. That is, the right insight, yielding a good starting point for an eventual fusion of horizons, involves identifying what something in the puzzling life of an alien people can usefully be contrasted with in ours. In Gadamerian terms, what we are doing is identifying that facet of our lives that their strange customs interpellate, challenge, and offer a notional alternative to.

An example will show what is at stake here. A few years ago, a wildly reductivistic American social scientist produced a theory of Aztec sacrifice in which it was explained "materialistically" in terms of their need for protein. On this view, the right point of comparison in Spanish society would be their slaughterhouses rather than their churches. Needless to say, from such a starting point, one gets nowhere.

The fruitful supposition is that what went on atop those pyramids reflected a very different construal of an X that overlaps with what Christian faith and practice is a construal of in Spain. This is where thinking, enquiry, can usefully start. It has one very powerful – and in principle challengeable – presupposition: that we share the same humanness, and that therefore we can ultimately find our feet in Aztec sacrifice, because it is a way of dealing with a human condition we share. Once this is accepted, then the notion of two schemes, same X becomes inescapable. Only we have to be careful what we put in the place of the X.

In a general proposition, we might say: "dimension, or aspect of the human condition." In the particular case, it is much more dangerous to specify. "Religion" would be an obvious candidate word. But the danger is precisely that we happily take on board everything that this word means in our world, and slide back toward the ethnocentric reading of the Conquistadores. So we perhaps retreat to something more vague, such as "numinous." But even this carries its dangers.

The point is to beware of labels here. This is the lesson to be learned from attacks on the scheme–content distinction. But that the Mass and Aztec sacrifice belong to rival construals of a dimension of the human condition for which we have no stable, culture-transcendent name, is a thought we cannot let go of, unless we want to relegate these people to the kind of unintelligibility that members of a different species would have for us. If rejecting the distinction means letting this go, it is hardly an innocent step.

III

The conception of horizons and their fusion shows how the "science" we have of other times and people is, like the understandings we come to, party-dependent. It will differ both with the object and the subject of knowledge.

But how about the analogue to the other property of understandings I mentioned above, that they may involve our changing our goals? The analogous point here is that in coming to see the other correctly, we inescapably alter our understanding of ourselves. Really taking in the other will involve an identity shift in us. That is why it is so often resisted and rejected. We have a deep identity investment in the distorted images we cherish of others.

That this change must occur falls out from the account of the fusion of horizons. To return to our example: we come to see that attributing "opinions" to them is distortive. But we only ever did so originally, because it seemed to go without saying that this is what it meant to have beliefs in certain areas. In order to get over the distortion, we had to see that there were other possibilities, that our way of being is not the only or "natural" one, but that it represents one among other possible forms. We can no longer relate to our way of doing or construing things "naively," as just too obvious to mention.

If understanding the other is to be construed as fusion of horizons and not as possessing a science of the object, then the slogan might be: no understanding the other without a changed understanding of self. The kind of understanding that ruling groups have of the ruled, that conquerors have of the conquered – most notably in recent centuries in the far-flung European empires – has usually been based on a quiet confidence that the terms they need are already in their vocabulary. Much of the "social science" of the last century is in this sense just another avatar of an ancient human failing. And indeed, the satisfactions of ruling, beyond the booty, the unequal exchange, the exploitation of labor, very much includes the reaffirmation of one's identity that comes from being able to live this fiction without meeting brutal refutation. Real understanding always has an identity cost – something the ruled have often painfully experienced. It is a feature of tomorrow's world that this cost will now be less unequally distributed.

The cost appears as such from the standpoint of the antecedent identity, of course. It may be judged a gain once one has gone through the change. We are also enriched by knowing what other human possibilities there are in our world. It cannot be denied, however, that the path to acknowledging this is frequently painful.

The crucial moment is the one in which we allow ourselves to be interpellated by the other; in which the difference escapes from its categorization as an error, a fault, or a lesser, undeveloped version of what we are, and challenges us to see it as a viable human alternative. It is this that unavoidably calls our own self-understanding into question. This is the stance Gadamer calls "openness." As against the way I stand to what I see as an object of science, where I try to reflect myself out of my "relation to the other ... becoming unreachable by him" (TM 360). "Openness to the other, then, involves recognizing that I myself must accept some things that are against me, even though no one else forces me to do so" (TM 361).

Gadamer's argument in *Truth and Method* deals with our understanding of our own tradition, the history of our civilization, and the texts and works that belong to this. This means that what we study will be in one way or another internal to our identity. Even where we define ourselves against certain features of the past, as the modern Enlightenment does against the Middle Ages, this remains within our identity as the negative pole, that which we have overcome or escaped. We are part of the "effective history" (*Wirkungsgeschichte*) of this past, and as such it has a claim on us.

My point in this essay has been that Gadamer's account of the challenge of the other and the fusion of horizons applies also to our attempts to understand quite alien societies and epochs. The claim here comes not from their place within our identity, but precisely from their challenge to it. They present us different and often disconcerting ways of being human. The challenge is to be able to acknowledge the humanity of their way, while still being able to live ours. That this may be difficult to achieve, that it will almost certainly involve a change in our self-understanding and hence in our way, has emerged from the above discussion.

Meeting this challenge is becoming ever more urgent in our intensely intercommunicating world. At the turn of the millennium, it is a pleasure to salute Hans-Georg Gadamer, who has helped us so immensely to conceive this challenge clearly and steadily.

NOTE

1 "On the Very Idea of a Conceptual Scheme," in *Inquiries into Truth and Interpretation* (Oxford: Clarendon Press, 1984), p. 198.

7   Lyric as Paradigm: Hegel and the Speculative Instance of Poetry in Gadamer's Hermeneutics

I

"Art lies in its fulfillment" – "*Die Kunst ist im Vollzug.*" This laconic statement from the late essay "Wort und Bild – 'so wahr, so seiend'" (GW 8, 391) summarizes a facet of the hermeneutic experience that receives special emphasis in the final phase of Gadamer's thought. As my provisional translation suggests, the statement, in its concise German form, defies translation. The fulfillment Gadamer has in mind is not the act by which an artist completes a work of art but rather that fulfillment, in the sense of a carrying out, or realization, that occurs every time a work is understandingly read, heard, or seen. In this essay I shall probe the hermeneutic scope of what Gadamer calls this fulfillment, or carrying out, of the work of art. Taking a cue from Gadamer himself, I shall use lyric poetry as the paradigm for such fulfillment, although the conclusions reached will obtain for Gadamer's understanding of aesthetic experience in general. My essay begins, then, with the cardinal features of the hermeneutic experience as a linguistic phenomenon and then moves on to an in-depth look at the properly speculative dimension of poetic speech.

For Gadamer, poetic language is not exceptional but rather representative of language use in general insofar as achieves a certain ideality. That ideality consists in its sustaining in itself "the continuity of memory." Rather than document the past in the way of a fragment, the poetic text positively brings the past down to us as something contemporaneous with us (TM 390–1). That is why it is said that every genuinely poetic text addresses the present as something present. The poetic text is therefore paradigmatic for the hermeneutic experience by virtue of its interpretability: addressed to every succeeding present, it is applicable to every succeeding present. From this it does not follow of course that the text's meaning is merely a function of any given present's self-understanding. That kind of existentialist relativism is given the lie by Gadamer's observation that interpretive concepts, which succeed in bringing the "what" of a text to light, have the paradoxical virtue of disappearing behind that "what" (TM 398).

These two paradigmatic aspects of poetic language, its ideality, and its applicability to every successive present, are related to the fundamental ontology of language set forth in the second division of the final part of *Truth and Method*, "The development of the concept of language in the history of Western thought." In the section there on Greek thought, Gadamer investigates, on the basis of a highly discriminated reading of the *Cratylus*, the alternative views of language as image (*eikon*) and sign (*semeion/semainon*). He exposes the weaknesses of both views as they are argued in Plato's dialogue, but he does so, notably, in order to recuperate something of the former. Toward the end of his discussion of Greek thought, Gadamer notes that "in all discussion of language ever since, the concept of the image...has been replaced by that of the sign..." (TM 414). Gadamer is therefore registering an event of epochal moment when he punctuates his treatment of ancient Greek thought with the judgment that the critique of names in the *Cratylus* "is the first step toward modern instrumental theory of language...Wedged in between image and sign, the being of language could only be reduced to the level of pure sign" (TM 418). Against this abstract view of language use, Gadamer urges a qualified return to the sense of language as copy or image (TM 416). Clearly, what Gadamer means by image is not a copy in any sense of equivalence of word and thing. What he intends instead is a sense of the revelatory, or showing, power of discourse (*logos*), as distinct from words regarded as pure signs. If the world is only world insofar as it is spoken in language, language, too, is only language to the extent that it speaks world (TM 443). That is why, as Gadamer says, a poetic text does not simply document a past world but positively delivers that world to us. This, and not any arbitrary prerogative of the present, is what makes for the text's interpretability.

Hence, in the essay cited at the beginning, "Wort und Bild – 'so wahr, so seiend,'" Gadamer explicates his statement "art lies in its fulfillment" to mean "[t]he truth that we seek in the testimony of art is the truth that can be attained in art's fulfillment" (GW 8, 394). This view of art's truth as something that is fulfilled by the one who contemplates it should be related to the line Gadamer draws at the end of *Truth and Method* to the connection made in the *Phaedrus* between participation (*methexis*) and the being of the beautiful as self-presentation (TM 481). The beautiful has to be understood as an image (*eikon*) that shines forth and is beheld. As Gadamer notes, in the case of the beautiful it makes no sense to ask whether what appears in the image of the beautiful is the thing itself or a copy because the beautiful has the purely evidential character (*das Einleuchtende*) of what shines forth (*Vorscheinen*) (TM 483–5). By appealing to the ancient experience of the beautiful as what in the rhetorical tradition was called the purely evident, that which without being proven or absolutely certain nevertheless asserts itself, Gadamer provides the ontological basis for his own concept of "aesthetic nondifferentiation" or the nondistinction "between the particular way the work is realized and the identity of the work itself" (RB 29; see also TM 117). The epochal moment, if I may put it this way, of Gadamer's own recourse to the Greek concept of beauty as truth (*aletheia*), as "the way in which goodness appears," lies in his joining of that concept to the issue of language (TM 487). My joining of the issue will consist in demonstrating the relevance of poetry to Gadamer's reframing of the question of aesthetics.

II

Although widely recognized as the late twentieth century's most authoritative interpreter of hermeneutics, the relevance of Hans-Georg Gadamer's thought to literary theory and poetics has only received intermittent attention. This is true of even such an appreciative a work as Joel Weinsheimer's *Gadamer's Hermeneutics*, which does not enter at any length into the question Gadamer always kept in view: what is the special relationship between poetic discourse, above all the lyric, and speculative philosophy?[1] This relation is essential to an understanding of Gadamer's hermeneutics insofar as Gadamer regarded poetic language as a fundamental instance of the hermeneutic experience, not simply as one subject among others to which hermeneutics gets applied. The hermeneutic relevance of poetic discourse to philosophy lies not in its engagement of philosophical themes and topics but rather in the properly speculative instance of its own discourse. It is with this basic thesis in mind that one must approach Gadamer's claim that poetry has its own speculative character.

Approaching Gadamer's own argument for this thesis requires a preliminary clarification. Two developments have impeded literary theory's recognition of Gadamer's contribution. First, recent theories of literature have been mainly developed with reference to narrative literature at the expense of the lyric. (The influential but also exceptional status of Paul de Man, whose works were largely devoted to lyric poets, marks him as a transitional figure between an older, phenomenological, and immanentist critical method on the one hand and poststructuralism on the other.) Second, and more important, in its most speculative forms, literary theory has tended to give privilege of place to negativity; in particular, to the presumed renunciation within poetic discourse itself of any claim to ontological reference. In the purest forms of deconstruction, the works of Jacques Derrida and Paul de Man, this spirit of renunciation goes back to a reading of Mallarmé and Hegel. As regards the first development, the privilege enjoyed by narrative has to do with the recent interest in modes of emplotment, in the leading tropes governing a text's order of presentation. At the same time it is a reaction against the privilege given to the lyric genre by T. S. Eliot and the New Criticism. This criticism cannot be leveled against Gadamer inasmuch as his preference for the lyric is founded on properly philosophical grounds rather than on the cultural and historical prejudices that influenced Eliot and New Criticism. This point leads me directly to the second. Because Gadamer's interest in the lyric is speculative, Gadamer is deeply cognizant of the role of negativity in poetic discourse, as his treatment of Mallarmé's poetry – the paradigm case for the negativity of poetic saying – makes apparent. Because I go into this discussion below, it is sufficient here to note that Gadamer dissents from the view, shared by deconstructionists and Sartre alike, that Mallarmé is *the* poet of ontological derealization. Gadamer's dissent, however, is in no way simple. Far from being made from the point of view of an aesthetic idealism, it is developed from his own well-known understanding of Hegel's speculative dialectic. If negation is the motor of the dialectic, nevertheless its force is never absolute. On the contrary, where there is negation, there is always, at the same time, a minimal claim to ontological reality. As it pertains to Mallarmé, Gadamer's argument is that his poetry represents a limit case in that it complements Hegel's speculative dialectic. In pushing the grammar of predication to the breaking point, Mallarmé imitates Hegel's most radical intentions in the field of logic: both push predication to its limits, but both intend something that will not be falsified, something indeed that both called the idea. In making this kind of argument for the speculative relevance of the lyric, Gadamer lays out an argument for the truth of poetry, an argument that negotiates the straits between idealism and what must be called the dogmatic skepticism of deconstructionist and much poststructuralist theorizing.

By contrast I shall be arguing here for the positive ontological stake of poetry on the basis of several repeated claims in Gadamer's work. The first is his claim that poetry always has a revealing, or "showing," character. It is the character of poetic language to serve as the "pledge" for that which it brings to presence in the way of language. Gadamer makes this point by way of Hölderlin but in a way that makes clear that what holds for Hölderlin is paradigmatic for all poetry. Second, at least since Romanticism and certainly since Mallarmé, poetry has been marked by a growing strangeness to the world. The strangeness has a certain negative force that has to be rightly gauged and understood. At stake in the negativity of modern poetry – the examples I shall refer to here are Mallarmé and Rilke – is not a wholesale denigration of the world but, much rather, a rethinking and rearticulation of worldliness. Third, and last, these two claims are related to the interpretation given to Hegel's aesthetics by Gadamer. By treating these three claims together, I wish to make a synthetic point about the speculative instance of poetry never made as such in Gadamer's writings.

III

At the beginning of his essay "On the Contribution of Poetry to the Search for Truth" Gadamer asserts that "poetry is language in a preeminent sense" (RB 106). In the same essay he refers to Luther's phrase *"es steht geschrieben"* ["it stands written"] in order to affirm the completeness of the poetic word. Poetry requires nothing beyond its own utterance to secure the reality of its language: "it bears witness to itself and does not admit anything that might verify it" (RB 110). Although he does not mention it, Gadamer certainly knows that this topos was adopted by Hölderlin in the conclusion to his great hymn "Patmos." There the poet names the "cultivation of the firm letter and the interpretation of what is" as the proper office of poetry.[2] Hölderlin had anticipated the hymn's turn of phrase in a well-known letter of November 1802 to Casimir Böhlendorff, where he defined "art's highest quality" as its "holding everything steady in itself, so that security in this sense is the highest form of the sign."[3] What is it that is thus secured and preserved in poetic speech and what is its relevance to philosophic discourse?

Gadamer, like Heidegger before him, insists that interpretation ideally disappears before the voice of the text. "Interpretive words should...disappear after they have evoked what they mean. If one reads the poem again, then one should not remember what has been said about it, but rather one should have the impression: there it stands. It is there in the words of the poem and not in what someone has said about it" (EPH 76). Among literary critics, this kind of viewpoint has frequently been misunderstood to mean that a purely receptive passivity on the part of the reader before the ideal object of interpretation is being advocated. Or, more subtly, Gadamer is accused of advocating an iconic ideal of objective interpretation – the text speaks finally for itself without any external aid or supplement – that conflicts with his own hermeneutic precepts of conversation and variability. In fact, though, neither of these seemingly critical views comes near doing justice to Gadamer's understanding of the peculiar achievement of poetry. The disappearance of interpretation is a hermeneutic moment. Not an expression of interpretation's redundancy or its factitiousness, the moment of disappearance is rather the phase in which understanding of the poem becomes participation in its meaning. From that moment the poem is part of us, its language accompanying and informing our experience of the world.

When Gadamer says that poetry is language in a preeminent sense, he directs attention to the peculiar completeness of the poetic word. Whereas the ends of communication demand that we alter our language if it does not achieve its intended effect, no one confronted with a difficult poem thinks of altering its language, just as no one confronted with a difficult saying in the Bible thinks of altering the Biblical text. When one reads a poem, its words do not stand for something else; they are themselves the instantiation of a presence that every interpretation intends but for which none is a substitute (RB 110). Referring to Aristotle, Gadamer reasserts that "[p]oetic language stands out as the highest fulfillment of that revealing [*deloun*] which is the achievement of all speech" (RB 112).

What is this revealing? Certainly it has nothing to do with the reference to positivities. Taking a cue from Dilthey and Heidegger, Gadamer argues that poetry's revealing takes place at the level of a world. But the world the poem reveals is not dependent upon existing objects. Nor, for that matter, does it have anything to do with the simulated wholes made available to us through increasingly refined means of technical reproduction. Those ersatz-wholes are merely the virtual reproduction of totalities of objects, whereas what the poem opens up to us simulates nothing and cannot be measured against anything else. Hence Gadamer's deeply consistent defense of the notion of mimesis, which, as he shows, has nothing to do with verisimilitude or the reproduction of an original.

For the [poetic] word enjoys unlimited power and ideal perfection. Poetry is something that is made in such a way that it has no other meaning beyond letting something be there. There is no respect in which a linguistic work of art has to be there *for* anything. It is thus properly speaking something "made."

But it also fulfills what we mean by *mimesis* in a specific way what means... [for] the meaning of the word "*mimesis*" consists simply in letting something be there without trying to do anything more with it. (RB 119)

Gadamer links the notion of mimesis to expressiveness and recognizability. Expressivity, as he already argued in *Truth and Method*, is not an internal experience made exterior but rather the capacity to make an impression – to give an imprint one might say – that we do not translate back into a psychological attitude on the part of the artist. On the contrary, the expressiveness of art has to do with its capacity to open up before us a possible world. Similarly, Gadamer's notion of recognizability has nothing to do with an artistic representation's being referred back to either a given or a posited reality. Gadamer writes indeed that "poetry participates in the truth of the universal" (RB 120). This comes about because art, even when handling the contingent, frees itself from contingency, becoming something abiding, and thus recognizable. Recognizability does not of course preclude interpretative difficulties. Gadamer defines hermeneutics after all as the task that commences precisely when the possibility of understanding has been made difficult or questionable. Still, however difficult the access its object may become, art's representation is always in some minimal sense recognizable. Hence, Gadamer's defense in *Truth and Method* of the concept of *mimesis* as "aesthetic nondifferentiation:" the nondistinction between what is represented and its representation. The expressiveness of art is the presence of something meaningful and recognizable in its own right. Herein lies the poetic and hermeneutic relevance of Gadamer's concept of aesthetic nondifferentiation. The instance of aesthetic presentation, or *Darstellung*, is not measured according to its difference from the represented but rather by its standing in for the represented in such a way that the form of the represented, in the sense of *eidos*, is not missed. This standing-in-for constitutes its own form of negativity, a negativity that Gadamer positions within the reflexive movement of thought in general instead of restricting its relevance to the sphere of textual self-reference. A similar order of thinking obtains for the Hegelian concept. Both are only proven true when taken at their word.

The relevance of the principle of nonverifiability to the concept of worldliness is exemplified by the first of Rilke's *Sonnets to Orpheus*, in which the poet immediately sets to work on his redefinition of the Orpheus myth. No longer the magical mastery of nature, Orphic singing now consists in the purely aural existence of what is sung. The tree that rises up before us is the tree fashioned in the word:

Da stieg ein Baum. O reine Übersteigung!
O Orpheus singt,! O hoher Baum im Ohr!
Und alles schwieg. Doch selbst in der Verschweigung
ging neuer Anfang, Wink und Wandlung vor.
["There arose a tree. Oh, pure transcendence!
Oh, Orpheus sings!, Oh tall tree in the ear!
And all was still. But even in this suspension
new beginnings, signs and changes were."]

The tree, which is most purely tree, is that one that rises up in the ear, articulated by song. This tree, purely intended like Mallarmé's absent flower, is not subject to verification or to doubt. In what world, according to what criteria, would one judge the truthfulness of this tree? Rilke's language instances Gadamer's assertion that the language of modern lyric is paradigmatic precisely in the way that in setting something forth it also retreats back into itself. In poetry's moment of showing, its *deloun*, there resides at the same time a moment of occlusion. For Gadamer, this moment of withholding in showing forth is an aspect of poetry's essential worldliness. For just as what makes a world is not any collection of enumerable positivities, so also what makes poetry essential language is its showing forth a whole whose sense exceeds the grammatical or even semantic sense of its statements.

The relevance of poetry's speculative instance to philosophical discourse proper remains to be defined. In several of his studies on poetry, Gadamer refers to Husserl's remark in *Ideas Pertaining to a Pure Phenomenology* that poetry spontaneously performs the eidetic reduction, or epoche (RB 112). Gadamer subscribes to Husserl's view, but with the caution that, taken in itself, the remark constitutes a half-truth. For if it is true that the poetic word accomplishes "a spontaneous intentional fulfillment" in suspending the positive and giving us an image raised above concrete particularity, it also accomplishes more than this. For the poetic word accomplishes a realization whose reality nonetheless is not dependent upon given, empirical reality, upon what Hegel criticized as the dogma of external perception. This comes about on account of the double movement of poetry. In the essay "Philosophy and Poetry," Gadamer describes the double movement of poetic significations as follows: "There is not a single word in a poem that does intend what it means. Yet at the same time the word sets itself back upon itself to prevent it slipping into prose and the rhetoric accompanying it" (RB 136). Now it may seem that what Gadamer describes as a danger to be avoided is, from the Hegelian perspective, precisely the destiny of poetry, namely, that it become the prose of philosophical, or, in Hegel's terms, scientific discourse. But from Gadamer 's vantage point this is only true if we read Hegel's philosophy in naively teleological terms as the prescription for a certain historical development. However, if we read it in the way that has been sketched here, that is, as a response to as well as a criticism of Hegel, then Gadamer presents us with a sophisticated hermeneutics of modern poetry, a genuine alternative to the reading of Hegel – and of Hölderlin, Mallarmé, and modern poetry – in Paul de Man and sundry forms of deconstruction.

In the poetic word "something is always being understood" (PL 251). However splintered and fragmented poetic language may become, it is always presenting something to us, "always bestowing a certain intimacy with the world of meaning" (PL 251). In this way, Gadamer's hermeneutics of modern poetry preserves something of Husserl's phenomenological reduction. To be sure, poetry's performance of the reduction is not to be understood in Husserl's exact sense. But this is also where Gadamer's reminder of the ideality of poetic speech enters. What poetry presents (das Dargestellte) and its presentation (die Darstellung) are the same. An example here is Hölderlin's prophetic language about the gods. We do not take Hölderlin's language seriously as the prediction of a future event. But we do take it seriously as poetry, and when we do, then we recognize the anticipation enunciated in this poetry as something already completed in the poem (PL 252). But this only comes about when we as readers are able to let the text come forth as "an authoritative whole" (PL 252). Gadamer calls such completed anticipation evocation. It is the third phase of a hermeneutic process that begins with intention and fulfillment (Husserl) and proceeds to schematization. In this process what stands out at the end is precisely the literary text in its written character as literature; that is, in its character as something being written thus and not otherwise. Hence, Gadamer's attention to the trans-religious significance of Luther's topos "it stands written." To this degree the text may be said to fold back upon itself, though not simply in the finally trivial sense of a self-mirroring, but rather in the sense that the language of the text acquires a stipulative force: it provides the condition for any further mediation: "It is what is ... language here obtains a unique value permanence ever emerging into its own presence" (PL 253).

Elsewhere Gadamer has referred to a "forgetfulness of language" as a facet of aesthetic nondifferentiation: "What makes understanding possible is precisely the forgetfulness of language, a forgetting of the formal elements in which the discourse of the text is encased" (DD 32). Here Gadamer keeps sight of a distinction that has been lost at times in recent literary criticism, namely, the distinction between the text as wording and the text as what is said. The latter may be impugned of course as a version of metaphysical presence. Gadamer, however, has rightly suggested that that there is something facile and compulsive about deconstruction's obsession with the matter of presence. Hermeneutics has never made the claim that the text's or the author's voice is some kind of privileged presence in which meaning resides. Gadamer reminds us, on the contrary, that the poetic text is *Zeitigung von Sinn*: it is always the "temporalization of meaning" as event (GW 9, 337).

Now it is precisely the event character of modern poetry that marks it out as *semantische Poesie* (GW 9, 339). That the language of modern poetry is no longer derived from legend, myth, and salvation history, nor yet from the classical rhetorical topoi is what names the transition from traditional to modern poetry, or, as we shall see, from pre-Hegelian to Hegelian understanding of art. This holds true regardless of whether a modern poet still invokes the legends or myths of the past. Poetry has become the poetry of meaning: Where there is no longer a common experience or a common memory of events, then meaning is no longer something assumed but rather something in need of a voice:

> ...it is the poet's task nevertheless to bring the unity of a saying – of his saying – to speech. A poem is and remains a gathering of meaning, even when only a gathering of meaning fragments. The question of the unity of its meaning remains standing as an ultimate question that receives its answer in the poem. (GW 9, 339)

This means that poetry has, like philosophy, its speculative claim, for it intends a certain *Sinnsrichtung*, or directionality. This indication of direction however is something that only comes to be as language, as a gathering of meaning, in the poem. Gadamer says that poetry is always "a thinking word on the horizon of the unsaid" (*ein Wort im Horizont des Ungesagten*) (GW 9, 343). As an articulation of the unsaid, the poem is always conversation with the future, hence with its potential reader.[4]

It is on account of his concern for the continuing claim of poetry in the wake of the fragmentation of cultural memory, that Gadamer sees a peculiar legitimacy in the project of Mallarmé's *poésie pure* (RB 136). Here Gadamer draws the parallel of Mallarmé and his heritage to Hegel. Pure poetry and the speculative concept share two things in common: both represent limit cases and neither admits of falsification. Because both operate at a maximum distance from everyday meaning and language, the eminent character of each is that they are a priori nonfalsifiable. Neither can be controverted by an appeal to referential or empirical reality. It is only by entering into them, only by participating in the movement of their discourse, that one can come to a recognition of their speculative truth.

It is important to sketch briefly what may have motivated Gadamer's making reference to Mallarmé at all, a poet to whom he otherwise gives little notice. The answer to this question lies in Gadamer's own observation that Mallarmé represents a limit case for the kind of language described above. This is to say that Mallarmé elaborated a language that seems at once to bring something otherwise inaccessible into presence and yet to defeat any attempt to name that presence or to assign it any reality outside the purely linguistic structure of the work. Mallarmé's work thus seems to confirm and deny at once Gadamer's claim that even the "purest" poem reveals something, that it has a content not reducible to a perceived aesthetic quality. This contradiction is a problem Gadamer already addressed in *Truth and Method* as the problem of aesthetic differentiation: aesthetic differentiation gives the work of art its independent status but in doing so abstracts the work of art from its relationship to the world (TM 85). Gadamer's writings after *Truth and Method*, however, including the "Afterword" that appears in later editions of that work, make clear that this representation of the problem demands a further working out. Significantly, Gadamer has confronted this problem by way of a recourse to Hegel's aesthetics. Gadamer is thinking specifically of the Hegelian argument that, since the emergence of revealed religion and of philosophy as a science (*Wissenschaft*), art has become nothing but art insofar as it has been relieved of its service to religion and myth. Yet this "nothing but" harbors its own new set of possibilities for art. Above all, Gadamer sees art's self-reflexive character as something more essential than a sign that art, after Hegel, finds itself in a late phase of its development. Instead, Gadamer emphasizes that if this development represents the ending of one phase in the history of art, it also represents a transition to a new phase. He calls this "the transition from reflective art to the art of reflection" because in this new phase poetry in particular moves into a newly autonomous relation to speculative thought (TM 574). In other words it is not just that the discourse of science, or *Wissenschaft*, comes into its own with modernity, but that the language of art, for which lyric poetry is paradigmatic, also comes into its own for the first time. Gadamer's reference to Mallarmé must be situated in this context, Regarding this context, Gadamer cites Reiner Wiehl's thesis that the common speculative thread in poetry and dialectical thought is the concept of action: "The lyric is the presentation of the pure speech act, not the presentation of an action in the form of the speech act" (TM 575).

As pure speech act, the lyric is where "linguisticality emerges as such for the first time" (TM, 574). That Hegel himself did not appreciate this potential in the lyric is not of moment. The decisive thing, as Gadamer says, is the confluence of reflective art, or poetry's awareness of its own linguistic instance, with the art of reflection, or the speculative instance as such.

In texts such as "Are the Poets Falling Silent?" (EPH 73–82), "Poem and Dialogue" (GW 9, 335–46), and "Philosophy and Literature," Gadamer has drawn attention to two salient features of Hegel's thought that are of consequence for the philosophical interpretation of modern poetry. The first is what Gadamer calls the secondary and less noticed aspect of Hegel's pronouncement; namely, that art has not only become something past but that this pastness has to do with art's being definitively shorn in the modern age of its traditional relationship to Greco–Christian religion and mythology. The consequences of this are some of modern poetry's outstanding characteristics: that it has become what Gadamer calls *semantische Poesie*, poetry wholly thrown back upon the resources of the word, and that it is thoroughly marked by what Gadamer calls an extreme discretion and reserve in any of the semantic registers formerly associated with religion and myth. The second feature is strictly related to the first. It is what must be called the speculative thrust of poetry, an idea whose groundwork was laid in Gadamer's discussion of speculation in *Truth and Method*.

More than one hundred years after the poet's death, Mallarmé's poetry remains the most enigmatical illustration of the lesson Gadamer draws from Hegel's aesthetics. For it is Mallarmé's text that exemplifies as well as any the aestheticist claim that poetry is a self-sufficient, or auto-telic, activity. And yet at the same time it is a poetry that in its very negativity, in its repudiation of any reference beyond itself except the vague "idea," nevertheless suggests a kind of revelation, so that we are compelled to speak paradoxically of a negative manifestation, or showing, in it. In Gadamer's terms, poetry's coming into its own, its discovery of the instance of its own speech, coincides with, or is indeed the same as, the discovery of its inherent negativity. The result is a poetics in which the impossibility of predication becomes a constitutive, structural feature of poetic language. Mallarmé's poetry intends something, but it is a thing apparently voided of all earthly or worldly qualities: "the flower absent from every bouquet," as he famously declared. For Gadamer, though, this negativity cannot, by virtue of its very linguistic character, signify a total obliteration of the notion of showing or content. And yet to judge from literary studies of the last several decades that has judged to be the consequence of Mallarmé's poetics, as if the "flexion" in Mallarmé's reflexivity pointed in only one direction, namely, to the impossibility of the sign's transcendence to anything outside its own universe of signs. And in fact this one-sided and, in Gadamer's terms, decidedly unspeculative reading of Mallarméan reflexivity betrays the "revolt" that Julia Kristeva has argued to be the defining feature of the poet's enterprise. Kristeva finds that Mallarmé revolutionized the nature of the sign by fragmenting and indeed "pulverizing" the grammar of poetic statement.[5] This revolution entails, to be sure, a moment of voiding, that hollowing out of the signifier that is now long since the signature of poststructuralist theory. Yet it also entails, as Gadamer reminds us, a moment of gathering that Mallarmé, in a text called "Sollenité," did not hesitate to call wealth (*richesse*).[6]

Gadamer does not dwell on the radical negativity of Mallarmé's project for a *poésie pure* for good reason. Mallarmé mistakenly believed that his discovery of an ontological nothingness, a discovery documented in letters to his friend Henri Cazalis in the late 1860s, was coincident with the concept of negation found in Hegel's *Logic*. Gadamer does not pursue this connection at all because his intention is to show what is permanently valid in Mallarmé's and Hegel's respective practice. And only at this level do their respective modes of negation illuminate each other. The aim of Mallarmé's pure poetry is to say what, in any positive sense of the word, is not. Contrary though to certain assumptions in literary theory, that aim is not coextensive with dogmatic assumptions about the unhinged, or "free-floating" status of the signifier vis-à-vis the signified. That is, when Mallarmé speaks of the power of poetic syntax to elide reference, he does not point merely to its self-referential quality. So Mallarmé's famous note that what a purified poetic language evokes is "the flower missing from every bouquet" is not in fact an assertion that poetry delights in the ringing of a bell in an ontological void. The whole sentence in which that figure appears reads as follows:

Je dis: une fleur! et, hors de 'oubli oùma voix relègue aucun contour, en tant que quelque chose d'autre que les calices sus, musicalement se lève, idée même et suave, l'absente de tous bouquets.

["I say: a flower! and, out of the forgetfulness where my voice banishes any contour, inasmuch as it is something other than known calyxes, musically arises, an idea itself and fragrant, the one absent from all bouquets."][7]

An essential nuance of Mallarmé's prose is that the thing evoked here is not "the absent flower" but rather simply "the absent one," *l'absente* – precisely that thing, now nothing, which can only appear as idea. This is the special generality of ontological reference that Mallarmé's poetry only lets rise with a severe restraint. But let it rise it does. The negation effected by Mallarmé's phrasings has the effect of absence, but it is an absence "inseparable from the highest generality of speech."[8] The elision of concrete, positive reference is not the obliteration of reference altogether but rather the reduction that "must take place before the word's 'pure notion' can emanate from it."[9] The effect of poetic negation is to release a quality not otherwise discernible:

A quoi bon la merveille de transposer un fait de nature en sa presque dis-parition vibratoire selon le jeu de la parole, cependant; si ce n'est pour qu'en émane, sans la gêne d'un proche ou concret rappel, la notion pure?

[What purpose is served by the miracle of transposing a natural fact into its almost vibratory disappearance by means of the word's action, however; if it is not that there may proceed from it, without the embarrassment of an immediate or concrete reminder, the pure notion.][10]

If, as Gadamer argues, the mutual relevance of Hegel and Mal-larmé lies in their pushing the speculative instance of philosophi-cal and poetic discourse to their respective limits, then it follows, as Gadamer also suggests, that their respective modes of discourse open up a new plane of reference in the modern world, a plane of reference that the Romantics only partially began to explore as an expanded subjectivity.[11] I quoted above Albert Cook's remark that the negativity or absence perceived to dwell in Mallarmé's speech is "inseparable from the highest generality of speech." That remark is actually part of a larger claim by Cook that "there is something quite special about the 'generality' of signification in modern writing."[12] Gadamer's reading of Hegel's aesthetic develops what Cook had intu-ited. Rather than simply take Hegel at his word that "art in its highest calling is a thing of the past," Gadamer gives to Hegel's proposition his own speculative turn. If art has taken flight from the visible, manifest world of cult and myth, it does not follow that art simply disappears or that it simply continues its same mode of existence in a diminished key. As I have noted, Gadamer's own post-Hegelian thesis is that art's becoming a thing of the past, its so-called death, is simultaneously its release into a new mode of being and signification. The earmark of this new mode of being is precisely the diffuse and generalized level of reference that typifies so much modern poetry that has any kind of speculative bent. That diffuseness and invisibility moreover consists in an invisibility that Gadamer observes is the mark of a world from which the former language of cult and myth have receded. Yet that does not mean that cult and myth are henceforth meaningless, no more than Mallarmé's syntactic transformation of objects into musical effects means that his poetry no longer has any referent outside itself. What it does mean is that their abode is henceforth the invisible. This word, however, cannot be understood as the simple opposite of the visible, external, and material. It is a matter much rather of finally grasping that things have in their same material exteriority an invisibility that has first of all to be articulated. To articulate that invisibility, and in that sense to "find" it, is the appointed task of a post-Hegelian aesthetic. Gadamer's own speculative turn on Hegel is his insight that in ceasing to inhabit the visible world in the traditional manner of religion and myth, art does not cease to be art and become instead a form of philosophy but enters rather into a new dispensation.

The poet in whom Gadamer sees this change to a new dispensation being most thoroughly worked out is Rilke. I therefore wish to show how what Gadamer says about Rilke illuminates his other argument about Hegel and Mallarmé.

Gadamer has singled out "mythopoeic reversal" (Umkehrung) as a central feature of Rilke's poetry.[13] The reversal described in Rilke's poetry is one from world into myth: the world of the human heart is set over and against ourselves as a mythical world. Thus, the shock over the death of a young person becomes the shape of the young person him or herself; the lament or mourning that fills the human heart becomes a shape, or figure, that the young person follows. In other words, our own suffering gets metamorphically represented as the suffering of another. Rilke's angels are obviously the highest instance of such reversal. The angels are human affect that goes beyond the human capacity to comprehend itself. The conclusion of the second Duino Elegy gives a concise instance:

Denn das eigene Herz übersteigt uns
noch immer wie jene. Und wir können ihm nicht mehr
nachschaun in Bilder, die es besänftigen, noch in
göttliche Körper, in denen es größer sich mäßigt
[For our heart overcomes us
just as it did those others. And we can no longer
gaze after it into figures that soothe it, or godlike
bodies, in which it achieves a greater restraint].[14]

This idea might appear to have no complement in Mallarmé, yet there is parallel in his conversion of the particular into a generality that resists denotation. Mallarmé's generalized references are not simply abstractions from the particular, a kind of elaborate Mannerist conceit. Their abstraction depends instead upon a rigorous suspension of any ontological reference to particulars, a suspension that rises to the level of ideas. Mallarmé practices an attenuation of concrete reference leading to absence, but it is an absence from which emanates *l'idée même*.

Gadamer's definition of myth establishes a common ground for the two poets' respective endeavors: all poetic speech is myth to the extent that it affirms itself through nothing else but its being said (LPD 158). In this utter absorption into the moment of being said is something of the self-forgetfulness of myth. Here a special hermeneutic problem arises to which Gadamer calls attention. Rilke's figures of angel, child, and lament cannot be translated back into the experiences of which they are already translations. That is the historical difference that separates Mallarmé and Rilke from even as forward-looking a poet as Hölderlin. In Hölderlin the antique gods serve, for the last time, as adequate vessels for the translation of human experience into mythopoeic form. Mallarmé and Rilke, however, beginning from a recognition of the historical inadequacy of traditional mythology and refusing a post-Romantic expressionism, project a sphere of signification that nullifies distinctions between subject and object, inside and outside, life and death. The passage quoted above from the second Duino Elegy says the thing exactly: in being metamorphically opposed to ourselves as something other, as something myth-like, our own heart is not simply being figuratively transposed in the allegorical mode that traditionally informed myth and religion. Once the movement of reversal is begun, there is no way back from it but only the venturing into those open spaces that claim Rilke's poetry. In the same way, Mallarmé's poetic objects cannot be translated back into the concrete objects from which they are abstracted: there is only the resonant space beyond that his evocations open up. But in each case, the mere fact of the poem being spoken has brought something new into being. One can only let what is articulated in these poems be present for us, and that, for Gadamer, is what brings this poetic discourse into the neighborhood of speculative discourse.

Neither Rilke nor Gadamer is suggesting that poetry does or should become less worldly. It is a matter instead of a rethinking of the concept of worldliness. Rilke's insight, and Gadamer's complementary insight in his concept of reversal, is that in this new dispensation things will not continue to exist as they once did but will be translated to an invisible level of being. What kind of dimension of being this is, is precisely the riddle to which the *Duino Elegies* are addressed. In the eighth elegy, Rilke defines it in negative terms that nevertheless affirm:

Wir haben nie, nicht einen einzigen Tag,
den reinen Raum vor uns, in den die Blumen
unendlich aufgehn. Immer ist es Welt
und niemals Nirgends ohne Nicht: das Reine
Unüberwachte, das man atmet und
unendlich *weiß* und nicht begehrt
[We never have, not for a single day
that pure space before us, into which flowers
endlessly open: always there is world,
and never nowhere without no: that pure,
unsuperintended element one breathes
and endlessly knows and never covets].[15]

By opposing "world" here to "pure space," Rilke executes his own dialectical reversal. For it is obvious that Rilke is not abjuring or depreciating the phenomenality of the world. Instead, he is unfolding its hidden side: the pure draft of the open against which things – flowers, for example – first emerge. What is worldly is negated by this "pure space" but in being negated it is also released into an openness that is endlessly open. Rilke's flowers that endlessly bloom may remind us of Mallarmé's absent flower. These are not mere abstractions from the world of objects and things but rather projections of a signifying space in which worldly objects are both saved and annulled. This is the subject on which I want to dwell by way of a conclusion.[16]

IV

That poetry since Hegel has become a more inward art coincides with the severance of poetry from the discourse of religion and myth. This severance has undeniably resulted in a poetry more modest in its claims on public attention. Paradoxically, however, it has also resulted in a poetry more radical in its purchase upon the world. Not the least of Gadamer's contributions is his detection in Rilke, a poet surely ignorant of Hegel, of an answer to the Hegelian prophecy on the future of art that is simultaneously a speculative working out of that prophecy.

In his essay "On the Contribution of Poetry to the Search for Truth" Gadamer draws the connection between poetry's speculative relevance and the concept of world. There he links poetry to an *Einhausung*, or making oneself at home, specifying though that what appears in the poem "is not the world nor this or that thing in the world" (RB 115). This passage is worth pausing over on account of Gadamer's very careful phrasing. For Gadamer actually distinguishes the moment of poetic showing from this process of sharing a world. He says in fact that poetry stands over against this process, "like a mirror held up to it" (RB 115). This is a most telling choice of words. What Gadamer means here is not, as the words quoted already attest, that poetry reproduces the appearances of the world. On the contrary, the mirroring that poetry does has the sense of speculation that Gadamer first examined in the final part of *Truth and Method*. Poetry is speculative discourse in that standing over against the world it opens up to us the "nearness or familiarity" in which something like a world can be first be experienced and become the object of sharing. Poetic language is in this "eminent" sense language: it discloses not a world so much as the being of world, the phenomenon of worldliness. It is this feature of poetic language that keeps it in the neighborhood of speculative language. This naturally does not mean that there are no criteria for establishing poetic worth. What a poem offers may turn out to be hollow – as Gadamer says, it may merely sound like poetry, be a mere echo of poetry. But as poetic discourse it is not, in itself, falsifiable (RB 139).

Moreover, this articulation of experience is never sufficient to itself, but instead always intends something beyond itself: "Everything that goes under the name of language always refers beyond that which achieves the status of a proposition" (DD 25). This idea is implicit to all great poetry but it has received a particular relevance in the modern poetry of, say, Hölderlin, Mallarmé, T. S. Eliot, and Paul Celan, where what is said is crafted from the beginning as fragmentary utterance. This gives rise to the paradoxical but thoroughly consistent hermeneutic tenet that when we do not understand what is said in the poetic text, we must return to the text itself. Returning to the text, though, is only productive as long as we are willing to be transported into that other realm, the beyond of language that the poetic text reveals: " ... Everything that is fixed in writing refers back to what was originally said, but must equally as much look forward; for all that is said is always already directed toward understanding and includes the other in itself" (DD 34). For this reason Gadamer says of poetic texts that they "are only authentically there when they come back into themselves," a phrasing reminiscent of Heidegger's thesis in "The Origin of the Work of Art" that works of art, in bringing forth a world, simultaneously retreat into a space that he calls "earth." Both point to a basic feature of literary art: as language poetry is oriented toward sense and meaning, but as art it entertains a peculiar kind of self-insistence. In literature, the teleology of meaning is discernible but limited. Here a certain overlap with the deconstruction of Paul de Man is noticeable, and yet we must be on our guard. For Gadamer it does not follow that the concept of meaning is therefore totally overturned, making it impossibly unreliable. It means, on the contrary, that we are compelled to find the text's meaning in itself, in its own peculiar mode of bringing to presence that which admits of no other saying than in speculation.

This point requires further refinement. In reasserting the internal teleology of the work of art, Gadamer revisits the Kantian aesthetic and its formula of a finality without purpose. Never content though with the pure negativity of the Kantian formula, Gadamer found a certain corrective and expansion in Hegel. As Charles Taylor points out, in Hegel's thought, Kant's finality without purpose becomes "self-purpose."[17] In this way art participates in the internal teleology of *Geist* and becomes an agent of "ontological vision." This is what Taylor calls the "expressivist" dimension of Hegel's thought, precisely the thing missing in the Kantian aesthetic. Gadamer picks up this same motif in Hegel with his idea that the work of art does not represent something but rather shows it, presents it. In Taylor's resumption of Hegel, art is a mode of consciousness of the Idea, not its representation. Because art is an embodiment of the Idea rather than its conceptual expression, there is no standard or measure external to the work by which it can be judged or measured. As already noted, though, that is not a merely negative proposition. Because, as Gadamer says, "[t]he whole of being and its categorical conceptualization is nowhere given," the whole of the relation of being is only articulate in the nonfalsifiable discourse of speculation, whether the discourse of poetry or that of philosophy (PL 257).

In the time elapsed since Hegel the space in which poetry is heard and received has of necessity grown smaller and more modest as well. In this modesty is a clue to Gadamer's interest in Rilke, whom he interprets in a more cautious and in some respects more instructive manner than does Heidegger. As we have seen, Gadamer draws attention to the fact that in Rilke the invisible realm has become the home of poetry. If, as Rilke says, things have lost the presence they once had in our world, they can only regain that status at the other, enhanced level of poetic speech. In this way, Rilke responds for Gadamer to the challenge implicitly issued by Hegel and Mallarmé. And here the two sides of Gadamer's interest in the instance of lyric discourse are revealed to have a common root. Modern poetry's apparent inward turn, its apparent concern with itself alone, is actually the sign of poetry having entered its own sphere. Its separation from religion, myth, and the visible world itself marks the beginning, not the end, of its self-realization, a self-realization in which it shares with speculative discourse a transcendence of the limits of verification.

In this context, it is worth underlining the fact that when Gadamer observes that the Hegelian prophecy on the future of art is predicated on an uncoupling of art's historical relationship to cult and religion, he is not simply repeating the aestheticist view that art can displace religion. Nor is he taking Arthur Danto's view that the destiny of the work of art is to become philosophy.[18] Even where that might appear to happen, as in Mallarmé, the equivalence is not simple. Gadamer's reading of Hegel is dialectical, and indeed in a way that necessarily affects a reading of Mallarmé. Gadamer's interpretations of Hölderlin and Rilke show that the historical uncoupling of poetry and religion, indeed of poetry and myth, is at once an undoing and a transformation of that relationship so that the religious element finds a new home in the inward dimension of poetic speech. Of course, this further dialectical turn that Gadamer gives to Hegel goes beyond

Hegel himself. And yet it also preserves, in an eminent manner, an integral aspect of Hegel's aesthetic. For Gadamer, as for Hegel, poetry "after" Hegel – "after," because this is in fact poetry beginning with Hölderlin – is in its vocation (*Bestimmung*) more truly philosophical than it ever had been in the past. Where Gadamer naturally differs from Hegel is in his insight that poetry's realization of its speculative vocation takes place not in the medium of prose but precisely in the medium of lyric. The genre that has traditionally been regarded as the most musical and inward of the literary genres is the genre in which in late modern times the speculative relevance of poetry is most originally broached.

I have tried here to expand the parameters of Gadamer's Hegel interpretation by placing special emphasis on the relevance of poetry's speculative instance to the theme of worldliness. In this I have sought to correct a certain misunderstanding. The privative nature of much of the greatest modern poetry – its air of jealously guarded reserve, especially with respect to the sacred and to any reality transcending the language of the poem – has misled more than a few into the belief that modern poetry seeks an estrangement from the world. Gadamer, however, understands that that poetry's reserve is actually its way of refounding a notion of worldliness. Rilke articulated that need for a refounding in the seventh Duino Elegy:

Nirgends, Geliebte, wird Welt sein, als innen.
Unser Leben geht hin mit Verwandlung.
Und immer geringer schwindet das Außen
[Nowhere, beloved, will there be world but within.
Life passes with transformation.
And, ever diminishing,
The world outside fades away].

By this point it should go without saying that what Rilke means by "within" (*innen*) is not a Romantic interiority. Neither interior nor exterior, Rilke's *innen* corresponds to the plane of signification adumbrated but, as Gadamer shows, only partially grasped in Hegel's *Aesthetics*. Poetry's participation in the severance of *logos* from myth and cult does not spell what Gadamer calls the silencing (*Verstummung*) of the poets but rather the release of poetry into a new dispensation. The Hegelian dialectic and Mallarmé's *poésie pure* confirm that this new dispensation works indefectibly under the sign of negation, yet with a new twist. Once again, it is Rilke, who certainly knew nothing of Hegel, who supplies the adequate word:

Immer ist es Welt
und niemals Nirgends ohne Nicht.
[Always it is world
and never nowhere without negation.]

This "nowhere" that would nevertheless be without negation, *ohne nicht;* this nowhere that is a negation beyond absence, this is what names the post-Hegelian space in which worldliness may henceforth abide. Worldliness having been made more and more tenuous by the universal commodification of all objects and goods, it becomes the place of poetry to return to objects a world in the space of poetry. As Gadamer shows, that is a linguistic turn of another kind.

NOTES

1 Joel Weinsheimer, *Gadamer's Hermeneutics*, (New Haven: Yale University Press, 1985).

2 Friedrich Hölderlin, *Poems and Fragments*, translated by Michael Hamburger (London: Routledge, 1966), pp. 476–7: "daß gepfleget werde/Der veste Buchstab, und bestehendes gut gedeutet."

3 "... das Höchste der Kunst, die ... alles stehend und für sich selbst erhält, so daß die Sicherheit in diesem Sinne die höchste Art des Zeichens ist." See Friedrich Hölderlin, *Essays and Letters on Theory*, translated by Thomas Pfau (Albany: SUNY Press, 1988), p. 153.

4 It is because Gadamer approaches poetry, and interpretation in general, with this open temporal horizon in mind that he is perplexed by Derrida's, and poststructuralism's, obsessive concern with the phantom of presence, or logocentrism.

5 Julia Kristeva, "The Revolt of Mallarmé," in Robert Cohn and Gerald Gillepsie, *Mallarmé in the Twentieth Century* (Teaneck: Fairleigh Dickinson University Press, 1998), pp. 33, 36. See also *La révolution du langage poétique* (Paris: Editions du Seuil, 1974).

6 "Signe! au gouffre central d'une spirituelle impossibilité que rien soit exclusivement à tout, le numérateur divin de notre apothéose, *quelque suprême moule qui n'ayant pas lieu en tant que d'aucun objet qui existe:* mail il emprunte, pour y aviver un sceau tous gisements épars, ignorés et flottants selon quelque richessse, et les forger." Stéphan Mallarmé, *Igitur, Divagations, Un Coup de dés* (Paris: Gallimard, 1976), p. 234.

7 Stéphan Mallarmé, *Mallarmé*, edited and translated by Anthony Hartley (Harmondsworth: Penguin, 1965), pp. 174–5.

8 Albert Cook, *Prisms: Studies in Modern Literature* (Bloomington: Indiana University Press, 1967), p. 43.

9 *Ibid.*, p. 44.

10 *Mallarmé*, p. 174.

11 This "expanded subjectivity," a phrase I take from Novalis, is treated by Charles Taylor in *Sources of the Self* as the "expressivist" current in modern culture. According to Taylor, the expressivist need has nourished the Romantic and post-Romantic tradition of "epiphanic art," that gives a form to experience not otherwise available in the world. Taylor locates Mallarmé inside this tradition as an instance of "negative epiphany." While I agree that Mallarmé's example is, from the Romantic perspective, negative, I think Taylor implicitly misses the point Gadamer makes; namely, that the poetry of a Mallarmé or a Rilke is not subject to verification according to traditional concepts of subjectivity and objectivity, not even the Romantics' "expanded subjectivity."

12 Cook, p. x.

13 See "Mythopoietic Reversal in Rilke's *Duino Elegies*," translated by Robert Paslick, in *Literature and Philosophy in Dialogue*, edited by Dennis Schmidt (Albany: SUNY, 1994), pp. 153–71. Cited in text as LPD.

14 Rainer Maria Rilke, *Duino Elegies*, translated by J. B. Leishman and Stephen Spender (New York: Norton, 1939), pp. 32–33; translation slightly altered. The "others" in this passage, "jene," refers to "lovers," "*Liebende.*"

15 *Ibid.*, pp. 66–7, translation altered.

16 Two points merit mention here. First, Rilke's concept of the open is not virtual. The open is a space that has dimensionality, though its dimensionality is not, to be sure, of a measurable kind. The open is the invisible side of worldliness. Second, the fact that Rilke conceives of the open as a space is surely significant. It has a bearing, only partially acknowledged in my view, on the late Heidegger's preoccupation with the nature of spatiality. It has an obvious bearing, moreover, on the matter of signifying space: What kind of space is it that poetry opens up to us? On this score I rather doubt that Derrida's concept of "spacing," or "espacement," is adequate to what Rilke achieves in his poetry.

17 Charles Taylor, *Sources of the Self: The Making of Modern Identity* (Cambridge: Harvard University Press, 1989), p. 470.

18 See, for example, Arthur Danto's *The Philosophical Disenfranchisement of Art* (New York: Columbia University Press, 1986). Needless to say, I find Gadamer's reading not only subtler but also more truly Hegelian.

8 Gadamer, the Hermeneutic Revolution, and Theology

THE CONTEMPORARY REVOLUTION IN HERMENEUTICS

The twentieth century's hermeneutic revolution marks the third great turning point in the development of hermeneutics in Western culture.[1] Its founders were the theologian Karl Barth and the philosopher Martin Heidegger. In his fundamental book, *Truth and Method*, Gadamer acknowledges that Martin Heidegger is the *fons et origo* of this great turning point in hermeneutics.

The first turning point came after the establishment of the canon of Sacred Scripture and the dogmatic creeds of the great ecumenical councils, with Augustine of Hippo's *De Doctrina Christiana*. This work on biblical interpretation shaped the world of Christian learning, including medieval and early Reformation theology. Its hermeneutics was rooted in liturgical practice, especially baptism and eucharist, and in the Christian praxis of love.[2] It took creeds and a dogmatic theological context for granted. It was a hermeneutics of consent.[3]

The second great turning point in Western hermeneutics arrived with the Enlightenment and received its classic expression in Baruch Spinoza's *Theologico-Political Treatise*.[4] In time, and through Marx, Nietzsche, and Freud, it has become known as the hermeneutics of suspicion.[5] From the eighteeth century to the present this approach has dominated historical method and the critical retrieval of historical texts, church history, and the history of dogma independent of the auspices of ecclesiastical authority. Gotthold Lessing's "gaping abyss," which historical–critical method tries to close, was created when the presuppositions of Enlightenment epistemology formulated by the early modern thinkers Descartes, Locke, and others – the subject-object split and the 'problem of the bridge' – were applied to the relationship between the contingencies of history and the truths of faith.

Later, Kant sought the limits of reason in order either to "*make room for* faith" or to "*eliminate* faith," the word *aufräumen* in the *Vorrede* to edition B of *The Critique of Pure Reason* is ambiguous. In any case, Kant provided philosophical underpinnings for the classical Protestant doctrines of *sola fide, sola gratia*, and *sola scriptura*. His thought led to liberal Protestant difficulties with relativism (e.g., Troeltsch's 'Christ without absolutes'), historicism (e.g., the so-called quest for the historical Jesus from Strauss through Harnack and Schweitzer to Bultmann, and after) and subjectivism (as in the grounding of theology by Albrecht Ritschl and Wilhelm Hermann on 'religion within the limits of reason alone,' reducing it to imagination and subordinating it to morality).[6] These liberal approaches to theology nourished the *Kulturprotestantismus* against which Karl Barth rebelled on the eve of World War I.[7]

Karl Barth and Martin Heidegger inaugurated integral hermeneutics, which incorporates both the hermeneutics of consent and the hermeneutics of suspicion. Barth's revolt was sparked by his discovery in 1914 that theologians and teachers he admired were among the ninety-three signatories to a blatant manifesto in support of the Kaiser's war policies.[8] Barth's position relied on the writings of the later Schelling's Danish Lutheran student, Søren Kierkegaard. From invective against the bourgeoisification of the Danish Lutheran church through critique of Hegel, to his depiction of the existential plight of the New Testament interpreter in *Concluding Unscientific Postscript*, Kierkegaard's works were causing a sensation in the world of German-speaking philosophy and theology (HW 2).

Kierkegaard profoundly influenced the early dialectical theology of Barth's *Epistle to the Romans* (1919).[9] The rallying point of the hermeneutic revolution initiated by Barth's commentary on Romans (and documented in the prefaces he wrote for its successive editions) is the German, *Sachkritik*.[10] The German word *Sache* means thing, subject matter, content, business, real issue at stake (in Latin, *res* or *causa*). The word *Sache* recurred when Husserl and the phenomenological movement made "*Zu den Sachen selbst!*" or "Back to the things themselves," the motto for their revolt against dominant neo-Kantianism.[11]

In theological hermeneutics, *Sachkritik* means moving from the past of the text to the present situation of preaching through contact with the reality about which the text is speaking. In philosophy, Husserl accused the neo-Kantians of beginning with the roof. He resolved to begin with the foundations by not using the vague and unverifiable abstractions of academic psychologism and neo-Kantian theories of consciousness, but returning to what can be shown experientially. Husserl focused on the phenomenology of perception, which he eventually developed in a Fichtean, transcendental direction.

"Back to the things themselves" was more profoundly interpreted by Husserl's student and research assistant, Martin Heidegger. He wondered about the ontological status of Husserl's transcendental ego, thereby radicalizing the phenomenological movement.[12] He regarded the import of *Sache* through the prism of two Greek words that denote more than the isolated objects of sense perception privileged by Husserl: *pragmata* (objects constituted through action), and *pathemata tes psyches* (objects of deep practical concern).[13] Here the *Sache* of theological *Sachkritik* met the *Sache* of phenomenology.

The concerns of the greatest Protestant theologian and the most influential twentieth century philosopher came together in a revolution in the reading of the classic texts of Western culture. Barth and Heidegger agreed that our concrete solution to the problem of living is integral to our interpretation of any classic text; careful reading engages the way we personally and communally ask the practical and political question about the right way to live in order to resolve the issue of what is of utmost concern to us.

THE CHRISTIAN ROOTS AND AMBIGUOUS
RELATIONSHIP TO ARISTOTLE OF
HEIDEGGER'S REVOLUTION

Heidegger's *Being and Time* (1927) was about "fundamental ontology," even though most philosophers since Kant held that you just do not *do* ontology. Ontology means the transformation of premodern metaphysics or philosophy of being *qua* being initiated by Scotus, resumed in early modern times by Francisco Suarez, and carried on after Leibniz in the *Schulmetaphysik* of Kant's predecessors, Alexander Baumgarten and Christian Wolff.[14] Kant had demolished ontology as a precritical science of being, because ontology did not satisfactorily answer the question about knowing (How do we know we know?). Why, then, was Heidegger concerned with ontology?

Heidegger's preoccupation with ontology is related to his Roman Catholic provenance, and early contact with the Suarezian "manual tradition" in Catholic theology.[15] As a young student he read Brentano's 1862 book about the multiple significance of being according to Aristotle and his teacher Carl Braig's Vom Sein. Abriss der Ontologie (1896). Although he started under the auspices of Roman Catholic scholastic philosophy, his doctoral dissertation on psychologism's doctrine of judgment (1914) was also influenced by neo-Kantianism, especially Hermann Lotze's notion of logical validity as distinct from existence. In his habilitation on De modis significandi (a work then attributed to Duns Scotus) this neo-Kantian influence expanded beyond Heinrich Rickert to Emil Lask. He reduced the Scotist doctrine of the categories and of meaning to a theory of meaning rooted in a neo-Kantian reinterpretation of the traditional transcendentals (the true, the good, the one). The transcendentals penetrate all the categories we use in saying something about anything; for the neo-Kantian transcendental philosophy of consciousness, they constitute the meaning of objectivity (the meaning of any object). With Lask's help, Heidegger explored how the meaning of being, or of the Being of beings, can be presented to us in and through the validity of judgment.[16] Heidegger's 1916 conclusion to that work invoked Husserl's notion of intentionality to argue the need to go beyond transcendental logic to a phenomenology of the judging subject in order to fill in the lacunae of Scotist (and scholastic) metaphysics and neo-Kantian epistemologies.

Tracing the paths from Heidegger's early works to Being and Time is an adventure for those interested in the achievements of Heidegger's most influential students from those years: Hannah Arendt, Hans-Georg Gadamer, Karl Löwith, Leo Strauss, and Gerhard Krüger. Before the posthumous publication of most of Heidegger's early courses from Freiburg and Marburg, and from Freiburg again, there were inklings of their content in his curriculum vitae and published letters, in the witness of older students, in intellectual biographies by Otto Pöggeler and William Richardson, and later, in information gleaned by scholars with access to certain scripta of the young Heidegger, such as Karl Lehmann, Thomas Sheehan, and Jacques Taminiaux. More recently, Hugo Ott, Theodore

Kisiel, and John van Buren have filled in the details of the itinerary to his *magnum opus*, going beyond the earlier focus on Heidegger's tutelage to and criticism of his older contemporary, Edmund Husserl. These more recent findings cast new light on Heidegger's path "From One Idea of Phenomenology to the Other," in Taminiaux's phrase.[17]

Heidegger struggled to break free from the dogmatic metaphysics of the Roman Catholic scholastic philosophy and theology in which he was inculturated, by recovering primitive or primal Christianity – a deepened sense of the unmanipulable momentousness of grace that arrives "like a thief in the night" (1 Thessalonians 5:2).[18] In his maturity he said he was "driven onto the path of thought especially by the question about the relationship between the Word of Holy Scripture and theological-speculative thought."[19] Heidegger also had a fateful encounter with Aristotle.[20]

By 1919, Heidegger's break from the dogmatic metaphysics of Roman Catholic scholastic philosophy was complete.[21] He wrote to Fr. Engelbert Krebs on 9 September 1919: "Epistemological insights encroaching upon the theory of historical knowledge have made the *system* of Catholicism problematic and unacceptable to me – but not Christianity and metaphysics (though the latter in a new sense)...."[22] From the time of his War Emergency Seminar and Summer Semester courses of 1919 and his initial firsthand readings of Aristotle, he began to withdraw from both Husserl's option for *Philosophy as a Rigorous Science* (1911), and from the alternative neo-Kantian philosophies, comprehensive world-view philosophies, or philosophies of life.[23] This is documented in the 1920 lectures, "Phänomenologie der Anschauung und des Ausdrucks."[24] Philosophy is rooted in the basic experience of concern for itself and its motive is the restlessness of one's own *Dasein*. Facing this motive evokes the definitive breakthrough to facticity, *faktisches Leben*, "the full, concrete, historical, factical [*faktische*] self, accessible to one's own historically concrete experience."[25] The sheer earnestness is spellbinding: "The genuine foundation of philosophy is the radical existential grasp and the precipitation in time of questionability; to call oneself and one's life and one's decisive performances into question is the basic concept of every and even of the most radical illumination."[26] From then on, it was said, "the name [of Heidegger] travelled throughout the whole of Germany like the rumor of a hidden king."[27]

During most of the period before the publication of *Being and Time*, Heidegger focused on facticity – human being in its contingency as concretely available to us – with a view to elaborating the structures of concrete caring (*Sorge*).[28] His aim was to depart from the concreteness of our experience of the world mediated by meaning in order to discover the proper mode of human facticity's givenness – its accessibility and its adequate expression. He was determined to discover terms and relations that would be adequate to and not deform the original complex of concrete experience in its matrix of motives and tendencies.

Heidegger's meditation on the theory of categorial intuition in Husserl's sixth *Logical Investigation* helped him to "conceive of Being as beyond beings, yet manifesting itself in an understanding of Being which permeates all our comportments."[29] In his phenomenology, Husserl wanted to establish "philosophy as a rigorous science" by means of a transcendental reduction to the apodicticity of self-consciousness; he erected a program of "constitutive" phenomenology based on the evidence of the transcendental ego. Wilhelm Dilthey, who thought he could achieve a critique of historical consciousness by combining Schleiermacher's hermeneutics with a neo-Kantian epistemology of historiography, helped Heidegger link his own radical break with Husserl to the hermeneutical disciplines of theology and history. Henceforth, the *hermeneutics of facticity* is the beginning of philosophy.[30]

For Heidegger, *Dasein* is not a Cartesian subject but a being-present-to-a-world constituted by meaning. That odd term "facticity" (first used in theological debates concerning Christian belief in the Resurrection) points to everything about our experience that resists understanding and clear and precise conception. Instead of consciousness or self-consciousness in the Kantian sense of those terms, facticity highlights *Dasein*'s existence as a compact interplay between motivation (*Rück-griff*) and anticipation or spontaneous tending-towards (*Vor-griff*). Its meaning therefore is performative, an enactment (*Vollzug*) that relates (*Bezug*) motives to tendencies. Concepts or definitions (*Begriff*) and sense perceptions (*Anschauung*) are relatively minor parts of human life as inherently meaningful and concretely expressing itself. As meaningful, life speaks its own language and expresses itself in concrete situations. Life experiences itself and understands itself concomitantly with and through its anticipatorily structured flow, in an implicit, tacit, and nonthematic reflexiveness. This combination of performance and relating constitutes history as meaningful.[31]

Dilthey also drew Heidegger's attention to Graf Yorck von Wartenburg.[32] Wartenburg's concern for "historicity" led him to the young Luther's evangelical *fides ex auditu*, which Heidegger took as a model for philosophy as cooperating with and accompanying one's personal life experience in a mode of heightened vividness and interiority. He appreciated primitive Christianity's insight into the primordiality of self-experience and into the fact that "life has the character of a coming to a head in the *Selbstwelt*."[33] From Luther, Heidegger learned the contrast between the *theologia gloriae*, which turns the wine of the passion and death of Christ into the water of Aristotelian metaphysics, and the *theologia crucis*, which clings to life in the shadow of the cross. Luther, Paul, Augustine, and Kierkegaard taught him about the crucial condition of "fallenness."[34]

In particular, Augustine's *inquietum cor* helped Heidegger realize that what typifies the self as the *Grund-situation* and *-erfahrung* of philosophy is the restlessness (*Beunruhigung*) of human presence-to-self-in-the-world. The troubledness or persistent concern (*Bekümmerung*) of factual, lived experience is philosophy's point of departure and return; to begin with, it is conscious and operative (*actu exercito*) and not objectively known. It is *Vollzugssinn*, the meaning immanent in what we do, perform, suffer – what we encounter in our depression and elation.[35]

Heidegger saw in Augustine's contrast of the two modes of concern for life an example of either access to performative meaning or loss of it through misguided attempts to objectify it: detached, noble appreciation of beauty and goodness (*frui*); or utilitarian exploitation (*uti*). Heidegger's analysis of facticity also integrated other Augustinian motifs from *Confessions* X: becoming a question to oneself (*quaestio mihi factus sum* [chapter 33]); becoming a burden to oneself (*oneri mihi sum* [chapter 28]) because of temptation; and becoming sensitive to the conditions that lead to our being *defluxus in multum* or distracted by the multiplicity of various possibilities and meanings. Heidegger took up Augustine's chaste fear (*timor castus*), which led eventually to the role of the this-worldly experience of death in his thought. In time, Heidegger would remove the focus of unrest about one's own life from the Christian context of revelation, grace, and the forgivenness of sins.

When Heidegger turned to Aristotle, he became convinced of the so-called "a-theistic" character of philosophy: It is

"atheistic" not in the sense of a materialism or any similar theory. Any philosophy that is what it is and understands itself, has to know, as the factical How of its life-interpretation (and precisely when in doing so it still has a presentiment of God) that, in religious terms, the performative wresting back of its life is a raising the hand against God. Only in this way does it maintain its honor, i.e., in accord with the possibility before God available to it as such; here atheism conveys: holding oneself free from the misguided state of concernedness that merely discusses religiosity.[36]

In Heidegger's elaboration of the hermeneutical situation for reading Aristotle, the language of restlessness and concern (*Beunruhigung, Bekümmerung*) gave way to that of care (*Sorge*); the entanglements of temptation and the burden (*molestia*) weighing on Augustine's self as a question to itself were displaced by neutral, existential categories of life. We still may overhear Paul, Augustine, and Luther in Heidegger's meditative exegesis on *Nicomachean Ethics* II, 5 (1106b, pp. 28–34) that became the central motif of his Aristotelian reorientation.[37] The passage in Aristotle reads:

Again, it is possible to fail (*harmartanein*) in many ways (for evil belongs to the class of the unlimited, as the Pythagoreans conjectured, and good (*agathon*) to that of the limited), while to act rightly (*kathortoun*) occurs in one way only (*monachos*). (Hence the one is easy, the other difficult: it is easy to miss the mark, hard to hit it.) And for this reason it is characteristic of vice (*tes kakias*) to have excess (*huperbole*) or defect (*elleipsis*), and of virtue (*tes d'aretes*) to hold to a mean (*mesotes*).

The hermeneutic situation for reading Aristotle was flawed by different ways of "missing the mark" (*hamarteinein, Verfehlen*): just as in their living, people become lost in the multitude of possible and purportedly meaningful pursuits, and yield to what is "easy," philosophically trained interpreters were proponents of the then popular philosophies of value, or of life, or of science.[38]

When specifying the heart of factical life as care (*Sorge*), the young Heidegger immediately adds, "Living is caring, and the inclination is to make-it-easy-for-ourselves, to escape."[39] If human living bears within itself an inevitable inclination (*Neigung*) toward ruin (*Ruinanz*), philosophical interpretation must resist the drift toward ruin – a countermovement enacted in making one's own the mode of access to what can be questioned.[40] "This fundamental direction of philosophical inquiry is the object in question, factical life, not as imposed or clamped on from outside, but to be understood as the explicit grasp of a basic having-been-set-in-motion (*Bewegtheit*) of factical life, which exists in such a manner that it is concerned about its Being in the concrete time-conditioned generation (*Zeitigung*) of its Being, and that is also the case wherever it goes astray."[41] If we cannot attain lucid self-transparency, we can penetrate our inclination toward fallenness, become aware of escape routes into illusory safety, and have the courage to risk the restlessness of life in the recognition that putative points of repose are delusory. As Gadamer writes:

Life is inclination, tendentiousness, covering over of its distance in relation to what it is persistently concerned about, and so seals itself off against itself that it does not come to light itself. In the facticity of care, cover-up of distance, yes, of the 'now this, now that' character of living, the task is posed to our performative thinking itself, to *Dasein* itself, to turn inward.[42]

This tension built into *Dasein* presages *Being and Time* on authenticity and inauthenticity. Even as Heidegger makes Rilke's conviction that "one lives so badly because one always arrives in the present unfinished, incapable, distracted" his own, the explicitly religious context of sin and grace and repentance as disclosed by faith vanishes altogether. In the end, says Gadamer,

It may be questionable how much the word '*Faktizität*' still possessed religious connotations for Heidegger as well. But it is certain that precisely in the area of religion the limits of apriorist thought were co-present. Above all, surely, '*Hermeneutik der Faktizität*' means that the self-interpretation of factually concrete life constitutes *Dasein* as human, and it is what any philosophizing must attach itself to.[43]

Of central importance for Gadamer, Aristotle helped Heidegger to transpose the ontological problematic of meaning from the neo-Kantian context of transcendental logic to the transcendental-ontic conception of the notion of the object.[44] The formerly Catholic Heidegger returned to an Aristotle freed from the neo-Thomism spawned by *Aeterni Patris* (1879) for aid in clarifying his task apart from revealed teachings and detached from any tradition that might have compelled him to trim his teaching to reconcile it with such truths.[45]

Heidegger frequently analyzed the dianoetic virtues in Book VI of *Nicomachean Ethics*. For Gadamer, Aristotle's distinction between *poiesis* and *praxis* (as in Heidegger's Winter 1924–5 Marburg lectures on Plato's *Sophist*) is a heuristic key to Heidegger's articulation of fundamental ontology. Aristotle states in the *Politics* (1254a) that "the mode of being of humans does not consist in producing (*poiesis*), but acting (*praxis*)."[46] In *poiesis*, a circumscribed clarity verging on univocity characterizes the object of production. This quality of exactitude (*akribeia*) governs the productive process from the conception of the plan through the choice of materials and tools to the completion of the product, which, as external to the producers, is the model for all that can be predicted and controlled (*NE* 1141a 30). The attitude proper to every aspect of production (plan, means/ends relationships, goal, execution, and completion) correlates with the "horizon of *Vorhandenheit*," whose primacy in the premodern and modern philosophic tradition Heidegger criticized.

The horizon of *Vorhandenheit* is manifest in modern philosophy's "turn to the subject," which privileged the question about knowing over the question about being, and took the shape of epistemology (in German, *Erkenntnistheorie*) (PH 130–81). Philosophy's first question became, How do we know we know the really real? Assumptions shared by Descartes, Kant, and the neo-Kantians motivate the epistemological question: (1) the subject/object split, as in Descartes' division between *res cogitans* and *res extensa*; and (2) the "problem of the bridge," in which the consciousness of the knower is imagined to be a container, and objects to be known are imagined to be "already-out-there-now." *Vorhandenheit* privileges images of presence as "already-out-there-now" or "already-in-here-now," where consciousness is "already-in-here-now." *The* issue is either how knowing "gets out there" validly? or how it "gets the objects in here"?

Heidegger interprets the premodern logical ideal of science explicated in Aristotle's *Posterior Analytic* in terms of the horizon of *Vorhandenheit*.[47] He conflates the qualities of univocity, permanence, and distantiation proper to the *bios theoretikos – sophia* (theoretical wisdom) and *episteme* (science) – with *poiesis*.[48] Logical technique's emphasis on the abstract universality and necessity proper to precisely and explicitly defined terms, and on the rigor and consistency of inference via correctly formed syllogisms exercised, such an imaginative power over philosophical endeavor that abstract deductivism and conceptualism, became the hallmarks of true knowledge.[49] A residue of this imbalance in the logical control of meaning, which handles only the domain of the static and closed, is the premodern deductivism of Scotus and Ockham and the modern stress on "system."

The web of presuppositions proper to the horizon of *Vorhandenheit* combines the "already-out-there-now" image of objectivity and the "already-in-here-now" image of consciousness with the static and closed character of exclusively logical control.[50] Focusing solely on the *products* of the mind's operation, it prescinds from all the preconceptual, prepredicative, informal, and tacit factors in the *performance* of understanding and judging correctly. Heidegger dismantles this dominative project rooted in an antecedent willingness to gain technical control over the entire range of human aspiration: to subject all of living and being to *Verfügbarkeit* – manipulative control and massive possessiveness. The human subject becomes the isolated lord and master of reality.

Under the sway of the horizon of *Vorhandenheit*, philosophers installed either a mistaken notion of object (in the case of the ancients) or an equally mistaken notion of subject (modern philosophy after Descartes) at the center of their enterprise. They were oblivious to the question about Being whose scope is radically disproportionate to that horizon.

Gadamer shows that Heidegger exploited Aristotle's criticism of Plato's Idea of the Good as separate and immutable, to deconstruct *Vorhandenheit* (GW 2, 484–7). Projected into the beyond in accord with a this-worldly "already-out-there-now" object, the idea of the good epitomizes forgetfulness of the meaning of Being. In Heidegger's critique of the history of philosophy's collapse of Being into *Vorhandenheit*, Aristotle's *phronesis* as an *allo genos gnoseos* (another kind of knowledge distinct from *techne*, and from *nous, sophia,* and *episteme*) functions as a model for the hermeneutics of facticity.[51] In Gadamer's words:

The elucidation of the modes of being true in Book VI of 'Nicomachean Ethics' had for Heidegger this significance above all, that the primacy of judgment, of logic, and of 'science' for the understanding of the facticity of human living reached a decisive delimitation in this text. An *allo genos gnoseos* came into its own right, which does not know objects and does not wish to be objective knowledge, but rather intends the clarity proper to factically lived *Dasein*. So besides Aristotle's *Ethics* the *Rhetoric* was important for Heidegger, because it knows about *pragmata* and *pathemata* – and not about objects. (HW 172)

Phronesis is a habitual sense for the do-able, a care for what is prac- tically good here and now, whose mode of "trueing" (*aletheuein*) can be adequately conceived neither in terms of looking at the already- out-there-now nor in terms of producing. The model of producing spontaneously locates the overall form of Being-in-the-world in a will's power to project the "world" proleptically in willing itself. The model of *phronesis* focuses on making preferential choices in light of the *hou heneka* – the that-for-the-sake-of-which everything and anything is chosen.[52] The realization that comprehensive reflec- tion on Being is inextricably tied up with our prudential sense for the do-able signals the radicality of Heidegger's dependence on Aristotle in the early Freiburg and Marburg periods. In the realm of our pas- sions and of our practical ends, to find our direction in the mean we have to make an *Urentscheidung*, a fundamental option for the "one thing needful." The hermeneutics of facticity is directly inspired by the dianoetic and ethical virtue that discovers a decisive orientation, establishes our basic disposition in relation to the striving and desir- ing that moves us to action according to the right *logos*, and keeps us faithful to it.[53]

Being and Time's reappropriation of *phronesis* becomes ambigu- ous when Heidegger replaces the notion of the good implicit in Aristotle (and explicit in Plato) with the anticipation of death. The resolute facing of death parallels the *phronimos's* insight into the good here and now, because, like the good as the comprehensive end of human living, death can only be known provisionally. This parallel may obscure the differences, so that it becomes ambiguous whether the standpoint of producing does not ultimately prevail in *Entschlossenheit* or resoluteness.[54]

Heidegger's recognition of the open texture of our implicit, tacit, anticipatory knowledge of the good admits of either a Nietzschean

interpretation in terms of radical historicism or a Kantian interpretation as asymptotic goal. If Heidegger follows Nietzsche, resoluteness enacts the primacy of self-will, and his atheism becomes
Nietzschean. Thus, Karl Löwith links Heidegger's existential ontology to Carl Schmitt's "decisionist" political theory:

a decisionism that shifts the 'capacity-for-Being-a-whole' of the *Dasein* that
is always one's own to the 'totality' of the state that is always one's own.
To the self-assertion of one's own *Dasein* corresponds the self-assertion of
political existence, and to 'freedom toward death' corresponds the 'sacrifice
of life' in the political exigency of war. In both cases the principle is the
same, namely 'facticity,' what remains of life when one does away with all
life-content.[55]

Gadamer reads Heidegger dialectically, in opposition to rationalist
illusions of adequate self-knowledge. Construing the anti-theological
tenor of a phrase in Heidegger's lecture notes: "From the Hermeneutics of Facticity back to A" (Aristotle), he writes:

When one starts from the hermeneutics of facticity, i.e., from the self-
interpretation of *Dasein*, then it is evident that *Dasein* always projects itself towards its future and thereby becomes aware of its finitude. This is
what Heidegger in his renowned trope, "*Vorlaufen zum Tode,*" characterized as the authenticity of *Dasein*. So the Being in the 'there' (*Da*) is *Dasein*
between two opacities, its future and its origins. The hermeneutics of facticity teaches us this. It aims at the concept radically counter to Hegel's
absolute spirit and its self-transparency.[56]

I would say that neither interpretation resolves the ambiguity in
Heidegger's undertaking. Clearly, Gadamer's independent work uses
what is positive in Heidegger in a manner more consonant with
Kierkegaard and Dilthey than with Nietzsche.

PHRONESIS AND GADAMER'S
INTEGRAL HERMENEUTICS

In 1960, Hans-Georg Gadamer published his fundamental work,
Truth and Method. Instead of a theory of interpretation in the abstract *de jure* style of post-Kantian philosophy – and of his contemporary from the Cassirer school, Emilio Betti – Gadamer's philosophy
is factually grounded in his practice of appreciating works of art, doing history, and interpreting texts.[57] Heidegger perhaps did succumb

to Nietzschean suspiciousness when he studied texts in order to dismantle them as instances of the forgetfulness of Being. Yet Heidegger's early analysis of Aristotle's *phronesis* helped Gadamer see that Aristotle's practical philosophy exemplifies integral hermeneutics.[58] When he makes *phronesis* the heart of his philosophical hermeneutics, Gadamer removes all the ambiguity from Heidegger's insight into the relevance of *phronesis* for a philosophy of human historicity.

Interpreting Aristotle's passage on finding the mean in a preferential choice of the good, Heidegger highlights the contrast between hitting the mark in right action and missing the mark by excess (hyperbole) or defect (ellipsis). To fall prey to carelessness, he said, is to

become hyperbolic and to confirm a more facile fulfillment and overweening concern, i.e., to maintain and preserve one's *Dasein*. Hyperbolic *Dasein* manifests itself at once as elliptical: it heads away from the difficult, from that which is *monachos*, simple, (without short-cuts), it does not set any end for itself, it will not commit itself to a primal decision, and (be repeatedly) committed to it.[59]

Heidegger pushes this motif in the direction of *Dasein*'s "capacity-for-Being-a-whole" and its eventual resolute choice of itself. If, as Karl Löwith believed, this choice confronts simply nothingness, it lacks ethical bearing. Gadamer dwells instead on the *logos* immanent in praxis and apprehended by *phronesis*, as a mode of *aletheuein* – uncovering the truth in action – incompatible with theoretical science or wisdom. The contingent intelligibility and truth at stake eliminates all decisionism from Gadamer's appropriation of practical wisdom. Recalling Heidegger's explication of the dianoetic virtues (in *Nicomachean Ethics* VI), he speaks of five modes of being true as "an *allo genos gnoseos* that does not know objects and does not want to be knowledge, but intends the clarity possible to factically lived *Dasein*" (HW 139–52). Gadamer learned from Heidegger to appreciate the Greeks' closeness to concrete, factual human life in contrast to scientism and neo-Kantian epistemology. Heidegger's interruption of the dominance of propositional truth and apodictic foundationalism led Gadamer to use practical reason to explore the primacy of hermeneutic reason.

We see Gadamer's rather different approach to Aristotle's practical philosophy in the 1930 essay, "Praktisches Wissen." Discussing dialogues where Plato discusses true usefulness, he shows how Platonic ethics is rooted in "intelligence" rather than concepts and theories. His treatment of Aristotle begins, "Only friends can give counsel. This is why *synesis*...is one form of practical-dianoetic virtue in Aristotle."[60] Typically, he takes Plato seriously by emphasizing the explicitly communicative and other-oriented dimensions of deliberative excellence in Aristotle's analysis of *phronesis* (HW 81–93).[61]

Gadamer agrees with Leo Strauss in opposing Heidegger's caricature of Plato. If Plato's idea of the good is the epitome of the forgetfulness of Being for Heidegger, Gadamer showed the Platonic 'Idea' is neither an intelligible content nor, as the neo-Kantians would have it, a prefiguring of a law of nature in modern physics. The hypothesis of ideas is "not so much a 'doctrine' but a direction of inquiry, the development and discussion of whose implications was the task of philosophy, which means, of course, Platonic dialectic"(GW 2, 502).

Plato does not pursue politics in accord with the principles of a theory of ideas – just as little did he give lessons in a doctrine of ideas. The path on the heights toward the vision of a place beyond the heavens is one and the same as the path in the depths proper to a care left over to oneself about one's own Being. Philosophy is not politics for the reason that Plato believed naïvely in an abstract synthesis of the cosmic and the human good, but because the philosopher and the true statesman live in the same care. In both there must be true knowledge, and that means: they must know the good. But one cannot know the good from a distance and for everybody, but only for oneself originally. Only out of this concern for one's own self (the 'soul') does there grow true knowledge, whose truths are fruitful, and this persistent concern is philosophy. (GW 5, 239)

For Plato, then, "Practical knowledge is not reinterpreted in the theory of ideas; on the contrary, even still in the Socratic mode of practical knowledge, the theory of ideas, the knowledge of everlasting being, is immersed in the concrete knowledge of man" (GW 5, 239). Unlike Strauss, Gadamer highlights *phronesis* as "the reasonable ability to reflect on what is useful for oneself – namely, for one's own *Existieren* (EN 1140a 25, *eu zen*)." "Ability to reflect is the only relevant ability, for there is no knowledge of what is good for one's own existing available in advance" (GW 5, 241). Like Strauss, Gadamer is explicit about how practical wisdom as "the sense for oneself and one's own best" is political, embracing the sense for economics, for the politically advisable, for justice, for organization or lawmaking. The practically wise person discovers what is best for himself in what is common to the *polis*, and insofar as this is true, it is what the *polis* needs.

Gadamer specifies the role of *nous* or intelligence in the exercise of practical wisdom as a "seeking and deliberating resolution" of the issue: what is to be done? It has to will the end, the ultimate good as the goal of action apprehended without demonstration. In letting the proximate means for fulfilling the goal occur to our intelligence in the particular present situation, we apprehend the end more determinately at the same time. The intelligibility grasped by it is not something given, but something to be done that enables both the ongoing discernment and achievement of the good.

In *Being and Time*, Heidegger equated practical wisdom with conscience and then isolated it in relation to nothingness.[62] For Gadamer, sound judgment involves performatively deliberating with ourselves about our own affairs; it implies the ability to take counsel or deliberate with others and understand their practical judgments. *Synesis* is the ability to understand by which we follow others as they disclose their deliberations about what is best for them, by applying our own knowledge in the practical sphere about the situation of the others. "Only when one puts oneself in the position of the other and inquires into what is best for oneself does one have the understanding and judgment for the other that is required" (GW 5, 245–6). This communicative dimension of practical wisdom makes it the hermeneutical virtue *par excellence*.

For Gadamer, the paradigm of the hermeneutics of facticity and the key to the analysis of *Dasein* is sound judgment, which realizes itself discursively in existential dialectic. Plato's *Republic* (521c, 5–8) states what is at stake in dialectic: "This ought not to be so easy and trivial as the spinning of a shard, but it is the conversion of the soul (*psyches periagoge*) from the day that is like night to the real day – the way out toward being as such, what we call genuine philosophy." Gadamer devoted a lifetime's attention to the parallel between *phronesis* as it discovers the one thing needful time after time and the primacy of the question in true dialectic. So understanding every formulated and affirmed answer draws us into a further question. Placing dialectic as the human capacity to hold a conversation and give a reasonable account at the center of the hermeneutics of facticity discloses fidelity to the idea of the good as being faithful to one's questions through time. In Gadamer's Heidegger-inspired reconstruction of Plato's dialectic, self-understanding in terms of the highest possibility of Being becomes human *Dasein's* ongoing being-in-the-truth.[63]

Gadamer's philosophy as hermeneutical makes sense out of the way human beings make sense of their lives by anticipating the future in the light of the past. As a second-order understanding, philosophy reduplicates the structure of the hermeneutic circle enacted in human existence itself. Both life and philosophy are a *fides quaerens intellectum*: faith seeking understanding.

THE CENTRALITY OF CONVERSATION
FOR INTEGRAL HERMENEUTICS

Barth and Heidegger revolutionized philosophy and theology by reading the originative classics of Western culture with the realization that the interpretation of any classic text depends on the readers' concrete solution to the problem of living, and their asking and answering the question about the right way to live, thereby personally deciding the issue of concern. *Truth and Method* gives the philosophical basis of this revolution by using Heidegger's hermeneutics of facticity (WM 250–61/TM 265–71) to overcome aesthetic, Romantic, and historical consciousness. In its three parts, *Truth and Method* advances (1) a critique of aesthetic consciousness in the light of an ontology of the work of art; (2) a critique of historical consciousness in the light of an ontology of *Verstehen* and of effective-historical consciousness; and (3) an ontology of language.

In *Unterwegs zur Sprache* (1959), Heidegger criticized the entire vocabulary in *Being and Time's* analysis of facticity as still too embued with Husserlian and Idealist transcendental subjectivity, explicit self-consciousness (reflective self-awareness), and self-possession. After his "turning" (in the early 1930s) Heidegger condemned all conventional philosophical conceptualities as tainted by the biases of one or another "language of metaphysics," which he was striving to overcome.[64] Gadamer says he was in a "linguistic emergency" (*Sprachnot*) (HW 118).

Gadamer's disagreement here is emblematic of the tenor of his *integral* hermeneutics. He denies that there is a "language of metaphysics" whose vocabulary is automatically "used up," because at root any language is dialogical. The so-called "language of meta-physics" only makes sense in light of the questions that were being asked and answered in it. Re-asking the questions to which linguistic statements are intended to be answers helps us realize that language is a horizon framing our asking and answering of questions; recovering the questions liberates language by de-rigidifying and de-scholasticizing it. In philosophy, such inquiry cannot dry up or freeze. Language's true point of access is the interplay of questions and answers (GW 2, 10–12).

This disagreement with Heidegger exemplifies his more general critique of the "prejudice against prejudice." It marks the parting of the ways among Heidegger's postmodern followers. Those such as Gadamer, Paul Ricoeur, Emmanuel Lévinas, David Tracy, Jean-Luc Marion, Michel Henry, and Jean-Louis Chretien radicalize Heidegger in an integral hermeneutics open to religious, Jewish and Christian, meanings and values. Genealogists and deconstructionists such as Michel Foucault, Jacques Derrida, and Gianni Vattimo remain in the throes of the hermeneutics of suspicion (although Derrida and Vattimo have recently shown an interest in religion, rather in the sense of Vattimo's title, *Credo di Credere*).

The chief issue for theology today is whether theologians can listen openly and critically to their traditions. Gadamer's radical breakthrough to hermeneutic consciousness, which resumes Heidegger's hermeneutics of facticity in the context of art and the historical and humane sciences (the *Geisteswissenschaften*, *belles lettres*, humanities), illuminates this issue. Generalizing Heidegger's language of *Ereignis*, *Lichtung*, and *Es gibt...*, and his speech about language as the house of Being and human beings as the shepherds of Being, Gadamer insists "Human beings are what they are in constantly affecting the world and in constantly experiencing the effect of the world upon themselves. Not in the isolated freedom of being-over-against, but in daily relation-to-world, in letting ourselves in for the conditionings of the world do human beings win their own selves. So, too, do they gain the right position of knowing" (LPD 16, translation altered).

Gadamer demystifies Heidegger's insight into language: human beings live within language as the air they breathe rather than as an instrument they deploy at will. They exist conversationally in relation to everything that is. Relating truth as "dependent upon the temporal-historical movement proper to *Dasein*" to reason as "the self-empowered capacity to perceive truth and make it binding," Gadamer affirms that reason is "made possible by what it is not."[65] He rejects critical theory's fear that the existential conditionedness of reason or truth renders them mere "tools in the service of a higher, unconscious, and irresponsible power...."[66] "It is the essence of our reason and our spirit to be capable of thinking against what is to our own advantage, to be able to detach ourselves from our needs and interests and to bind ourselves to the law of reality."[67] By reason we have the capacity to acknowledge reality even against our own self-interest: "To be taught, even against our own subjectively certain convictions – that is the way of mediation of authentically historical truth."[68]

Our first learning to speak is less an intentional process than a "game of imitation and exchange" (GW 2, 5). "In the receptive child's drive to imitate the forming of sounds," Gadamer says, "the enjoyment in such forming of sounds is paired with the illumination of meaning. No one can really answer in a reasonable manner the question of when their first understanding of meaning occurred." Theologian Austin Farrer put this beautifully:

Our humanity is itself a cultural heritage; the talking animal is talked into talk by those who talk at him.... His mind is not at first his own, but the echo of his elders. The echo turns into a voice, the painted portrait steps down from the frame, and each of us becomes himself. Yet by the time we are aware of our independence, we are what others have made us. We can never unweave the web to the very bottom.... Nor is it only parental impresses of which we are the helpless victims. How many persons, how many conditions have made us what we are; and, in making us so, may have undone us.[69]

"It made sense" as Gadamer said of *Truth and Method*, "to bring the game-play of language into closer connection with the game-play of art in which I had contemplated the parade example of the hermeneutical. Now to consider the universal linguistic constitution of our experience of the world in terms of the model of game-play certainly does suggest itself."[70]

If we learn everything in language-games, then the language-game, like game-play (*Spiel*) in general, only starts when players become serious by not holding themselves back in "just playing" (PH 66).

Language for Gadamer means language-in-use, never a set of tools such as vocabulary, grammar, syntax, and so on. Language is used in conversation. Structured as game-play, conversation constitutes language concretely as language-games.[71] "The life of language consists" as Gadamer says, "in the constant further playing out of the game we started when we learned to speak.... It is this continuously played game in which the mutual life together of people is played" (PH 66).

Conversation as game-play has the spirit of "lightness, freedom, and the luck of success – of being fulfilling, and of fulfilling those who are playing," especially when we achieve mutual understanding:

Mutual understanding happens by the fact that talk stands up against talk, but does not remain static. Instead, in talking to each other we pass over into the imaginative world of the other, we as it were open ourselves up to them, and they do so to us. So we play into each other until the game of giving and taking, the conversation proper, begins. No one can deny that in such real conversation there is something of chance, the favor of surprise, finally also of lightness, yes, even of elevation, which pertains to the nature of game-play. And truly the elevation of conversation is experienced not as a loss of self-possession, but, even without ourselves actually attending to it, as an enrichment of ourselves (PH 56–57).

As we come together in conversation, and are now...led on further by the conversation, then what is determinative is no longer people as holding themselves in reserve or as willing to be open, but the law of the subject matter about which the conversation is going on, which releases speech and response and finally plays everyone into itself. So wherever a conversation has been successful, afterwards everyone is, as we say, filled with it. The play of speech and response is played out further in the inner conversation of the soul with itself, as Plato so beautifully named "thinking." (GW 2, 152)

By focusing on the role of conversation in human life and thought, philosophy goes beyond either phenomenology of perception or logical preoccupation with concepts, propositions, and inferences. The conversational point of departure finds the root of all answers in questions. Gadamer relishes the great British historian and philosopher R. G. Collingwood's articulation of "the logic of question and answer" (WM 351–60/TM 369–79), but goes further than Collingwood to show that 'logic' as concretely enacted in dialectic or friendly conversation, and structured as a game, so that when understanding occurs and grows in the to and fro of question and answer, this "happens from the side of the things themselves. The subject matter 'yields' questions" (GW 2, 6).

When we truly converse, we understand and interpret at once. Both English words correctly translate Gadamer's key term *Verstehen*. The German word covers not just the act of insight but also the act of articulation or *Auslegung* by which we talk to ourselves, laying out in language what we actually understand. "Interpretation belongs to the essential unity of understanding. Whatever is said to us must be so received by us that it speaks and finds a response in our own words and in our own language" (PH 57).

Understanding always involves interpretation, and this is preeminently true in understanding texts:

> Whoever wants to understand a text always performs a projection. We project a meaning of the whole, as soon as a first meaning is manifest in the text. Such a meaning in turn only becomes manifest because one is already reading the text with certain expectations of a determinate meaning. Understanding what is there to be understood consists in working out such a projection which of course is constantly revised by what emerges in penetrating its meaning further.... [A]ny revision of the projection exists in virtue of the possibility of casting up a new projection; ... rival projections towards the elaboration can be generated one after the other, until the unity of sense is fixed unequivocally; ... the interpretation is initiated with anticipatory notions that are replaced by more adequate ones: precisely this ongoing newly-projecting that constitutes the movement of meaning proper to understanding and interpreting is the process that Heidegger describes.[72]

Whenever we read a text "there is no author present at the discussion as an answering partner, and no subject matter present which can be so or otherwise. The text as a work stands on its own." Does this mean that there is no dialogue? Not at all.

It seems that here the dialectic of question and answer, in so far as it has any place at all, is only available in one direction, which means from the side of the one seeking to understand the work of art, who questions it and who is called into question by it, and who tries to listen for the answer of the work. As the person one is, one may, just like anyone thinking, be the inquirer and responder at once, in the same manner as happens in a real conversation between two people. But this dialogue of the understanding reader with himself surely does not seem to be a dialogue with the text, which is fixed and to that extent is finished. Or is this really how it is? Or is there an already finished text given at all?

In this case the dialectic of question and answer does not come to a stand-still.... The reception of a poetic work, whether it be by our outer ear or by that inner ear that listens attentively when we are reading, presents itself as a circular movement in which answers rebound into further questions and provoke new answers. This motivates our abiding with the work of art, of whatever kind it may be. Abiding is obviously the authentic characteristic in the experience of art. A work of art is never exhausted. (GW 2, 9)

For Gadamer, the process of translating the meaning of something in one language into the terms offered by another language is an exaggerated case of what happens as we make our way through life in general. Human living is conversational so that we constantly make sense of what presents itself in the foreground of our experience in terms of our linguistic horizon. By a process of trial and error, we try to find the right word with which to articulate and communicate our experience (both to ourselves and to others), and we rarely, if ever, achieve a definitiveness beyond all provisionality. As Gadamer tells us:

If any model can really illustrate the tensions residing in understanding and interpretation, it is that of translation. In it the strange or alien is made our own as strange or alien, and that means neither that it is just permitted to stay alien, nor that it is constructed in one's language by a sheer imitation of its very strangeness; but in [translation] the horizons of past and present are merged in an ongoing movement as it constitutes the very nature of understanding and interpretation (*Verstehen*). (GW 2, 436)

GADAMER AND INTEGRAL
CHRISTIAN HERMENEUTICS

Rowan Williams suggests that Wittgenstein and Dietrich Bonhoeffer converged on the view of human living we can now recognize is Gadamer's:

Wittgenstein and Bonhoeffer more clearly presuppose that to interpret the symbolic, linguistic, and behavioral complex that 'addresses' us in the human world is to have one's own pattern of speech and action conditioned (not determined) by it, to be provoked (called forward) by the ways in which it touches, confirms, resonates, or questions what we have done and said. To interpret means interweaving a text (words and actions, words *and* actions) with our human project, acquiring a partner, a pole of difference that refuses to allow our "project" to return endlessly on itself, as if it were indeed generated from a well of unsullied interiority, "self-consciousness."[73]

Gadamer recognizes that life is a process that displaces the subject from centrality. Human beings become themselves by playing into a direction of meaning and value moving through the interplay of subjects with the world. The game-play structure of life is also disclosed in the Christian experience of grace and faith. As Williams says of achieving human wholeness, "in... belonging to God, a wholeness is achieved in trust or hope rather than analysis":

My own identity's "ungraspable" quality thus becomes not an elusive level of interiority, but the unknowable presence of the creator's absolute affirmation, the mysteriousness of grace, past, present, and future, not of the "true self' as a hidden thing. My unity as a person is always out of my field of vision (I can't see my own fact), just as the divine condition for there being fields of vision at all, for there being a world or worlds, is out of my field of vision (I can't see my own origin).[74]

Gadamer in parallel fashion states:

All understanding in the end is self-understanding, but not in the mode of a prior or finally achieved self-possession. For this self-understanding is always realized only in the understanding of a subject matter, and does not have the character of a free self-realization. The self that we are does not possess itself. One could better put it that instead it happens. And that is what theology really says, that faith is just such an event, in which a new man is founded. And it says further that it is the Word that needs to be believed and understood and by which we overcome the abysmal lack of self-knowledge in which we live. (PH 55)

Gadamer criticizes the ideas about self-understanding of Rudolf Bultmann (another theorist of hermeneutics influenced by Heidegger) for being too tainted by an idealistic subjectivism and existentialism. Transposing self-understanding into the game-play structure of human life, he considers the relationship of Christian faith to human understanding and interpretation.

Whatever is said to us we must receive into ourselves so that it speaks to us and finds a response in our own words in our own language. This holds utterly true for the text of proclamation which cannot really be understood if it does not appear as being said to our very own selves. Here it is the sermon in which the understanding and interpretation of the text attains its full reality. Neither the explicating commentary nor the exegetical labors of the theologians, but the sermon stands in the immediate service of the proclamation inasmuch as it not only mediates the understanding of what the Holy Scripture tells us, but witnesses to it at the same time. However, the proper fullness of understanding lies not in the sermon as such, but in the manner in which it is accepted as a call that impinges on each one of us. (PH 57–58)

Gadamer objected to Bultmann's overemphasis on historical–critical mediation of New Testament texts. Once he half-jokingly told me, "Bultmann forgets that the books of the New Testament are not *books* in the ordinary sense of the term." He was agreeing with Franz Overbeck and Helmut Kuhn that these texts belong to the genre of *Urliteratur*. This implies that "If, under the meaning of the text, we understand the *mens auctoris*, i.e., the 'verifiable' horizon of understanding of any given Christian writer, then we accord the authors of the New Testament a false honor. Their proper honor ought to lie in the fact that they announce the tidings about something that surpasses the horizon of their own understanding – even if they happen to be named John or Paul" (PH 210). Gadamer appeals to a similar aspect of "hearing the Word" in showing in terms of the concrete experience of word how language works:

When I say 'word' (*das Wort*), I do not mean the word whose plural are the words (*die Wörter*) as they stand in the dictionary. Nor do I mean the word whose plural are the words (*die Worte*) which with other words go to make up the context of a statement. Rather I mean the word that is a *singulare tantum*. That means the word that strikes one, the word one allows to be said to oneself, the word that enters into a determinate and unique life-situation; and it is good to be reminded that behind this *singulare tantum* stands ultimately the linguistic usage of the New Testament. (GW 2, 192)

Gadamer points out three characteristics of the New Testament as an instance of *Urliteratur*. First, the authors of the Holy Scriptures "present themselves as faithful witnesses of an authentic tradition which begins with the first community and with the immediate witnesses," and so they are less authors, strictly speaking, than intermediate witnesses. For Gadamer, not every religious message counts as witness, but witness is the distinguishing mark of the Christian message or gospel. It witnesses to the passion of Jesus and the resurrection promise of salvation. "It is an authentic witness because it refers to a particular event: the death of Jesus on the cross. It is a human being who suffers the death of a criminal and who in full awareness of being the Son of God and of being God, insists on the title "Son of Man" and accepts the fate of creatures."[75]

Second, the New Testament has the status of an "eminent text" (GDE 41–2). There are three categories of such texts: (1) *announcements* or promulgations of the kind common in law, such as verdicts or statutes; (2) *affirmations* such as are found in poetry (works of art "made out of" language) and philosophy; and (3) *addresses* such as religious texts, especially the Jewish and Christian Scriptures, and the preaching/hearing by which they are applied. For Gadamer an "eminent text" is one that "capture(s) a purely linguistic action and so possesses an eminent relationship to writing and writtenness. In it language is present in such a way that its cognitive relationship to the merely given outside the text disappears just as much as does its communicative relation to the one originally being addressed" (TM 576, GW 2, 475). According to Gadamer, as an eminent text the Christian scripture has a normativity that is virtually equivalent to that justified under the heading of inspiration:

The primordial question to which the text has to be understood as an answer has here... by reason of its origin an inherent supremacy and freedom.... [T]he classical text is "telling" only when it speaks "primordially," i.e., "as if it were spoken just to me alone." This does not at all imply that what speaks in this way is measured against an extra-historical concept of norm. Just the contrary: what speaks in this way thereby posits a standard. Herein lies the problem. The primordial question to which the text is to be understood as an answer in such a case lays claim to an identity of meaning which always has already mediated the distance between presence and past. (TM 577–8, GW 2, 476)

The "eminent text" therefore entails "an exceptional mode of historical being, the historical enactment of preservation which – in ever renewed corroboration – allows something to be true" (WM 271/TM 287). It is proper to such a work to have "an identifiability, a repeatability, and a worthiness to be repeated" that only can be predicated of something that once functioned in the past and continues to function in any succeeding temporal context in an originative way. This means that it is normative, but constantly also becomes constitutive of ourselves. Luther saw this when he said that the gospel has a *pro me* character. When we come into contact with the gospel as an eminent text we sense our "immediate and binding affinity" to a reality that "as past is at once unattainable and presently relevant" (WM 273/TM 289). The gospel, "far from being evidence documenting something bygone that we may not care to interpret and make our own, is already speaking to us and every person in history in a way that is uniquely appropriate to that particular place and time" (WM 274/TM 289). This means that as an eminent text, the gospel has an autonomous meaning that is self-interpreting and self-authenticating.[76]

Third, the Christian message as the proclamation of the good news and the messianic promise does not have the status of a symbolic form of recognition common to all religious traditions. Instead, the meaning of the Christian message "This is you" in the context of the incarnation and Easter has the status of *sign*. "A sign is something only given to one who is ready to accept it as such" (RB 152). According to Gadamer, "the uniqueness of the gospel message lies in the fact that it must be accepted against all expectation and hope," because "the claim of the Christian message... is that it alone has really overcome death through the proclamation of the representative suffering and death of Jesus as a redemptive act" (RB 151). In Gadamer's radical expression:

It is not the infinite wealth of life possibilities that is encountered in [the Christian] "this is you," but rather the extreme poverty of the *Ecce homo*. The expression must be given a quite different emphasis here: "this is you" – a man helplessly exposed to suffering and death. It is precisely in the face of this infinite witholding of happiness that the Easter message is to become "Good News" (RB 151).

As a sign, Gadamer tells us, this "is not something that takes the place of seeing, for what distinguishes it precisely from all reports or from its opposite, silence, is the fact that what is shown is only accessible to the one who looks for himself and actually sees something there" (RB 152).

CONCLUSION

Beyond these quite insightful suggestions about the interpretation of Christian themes, Gadamer culminates the hermeneutic revolution started by Barth and Heidegger. That revolution critically transposed reading from the modern framework of epistemology onto the plane of personal and communal identity and orientation. By retrieving and developing Aristotle's notion of *phronesis* more adequately than Heidegger, Gadamer performs hermeneutics integrally, combining critique with creative assimilation. He integrates the

Platonic–Aristotelian idea of the good into a conversational model of understanding and interpretation, of judgment and discernment. Integral hermeneutics overcomes the monological bias of the horizon of *Vorhandenheit*, and corrects rationalist misunderstandings of premodern and modern philosophy. Hermeneutic philosophy shows that, even independently of divine revelation and grace, the human quest for meaning is shaped as "faith seeking understanding." In making manifest the ever mysterious nature of human self-understanding in time, Gadamer opens up philosophy to theology, and challenges theology to be philosophical.

NOTES

1 See Hans-Georg Gadamer, "Klassische und philosophische Hermeneutik (1968)," *Gesammelte Werke 2: Hermeneutik II.* (Tübingen: Mohr Siebeck, 1985), pp. 92–117. For a general introduction to the development of (especially philosophical) hermeneutics, see Jean Grondin, *Introduction to Philosophical Hermeneutics*, translated by Joel Weinsheimer (New Haven: Yale University, 1994).

2 Ernest Fortin, "Augustine and the Hermeneutics of Love: Some Preliminary Considerations," *The Birth of Philosophic Christianity. Studies in Early Christian and Medieval Thought*, Ernest L. Fortin: *Collected Essays*, Vol. 1, edited by Brian Benestad (Lanham: Rowman and Littlefield, 1996), pp. 1–19.

3 Ben F. Meyer. "Conversion and the Hermeneutics of Consent," *Critical Realism and the New Testament* (Allison Park: Pickwick Publications, 1989), pp. 57–75.

4 On Spinoza, see Hans-Georg Gadamer, *Wahrheit und Methode. Grundzüge einer philosophischen Hermeneutik* (Tübingen: Mohr Siebeck, 1962), pp. 169–172; in English translation: *Truth and Method*, second, revised edition, translation revised by Joel Weinsheimer & Donald Marshall. (New York: Crossroad, 1991), pp. 181–4. [In the text, I have often used my own translations. I will refer in the text to *Wahrheit und Methode* as WM and give cross references to *Truth and Method* as TM.] See also Leo Strauss, *Spinoza's Critique of Religion* (New York: Schocken Books, 1975); *Persecution and the Art of Writing* (Glencoe: Free Press, 1951); Nicholas Boyle, "Lessing, Biblical Criticism and the Origins of German Classical Culture," *German Life and Letters*, 34 (1981), 196–213.

5 Paul Ricoeur, *Freud and Philosophy: An Essay on Interpretation*, translated by D. Savage (New Haven and London: Yale University Press, 1970). Also, Gadamer, "The Hermeneutics of Suspicion," in *Hermeneutics:*

Questions and Prospects, edited by Gary Shapiro and Alan Sica (Amherst: University of Massachusetts Press, 1984).

6 Sarah Coakley, *Christ Without Absolutes: A Study of the Christology of Ernst Troeltsch* (Oxford: Clarendon Press, 1988). See also Stephen Niell and Tom Wright, *The Interpretation of the New Testament 1861 to 1986* (Oxford: Oxford University Press, 1988); and Ben F. Meyer, *Critical Realism and the New Testament*.

7 See Eberhard Busch, *Karl Barth: His Life From Letters and Autobiographical Texts*, translated by John Bowden (Philadelphia: Fortress, 1976); and Hans W. Frei's review in *Types of Christian Theology* (New Haven: Yale University, 1992), pp. 147–63.

8 Busch, *Karl Barth*, pp. 60–125.

9 Karl Barth, *Römerbrief* (Zurich: Zollikon, 1984 [1922]).

10 James M. Robinson, "Hermeneutics Since Barth," *The New Hermeneutic* Eds. J. M. Robinson, J. B. Cobb (New York: Harper & Row, 1964), pp. 1–77.

11 Gadamer relates that "Thomas Sheehan once told me that Heidegger once showed him an off-print of Husserl's Logos Essay of 1910, 'Philosophy as a Rigorous Science.' There is a passage there where Husserl says: our method and our principle must be *'Zu den Sachen selbst'* – and there the young Heidegger had written in the margin: 'We desire to take Husserl at his word.'" See HW 171 and PH 130–81.

12 "In a marginal note on Husserl's draft for the article on phenomenology in the Encyclopedia Britannica, Heidegger asks a question that touches the characteristically modern ambiguity at the center of Husserl's position: 'What is the mode of being (*Seinsart*) of the absolute ego: in what sense is it the same as the factual I, in what sense is it not the same?'" Thomas Prufer, "A Protreptic: What Is Philosophy?" *Studies in Philosophy and the History of Philosophy* (Washington, DC: Catholic University of America Press, 1963), pp. 1–19, cit. 15–16: The reference for the inner quote (note 50) is to *Tijdschrift voor Philosophie*, XII (1950), p. 268.

13 M. Heidegger, *Sein und Zeit*, 7th ed. (Tübingen: Max Niemeyer Verlag, 1953), p. 68; in English translation by J. Macquarrie and E. Robinson, *Being and Time* (London, SCM, 1962), pp. 96–7. See also Leo Strauss, "A Giving of Accounts" with Jacob Klein, *The College* (Annapolis and Santa Fe) 22 no. 1 (April), pp. 1–5; and Don Ihde, "Language and Two Phenomenologies," *Southern Journal of Philosophy* (Winter, 1970), 399–408.

14 Jean-Francois Courtine, *Suarez et le système de la métaphysique* (Paris: Presses Universitaires de France, 1990); and Olivier Boulnois, "Quand commence l'ontothéologie?" Aristote, Thomas d'Aquin et Duns Scot,"

Saint Thomas et l'onto-théologique, Actes du colloque tenu à l'Institut catholique de Toulouse les 3 et 4 juin 1994, *Revue Thomiste* XCV (1995/1), 85 ff.

15 John Van Buren, *The Young Heidegger: Rumor of the Hidden King* (Bloomington: Indiana University, 1994), pp. 133–56; Walter Strolz, "Herkunft und Zukunft: Martin Heideggers frühe Auslegung urchristlicher Lebenserfahrung," *Herder Korrespondenz* 4 (1996), pp. 203–7.

16 Manfred Riedel, "Hermeneutik oder Gesprächsdialektik. Gadamers Auseinandersetzung mit Heidegger," in *Hören auf der Sprache, Die akroamatische Dimension der Hermeneutik* (Frankfurt: Suhrkamp, 1990), pp. 96–130; and Stephen Crowell, "Making Logic Philosophical Again," *Reading Heidegger from the Start: Essays in His Early Thought,* edited by T. Kisiel and J. van Buren (Albany: SUNY Press, 1994), pp. 55–72.

17 Jacques Taminiaux, *Heidegger and the Project of Fundamental Ontology,* translated and edited by M. Gendre (Albany: SUNY Press, 1991) pp. 1–54.

18 See John van Buren, "Martin Heidegger, Martin Luther," in *Reading Heidegger from the Start* (note 47), pp. 159–74; and Theodore Kisiel, "Heidegger (1920–21) on Becoming a Christian: A Conceptual Picture-Show, *Ibid.,* 175–91; and "Theological Beginnings: Toward a Phenomenology of Christianity," in *The Genesis of Heidegger's Being and Time* (Berkeley, Los Angeles: University of California, 1993), pp. 69–115, on the years 1915–19.

19 M. Heidegger, *Unterwegs zur Sprache* (Pfullingen: Neske, 1982 [7th ed.]), p. 96.

20 Franco Volpi, *Heideggere Aristotele* (Padova: Daphne Editrice, 1984); "Dasein comme praxis: L'assimilation et la radicalisation heideggerienne de la philosophie pratique d'Aristote," in *Heidegger et l'idée de phénoménologie,* (Dordrecht: North Holland 1998), pp. 2–41; for the English translation see: "Dasein as *praxis*: the Heideggerian assimilation and the radicalization of the practical philosophy of Aristotle," in *Reading Heidegger from the Start,* pp. 90–129. See also Walter Brogan, "The Place of Aristotle in the Development of Heidegger's Phenomenology," in *Reading Heidegger from the Start,* pp. 213–27.

21 Hugo Ott,"The struggle with the faith of my birth," *Martin Heidegger. A Political Life,* translated by Allan Blunden (London: Harper Collins/ Basic Books, 1993), pp. 41–121. Note the statement by Karl Löwith's *Mein Leben in Deutschland vor und nach 1933* (Stuttgart, 1986), p. 45 cited by Ott at 121: "A Jesuit by education, he became a Protestant through indignation; a scholastic dogmatician by training, he became an existential pragmatist through experience; a theologian by tradition, he became an

atheist in his research, a renegade to his tradition cloaked in the mantle of its historian."

22 Cited by Bernhard Casper, "Martin Heidegger und die theologische Fakultät Freiburg 1909–23," *Kirche am Oberrhein*, edited by R. Bäumer et al., (Freiburg, 1980), pp. 534–41 at 541; H. Ott, *Martin Heidegger. A Political Life*, pp. 106–7.

23 M. Heidegger, *Zur Bestimmung der Philosophie. Gesamtausgabe*, 56/57, edited by Bernd Heimbüchel (Frankfurt: Klostermann, 1987).

24 Frithjof Rodi, "Die Bedeutung Diltheys für die Konzeption von 'Sein und Zeit. Zum Umfeld von Heideggers Kasseler Vorträgen (1925)," *Dilthey Jahrbuch für Philosophie und Geschichte der Geisteswissenschaften* 4 (1986-87), 161–77 at 168.

25 M. Heidegger, *Wegmarken, Gesamtausgabe*, 9, edited by F. W. von Herrmann (Frankfurt: Klostermann), p. 30; Kisiel, "The Deconstruction of Life (1919–20)," *The Genesis of Heidegger's Being and Time*," pp. 116–48.

26 M. Heidegger, *Phänomenologische Interpretationen zu Aristoteles: Einführung in die phänomenologische Forschung, Gesamtausgabe* 61, edited by W. Bröker and K. Bröker-Oltmanns (Frankfurt: Klostermann 1985), p. 35.

27 T. Kisiel, "Das Entstehung des Begriffsfeldes 'Faktizität' im Frühwerk Heideggers," *Dilthey Jahrbuch* 4 (1986–7), 91–120 at 92.

28 T. Kisiel, "On the Way to *Being and Time*: Introduction to the Translation of Heidegger's Prologomena zur Geschichte des Zeitbegriffs," *Research in Phenomenology* 15 (1985), 193–226; "The Genesis of *Being and Time*," Man and World 25 (1992), 21–37; and "Why the First Draft of *Being and Time* Was Never Published," *Journal for the British Society for Phenomenology* 20/1 (January 1989), 3–22.

29 Jacques Taminiaux, "The Reappropriation of the Nicomachean Ethics: *Poiesis* and *Praxis* in the Articulation of Fundamental Ontology," *Heidegger and the Project of Fundamental Ontology*, 111–43 at 115; J.-F. Courtine, "Martin Heidegger's 'Logical Investigations.' From the Theory of Judgment to the Truth of Being," *Graduate Faculty Philosophy Journal* 18/2-20 (1997).

30 See T. Kisiel, *The Genesis of Heidegger's Being and Time*; "Das Entstehung des Begriffsfeldes 'Faktizität' in Frühwerk Heideggers," *Dilthey-Jahrbuch* 4 (1986–7), 91–120; "The Missing Link in the Early Heidegger," *Hermeneutic Phenomenology*, edited by J. Kockelmanns (Washington, DC: University Press of America, 1988), pp. 1–40; and "Why the First Draft of *Being and Time* Was Never Published," *Journal of the British Society of Phenomenology* 20/1 (1989), 3–23; "Why students of Heidegger will have to read Emil Lask," *Man and World* 28 (1995), 197–240.

31 Kisiel, "Die Entstehung des Begriffsfeldes 'Faktizität'...," p. 103.

32 Hans Ruin, "Yorck von Wartenburg and the Problem of Historical Existence," *Journal for the British Society for Phenomenology* 25/2 (1994), 111–130.

33 Cited in Kisiel, "Die Entstehung des Begriffsfeldes 'Faktizität'...," pp. 104–5; see also 117–8; and Christoph Jamme, "Heideggers frühe Begründung der Hermeneutik," *Dilthey Jahrbuch* 4 (1987-87), 72–90 at 78–9.

34 William J. Richardson, "Heidegger's Fall," *American Catholic Philosophical Quarterly* 49/2 (1995), 229–53.

35 Carl Friedrich Gethmann, "Philosophie als Vollzug und als Begriff. Heideggers Identitätsphilosophie des Lebens in der Vorlesung vom Wintersemester 1921/23 und ihr Verhältnis zu 'Sein und Zeit'," *Dilthey Jahrbuch* 4 (1986-7), 27–53.

36 M. Heidegger, "Phänomenologische Interpretationen zu Aristoteles (Anzeige der hermeneutischen Situation)," edited by Hans-Ulrich Lessing, *Dilthey Jahrbuch* 6 (1989), 235–74 at 246. See Thomas Sheehan, "*Hermeneia* and *Apophansis: The Early Heidegger on Aristotle*," *Heidegger et l'idee de la phenomenologie* Eds. F. Volpi et al. Phenomenologica, Vol 108. (Dordrecht: Kluwer, 1976), pp. 252–71; Rudolf A. Makreel, "The genesis of Heidegger's phenomenological hermeneutics and the rediscovered 'Aristotle introduction' of 1922," *Man and World* 23 (1990), 305–20.

37 Heidegger, *Phänomenologische Interpretationen zu Aristoteles*, 108.

38 Manfred Riedel, "Seinsverständnis und Sinn für das Tunliche, Der hermeneutische Weg zur praktischen Philosophie," *Hören auf die Sprache*, pp. 131–63 at 142–3.

39 Heidegger, "Phänomenologische Interpretationen zu Aristoteles," p.109.

40 Heidegger, *Ibid.* 153. William Richardson, in "Heidegger's Fall," gives us a compendious summary of the dynamics of 'ruination,' pp. 242–3.

41 M. Heidegger, "Phänomenologische Interpretationen zu Aristoteles," p. 238.

42 Gadamer, "Der eine Weg Martin Heideggers," GW 3, 417–30 at 422; for the English translation, "Martin Heidegger's One Path," in *Reading Heidegger from the Start*, pp. 19–35.

43 Gadamer, "Erinnerungen an Heideggers Anfänge," GW 10, 6.

44 Riedel, "Hermeneutik und Gesprächsdialektik. Gadamers Auseinandersetzung mit Heidegger," *Hören auf die Sprache*, p. 104.

45 Riedel, *Ibid.*, p. 105, describes how Heidegger thought of his task: "asking about the Being of factical life in each one's own proper world, in the possible and (and real) *Lebenswelt*, toward which it comports itself in understanding and action; and... asking about the relational and

performative meaning of this comportment" in terms of the "singular having-been-set-in-motion (*Bewegtheit*) of factical life, which is
'enacted' (that is to say, 'is') '*in it*-self as it-self *for it*-self *proceeding
from it*-self, and in all this, *against itself*,' 'with the goal of determining
the meaning of 'Is.'" (The internal quotation is from Heidegger,
"*Phänomenologische Interpretationen zu Aristoteles*," 131.)

46 Taminiaux, "The Reappropriation of the Nicomachean Ethics: *Poiesis*
and *Praxis* in the Articulation of Fundamental Ontology," *Heidegger and
the Project of Fundamental Ontology*, p. 124.

47 Patrich H. Byrne, *Analysis and Science in Aristotle* (Albany: State
University of New York Press, 1997).

48 Taminiaux, *Heidegger and the Project of Fundamental Ontology*,
pp. 113–4.

49 Gadamer, "Rationalität im Wandel der Zeiten," GW 4, 23–36.

50 Fred Lawrence, "The Horizon of *Vorhandenheit*," *Believing to Understand: The Hermeneutic Circle in Gadamer and Lonergan* (unpublished
Doctoral Dissertation, University of Basel, 1976), pp. 13–55 [to appear
from University of Toronto Press].

51 Aristotle, *Nicomachean Ethics* VI, 5 1140a 24ff; 9, 1141b 33ff.

52 *Being and Time*'s transposition of this is "resoluteness" toward oneself,
the proleptical projecting of "wanting to have a conscience" that first
provides one's ability to be a whole (in the anticipation of death) its full
"transparency." (Riedel, *Hören auf die Sprache*, pp. 127–8.)

53 Aristotle, *Nicomachean Ethics* II, 2, 1103b 32, 34; 1106a 1–4; Riedel,
Hören auf die Sprache, pp. 143–5.

54 Riedel, *Hören auf die Sprache*, p. 127: "the roots of the transcendence in
practice from the viewpoint of *poiesis* – as if the idea of the good is determined from the horizon of producing. That motivates the emphasis
on the project-character of understanding, the orientation of action by
the projecting (and ultimately in terms of the self-project) of the that-for-
the-sake-of-which. This good is displaced back into Dasein." See Stanley
Rosen, "Heidegger's Interpretation of Plato," *The Quarrel Between Philosophy and Poetry: Studies in Ancient Thought* (New York, London:
Routledge, 1988), pp. 127–7.

55 K. Löwith, "The Occasional Decisionism of Carl Schmitt;" "Postscript:
The Political Decisionism of Martin Heidegger and Friedrich Gogarten's
Theological Decisionism;" and "European Nihilism: Reflections
on the Spiritual and Historical Background of the European War,"
Martin Heidegger and European Nihilism Ed. Richard Wolin, trans.
Gary Steiner (New York: Columbia University, 1995), pp. 137–69, 173–
234 at 215.

56 Gadamer, "Hermeneutik und ontologische Differenz," GW 10, 68–9.

57 Emilio Betti, *Die Hermeneutik als allgemeine Methodik der Geisteswissenschaften* (Tübingen: Mohr Siebeck, 1962).

58 See Gadamer's, "Hermeneutics as Practical Philosophy," and Hermeneutics as a Theoretical and a Practical Philosophy," in *Reason in the Age of Science,* translated by F. Lawrence (Cambridge: MIT Press, 1981), pp. 88–112, 113–38.

59 Heidegger, "Phänomenologische Interpretationen zu Aristoteles," p. 109.

60 Gadamer, "Praktisches Wissen," GW 5, 239.

61 On the theme of Gadamer vis-a-vis Plato, Francis Ambrosio, "Gadamer and Aristotle: Hermeneutics as Participation in Tradition," *Proceedings of the ACPA* 62 (1988), 174–82; and "Gadamer, Plato, and the Discipline of Dialogue," *International Philosophical Quarterly* 27 (March 1987), 17–32; Robert J. Dostal, "Gadamer's Continuous Challenge: Heidegger's Plato Interpretation," *The Philosophy of Hans-Georg Gadamer,* The Library of Living Philosophers, volume 24, ed. Lewis Hahn (Chicago and LaSalle: Open Court, 1997), pp. 289–307; Pierre Fruchon, "Herméneutique, Langage et Ontologie: un discernement du platonisme chez H.-G. Gadamer," *Archives de Philosophie* 36 (1973), pp. 529–68, 37 (1974) pp. 223–42, 353–75, 533–71; Jean Grondin, *Hermeneutische Wahrheit? Zum Wahrheitsbegriff Hans-Georg Gadamers* (Forum Academicum, 1982); Paulette Kidder, "Gadamer and the Platonic Eidos," *Philosophy Today* (Spring 1995), pp. 83–92; Walter Lammi, "Hans-Georg Gadamer's Platonic *Destruktion* of the Later Heidegger," *Philosophy Today* (Fall 1997), 394–404; Thomas Prufer, "Husserl, Heidegger Early and Late, and Aquinas," and "Scholium III (Chapter 12): Heidegger between (Gadamer's) Plato and Aristotle," *Recapitulations: Essays in Philosophy* (Washington, DC: Catholic University of America Press, 1993), pp. 72–90 and 110–12. P. Christopher Smith, *Hermeneutics and Human Finitude: Toward a Theory of Ethical Understanding* (New York: Fordham University Press, 1991); "The Ethical Dimensions of Gadamer's Hermeneutical Theory," *Research in Phenomenology* 18 (1988), 75–91; "H.-G. Gadamer's Heideggerian Interpretation of Plato," *Journal for the British Society for Phenomenology* 12 (October 1981), 211–29; Catherine Zuckert, *Postmodern Platos: Nietzsche, Heidegger, Gadamer, Strauss, Derrida* (Chicago: University of Chicago Press, 1996).

62 Jean-Luc Marion, "The *Ego* and *Dasein*," *Reduction and Givenness: Investigations of Husserl, Heidegger, and Phenomenology,* translated by T. A. Carlson (Evanston: Northwestern University Press, 1998), pp. 77–107, esp. 101–2.

63 Gadamer, *Plato's Dialectical Ethics: Phenomenological Interpretations Relating to the Philebus,* translated by R. M. Wallace (New Haven: Yale University Press, 1991); *Dialogue and Dialectic: Eight Hermeneutical*

Studies on Plato, translated by P. C. Smith (New Haven: Yale University Press, 1980); The *Idea of the Good in Platonic-Aristotelian Philosophy*, translated by P. C. Smith (New Haven: Yale University Press, 1986).

64 For an intellectual biography of Heidegger, see Otto Pöggeler, *Der Denkweg Martin Heideggers* (Pfullingen: Neske 1963, 1st ed.; 2nd ed. 1983 includes the important *Nachwort* [pp. 319–55]).

65 H.-G. Gadamer, "Über die Ürsprunglichkeit der Philosophie: I. Die Bedeutung der Philosophie für die neue Erziehung, II. Das Verhältnis der Philosophie zu Kunst und Wissenschaft," *Kleine Schriften I: Hermeneutik* (Tübingen: Mohr Siebeck, 1967), pp. 11–38 at 17, 19.

66 *Ibid.*, p. 18.

67 *Ibid.*, p. 20.

68 *Ibid.*, p. 21.

69 Austin Farrer, *Love Almighty and Ills Unlimited* (London: Collins/ Fontana, 1967/1966), p. 114.

70 I often translate the German word *Spiel* as game-play in order to suggest the game aspect of language-games, of sports, but also of "the game of life"; then, too, besides denoting the activity of playing in games and acting, play denotes drama, whether as artwork or as the drama of human existence. See Gadamer on game-play, WM 97–127/TM 101–34.

71 Gadamer finds himself in agreement with Wittgenstein, who hit upon the same insight completely independently. See PH 173–7.

72 GW 2, 59–60, translation my own. For an English translation of the essay, "On the Circle of the Understanding," see *Hermeneutics Versus Science?*, edited and translated by John Connolly and Thomas Keutner (Notre Dame: University of Notre Dame Press, 1988), pp. 68–78, especially 71–2.

73 Rowan Williams, "Suspicion of Suspicion: Wittgenstein and Bonhoeffer," *The Grammar of the Heart. New Essays in Moral Philosophy and Theology*, edited by Richard H. Bell (San Francisco: Harper & Row 1988), pp. 36–53 at 48.

74 *Ibid.*, p. 43.

75 Gadamer, "Temoignage et Affirmation," *La Testimonianza* Ed. E. Castelli (Instituto de Studi Filosofici: Rome, 1972), pp. 161–5 at 164.

76 As Gadamer says, "The classical ... is as Hegel says, 'that which signifies itself and so also interprets itself'. – Ultimately this means: the classical is what preserves itself, *because* it signifies itself and interprets itself ..." (WM 273–4/TM 289).

9 Hermeneutics in Practice: Gadamer on Ancient Philosophy

For Hans-Georg Gadamer, ancient philosophy consists, first and foremost, of the writings of Plato and Aristotle. As he points out in the lectures he gave on *The Beginning of Philosophy*, they left us the first complete texts. What we know of the "presocratics" is derived from fragments, many taken (out of context) from the texts of Plato and Aristotle. The meaning of these fragments can be determined, Gadamer argues, only by looking at them in their context, both textual and historical. To discover the "beginning of philosophy," Gadamer thus insists that we must proceed through a study of the writings of Plato and Aristotle.[1] Because Aristotle was a student of Plato who, despite his criticisms of his teacher, perpetuated the Platonic method of investigating things through *logos*, we must begin, indeed, primarily with Plato.

That is what Gadamer himself did. His first book, entitled *Plato's Dialectical Ethics*, was primarily a study of the *Philebus*. From the very beginning, Gadamer announced, he was interested in Plato's philosophy as it speaks to us today (PDE 7). Writing directly under the influence of his teacher, Martin Heidegger, Gadamer thought that he was able to recapture the original experience of philosophy by reading the dialogues – the equivalent as it were, in Edmund Husserl's terms, of returning to the things themselves. As a result, even though Gadamer's understanding of some important aspects of Plato's philosophy changed (particularly with regard to Plato's relation to Aristotle), Gadamer continued to find the first and perhaps purest expression of the character and grounds of his own work in Plato.[2]

In this essay, I will, therefore, begin by describing Gadamer's initial understanding of the nature and significance of Platonic philosophy in terms of dialogue and dialectic. Then I will give a brief account of Gadamer's explication of his own interpretative method in *Truth and Method*. Third, I will trace the way in which Gadamer changed his understanding of Plato, particularly in relation to Aristotle, as a result of his reflections on his own practice. Fourth, I will show how this new understanding of Plato provides the ontological foundation for Gadamer's own "hermeneutics." Finally, I will present some thoughts on the significance of the new reading Gadamer suggests not merely of Plato, but of the Western philosophical tradition as a whole. Gadamer's readings of ancient philosophers constitute not only a fundamental challenge to, but also a useful correction of, the mode of interpretation still dominant in Anglo-American philosophy. Unfortunately, I conclude, Gadamer does not go far enough. Fortunately, for us – and in accordance with Gadamer's own interpretive principles – there is further work to be done.

THE ORIGIN OF KNOWLEDGE IN DIALOGUE

In his first book, *Plato's Dialectical Ethics*, Gadamer contrasted Plato's presentation of his own philosophical intentions through a literary representation of Socrates' entirely unliterary and undogmatic existence with Aristotle's conceptual analysis.

> The conclusion that Aristotle misunderstood Plato is rightly felt to be impossible. But it is equally certain that in [Aristotle] what is truly Platonic does not make itself felt in the positive character that it still has even today, for us. Aristotle projected Plato onto the plane of conceptual explication ... [T]his projection cannot catch the inner tension and energy of Plato's philosophizing .... [T]he part of lived reality that can enter into the concept is always a flattened version – like every projection of a living bodily existence onto a surface. (PDE 7)

The part of "lived reality" Gadamer thought most important to recapture was, indeed, the centrality of dialogue in human attempts to understand the world.

Reading Plato in light of Heidegger, Gadamer proclaimed: "Philosophy, for Plato, is dialectic. Dialectic, as effort directed at the *logos ousias* (word or reason of being), is determined by the meaning of being" (PDE 8–9). As Socrates tells his auditors in the *Phaedo* (and Heidegger argues in *Being and Time*), being itself is not directly cognizable. The intelligibility of the world in which we find ourselves becomes manifest only indirectly through language or *logos*. Socrates' famous turn to an examination of the *logoi* thus represents *the* beginning of philosophy.

As Aristotle observes in the first sentence of his *Metaphysics*, human beings seek knowledge. We seek knowledge of the things around us, Gadamer explains, not merely so that we can use or manipulate them; we want to become familiar and so feel at home in all parts and aspects of our world. Our distinctive ability to speak is both the sign that we already possess some understanding and the means by which we can acquire more. Our ability to designate not only specific things with proper names but also classes of things with words reflects an ability to perceive that which makes the thing or things what they are, that which gives them their unity or identity as such. In itself, this ground of unity or identity is not visible or sensible; it is rather the intelligible ground of our ability to perceive different things as different, and not simply an unending, undifferentiated flux of sensations.

Human beings admittedly do not agree on what we see or how we understand things. That is why we come together to converse about them (or converse with ourselves silently in thought). The point of such conversations is, however, to bring out the truth about the things by sorting out the various claims made about them. We know that we have arrived at that truth when we come to an agreement about what we see disclosed. Socratic conversations thus gave rise to Aristotelian science. In and of itself, however, science is something less than a full conversation among living people. In scientific "conversations," inferences, or deductions, the interlocutor is a sort of generic, ideal figure who agrees to what has been established on the basis of accurate observation and reason. Because observation and reason are and ought to be impersonal, the specific characteristics of the interlocutor are irrelevant. In actual conversations, however, those speaking do not merely talk about the things; they also express themselves. In the actual process of conversing, people seek to learn not only about the things in question but also about themselves, as individuals and as a group or kind. This is what happens or should happen in genuine conversations. There are, Gadamer recognizes, other kinds of verbal exchanges. Acting out of certain passions, people may also seek to dominate or to refute, for the sake of refuting rather than for the sake of forwarding the investigation of the matter at hand. These are the degenerate, inauthentic, or "sophistical" kinds of arguments Socrates had to defeat in order to show his interlocutors that they were, in fact, ignorant and that they needed to seek knowledge along with him.

As Socrates indicates in his autobiographical statement in the *Phaedo* and argues more explicitly in the *Republic*, to know what something is, is to know what it is good for – as Aristotle would say, its "final cause" or use. In the *Phaedo*, Socrates thus not only puts forward his hypothesis about the ideas as the source of the character or being of things, as what makes things great, beautiful, or ... (as opposed to things being defined by their relations to others). He also suggests that we need to see how these ideas are related to one another, in particular, whether some do not encompass others. That which encompasses them all, that which explains and justifies all other things and does not itself require further justification, he argues more explicitly in the *Republic*, is the idea of the good. The process of dialectic sketched in the *Republic* thus involves an ascent to the most general cause and a descent to particular things. As Plato makes clear in the *Sophist*, it is not possible to understand the ideas in isolation; on the contrary, it is necessary to understand how they are related to each other. One must dialectically both gather things together according to what they share in common and discriminate among them according to their differences. Even the Good itself, as he explicates it in the *Philebus*, consists of a mixture of knowledge and pleasure.

Although for Plato the good is the chief ontological principle, Gadamer reminds his readers, the good becomes manifest only through an investigation of the actual, factual possibilities of human existence (*Dasein*), which are finite and temporal. In the two essays he published on Plato's *Republic* during the Third Reich, Gadamer thus attempted to show, first, how the radical reforms Plato proposed there constituted his response to the corruption of traditional Greek education by the sophists; that is, Gadamer tried to set Plato's dialogue in its own historical context. Then in "Plato's Educational State" he argued that the purpose of making mathematics the core of the new education was to turn the minds of future rulers away from sensible things to the purely intelligible. This turning of the soul was necessary not for the sake of making the philosopher-kings abstract theorists, however, but to free them from the influence of flattery and power politics. That was a lesson applicable to Gadamer's troubled age as well.[3]

MAKING EXPLICIT THE PRINCIPLES OF HIS OWN HERMENEUTICS

Reflecting on his own hermeneutical practice in *Truth and Method* more than a decade later, Gadamer defended his emphasis on discovering what remains true for us in older texts and his tendency, therefore, to amalgamate past with present (in this case, Plato with Heidegger). Gadamer insisted, moreover, that he was not merely laying out a method of reading texts. For Gadamer, "hermeneutics" describes the way in which human beings come to terms with themselves, each other, and the world in practice.

Redescribing what Heidegger called the "thrown" character of human existence, Gadamer pointed out that we all find ourselves born into a specific family at a certain place and time that we did not choose. The character of the people and circumstances in which we find ourselves has been shaped, moreover, by past events and the cumulative interpretation of their meaning we call our "tradition." In order to understand our "situation," which is to say ourselves and our world, we need, therefore, to acquire knowledge of this tradition. If we merely look back or upon the component parts of this tradition from the perspective of our current concerns and understanding, however, we do not move beyond the horizons of those current concerns. We do not even notice the horizon or limitations on our present understanding. For that we need to be "brought up short" by a perception of the fact that other people at other times saw things fundamentally differently. Why? Were they right? Only by regarding the past in its own terms, as different from the present, *and* as representing a potentially truer understanding of things will we perceive the limitations of our own unavoidable present-mindedness and, possibly, move beyond those limits to a wider, more encompassing view.[4] Simply viewing the past in its own terms will not suffice. Historicism or the historical consciousness is a peculiarly modern phenomenon. Insofar as it treats the past as simply past, as the product of a set of circumstances and expressing an understanding of the world that cannot possibly be duplicated in the present, an exclusively historical or scholarly reading of a past text precludes that text from challenging the truth of our current conceptions, including the historical insight itself. We do not learn anything new, which is to say that we do not really learn anything at all, about ourselves or the part of the tradition that shaped us contained in the particular text. To expand our horizon, we must not only identify the way in which things from the past are different; we also have to ask how they can be combined with or otherwise affect our current understanding. That is, in Gadamer's now-famous terminology, we must ultimately seek to fuse horizons.

In fact, Gadamer argues, such fusions are a part of our everyday experience. Confronted by new circumstances, we regularly have to try to apply and so extend what we have learned from the past. In the process, our understanding of ourselves and the world changes as we incrementally integrate current experiences with past memories. We see this process of gradual change through accumulation and selective deletion especially clearly in the medium of all understanding – language. New words are invented, others are taken over from foreign languages, some drop out. Over time, not merely the specific words, but the grammatical structure and even, finally, as in the transition from Latin to Italian, the whole language is altered. There is no progressive movement toward one all-encompassing language or understanding; but in opposition to Heidegger, Gadamer emphasizes, it is possible to translate texts from one language into another. In other words, no language is completely self-contained, impervious, or impenetrable by others. Meanings do change somewhat in the process of translation. There is no universal language, just as there is no universal, all encompassing view or viewpoint. Each is bounded by a horizon set in time and space.

UNDERSTANDING PLATO IN LIGHT OF ARISTOTLE'S CRITIQUE

Having emphasized the importance of reading past texts in their own terms as a step in coming to understand them as well as the tradition of which they and we are a part, Gadamer concluded, his previous reading of Plato had been somewhat defective. In *Plato's Dialectical Ethics*, he had used the tools of phenomenology in attempting to tie

Plato's dialectic to Socratic dialogue. In the process "Plato's doctrine was pushed all too much into the background" (DD 125). Resting his analysis on the literary difference between Plato's dialogues and Aristotle's treatises, Gadamer admitted, he had also "tried ... to circumvent the problem [of Aristotle's critique of Plato's doctrine of the ideas] by establishing that one first finds a definite, fully developed awareness of what a concept is as such, only in Aristotle." Reading the ancient philosophers in their own historical context, he now thought, "any interpretation which properly adheres to the subject matter under investigation here must start with the assumption that Aristotle's critique of Plato relies on something essential which he has *in common* with Plato." Despite "Aristotle's critique of the doctrine of ideas, ... the tendency to *harmonize* Plato and Aristotle predominated overwhelmingly in ancient times" as well as in "the Middle Ages despite all the disputes among schools which pervade that period" ("Amicus Plato Magis Amica Veritas," DD 194, 198). The tendency to contrast, if not oppose, Plato and Aristotle arose only in modern times in conjunction with the attempt of natural scientists such as Galileo to promote a mathematically based physics that could be associated with Plato, in place of the teleological view of nature, defended by Aristotle.

What Aristotle had in common with Plato, Gadamer argues, was "the 'turn' to the *logoi* known to us from its literary formulation in the *Phaedo*. Rather than naively or unreflectively trying to investigate natural events, both Plato and Aristotle asked (reflectively) how we come to know about them. Speech or *logos* was the vehicle or medium. "When he asks about the being of what is, Aristotle [also] begins with the question of how we speak about it" ("Amicus Plato Magis Amica Veritas," DD 198–9). Aristotle presents his critique of Plato's doctrine of the ideas in the *Metaphysics* as part of his survey and analysis of what has previously been said in response to the question, what makes something be what it is. Insofar as Aristotle himself claims that *todi ti* (this [thing] here) is what really is and grants the *eidos*, which answers the question, what (*ti esti*), only secondary status, he seems to move away from the *logos*. But in fact, Gadamer claims, Aristotle thus reveals the ultimate structure of all speaking. According to Plato as well, we are always speaking about some *thing*. Insofar as Plato analyzes the *logos* as the *koinonia* (community or coexistence) of ideas, he does not make it sufficiently clear that *logos* always refers to something outside of the speech itself. Rather than flattening out the multifaceted existential truth of Plato's literary presentation of the life of Socrates by transforming it into concepts, Gadamer argued in essays he wrote after *Truth and Method*, Aristotle filled out Plato's insight into the way *logos* reveals the meaning of being by applying it to nature and thus making it concrete.

As Aristotle indicates in his critique of the doctrine of ideas in the *Metaphysics*, Plato's understanding of the intelligible order of the world was essentially mathematical. But, Gadamer insists, it is important to understand what "mathematical" means. In many of the dialogues, Plato uses mathematical concepts, such as equality, as prime examples of supersensible, purely intelligible being (or "ideas" [*eide*]) that nevertheless help illuminate the order of the sensible world. In Book VII of the *Republic*, he also shows that the different concepts and forms of mathematics have an intelligible order or relation to each other. "Number, line, plane, and solid, each of which depends upon the previous one, have a natural order which gives a sequential structure to the mathematical sciences" (DD 202). Nevertheless, Gadamer argues in opposition to commentators such as Julius Stenzel, Plato did not think it was possible to deduce a rigid system or pyramid of ideas. The way in which mathematics provides a model of the intelligibility of the whole as it becomes manifest in *logos* is not in the logical deductions of more specific corollaries from general axioms as in geometry. It is rather in the concept or structure of the *arithmos* [number] as a unity of many.

As Plato presents it in the *Sophist* and *Statesman*, the process or method through which we discover what something is appears to be mathematical insofar as it is a process of division. Cutting things through the middle, we find out what something is by separating it gradually, in stages, from what it is not. At first it seems that the process should in principle be capable of producing a definition of everything in terms of how it is like and unlike all other things. However, Gadamer observes, the fact that the diairetic divisions in these dialogues are shown to be gratuitous insofar as they have no inherent necessity and that, as Aristotle points out, the result is already anticipated by the steps in the division indicates "that the whole procedure is not intended to arrive at a rigid systematization, a pyramid of ideas." A complete explication of everything in terms of everything else could never be completed. "One must," Gadamer thus concludes, "consider Plato's real insight to be that there is no collected whole of possible explications either for a single *eidos* or for the totality of the *eide*" (DD 203).

"What *is* revealed [in the Eleatic Stranger's teaching about the *koinonia* of the *eide* and the way in which that *koinonia* is not merely reflected in, but makes *logos* possible] is that the number as the unity of many is the ontological paradigm." Number is the ontological paradigm in three different respects: (1) The units that constitute numbers, as well as the numbers themselves are, like the ideas, purely intelligible. (2) The number constituted by the units is not merely the sum of its parts. As a whole, it and its parts acquire a character different from the constituent elements taken separately. As Socrates observes in the *Hippias Major*, taken separately, one and one are both odd; added together, however, one and one make two, and hence are even. (3) It is always possible to generate a new number by adding a unit. The series of such numbers or wholes is, therefore, infinite.[5]

Once we recognize the *arithmos* structure of Plato's understanding of both being and *logos*, Gadamer suggests, we see that Aristotle's critique of the ideas constitutes a response to two basic questions: (1) "is the *logos* properly understood when it is taken to be a reflection or repetition of the intelligible sort of being characteristic of number?" And (2) "if one should not be satisfied with the mere metaphors of the *Timaeus* (the manufacturing of the All by a demiurge), how is one supposed to conceive of the idea's really being *para tauta*, 'alongside' the things here, and of its developing an efficacy of its own?" (DD 206).

"The extension of the concept of the idea to all that can be said and meant is an inescapable consequence of orienting one's thought to the logos," Gadamer insists. That is, indeed, the task that Aristotle set himself. To fulfill it, he had to change or develop Plato's notions of the way in which the being of anything was defined by the *eidos* and expressed in *logos*.

If each word pointed to the intelligible unity of a thing, Aristotle saw, there would be as many ideas as words. That was too many, he objected. Plato merely doubled the number of things to be understood. That objection sounds absurd, Gadamer comments, but it points to the real problem: How could the ideas, which are said to exist separately, in themselves, cause or otherwise account for everything that is? The ideas are supposed to account for the organization of nature into species or kinds. But even in this best case, Aristotle shows, the ideas do not provide an adequate account or explanation. The "idea" of the species does not perpetuate itself by producing another human being. To show how things could actually come into being (rather than merely tell a story about a "superartist" who uses the ideas as models) and so perpetuate intelligible kinds or species of things in sensible form, Aristotle added efficient and final causes to the material and formal elements to be found in Plato. Even more important, by sorting out the different meanings of "to be," Aristotle was able to develop his notions of *dunamis* (potential) and *energeia* (actualization) and so substitute a biological for a mathematical explanation of things which are. In the *Sophist*, Plato had argued, in opposition to Parmenides, that it was not illogical or contradictory to speak or think of "what is not," if "what is not" refers to what something is different from. In that case, the speaker or thinker is not simultaneously affirming and denying that something is. Aristotle observes that "is not" can refer, in addition to nonexistence and being-different, to "not being yet" (*steresis*). As a result, he was able to redefine the way in which the *eidos* defined what something was.

There is a not-being in the *eidos* which has to do not with its relationship to other *eide* but with existence itself or, . . . of being deprived of something, *steresis*. Every natural process runs its course between *steresis* and *eidos*, Not-being and Being. Such not-being of the existent thing is dependent upon its eidetic determination *insofar as the latter is missing* in it. To this extent it is indeed defined by the *eidos*.

In Aristotle the way in which natural things are defined by their *eide* is, therefore, no longer mathematical. "The living thing which emerges from the seed does not simply assume another eidetic determination and it is not simply something "different," something defined by essentially different determinations, though if viewed *mathematically* it would be." It is defined, rather, in terms of its transition from the immature to the ripe. As that which is immanent in the thing as its potential, the *eidos* exists nowhere else. There is no separate "world" of the *eide* existing apart from or in addition to the things or beings they define.

Having reconceived the way in which the beings are defined by their *eide*, Aristotle had to reconceive the way in which that definition is expressed in *logos* as well. Here, too, Gadamer suggests, he improved upon his teacher.

For in a strange way Plato"s thinking on the *eidos* tends to obscure the actual sense of the *logos* insofar as he conceives of it as the combination of ideas with one another. For the *logos* itself implies more than a fitting together, more than a sum of essences. It is always a reference to something, to something which is here and now, a "this here" (*todi ti*), of which not only its essential definition may be expressed but to which much else besides may be attributed which is precisely not constitutive of its permanent essence. (DD 213)

By showing how the *eide* were immanent in the things rather than self-subsisting, Aristotle was also able to bring out the referential and descriptive rather than merely reflective character of language. Instead of merely opposing or contradicting Plato, Gadamer concluded, Aristotle's critique not only brought out the basic character but also fulfilled the intention of Plato's teaching concerning the ideas, in some respects better than Plato himself.[6]

THE FUNDAMENTAL CHARACTER OF THE GOOD

The two respects in which Gadamer found Aristotle's articulation of the way in which beings were defined by their *eide* and expressed in *logos* superior to the mathematical understanding to be found in the dialogues pointed back to the reasons Gadamer had initially looked for an original understanding of philosophy in Plato's literary depiction of Socrates. If truth is disclosed only in language, through conversation, the search for truth must have its origins in the concrete concerns of human existence. As Plato showed in his depiction of Socrates, it did. Human beings have to make choices all the time, and these choices imply knowledge of what is good. To convince people to join him in seeking for knowledge, Socrates thus had to show his interlocutors not only that they did not really know what is good, but also that knowledge of the good is what they, like all other human beings, need and desire above all else.

Knowledge of the good is not like other forms of knowledge; it does not consist of generalizations from empirical data or experiences, nor does it constitute the application of general rules to particular situations, nor it is deductive like geometry. In sum, it is not nor can it be acquired through *techne*. As presented in the Platonic dialogues, knowledge of the good is both moral and ontological. It responds to our most urgent need and yet is somehow constitutive of the whole. It does not, however, involve cognition of an abstract or self-subsisting "idea" of the kind Aristotle criticizes in his works on ethics. On the contrary, Gadamer maintains, reading Plato in light of Aristotle's critique, "we see how close the knowledge of the good sought by Socrates is to Aristotle's *phronesis*" (IG 33–4).

Gadamer explicitly rejects attempts to read either Plato or Aristotle in terms of their purported intellectual development. Werner Jaeger's attempt to trace Aristotle's development from Platonist to empiricist collapses, Gadamer argues, when we recall that Plato himself gives many of the same criticisms of the doctrine of the ideas in the *Parmenides* that Jaeger claims Aristotle "developed" only later, after he ceased to be a student of Plato. Gadamer admits that the Platonic dialogues can be divided according to structure. "The 'aporetic' dialogues, in which Socrates refutes his interlocutors without finally giving an answer to the question posed, represent one clearly defined type of Socratic discussion" (IG 22). In the *Republic*, Socrates plays a new role when he positively describes the just state. He also begins to tell the great myths. Nevertheless, Gadamer insists, Socrates' refutations of his interlocutors' claims to know what is good or virtuous lead, logically, to his own positive teachings. From beginning to end, the Platonic dialogues are centrally concerned with the "question about the good and, in particular, about the good in the sense of *arete*, the 'best-ness' of the citizen of the *polis*" (IG 21). There is a development in the sense of explicating and expanding upon a central theme, but there is not a change of doctrine or fundamental understanding.

Plato first shows Socrates disputing the sophists' claim to purvey a new *techne* of virtue. In the *Protagoras* he not merely exposes the extremely common understanding of the good as pleasure that underlay their purportedly radical new teaching (and so provides support for his own later claim in book six of the *Republic* [493ff.] that the sophists merely catered to public opinion). He also paradoxically concludes that virtue is not teachable, despite his own arguments showing that virtue is knowledge.

Virtue is not teachable, Gadamer explains, because it requires knowledge of the good, and such knowledge is not technical or merely instrumental. Virtue requires knowledge of the end or goal, the good; the sophists merely taught their students new rhetorical means of achieving the old, conventional ends of political life in Greece-prominence and wealth.

In order to achieve knowledge of the good, Socrates urges his interlocutors, they have to seek self-knowledge through a dialectical examination of their own opinions. Although Socratic dialectic sometimes appears to be a kind of *techne*, Gadamer argues, the emphasis on seeking self-knowledge shows that it is not. Socrates' interlocutors often think that he controls the conversation because he asks the questions. When they insist, therefore, on changing roles, they show themselves unable to ask questions effectively, because they do not understand that in asking the questions the interrogator is questioning himself as much as his interlocutor. To ask a question one must, moreover, possess a certain kind of knowledge. "Seeking and learning presuppose that one knows what one does not know, and to learn that, one must be refuted. Knowing what one does not know is not simply ignorance. It always implies a prior knowledge which guides all one's seeking and questioning. Cognition is always re-cognition." In the *Meno* where Socrates re-raises the question concerning the teachability of virtue, he thus argues that all learning is re-collection. In questioning ourselves about what we think, we remind ourselves of something that we already in a sense knew. "Knowledge of the good is always with us in our practical life. Whenever we choose one thing in preference to another, we believe ourselves capable of justifying our choice" (IG 57). In dialectically examining the grounds of our choices, Gadamer argues, we simultaneously come to recognize who we are, that is, how we understand ourselves, in distinguishing our own opinions, thoughts, and choices from other possibilities. As an attempt to discover who we are and what is good for us, in contrast to the rhetorical art of acquiring influence over others purveyed by the sophists, "[d]ialectic is not so much a *techne*–that is, an ability and knowledge – as a way of being. It is a disposition, or *hexis* in Aristotle's sense of the word, that distinguishes the genuine philosopher from the sophist" (IG 39).

Gadamer responds to those who, relying on Aristotle's critique of "Socrates" in the *Nicomachean Ethics* (1144b ff.) for identifying virtue with knowledge, would maintain a distinction between Plato's "intellectualization" of virtue and Aristotle's concept of *ethos* by pointing out that the educational scheme outlined in the *Republic* involves years of training for the sake of inculcating certain opinions and habits, the basis and rationale of which become known, if at all, only much later. Aristotle's concept of *ethos* (habituation) "is in complete agreement with what Plato and Socrates intended to say and is implicit in the total 'intellectualization' of *arete* articulated in Plato's dialogues" (IG 60).[7]

As in the *Protagoras*, so in the *Republic* Socrates identifies all four of the virtues with knowledge. In the *Republic*, it becomes clear, however, that the kind of knowledge uniting and so constituting virtue is *phronesis*.[8] The meaning of *phronesis* in Plato is broader than it is in Aristotle, Gadamer admits. Plato extended the customary meaning of the word, which had a primarily practical sense, to include theoretical knowledge for the sake of showing the intrinsic relation between theory and practice. That relation is not what we moderns imagine when we speak about the application of general "theoretical" principles or precepts to specific situations "in practice." The purpose of the education future rulers in the *Republic* receive in science and dialectic is not to make them abstract theoreticians, mathematicians, or scientists; nor is it to provide them with useful knowledge (e.g., of astronomy for the sake of understanding the climate or of mathematics for the sake of deploying troops). The goal of their extended education is, rather, to make the rulers "reasonable." It is not so much a matter of acquiring a specific kind of knowledge as it is the formation of character. Like Aristotle, Plato understands virtue not to consist in reasoning or *logos* per se, but in acting with or according to reason (*meta logou*). So understood, *phronesis* is not merely different from both *techne* and *episteme*; it involves a more encompassing kind of knowledge. Socrates' quest for a definition of the good in human life thus leads to the broader, more "ontological" questions concerning the idea of the good raised in the *Republic*.

The question concerning the good in human life does not arise, Gadamer admits, directly out of the unity of the virtues asserted in Book IV. It seems, on the contrary, to arise almost as an afterthought in Book VI when Glaucon asks Socrates to show how the just city he has described could possibly come into being. The crucial requirement is that philosophers become kings. This requirement is paradoxical, because it is not at all clear how the theoretical studies of the philosophers would make them superior rulers.[9] In order to become philosophers, Socrates observes, future rulers need to study the sciences, especially mathematics, as well as the music and gymnastics required of the soldiers. The purpose of the mathematical studies Socrates outlines in Book VII is not to make the guardians expert mathematicians or even merely to teach them skills useful for waging war and managing property; it is, rather, as indicated by the allegory of the cave, to free their souls from an attachment to sensible things by introducing them to the purely noetic. By teaching them the difference between the enduring and the transitory, Gadamer argued in "Plato's Educational State," the guardians' education in mathematics immunized them against the temptations of people in power to use it to enrich themselves and to be seduced by flatterers. In this earlier essay, Gadamer thus emphasized the effects more than the content of the guardians' education.

In *The Idea of the Good in Platonic-Aristotelian Philosophy,* Gadamer points out that the guardians' study of mathematics is supposed to prepare them for a dialectical examination of the presuppositions, assumptions, or "hypotheses" of all the particular forms of knowledge, including mathematics, and that this examination is supposed to culminate in knowledge of the first and most fundamental of the ideas, the idea of the good. What that idea is, however, remains rather obscure.

The desirability of knowledge of the good is introduced in the *Republic* in terms of the human good, Gadamer emphasizes. In beginning to specify what the guardians will need to know, Socrates observes that many people would settle for the apparently noble or apparently just, but that no one would accept the only apparently good. Knowledge of what is truly good is, therefore, what all human beings most want. Most believe that the good is pleasure. Because people distinguish good and bad pleasures, that cannot be correct. Those with *phronesis* believe that it is knowledge. As Socrates pointed out earlier, knowledge (as opposed to opinion) is possible only of things that do not change. Knowledge must, moreover, ultimately be knowledge of the whole (if it is not to remain partial and hence potentially deceptive). Such knowledge constitutes the greatest learning (*megiston mathema*), because it involves or includes everything that is.

By comparing the good to the sun, which produces the light necessary not only for vision but also for growth, Socrates suggests that the good is the source of the necessary condition not only for knowledge of the truth but also for being itself. It is not clear, however, how the good makes either knowledge or intelligible existence possible. As the source, Socrates initially says that the idea of the good is "beyond" being. However, when he later describes the highest and last study as the dialectical investigation of everything that truly is, i.e., the ideas, he says that the good must be treated in "just the same way" (*hosautos*). Later commentators have mistakenly been tempted to take one of the suggested alternatives. Some, like the neoplatonists, have argued that as the source of intelligibility and being, the idea of the good is beyond both, not only ineffable, but also unintelligible. Others, like Aristotle, have argued that the good has no separate existence; like all other ideas, the good is to be found only in the various "goods" or good things. According to Gadamer, neither alternative is required by, or adequate to, the text.

Socrates was not able to explicate the meaning of his metaphor in conceptual terms. To do that, Gadamer suggests, we later readers need to employ Aristotle's distinction between *poiein* (doing or making) and *paschein* (suffering something) in delineating the structure of *nous* (intellect).[10] We also need to use the "indirect tradition," in particular Aristotle's account of Plato's teaching concerning the one and the indeterminate dyad, as an indication of the way in which one of his writings, the *Philebus*, sheds light on the content of his lecture, i.e., unwritten, oral teaching, "On the Good."

In the *Philebus*, the question concerning the good is taken up, as in the *Republic*, explicitly in terms of the human good. However, we are reminded, almost immediately, both of the universal nature of the good and the necessity of understanding it dialectically. As in the *Republic*, the question is whether the good is constituted by knowledge or pleasure. This time, however, the advocates of pleasure are not simply dismissed. On the contrary,

it seems as if two irreconcilable basic attitudes [a]re being pitted against each other here. For just as it steers the behavior of any living thing, the pleasure principle has a kind of obvious predominance, unlimited and overpowering, in the human being too. That one should argue for this principle in [rational] statement and answer would seem to be self-contradictory, and hence it is entirely consistent that those who do advocate it do indeed resist giving justification of their position. (IG 105)

Insisting that pleasure is obviously and entirely good, Philebus thus withdraws from the discussion. To engage the young man who replaces him as interlocutor in a dialectical examination of the cons- titution of the good, Socrates has to convince Protarchus to distin- guish among different kinds of pleasure – and of knowledge. Only by drawing distinctions can Socrates show him the true character or constitution of the Good (and everything else) as a mixture.

To show Protarchus the character or constitution of all things, Socrates introduces the doctrine of the four genera: the unlimited (into which pleasure is immediately placed along with other relative sensations like hot and cold, big and small, more or less); that which limits (including number); the mixture of the two that constitutes any particular thing; and its cause (nous). Plato distinguishes him- self from the Pythagoreans by adding the last two kinds and so dis- tinguishing, as they did not, between the noetic elements and the concrete manifestations of them. "This doctrine has far-reaching consequences for any appropriate understanding of Plato's dialectic and of the problems of chorismos (separation) and methexis (partici- pation)," Gadamer emphasizes. "If limit and determinacy do not ex- ist apart, for themselves, then neither does the entire noetic realm of the ideas – any more than do the ingredients of this potion of life that is supposed to be mixed. That the noetic world of num- bers and pure relationships belongs together with their dialectical opposite, the apeiron, implies that they are only abstracted aspects of this third thing called the 'mixed'" (IG 113). As we see in the particular case in question, pleasure and knowledge do not exist apart from one another. It is impossible to feel pleasure without awareness of it; likewise, it is impossible for a living being to have knowledge without taking pleasure in it. We ourselves are both. The distinctions we draw in our attempt to come to understand ourselves and the world through a dialectical investigation of the parts are noetic; they do not exist "somewhere" apart, in another world.

Parts become manifest and understood as such only in the context of the whole of which they are components. As that which makes any particular mixture "good," the good is not and cannot be simply "one." It is both "in" all those mixtures said to be good, and yet separable in thought from them. Insofar as it is purely noetic, the good is not visible as such. It becomes manifest, Socrates suggests, only in the measuredness or symmetry of the beautiful. (As Gadamer says in Heideggerian language, it shines forth or appears as the beautiful.) As Socrates indicates with the examples of writing and music, all arts (or kinds of knowledge) depend upon the identification of such an eidetic order or structure, in which the noetic elements are known only in relation to each other.

Because the *apeiron* is an element of all mixtures, the possible concrete manifestations and/or wholes to be dialectically analyzed is infinite. Each thing or being can be known only as a whole, but there are many, infinitely many wholes. The task of dialectic is, correspondingly, unending as well. In living things, of which we are one kind, the mixture is, moreover, subject to change. The question constantly arises, therefore, what should be added or subtracted. As Gadamer repeatedly emphasizes, human life is distinguished by the need to make choices. Dialectic is not, therefore, a *techne* like writing that one learns or that some know and others do not. "Thinking, to be sure, is an art, but [it is] an art that is practiced by everyone and that one is never finished learning. And how to live is just as little an art that one could ever be finished learning" (IG 121).

At this point, Gadamer's understanding of Plato with the help of Aristotle's conceptual analysis merges almost completely with his own understanding of the hermeneutical character of human existence. Our lives are defined by our understanding of ourselves and the world. We constantly have to re-evaluate and reconceive our understanding of ourselves and the world, however, in light of new experiences. We never begin merely with or as a "blank slate." We begin, rather, seeing things as they come to light in the horizon of our particular time and place. Like a series of numbers, each horizon constitutes a whole in itself. Each horizon can, however, be expanded and so changed as a whole through the process of addition or accretion. The series or number of possible horizons (views or understandings) is infinite. The *arithmos* structure Gadamer finds in

Plato not only describes but also provides the ontological foundation for his own hermeneutics. Gadamer makes the extent to which he understands his own thought to be a continuation and perpetuation of Platonic–Aristotelian philosophy explicit in the preface to *The Idea of the Good* when he urges his readers to

take what follows as an attempt to read the classic Greek thinkers...not from the perspective of the assumed superiority of modernity ...but instead with the conviction that philosophy is a human experience that remains the same and that characterizes the human being as such, and that there is no progress in it, but only participation. (IG 6)

RE-PRESENTING PLATO

By challenging the standard interpretation of Plato which identifies Plato with a "two worlds" view of intelligible and sensible experience and with a certain chronological development of his teaching concerning the ideas and which is still dominant both in Anglo-American schools of philosophy and on the continent, Gadamer asks his readers to reconsider and reconceive their understanding of the entire Western tradition.[11] As he intends, his work should provoke further study and thought. More detailed studies would be necessary, for example, to show that the questions Socrates raises about the character and unity of human virtue in the "early" elenchtic dialogues lead (necessarily?) to the broad ontological doctrines of the so-called "middle" dialogue, such as the *Republic* and *Phaedo*, and that the teaching concerning the ideas enunciated there is, in fact, basically the same as, or at least compatible with, what appear to be fundamentally different doctrines enunciated in "late" dialogue, such as the *Philebus* and *Sophist*.

In attempting to show the continuity not merely between Plato and Aristotle but between the ancient philosophers and modern thought, Gadamer makes sweeping claims and arguments that weave together a variety of texts. He often violates his own strictures about the need to read the dialogues as discrete works or wholes in which the character of the particular participants must be related to the specific setting and action. He does not pay any attention to the differences among Plato's philosophical spokesmen

(Parmenides, Socrates, Timaeus, the Eleatic Stranger, and the Athenian Stranger) or to the dramatic dating and setting of the dialogues. In amalgamating Plato and Aristotle, he is not content to point out the way in which both philosophers begin with an examination of the *logoi*. He also denies that the ideas have any kind of separate existence. As a result, he not only makes it difficult to understand why Plato and Aristotle both claimed that the theoretical life was superior to the practical, but he also obscures what would appear to be a fundamental difference between their ancient philosophy and his modern hermeneutics. According to Socrates in the *Republic*, the only sorts of things of which we can have real knowledge are those that never change (and are, therefore, eternal). Although Gadamer admits that the *eide* are purely noetic, it is difficult to see how he could admit the existence of any eternal truths or ideas. As Gadamer himself emphasizes, theory and practice tend to merge in his hermeneutics. Although Plato and Aristotle agree that the theoretical life involves the highest and most intense form of activity, both preserve the difference between theory and practice.

As Gadamer also sees, these ancient philosophers understood theory quite differently from us moderns. For them, the life of theory consisted of a life of contemplating the eternal truths. For those educated in modern natural science, theory consists of a set of generalizations that are to be tested or applied in practice. These different understandings of "theory" point, moreover, to the greatest provocation Gadamer provides his readers. In his recently published "Reflections on His Philosophical Journey," Gadamer explains that he turned to hermeneutics, in general, and the study of ancient philosophy, in particular, in order to find a means of uniting the various sciences in a way that had not proved possible for those who used modern natural science as a model of knowledge. Plato and Aristotle were able to give a unified understanding of the world and the various kinds of knowledge human beings can acquire of it, because they saw both the whole and its parts in terms of ends, purpose, or the "Good." Modern natural science explicitly broke with this "teleological" understanding. How then does Gadamer intend to bring it back within his general "hermeneutic"? He himself never explicitly says. Instead, we might say, he poses the question, the most important question faced by his contemporaries.

NOTES

1 In the lectures he gave on *The Beginning of Philosophy* in 1967 and, again, in 1988, Gadamer explained that there are three interconnected meanings of "beginning": that which comes first in time or history, that which is seen to be the point of origin from the perspective of the end, and that which finds itself in process without knowing where it is going. As Plato understood it, philosophy was an open-ended search for knowledge, not the attainment or possession thereof (BP 15–18, 20). Gadamer endorses Plato's "original" understanding of philosophy and thus the third sense of beginning; in contrast to Heidegger, Gadamer does not think that philosophy has or ever can come to an end. It cannot have a precise beginning in the second sense, therefore, or in the first. Cf. TM, "Foreword to the Second Edition," xxxvii–xxxviii.

2 "Reply to Donald Davidson," *The Philosophy of Hans-Georg Gadamer*, Library of Living Philosophers, vol. 24, ed. Lewis Edwin Hahn (Chicago: Open Court, 1997), p. 433: "[M]ore and more what both of us mean by philosophy is what we find in Plato."

3 The political relevance and significance of Gadamer's Plato studies under the Nazi regime have recently become a subject of some debate. See my *Postmodern Platos: Nietzsche, Heidegger, Gadamer, Strauss, Derrida* (Chicago: University of Chicago Press, 1996), pp. 78–84, Fred Dallmayr, "Hermeneutics and Justice," in *Festivals of Interpretation* (Albany: State University of New York Press, 1990), pp. 95–105; Theresa Orozco, "The Art of Allusions: Gadamer's Philosophical Interventions under National Socialism," trans. Jason Geiger, *Radical Philosophy: A Journal of Socialist and Feminist Philosophy* 78 (July/August 1993), pp. 18–41, and my reply in "On the Politics of Gadamerian Hermeneutics," Bruce Krajewski, ed., *Gadamer's Repercussions: Scaling Philosophical Hermeneutics* (Berkeley: University of California Press, 2001). See also Robert Dostal's comments in the first chapter of this volume.

4 Gadamer made the difference between what he means by reading a text in its own terms and Leo Strauss's insistence that we "understand an author as he understood himself" clear in TM 535 when he objected: [Strauss] seems to consider it possible to understand what one does not understand oneself but what someone else understands, and to understand only in the way that the other person himself understood. And he also seems to think that if a person says something, he has necessarily and fully understood 'himself' in the process." Gadamer argues, on the contrary, that "[w]hen we try to understand a text, we do not try to transpose ourselves into the author's mind but ... into the perspective within which he has formed his views" (TM 292). That is, we first have to try to understand the author

in his own historical context. However, "[j]ust as the events of history do not in general manifest any agreement with the subjective ideas of the person who stands and acts within history, so the sense of a text in general reaches far beyond what its author originally intended" (TM 372). According to Gadamer, we need to engage in a dialogue with the text and that means we must ask it or its authors questions. Those questions change, however, with the changing circumstances of the reader. So do the answers, therefore, and the meaning of the text. There are no eternal problems.

5 Gadamer owes much of his analysis of the *arithmos* structure of being, according to Plato, to Jacob Klein. In *Greek Mathematical Thought and the Origin of Algebra*, trans. Eva Brann (Cambridge: MIT Press, 1968), Klein argued that Plato had progressed beyond the Pythagoreans in two decisive respects. First, he had distinguished the intelligible units we use to count various things from the things themselves; the Pythagoreans had simply identified the two in their claim that everything was number. Second, he recognized the difference between the unity or character of the number and its constituent parts. This difference was crucial for understanding Plato's theory of the ideas, especially the *koinonia* of the *eide*. In the *Sophist*, Klein pointed out, being is shown to be identical with neither rest nor motion, but is said somehow to encompass both. The difference between this arithmological conception of being and the Greek concept of *arithmos* was simply that in the latter case the component units were all the same whereas in the former case the components were different. Gadamer goes beyond Klein (a) in attributing the same *arithmos* structure to *logos* and (b) in emphasizing the infinity of the number series.

6 In Heidegger's lecture course on *Plato's SOPHIST* in 1924–5 (trans. Richard Rojcewicz and Andre Schuwer [Bloomington: Indiana University Press, 1997]) he argued (pp. 5–9) that we (moderns) need to approach Plato through Aristotle, precisely because Aristotle worked out the meaning of Plato's insights more clearly on a conceptual level. In his writings on ancient philosophy after *Truth and Method*, Gadamer uses Aristotle's critiques of Plato in precisely that fashion, to bring out Plato's intended meaning. As Robert J. Dostal reports in "Gadamer's Continuous Challenge: Heidegger's Plato Interpretation," *The Philosophy of Hans-Georg Gadamer*, p. 290, Gadamer observed in his preface to the recently published sketch of Heidegger's 1922 Aristotle project: "When I today once again read this first part of the introduction to Heidegger's studies of Aristotle...it is as though I have rediscovered the clue to my own philosophical development." "Heideggers 'theologische' Jugendschrift," in Hans-Ulrich Lessing, ed., *Dilthey-Jahrbuch*, bd. 6 (Goettingen:

Vandenhoeck & Ruprecht, 1989), p. 229. In his autobiographical "Reflections on My Philosophical Journey," in *The Philosophy of Hans-Georg Gadamer*, pp. 10–12, Gadamer himself traces the fundamental elements of his later understanding of the commonality of Plato and Aristotle – their beginning with the *logoi* – as well as the distinction between *phronesis* and *techne* to Heidegger.

7 According to Gadamer, "The fact that Aristotle – in half agreeing with 'Socrates' – takes the paradoxical equation of virtue and knowledge in Plato and Socrates literally and 'corrects' their mistakes, can . . not be advanced as a counterargument. Aristotle has a way of taking statements not as they were intended, but literally, and then demonstrating their one-sidedness. Aristotle's use of dialectic consists in balancing off the one-sidedness of one person's opinion against the one-sidedness of someone else's. And while often doing violence in the process, he thereby succeeds in better articulating his own position and also in conceptualizing previously unquestioned presuppositions" (IG 60).

8 There is specific textual evidence for both Gadamer's claims that, according to Plato's Socrates, virtue must be first experienced as a kind of habit or characteristic attitude, in order to be understood later, and that the virtues are, really, *phronesis*. In Book III (409b–e) Socrates argues that, in contrast to the doctor who needs to see as many cases of disease as possible in order to learn how to cure them, the person who will become a judge must not be exposed to injustice until he or she is quite old. The person who learns early on how to calculate his or her advantage at the expense of others will never understand what justice is. Likewise in describing the character of the education of the philosopher-king with his famous image of the cave in Book VII, Socrates observes that "the other virtues of a soul, as they are called, are probably somewhat close to those of the body. For they are really not there beforehand and are later produced by habits and exercises, while the virtue of exercising prudence is more than anything somehow divine" (518e). Gadamer himself does not mention the discussion of the education of the judge in contrast to the doctor and refers to 518e only in passing. Only later in the chapter does he acknowledge that the definitions of the virtues in Book IV in terms of the city are all actually in terms of correct opinion, not knowledge. He blurs the difference here in order to emphasize the continuity from the "early" Socratic dialogues to the more "doctrinaire" *Republic* .

9 As in his earlier essays on the *Republic* (DD 48–50, 73–6), in IG 70, Gadamer argues that the description of the "city in speech" does not constitute a blue print for actual political reform. All the requirements for its actualization – the abolition of the family, the rule of philosophers, and the expulsion of everyone over ten years of age – are clearly impossible.

Implicitly contesting Leo Strauss's interpretation in *The City and Man* (Chicago: Rand McNally, 1964), pp. 52–130, and "Plato," in the *History of Political Philosophy* (Chicago: University of Chicago Press, 1963), 1st ed., pp. 7–63; however, Gadamer insists that the point is not merely to show the impracticality of the ideal. "Are we supposed to read this political utopia only negatively and be convinced by it only of the irreconcilability of theoretical and civic life? If so, a great expenditure of intelligence and wit has been wasted."

10 In explicating the meaning of Socrates' comparison between the sun and the Good, Gadamer argues, that the "light" in which the truth of beings becomes manifest is thinking. Beings are perceived as such only in thought. "In Aristotle too, "nous enables, 'makes' (*poiei*) thinking *hos hexis tis* (as a kind of condition), just as light 'makes potential colors into actual colors' (*De anima* 410a14 ff.)." (IG 88–9) It seems strange to this reader that Gadamer attributes this distinction between affecting and being affected only to Aristotle, because Socrates makes it both in arguing that soul is immortal in the *Phaedrus* (245c) and in explicating Protagoras' teaching in the *Theaetetus* (156a–b); the Eleatic Stranger also suggests it as definition of being in terms of power (*dunamis*) in the *Sophist* (247d–e). To be sure, Plato's Socrates himself does not understand being in this way. Gadamer does not usually differentiate Plato's philosophical spokesmen or the doctrines, however. On the contrary, he tends to combine them in his understanding of Plato's thought or intention.

11 Relying on Aristotle, *Metaphysics* 987a32–b10, 1078b122–1079a4, 1086a37–b11, scholars such as Terence Irwin, *Plato's Ethics* (New York; Oxford University Press, 1995) and Gregory Vlastos, *Socrates: Ironist and Moral Philosopher* (Ithaca: Cornell University Press, 1991) distinguish the "moralist" Socrates from Plato, the theorist of the ideas. Richard Kraut, "Introduction," *Cambridge Companion to Plato* (Cambridge: Cambridge University Press, 1992), sketches the common view not only of the difference between Socrates and Plato but also of the chronology of the composition of the dialogues.

10 Gadamer's Hegel

"So muße vor allem Hegels Denkweg erneut befragt wer-
den." ("Above all else, the path of Hegel's thought must be
interrogated anew.") *(GW 2, 505)*

I

Gadamer's philosophical hermeneutics is as much a reaction as an
initiation: a reaction against a relativistic historicism that "locked"
speakers and actors "inside" worldviews; a reaction against the over-
whelming prestige of the natural sciences and the insistence on
methodology inspired by that success; and a reaction against the
"bloodless academic philosophizing" of neo-Kantian philosophy
and its perennialist "great problems" approach to the history of
philosophy.[1] But in several of his autobiographical remarks, Gadamer
singles out an opponent that seems to loom oddly large in his remi-
niscences about provocations. "Using Heidegger's analysis, my starting point was a critique of German Idealism and its Romantic traditions" (PG 27), he writes in one such recollection. And in the same
essay, he writes of trying to avoid or to "forfeit" (*einbüßen*) "*the fun-
damentum inconcussum* of philosophy on the basis of which Hegel
had written his story of philosophy and the Neo-Kantians their history of problems – namely, self-consciousness" (PG 7). And later,

So I sought in my hermeneutics to overcome the primacy of self-consciousness, and especially the prejudices of an idealism rooted in consciousness...
(PG 27)

I want to explore in the following what Gadamer might mean
by giving to hermeneutics the task of "overcoming the primacy of

self-consciousness," and to ask whether it is really Hegel in his sights
as he attempts to do so.

II

We need first to attend to the conflicting strands of deep solidarity with Hegel, coupled with just as deep a rejection. With respect
to the former strand, there is much to cite. Indeed, the selection of
Hegel as such a principal opponent is somewhat odd because there
are so many passages throughout Gadamer's writings that warmly
embrace Hegel as a comrade-in-arms. While the major influences
on Gadamer's development of a philosophical hermeneutics are un-
questionably Plato, Aristotle, and Heidegger, Hegel is not far behind,
as the epigram above already indicates. This is so for a number of obvious and not so obvious reasons.

   In the first place, one would expect from Gadamer a sympathetic
embrace of Hegel's own reaction against Kantian formalism, an
embrace of Hegel's denial of transcendental subjectivity and pure
practical reason, an embrace of Hegel's attack on philosophies of
transcendence or "the beyond" (*Jenseitsphilosophie*), and so Hegel's
attempt to situate or embed the human subject in time, and an embrace of Hegel's attack on all attempts to understand concepts, or
language as means employed by a subject, or as rules applied by
a subject. The Heideggerian and Gadamerian "dialectic" between
"being in a world" (and being always already subject to a particular
life-world) and "having a world" (being a potentially critical, reflective subject of such a world) was already clearly announced by and
explored by Hegel (PG 36). And Gadamer sees that thereby Hegel
had already anticipated a great deal of the dialectic of later European philosophy. Hegel had understood that we would need a way of
achieving this rejection of formalism and this socio-historical
"embedding" without ending up with a kind of sociological, empirical, descriptive, nonphilosophical enterprise, and with a diverse
plurality of incommensurable language games (an option already on
the horizon in Herder). And all this must be accomplished without re-
animating a new hope for some decisive meta-language or transcendental philosophy of necessary conditions for the possibility of sense-
making, experience, practical life and so on; without re-animating a
new hope for temporally and methodologically stable conditions,

"scientifically" arrived at by a proper "control," or methodology (what turned out to be the neo-Kantian temptation).

It is thus no surprise that, in the exciting calls for a new "life" philosophy swirling throughout Germany in Gadamer's early adulthood, he would recall and astutely take his bearings from such a passage as the following from the Preface to Hegel's *Phenomenology of Spirit*.

The form of study in ancient times differs from that of the modern period in that study then was a thorough process of education appropriate for a natural consciousness. In specific probing of each aspect of its existence and in philosophizing about all that occurs, it generated for itself a universality actively engaged in the whole of its life. In the modern period on the other hand, the individual finds that the universal [*die abstrakte Form*] is already prepared for him. It would therefore be better to say that in his effort to grasp it and to make it his own he directly forces the inner essence into the open without the mediatory experience of the natural consciousness. Thus the generation of the universal here is cut off from the manifold of existence – the universal does not emerge out of that manifold. The task now is not so much to purify the individual of his immediate dependency on his senses and to raise him to the substance which thinks and is thought, as it is the reverse, namely, to actualize the universal and to infuse it with spirit by dissolving the fixed determinations of thought.[2]

Hegel's attempt to "infuse" the traditional categories of the understanding "with spirit" (*sich begeistern*) (HD 16), and so, in his *Phenomenology*, his attempt to understand the determinacy and authority of such discriminations by understanding the actual roles they play in a social community, and in their systematic inter-relatedness across many different activities of such a community, looks like an attempt to construe norms and principles as having a "life" of their own that in principle is quite close in spirit to Gadamer's two-pronged hermeneutical attack on transcendentalism and relativism.

Moreover, any claim that we have lost something "vital" that was a taken-for-granted aspect of ancient Greek life would obviously be welcome to Gadamer (whose great disagreement with Heidegger stems from Gadamer's resolute refusal to see his beloved Plato as "the origin of Western nihilism") and Gadamer indeed sometimes writes in almost a tone of gratitude for Hegel's philosophical rehabilitation of Greek thinkers as philosophers. He even goes so far as to refer to the Greeks "and their latest and greatest follower, Hegel"

(PG 15).[3] As we shall see shortly, Gadamer will disagree with Hegel's appropriation of the ancient art of dialectic, with Hegel's account of the deficiencies in the Greek theory of subjectivity, and with Hegel's readings of key passages, but he still credits Hegel, alone among the Titans of modern philosophy – Descartes, Spinoza, Leibniz, Locke, Hume, and Kant – with an appreciation of the "speculative" moment in Greek thought, an appreciation that remained unique in the history of modern philosophy until Heidegger.[4]

Indeed, only Hegel and Heidegger (and, one should now of course also say, Gadamer) have shown how philosophy itself should be understood not merely to have a history, but to be its history, that the work of philosophy itself is a speculative recollection of its history, and because it is so speculative and philosophical, it so "reconceptualizes" (aufhebt, cancels, preserves, and raises up) historical "thinking and knowing" that the objects of study should no longer count as merely historical texts. ("The first person who wrote a history of philosophy, that was really such, was also the last to do so – Hegel") (PG 35).[5] As we shall also see, there are various ways of comprehending philosophical recollection as a living conversation, ranging from Heidegger's "destruction" of the still living, still ontologically pernicious Western metaphysical tradition, to Hegel's developmental account of how "they" were trying, incompletely, to accomplish what "we" are still trying, more completely, to accomplish, to Gadamer's own account of the eternally inexhaustible residue of meaning in past texts and events, but the denial of any separation between philosophy and its history, and so the refusal to see past philosophers and writers as failed versions of us certainly unites them. At the end of the First Part of *Truth and Method* Gadamer writes,

Hegel states a definite truth, inasmuch as the essential nature of the historical spirit consists not in the restoration of the past but in thoughtful mediation with contemporary life.[6]

Finally, Gadamer makes clear that he understands the radicality of Hegel's enterprise; he especially understands how decisively Hegel broke with "the metaphysical tradition" so constantly under attack by Heidegger and his followers. Whatever Hegel is up to in his account of "spirit's experience of itself" in his *Phenomenology*, and in his treatment of "thought's self-determinations" in his *Science of Logic*, it cannot be understood as a continuation of the "substance metaphysics of the Western tradition" (PG 34). Gadamer realizes that Hegelian spirit, *Geist*, refers just as little to an immaterial substance as *Dasein* refers to human nature.[7] He notes that in pursuing his own life-long goal of attacking traditional, substance metaphysics, "I do not stand alone in all this; Hegel also held such a view" (PG 34).[8] He even goes so far as to write some things that stand in some considerable tension with what he also says about the need to overcome Hegel's absolutization of the principle of self-consciousness.

In particular, Hegel's powerful speculative leap beyond the subjectivity of the subjective Spririt established this possibility and offered a way of shattering the predominance of subjectivism ... Was it not Hegel's intention, also, [i.e., together with Heidegger after the latter's "turn" – RP] to surpass the orientation to self-consciousness and the subject–object schema of a philosophy of consciousness? (PG 37)[9]

III

That question is somewhat rhetorical, of course, and Gadamer's final answer is that whatever Hegel may have intended, his philosophy did *not* completely break free of "subjectivism," and for all his sympathy with the speculative, historical, "Greek," and anti-metaphysical, anti-subjectivist elements in Hegel, he cannot finally travel all that far down Hegel's *Denkweg*, the path of his thought.

For one thing, Gadamer is clearly a post-Heideggerian philosopher of finitude, in several different respects. He judges,

Kant's critique of the antinomies of pure reason to be correct and not superceded by Hegel. Totality is never an object, but rather a world–horizon which encloses us and within which we live our lives. (HD 104)[10]

He might have also added his frequent objections to the idea of such a totality as a *completion*, because any claim for an inner teleology and the completion of a development would have to be made from some position external to historical forms of life, arrived at by some reflective methodology, and it would have to suggest that understanding the past is less a matter of an unformalizable "conversation" and an eventual "fusion" of opposed horizons of meaning (*Horizontverschmelzung*), than it is a result of the application of some independent theory, with epochs as instances of moments in that theory.[11] Gadamer is forever returning to examples from art as

paradigmatic problems of understanding, insisting in such passages
that it would be ridiculous for someone to claim that Shakespeare
could be considered "superior" to Sophocles because farther along in
such a putative development.[12] Even more important, such an ideal
of a final, absolute self-consciousness, even as a regulative ideal, runs
counter to what Gadamer regards as Heidegger's successful demonstration of the unending, unresolveable interplay of "revealing" and
"concealing" in claims for truth.

Truth is not the total unconcealment whose ideal fulfillment would in the
end remain the presence of absolute spirit to itself. Rather Heidegger taught
us to think truth as an unconcealing and a concealing at the same time.
(PG 35)[13]

By contrast, Gadamer somewhat ironically embraces what Hegel
called the "*bad* infinite" when he claims that the "soul's dialogue
with itself" has no teleogical end point, no inner direction, and so is
inexhaustible. As Gadamer is wont to put it, the "otherness" of "the
other" in, say a conversation or attempt at a textual or historico-
cultural meaning, the opacity that originally called for interpretation, is never overcome, can only be partially "revealed" by another
sort of "concealing," contrary to Hegel's claim that in modernity
especially (in *some* sense brought to its full realization by Hegel)
human beings finally recognize themselves, make their own, what
had originally seemed, and is now no longer, other.[14]

Gadamer thus takes sides with the enormously influential (for all
later modern "Continental" philosophy) Schellingian and Kierkega-
ardian insistence on finitude against Hegel, and, on this score, is
particularly critical of an aspect of Hegel's project that he otherwise
praises – Hegel's attempted revivification of ancient dialectic. On
the one hand, in Gadamer's view, Hegel appreciated that the kind
of Eleatic dialectic on view in the *Parmenides* and in Zeno helps
one understand the "interweaving" of and "fluidity" among ideas
and especially the way in which statements about certain categorial
distinctions undermine the very distinctions themselves (the same
must be the same as itself, but also other than "other" and so forth)
and so seem to prompt a way of thinking about determinate meaning
very different from that possible in standard assertoric judgments.
And of course what Gadamer calls the "hermeneutic priority of the
question" would lead him to be quite sympathetic to the dialogic,

statement and counter-statement, question and answer model or origin for the Hegelian dialectic.[15] On the other hand, Hegel, for Gadamer, greatly exaggerated the possibility that some positive doctrine could actually result (for Plato, especially) from such contradictions, and so misinterpreted crucial passages, such as Plato's *Sophist*, 259b (HD 22). (According to Gadamer, Plato is there, in his famous parricide of Parmenides, attempting to dissolve the appearance of unavoidable contradiction with his distinction between "otherness" and "not being," not at all to embrace the results as the beginning of a new speculative doctrine.)[16] Gadamer agrees that the undecideability, aporia, and confusion that result from the Socratic elenchus in the dialogues, point to a positive result, but not a positive doctrine, or anything that can be stated as such. The real speculative moment in the dialogues is the dialogue drama itself which, for Gadamer, captures the unsayability but yet the presence of what cannot be said. Hegel, on the other hand, according to Gadamer, in passages that represent the extreme end of his criticism of Hegel, tried to present dialectic as a philosophical method, and in so doing fundamentally compromised his own insights about the limitations of language, the limitations arising from the historical embeddedness of *Dasein*, and the inherent limitations of natural consciousness itself. Hegel's dialectic is really a "splendid monologue," and "relies far more upon the principles of Cartesian method, on the learning of the Catechism, and on the Bible" (HD 7). Or: "In his [Hegel's] dialectical method I see a dubious compromise with the scientific thinking of modernity" (PG 45).[17]

Finally, the most comprehensive criticism of Hegel is intimated by Gadamer's report that one of the earliest influences on his work in ancient philosophy was Julius Stenzel, who observed in Greek philosophy what Stenzel had called "the restraining of subjectivity," what Gadamer refers to as the Greek "superiority ... in which out of self-forgetful surrender they abandoned themselves in boundless innocence to the passion of thinking" (PG 9). It is hard to imagine more un-Hegelian phrases than "self-forgetful surrender" and "boundless innocence," unless it is "the passion of thinking." What Gadamer is referring to here goes by the general term, "the problem of reflection," (or, said from the Hegelian side, the "impossibility of innocence") and for Gadamer and Heidegger, Hegel's account of the priority and status of reflection drastically qualifies his achievement in otherwise opening up ways of considering the actual "life" of human spirit without rendering that life an "object" of methodological study.

IV

And the problem is not an easy one to summarize, especially because Hegel considered himself a fierce critic of what he termed "finite" versions of "reflective" philosophies. We need first to note that the question opened up by Gadamer's restrictions on methodological access to the lived meanings of texts and utterances concerns the possibility of the intelligibility of experience itself. The issue is not a formal account of the interpretive human sciences; the issue is "ontological," or concerns human being itself. Our very mode of being is interpretive; we exist "understandingly," in an always already "understood" world. There is no way of conceiving a subject "before" any act of interpretation, and so no way of understanding the interpretations as accomplished by such a subject. The question Gadamer is posing about the role of reflection in this large context concerns then the right way to understand the "understandingly mediated," or, said in the German Idealist language, the self-conscious character of all experience, an issue given great weight by Kant, but already a key element in modern philosophy as such.

Locke had called reflection "that notice which the mind takes of its own operations," a view that typified the "theatre of the mind" approach of early modern philosophy, wherein what we were conscious of in ordinary consciousness could not be said to be spatio–temporal external objects in any immediate sense, but sensory effects, "ideas," "impressions," "representations" and so forth, such that the work of the understanding left us either, for the empiricists, "fainter" and, because more generalized, vaguer "ideas," or, for the rationalists, "clearer and distincter" versions of what were only imperfectly and deceptively apprehended immediately.[18] But for both camps, *consciousness itself was reflective*. (There was not first consciousness of objects in the sense of some direct "awakeness" as in the premodern tradition, and then, as a subsequent act, reflective attention to our own modes of apprehending. Being aware was being aware already of one's own mental items, *re*-presentings, which then had somehow to be reconnected to their real source or origin.)

This situation (and its resulting skepticism) was unbearable for Kant and in the course of rethinking it, he came to deny a touchstone for both earlier modern traditions: the possibility of some immediacy and givenness in experience at all, whether of the world or of the self. The mind was, Kant argued instead, active in *any* determinate experience and could not be said ever to apprehend directly a given content, even an idea or impression. This meant that the reflective nature of consciousness had to be put another way. In being aware of objects, say external objects, of "outer sense," the mind could still be said to be also "aware of itself," but this not because of awareness of inner content or of "a self." We are manifestly not aware of ideas or impressions of chairs when we are aware of chairs. We are aware of chairs, but we are also *taking* ourselves to be perceiving chairs, not imagining or remembering them, not perceiving stools or tables, and we are ourselves "holding" the elements of such thinkings together in time, all according to various rules that could not be otherwise if such contents are to held together in one time (or so Kant argued). We are conscious, in a way, self-consciously; we are adverbially self-conscious. In any act of intending, I am taking myself to be just thus and so intending, and there are elements of that "apperception" that cannot ever be said to be due to our contact with the world, but must be subjectively contributed.[19] This meant that there was an element of self-determination (a required active element that could not be attributed to the deliverances of the senses) in how I took myself to be engaging the world, and through Fichte and then Hegel, this acquired an almost mythic status as a "divine" sort of freedom. And this element, to come to the decisive point for hermeneutical theory, means that one cannot ever be said simply to be "in" a state of consciousness without also at the same time *not* being wholly "in" such a state, not being wholly absorbed in the intended object, except as an occasionally contingent and always recoverable self-forgetting. As Gadamer puts it in *Truth and Method*, speaking of a subject, understood as in Idealism as a reflective consciousness, "What is essential to it as consciousness is that it can *rise above* that of which it is conscious"(TM 341, my emphasis). One cannot likewise just be "carrying on," at some level unavailable to reflective consciousness, the practices and rules of a community life. In Hegel's account, *there is no such level unavailable to reflective life or the activity could not count as an activity belonging to us*, and therein lies the deepest disagreement between Gadamer and Hegel.

This approach ultimately meant that for the post-Kantians, especially Fichte and Hegel, the central act of consciousness was not a representing, or picturing, or grasping, or simply being in a state, but an activity, a construing thus and such, a judging, in *some* sense a making. (Hegel, for all the speculative qualifications, does not abandon this revolutionary Kantian insight, and that is partly what Gadamer means by saying that Hegel remains a philosopher of subjectivity.)[20] The position also required that the mind's relation to itself in such consciousness could not be accounted for in any standard bipolar (subject–object) model of intending. In judging, even in judging about ourselves, we are always judging self-consciously, and so reflectively, even while not judging *that* we are judging. (The judgment does not occur unless we judge, and still hold open the possibility of judging rightly or not, and we cannot *do* that without taking ourselves to be doing *that*.) At some appropriately defined level, the proper explanation of why we organize our experience the way we do, and hold each other to account the way we do, is that we, the subjects of experience, and not the contents resulting from our contact with the world, are "responsible" for such elements. When one begins (with Fichte) to insist that we cannot discover such rules "lying ready made in the mind," but must be understood to have instituted or founded or "posited" such rules, we have begun to move away from any finite reflective model, and have begun to attempt an absolute reflection, an understanding of the process itself of such self-regulation and its necessary moments.[21] The ineliminability of the reflexive character of experience is supposed to provide us with the supreme condition by appeal to which our own determinate requirements for experience can be nonempirically developed. And we have thus arrived at the beginning of Hegel's historical and "logical" account of how and why we hold each other to the norms we do.

This is the background behind many of the things Gadamer says about Hegel, reflection, and self-consciousness, and about this attempt, as he puts it, to develop "the entire content of knowledge as the complete whole of self-consciousness" (HD 77). For example:

That, according to Hegel, is the essence of dialectical speculation – thinking nothing other than this selfhood, thinking the being of self itself, in which the ego of self-consciousness has always already recognized itself . . . It (pure, speculative reflection) thus discovers in itself the origin of all further determination. (HD 19)

And, of course, however the particular transitions in Hegel's *Logic* are argued for, and however much Hegel attempts to avoid the traditional paradoxes in the subject's attempt to know itself absolutely, the whole idea of being able to make anything like the logical structure of intelligibility "for itself," or explicit, is a nonstarter for Gadamer. There is, in the first place, no way, he claims, to extract such normative dimensions from the "lived" language spoken in a community at a time (HD 95). If that is conceded, we can then appreciate the full force of Gadamer's Heideggerian objections. We are now (with any concession about the unformalizability or rendering explicit of the logical forms of language) prepared to say something like: "We do not speak such a language. It speaks us."[22]

Language completely surrounds us like the voice of home which prior to our every thought of it breathes a familiarity from time out of mind. (HD 97)

Demonstrating this point about the limits of reflection, with all its presuppositions, is what Gadamer meant by claiming that his task was the "overcoming of the primacy of self-consciousness." Such a result would involve acknowledging that the expression "the subject of thought and language" involves both a subjective as well as an objective genitive. The much cited summation of his position is from *Truth and Method*:

Understanding is to be thought of less as a subjective act than as participating in an event of tradition [*Einrücken in ein Überlieferungsgeschehen*], a process of transmission in which past and present are constantly mediated. This is what must be validated by hermeneutical theory ... (TM 290).[23]

Gadamer, in other words, would have us reverse the canonical relation between Hegel's *Phenomenology* and *Science of Logic*. It is in experiencing the insufficiencies of a disembodied account of our categorial requirements that we would *then* learn the necessity of returning to the lived experience of the "house of being," language. Were a more linguistically oriented *Phenomenology* to be the culmination of this antisystem, one small step would have been taken toward Gadamer's ultimate suggestion: "Dialectic must retrieve itself (*sich zurücknehmen*) in hermeneutics." (HD 99)

V

Before venturing a brief reaction of Gadamer's invocation of and separation from Hegel, I want to endorse enthusiastically the basic principle of his approach to all hermeneutics. There is no essential historical Hegel whose personal intentions we can retrieve, or whose historical world we can objectively reconstruct as the central necessary condition in understanding what his texts meant or mean, and there is no essential or core meaning-in-itself in Hegel's texts, eternally waiting to be unearthed. Gadamer is right: we can only look back at Hegel from where we are now, from within our own "horizon." As Gadamer has shown in a wealth of valuable detail, that does not mean that we cannot be confronted by an "alien" strange Hegel from whom we might learn something, or that the necessity of this "prejudiced" understanding prohibits a challenge to and development of our "fore-understandings." But, in my view, this means we ought, at the very least, to be much less confident that we simply long ago correctly boxed up and shelved "the Hegelian option" and can periodically drag it out and invoke his claims about "thought's self-determination," "development," "progress," "totality," or "Absolute Knowledge," as if straightforward candidates to be either accepted, rejected, or modified. We ought, at any rate, to be less confident about these matters than, it seems to me, Gadamer is. Consider Gadamer's laudatory characterization of Hegel as hermeneut, cited earlier.

Hegel states a definite truth, inasmuch as the essential nature of the historical spirit consists not in the restoration of the past but in thoughtful mediation with contemporary life (... *in der denkenden Vermittlung mit dem gegenwärtigen Leben*). (TM 168–69; WM 161)

The question of the modesty just mentioned is obviously most at issue in what one might mean by "thoughtful" (here the objections to Hegel's "dialectical methodology," and his developmental, progressive understanding of spirit, and notion of "totality" are relevant), "mediation" (the issue of *reflective* mediation and so the status of the *Logic*), and especially "contemporary life." There are several aspects of the last issue that raise the first questions for Gadamer's approach.

The "horizon" within which Hegel's philosophy re-emerged as of possible philosophical relevance for Gadamer and his contemporaries was first of all the systematic question of the human sciences, the *Geisteswissenschaften* And so Hegel's sensitivity to all the unique, nonreducible elements in such an understanding, to a "conversational logic" in interrogating the past, his insistence on a self-correcting process of historical change, his stress on taking everywhere account of what Gadamer calls "effective history" (*Wirkungsgeschichte*) in understanding our own situation, his entire systematic attempt to show that understanding other human beings and their cultural and political achievements could never happen were they to be understood as "objects," attracted a great deal of attention, if also qualification.[24]

But we might look at this as in a way only a first step in clearing a space for understanding the human *qua* human in the modern world. It is understandable that such an initial strategy would so heavily stress what cannot be comprehended by an objective methodology and that we would be occasionally tempted to argue for such a claim by arguing for a *fundamental* inaccessibility. But we stand now in some sense on the other side of the early debates with relativists and positivists and neo-Kantian, "scientistic" naturalists about the very legitimacy of the category of meaning and the relation between understanding (*Verstehen*) and explanation (*Erklären*). Our own "contemporary life situation" thus helps us to see other possibilities in Hegel than those of importance in Gadamer's appropriation and transformation of Hegel. The debate about what we now call "folk psychology" still goes on of course, and the notions of "person" or "*Geist*" or "*Dasein*," not to mention belief, desire, intention, and so forth, must apparently still contend with their naturalist opponents. But the original debate, which so decisively influenced Heidegger's early work in phenomenology and therewith Gadamer's project, was the psychologism controversy, and Husserl's response in his *Logical Investigations*. That debate made it appear that the alternatives were a psychologistic naturalism, versus some sort of realism about meaning, often a quasi-Platonic realism about meanings, commitment to intentional inexistence, ideal entities such as "values" in Scheler's "material ethics" and so forth. Much of Heidegger's animus against idealism and philosophies of subjectivity, and his own insistence on the question of being, draw their inspiration from such realist reactions. The effects of that early controversy can certainly be seen in Gadamer and in the various claims about what must be independent of, or what must precede and remain unreachable by, the constructions of subjectivity.[25] But the situation looks different now. For one thing, there are not many such Husserlian or Fregean realists around anymore. For another, the epistemological problems and the dogmatic implications of such a realism now appear impossible to overcome. For another, the linguistic turn, the success of various attacks on the dogmas of conventional empiricism and analytic philosophy, the influence of Quine's holism, Kuhn's attack on positivist history of science, and a great revival of philosophical Kant scholarship in the spirit of such a postanalytic turn, have all created a different way of understanding Kantian idealism and so a different way of understanding the post-Kantian idealist tradition. So what has drawn attention to Hegel in the last twenty-five years or so are two issues somewhat different from those that connect Gadamer to Hegel.

In the first place, Gadamer was so concerned to limit the pretensions of a "reflective philosophy" and so to insist on a kind of embeddedness and inheritance not redeemable "reflectively," in either Hegelian or left-Hegelian (practical) or Habermasean terms, that the curious, uniquely modern phenomenon first noticed with such brilliance by Rousseau is difficult to discuss in his terms. One can, to speak somewhat simplistically, come to understand and especially to experience virtually all of one's inheritance, tradition, life-world, and so forth, as coherent and intelligible but *not* "one's own," and so as, root and branch, *alien*. I can even, in some sense that requires much more qualification, become alienated "from myself," from my own life; indeed, paradoxically, can be the agent of such alienation. Or, said another way, all the formal conditions insisted on by modern democratic life as necessary for institutions to count as just (that is as somehow products of my will) can *all* be satisfied without any "identification" with such products; as if I made them, but do not see or experience that making as mine.[26] If there is such a phenomenon and if the language of identity and alienation is as indispensable as the language of rights or the language of finitude in understanding the modern social and political world, then the Hegelian language of subjectivity, reflection, and Geist's "reconciliation with *itself*" will also be ultimately indispensable.[27] And in the last twenty-five years or so, Hegel's approach has come to be more and more in evidence, especially in so-called "identity" or "recognition" politics.[28]

The second point can be made by reference to one of Gadamer's favorite images. When he wants to stress the unformalizable and largely unreflective character of everyday human experience of meaning, our mode of understanding, responding to, correcting, and ignoring meaningful utterances and deeds, Gadamer invokes the image of a game and the activity of play. And it is true that in "understanding" how to play the game and in actually playing it, I cannot rightly be said to be consulting the rules of play and/or reflectively "applying" them in practice. The founding argument of Heidegger in *Being and Time* about "being in the world" remains for much of the post-Heideggerian Continental tradition decisive on those points.[29] But this also means that such games (to be games) are normatively structured; there is a right and a wrong way to "go on," and the *active adherence* to such rules on the part of (what can only be described as) subjects doing the adhering makes the appeal to some sort of "entering a transmission event," rather than my sustaining a commitment, hard to understand. Such "game-playing" may not be rightly described as "guided" by individual subjects who make episodic, mental decisions, but game-playing is nevertheless certainly "minded" and normatively *guided* in some sense, and one of the topics of recent interest in discussions of Hegel has been attention to how he raises and discusses such questions, especially at the institutional level. (I don't mean to suggest that Gadamer denies this aspect of the problem, but I am not sure that his dialogic model of interrogation and "agreement" is adequate to account for it.)

Subjectivity in Hegel, even the collective kind that he is interested in, can then, on such a view of mindedness, be understood itself as a kind of collective human achievement (in no sense, as Gadamer would agree, a traditional substance), that achievement being the establishment of normatively successful, mutually bound communities. As Nietzsche also noted, we have *made* ourselves into creatures with the right to make promises (we are not "by nature" such creatures), and thus, by holding ourselves and each other to normative constraints, have made ourselves subjects and remain subjects only by finding ways to sustain such results.[30] *Geist*, Hegel regularly says in one of his most puzzling and paradoxical formulations "is a result of itself," or nothing but the achievement of such rule-following, reflectively rule-assessing communities, and that process must somehow be understood (at its most basic level) as a kind of continual negotiation about normative authority.[31]

Gadamer would be fine with the self-correcting, negotiating, aiming at agreement parts of all this, but without Hegel's argument for the relevance of criteria of genuine *success* in such attempts (ultimately the so-called "Absolute" viewpoint), we will end up with simply a narrative of what had been taken, as a matter of historical fact, to be failure, success, reformulation, and so forth (in so far as we, by our lights, could understand them now). And there is no reason in principle why such a narrative must be so radically distinct as a mode of knowledge; it seems compatible with a certain kind of cognitive, hermeneutically reflective, historical anthropology (which is what philosophical hermeneutics, without this normative animus, becomes).[32]

The idea of meaning or intelligibility in general as a *result* of normatively constrained or rule bound human practices, or the legacy of Kant's theory of judgment in Hegel (and paradigmatically in Fichte) is, I am claiming, the source of the deepest disagreement between the Idealist and the Heidegger-influenced hermeneutical project, inspired as the latter is by a very different notion of the understanding of meaning and ultimately of truth as "disclosedness" or "unconcealment," and so understanding as "itself a kind of happening" (PH 29).[33] On this Hegelian view, understanding cannot just happen (*geschehen*); it does not "occur" as we try to "occupy" or seize (*einrücken*) a place in a "transmission-event."

For reasons again having to do essentially with Kant (this time his theory of the unity of reason and the tasks of reflective judgment), this project assumes also a semantic holism, or understands any instance of a meaningful assertion to involve a variety of other implications and commitments without which such an assertion could not be properly made. And this raises the question of how to present an account of the form any such relation of implication, presupposition, inappropriateness, and so forth, would have to take were such interconceptual relations really to make possible meaningful assertions. Without attention to this sort of normative dimension and this sort of holism, the project of Hegel's *Logic* would have to look, as it so often has, like a kind of neo-Platonic theory of "concept emanation."

Gadamer's disagreement with this view is why he argues in *Truth and Method*, in a remarkable section on "The limitations of reflective philosophy," against all claims that nothing "prereflective" can determine or condition actions or utterances without our really having reflectively incorporated such a prereflective level, arguments based on the claim that otherwise such instances could not count as actions or utterances. He insists that these always rest on a kind of rhetorical trick of sorts, that though the argument is successful after its fashion, we know the claim isn't true (TM 341–46).[34] It is clearer, I think, with respect to the way the "ineliminability of reflection" thesis descends from Kant through Fichte to Hegel, and with respect to these issues of normative reflection, why one would want to say that the game we are playing with norms always involves a possible interrogation about reasons for holding such norms, and that *only* such reasons can "determine" our *commitment* to norms (or only beliefs can determine other beliefs).

From "where we stand now," the distinctiveness of the "human sciences," following this Hegelian lead, stems from the distinctiveness of human experience in being "fraught with ought" in Sellars's phrase, from the distinctive human capacity we might call our responsiveness to reasons, "ought's." Viewed this way, we can understand why "this is traditional," "this is the way we go on," and so forth, could never ultimately count as such reasons, however much time it takes us to learn that.[35]

NOTES

1 Hans-Georg Gadamer, "Reflections on my Philosophical Journey," in *The Philosophy of Hans-Georg Gadamer*, ed. Lewis Edwin Hahn (Chicago and LaSalle: Open Court, 1997) (PG hereafter, cited in the text), p. 9.

2 This is a very tough sentence to translate. "... *die Anstrengung, sie zu ergreifen und sich zu eigen zu machen, ist mehr das unvermittelte Hervortreiben des Innern und abgeschnittene Erzeugen des Allgemeinen als ein Hervorgehen desselben aus dem Konkreten und der Mannigfaltigkeit des Daseins.*" G. W. F. Hegel, *Die Phänomenologie des Geistes* (Felix Meiner: Hamburg, 1952), p. 30. Gadamer quotes it in "Hegel and the Dialectic of the Ancient Philosophers," in *Hegel's Dialectic: Five Hermeneutical Studies*, translated by P. Christopher Smith (New Haven: Yale University Press, 1976), p. 8. (HD, hereafter)

3 Gadamer means to echo here Heidegger's early remark, that Hegel is the most radical of the Greeks. See "Hegel and Heidegger," in HD 107.

4 A well informed study of the Hegel/Heidegger/Gadamer theme, with a focus especially on the common theme of Greek philosophy: Riccardo Dottori, *Die Reflexion der Wahrheit: Zwischen Hegels absoluter Dialektik und der Philosophie der Endlichkeit von M. Heidegger und H. G. Gadamer* (Heidelberg: Carl Winter, 1984). See especially Chapter Four, "Hegel und Gadamer," pp. 240–99.

5 Cf. also HD 104.

6 *Truth and Method* (New York: Continuum Press, 1989), hereafter TM, cited in the text, pp. 168–69.

7 One might say, going beyond Gadamer and anticipating what will be discussed below, that *Geist* refers instead to the collective achievement, in various "developing" ways, of a human community, communities more and more successfully self-authorizing and self-regulating over time. This would obviously require a book length gloss for it to become clear. For some indications, see my "Naturalness and Mindedness: Hegel's Compatibilism," *The European Journal of Philosophy*, vol. 7, n.2, (1999), pp. 194–212; also "Hegel, Freedom, The Will: *The Philosophy of Right*, #1–33," in *Hegel: Grundlinien der Philosophie des Rechts*, ed. Ludwig Siep, (Berlin: Akademie Verlag, 1997), pp. 31–53; and also "What is the Question for Which Hegel's 'Theory of Recognition' is the Answer?" in *The European Journal of Philosophy*, vol. 8, no. 2 (August 2000).

8 These claims are also somewhat confusing, because Gadamer also attributes to Hegel the intention of reviving "the logos-nous metaphysics of the Platonic–Aristotelean" tradition, but in a way "founded upon Descartes' idea of method" and undertaken "within the framework of transcendental philosophy." HD 78–9. This seems to me an impossible, internally inconsistent characterization.

9 Cf. also, in "Hegel and Heidegger": "For it is Hegel who explicitly carried the dialectic of mind or spirit beyond the forms of subjective spirit, beyond consciousness and self-consciousness" HD 104.

10 Cf. the discussion of Aeschylus on "learning by suffering" in TM, Gadamer's claim that "Real experience is that in which man becomes aware of his finiteness," p. 357, and the explicit contrast there with Hegel. Cf. the helpful discussion by Paul Redding in *Hegel's Hermeneutics* (Ithaca: Cornell University Press, 1996), Chapter Two, pp. 35–49.

11 The status of Gadamer's own proposals for a nonmethodological hermeneutics, and so his somewhat transcendental "theory of the possibility of meaning," and the examples cited to confirm it (not to mention the status of his model, Heidegger's *Daseinanalytik*), in the light of this critique of totality and theory, is another, complicated matter. Cf. his discussion

in TM, p. 341ff and his discussion in "The Scope of Hermeneutical Reflection," in *Philosophical Hermeneutics*, translated and edited by David E. Linge (Berkeley and Los Angeles: University of California Press, 1976), pp. 18–43 (hereafter PH, cited in the text). Gadamer himself has had to face charges of linguistic idealism (from Habermas) and an implicit teleology in his concept of a fusion of horizons (by Wolfhart Pannenberg), and he denies both ascriptions in this essay.

12 I note that the issue depends on what one means by "superior." With respect to the realization of art as such, Hegel goes so far as to defend the superiority of Greek art *as art* over modern. There is, though, another sense in which he claims that the ethical life behind Shakespeare's presentation and the kind of self-awareness visible in Hamlet, say, does represent an advance or moment of progress.

13 Cf. also TM, "To be historically means that knowledge of oneself can never be complete." p. 302.

14 As is often, indeed endlessly repeated, this hope for a kind of superceded difference and totality, especially when it reappears in Marx's theory of labor, is held to be responsible for "totalitarian thinking" of all sorts (cf. Gadamer, HD 98, on Hegel as forerunner of Marx and positivism!), notwithstanding Hegel's repeated insistence that the state of freedom in question, "being one's self in an another," still requires the self-other relation be preserved. Cf. Jürgen Habermas, *The Philosophical Discourse of Modernity*, translated by Frederick Lawrence (Cambridge: MIT Press, 1987), pp. 36, 42, 84; Theodor Adorno, *Negative Dialectics*, translated by E.B. Ashton (London: Routledge, 1973), pp. 22–3, and my "Hegel, Modernity, and Habermas," in *Idealism as Modernism*, op.cit., pp. 157–84.

15 Cf. TM, pp. 325–41.

16 On this score, about this particular passage, I think Gadamer is quite right. See my "Negation and Not-Being in Wittgenstein's *Tractatus* and Plato's *Sophist*," *Kant-Studien*, Bd. 70, 1979.

17 See also HD 79 and TM, "Hegel's dialectic is a monologue of thinking that seeks to carry out in advance what matures little by little in every genuine conversation." p. 369. From Hegel's point of view, in the terms he used early on to discuss such issues of finitude, what Gadamer is defending is a form of "faith" (*Glauben*), not philosophy or knowledge (*Wissen*).

18 John Locke, *An Essay Concerning Human Understanding* ed. A. S. Pringle-Pattison (Oxford: The Clarendon Press, 1967), I, p. 44.

19 I introduce and defend this "taking" and "adverbial" language in my *Kant's Theory of Form* (New Haven: Yale University press, 1981) and in Chapter Two of *Hegel's Idealism: The Satisfactions of Self-Consciousness* (Cambridge: Cambridge University Press, 1989).

20 It is also why Hegel's phenomenology is ultimately so different from Husserl's attempt to return to a kind of realism in his phenomenology. For a defense of this claim about the continuities in the Kant–Hegel relationship, see my *Hegel's Idealism, op.cit.*

21 Contra Heidegger, for the same sorts of reasons, we cannot be said to "find" such formal constraints in the world into which we have been "thrown."

22 Cf. "To What Extent Does Language Preform Thought," Supplement II to TM, pp. 542–49.

23 The passage is italicized in the original, WM 274–5.

24 A locus classicus: the discussion of "observing reason" in the *Phenomenology of Spirit*. Translated by A. V. Miller (Oxford: Oxford University Press, 1977), pp. 139–210.

25 I argue that this sort of Heideggerian critique of subjectivity confuses a compelling anti-Cartesianism with a much less persuasive anti-subjectivism, in my "On Being Anti-Cartesian: Hegel, Heidegger, Subjectivity and Sociality," in *Idealism as Modernism, op.cit.*

26 Gadamer has his own notion of a kind of emancipatory effect of hermeneutical reflection, the results of which assure that "... I am no longer unfree over against myself but rather can deem freely what in my preunderstanding (prejudice, *Vorurteil*) may be justified and what unjustified." PH 38. From a Hegelian (or critical theory) perspective the question of justification raised here, and its historical as well as logical presuppositions looks like a welcome return to traditional notion of reflection, but in the next paragraph, Gadamer makes clear that he considers this reflective justification to be only a "transformation" of some preunderstanding into another, or the "forming of a new preunderstanding." This seems to me to take back with one hand what was given by another, and is responsible for such Gadamerian claims as that every historian "... is one of the 'nation's' historians; he belongs to the nation," and so, whether he acknowledges it or not is "... engaged in contributing to the growth and development of the national state." Ibid., p. 28. Cf. Dottori, *op.cit.*, pp. 289–99.

27 I don't here mean the kind of experience Heidegger discusses in *Being and Time*, when "anxiety" detaches me in some way from my involvement in a world, and I experience the ground of my being as a "nullity." The phenomenon of alienation in modernity is, for want of a better word, considerably more dialectical. It is also not captured by Gadamer's invocation of Schiller's notion of disharmony and aesthetic harmony, cited as an issue of alienation in Gadamer's "Hegel and Heidegger" essay in HD 106. Schiller, in the seventeenth letter *On the Aesthetic Education of Man*, translated by Reginald Snell (New York: Fredrick Unger, 1965,

locates the origin of our unfreedom in "external circumstances," and "a fortuitous exercise of his freedom." p. 85. The puzzling issue in Hegel involves self-alienation, and is not fortuitous.

28 An important event in this development was of course the publication of Charles Taylor's influential *Hegel* (Cambridge: Cambridge University Press, 1975).

29 In PH, he makes two other important points about this game analogy. No one is "it," or has a privileged position (p. 32); and someone who keeps trying to question or undermine the motives of another play himself falls out of the game, becomes a "spoil sport" (p. 41). (Both claims lead to Gadamer's objections to Habermas's use of the psychoanalytic model of liberation.) One easy summation of Gadamer's Hegel criticism is that Gadamer is accusing Hegel in effect of being such a "spoil sport."

30 Friedrich Nietzsche, *On the Genealogy of Morals*, translated by Walter Kaufmann (New York: Vintage, 1969), Second Essay, #, p. 57ff.

31 *Hegel's Philosophy of Subjective Spirit*, translated and edited by M. Petry (Dordrecht: Riedel, 1978), p. 7. For more discussion and defense of such an interpretation, see "Naturalism and Mindedness: Hegel's Compatibilism," *op.cit.*

32 The direction suggested by this claim no doubt brings to mind Habermas's exchanges with Gadamer. See *Hermeneutik und Ideologiekritik* (Frankfurt: Suhrkamp, 1971), and PH 26–43. For the differences between the position that I am attributing to Hegel, and Habermas's position, see "Hegel, Modernity, Habermas," *op.cit.*

33 Cf. Chapter Three of *Hegel's Idealism*, op.cit., "Fichte's Contribution," and "Fichte's Alleged Subjective, Psychological, One-Sided Idealism," in *The Reception of Kant's Critical Philosophy: Fichte, Schelling, and Hegel*, edited by Sally Sedgwick (Cambridge: Cambridge University Press, 2000), pp. 147–70.

34 Cf. Gadamer's formulation of Heidegger's (and his) position in his "Hegel and Heidegger" essay. In discussing "fate" (*Geschick*) and "our being fated" (*Geschicklichkeit*), he writes, "... it is a matter of what is allotted [*zugeschickt*] to man and by which he is so very much determined [*bestimmt*] that all self-determination and self-consciousness remains subordinate" HD 109.

35 This of course still leaves a good deal unresolved about how any sort of "universal history" could be possible on such an interpretation, what the Hegelian account of totality would look like, how to understand the relation between thought and language in Hegel, and so forth. All that can be said here is that the direction sketched above does not, I think, lead to what Gadamer calls, "the total unconcealment whose ideal fulfillment would in the end remain the presence of absolute spirit to itself"

(PHGG, p. 35). There is no metaphysics of presence in one of Hegel's most sweeping and helpful characterizations of the task of the *Logic*, (*Hegel's Science of Logic*, translated by A. V. Miller (London: George Allen & Unwin, 1969)), that this "truth of actuality" must never be represented as a "dead repose," and that,

... by virtue of the freedom which the Concept attains in the Idea, the idea possesses within itself also the most stubborn opposition; its repose consists in the security and certainty with which it eternally creates and eternally overcomes that opposition, in it meeting with itself (p. 759).

11 Gadamer's Relation to Heidegger and Phenomenology

Gadamer's life and work is closely connected with and indebted to the life and work of Martin Heidegger. Gadamer's autobiography makes clear that the encounter with Heidegger in the early 1920s was quite literally fateful. Theirs was a lifelong personal and intellectual relationship. Throughout his published work and in his lectures and private conversation, Gadamer everywhere modestly acknowledges his deep debt to Heidegger. He tells us, for example, that *Truth and Method*, his magnum opus, was, among other things, an attempt to open the way for readers to the work of the later Heidegger.[1] In honor of Gadamer's 100th birthday in February 2000, Hermann Heidegger, Martin Heidegger's son, dedicated the 16th volume of Heidegger's *Collected Works* to Gadamer, "the oldest loyal pupil of my father."[2] Yet in many significant and fundamental respects, Gadamer's thought, life, and work did not follow the path of Heidegger. As we shall see below, Gadamer learned and borrowed much from Heidegger, but Gadamer's own characterization of the relationship between himself and Heidegger as one of constant challenge and provocation is perhaps the best short characterization of this complex relationship. Stylistically and substantively, the difference between their two modes of thought is the difference between a meditative thinker (Heidegger) and a dialogical one (Gadamer). Not unrelated to this difference is Gadamer's refusal to take Heidegger's lead to a kind of thought that is postphilosophical. This refusal has many ramifications.

SURPRISES AND DISAPPOINTMENTS:
THE HISTORICAL RELATIONSHIP TO
HEIDEGGER AND TO PHENOMENOLOGY

As discussed in the biographical essay that begins this volume, Gadamer first met Heidegger in Freiburg in the spring of 1923 after Gadamer had completed his doctorate under Paul Natorp in Marburg. He had come to Freiburg to study Aristotle with Heidegger and to acquaint himself more closely with phenomenology, a school of thought led by Edmund Husserl who was also in Freiburg and with whom Heidegger was closely affiliated. Gadamer enrolled in all the classes that Heidegger was offering that semester, and Heidegger immediately took him under his wing. Gadamer also enrolled in a seminar with Husserl, about which Gadamer likes to tell a story that marks a significant aspect of Husserl's phenomenological style for Gadamer. Once, after Gadamer asked Professor Husserl a question at the beginning of a seminar session, Husserl spent the rest of the session answering the question. Afterwards Gadamer overheard Husserl remark to Heidegger, who had been in attendance, that the day's seminar had yielded a marvelous discussion![3]

After this semester in Freiburg in which Gadamer studied Aristotle and other topics with Heidegger, including lectures on the hermeneutics of facticity, Heidegger accepted a position at Marburg and Gadamer returned with him. In the next years, Gadamer worked closely with Heidegger, although after Heidegger expressed reservations about Gadamer's abilities, Gadamer, whose confidence was shaken, concentrated on philology. After successfully passing the state examinations in classical philology, Gadamer, to his surprise, was invited by Heidegger to write a habilitation with him. Gadamer set out to write on Aristotle but ended up writing on the dialectical ethics of Plato and concentrating on the *Philebus*. Although the context for the habilitation, as Gadamer presents it in the introduction to the work, makes little reference to Heidegger, the analysis that Gadamer provides relies importantly on Heidegger. For example, Gadamer asserts, somewhat dogmatically, at the beginning of the work that the Greeks understood Being (*Sein*) as being-present-at-hand (*Vorhandensein*) – a thesis of Heidegger's that Gadamer will come to reject.[4] We should also note that the subtitle of his habilitation is "Phenomenological Interpretations Relating to the *Philebus*."

Central to Gadamer's account of the *Philebus* are the concepts of conversation, dialectic, and the world we have in common (*Mitwelt*). Shortly after completing his habilitation in 1928, Gadamer published a very positive review (1929) of Karl Löwith's *Das Individuum in der Rolle des Mitmenschen* (1928), also a habilitation with Heidegger and a work concerned with the philosophy of dialogue.[5] Interestingly enough, Gadamer's review never once mentions Heidegger, even though an important thesis of Löwith's treatise is the shortcoming of Heidegger's account of Being-with (*Mitsein*) in *Being and Time*.

In 1928, Heidegger returned to Freiburg to assume Husserl's chair, and Gadamer remained in Marburg where he began to establish his career as a philosopher. When Heidegger assumed the rectorship of Freiburg University in 1933 and became a public and official advocate for National Socialism, Gadamer broke off his contact with Heidegger. He renewed his relationship with Heidegger in the late 1930s, years after Heidegger had given up the rectorship and any public political role, and continued to remain in contact with him until Heidegger's death in 1976. Gadamer put together the first Festschrift for Heidegger in 1950, *Anteile*, and invited Heidegger regularly to visit his classes in Heidelberg.[6] Gadamer never wrote directly about Heidegger until Heidegger invited him to write an introduction for the publication of the second edition of the *Origin of the Work of Art* in 1960, the year in which *Truth and Method* appeared.[7] After 1964, essays on Heidegger appear regularly.[8]

Looking back over this life-long relationship, we can see that the "challenge" and "provocation" that Heidegger represented for Gadamer was both personal and philosophical. In the 1920s, Gadamer turned to classical philology because he was not confident that he could live up to the standard set by Heidegger. After his habilitation with Heidegger, Gadamer never published another book (discounting the two very small monographs on Plato and Herder, respectively) until *Truth and Method* in 1960. Gadamer reports that in the 1950s Heidegger urged him to write a substantive book and, further, that at this time he, Gadamer, always felt that Heidegger was "looking over my shoulder."[9]

In his autobiographical writings and interviews Gadamer reports that during their long relationship Heidegger provided him with a number of surprises and disappointments. He remembers being surprised when first reading *Being and Time* at its apparent Kantian transcendental framework. This "surprise" supports some of the recent work on the early publications and lectures of Heidegger that argue for a greater continuity in the development of Heidegger's thought than the standard secondary presentation of the 1960s and 1970s, which suggested a break between the "early" and the "later" Heidegger. The next surprise that Gadamer registers is also the first disappointment with Heidegger, i.e., Heidegger's engagement on behalf of the Nazis in 1933. Gadamer was not the only close associate who did not anticipate Heidegger's step into politics. Another surprise that Gadamer expresses follows from Gadamer's re-reading in the late 1980s of Heidegger's early and, until 1989, unpublished essay of 1922 that laid out a project that never came to fruition – a thoroughgoing phenomenological reading of Aristotle. This essay had been sent to Natorp via Husserl in the attempt to obtain a position for Heidegger in Marburg. This essay was passed on to Gadamer by Natorp at that time and importantly motivated him to go to Freiburg to study with Heidegger. Reading the essay, Gadamer much later reports, gave the young Ph.D. an "electric shock" (PA 47). Gadamer lost his copy of the essay and did not see it again until the late 1980s. What surprises Gadamer in his reading of the essay some sixty plus years later is the strong interest of the essay in the concepts of theory and science. Gadamer's own philosophical hermeneutics emphasizes the practical aspect of understanding and refers back to the treatment of understanding (*Verstehen*) in *Being and Time*, where Heidegger places all understanding in the context of an "in order to" (*um zu*), i.e., in a practical context. Although Gadamer in his introductory essay to the publication of Heidegger's essay in 1989 does not comment on it, Heidegger's essay treats theory as a sort of "tarrying" (*Verweilen*). This is the very concept with which Gadamer characterizes the encounter with the work of art – which encounter is paradigmatic for Gadamer of the event of understanding. We should also note that Gadamer considers this early essay by Heidegger one of Heidegger's most important works.[10]

Finally, a later disappointment with Heidegger that Gadamer registers is the lack of recognition that Heidegger accorded to *Truth and Method*. Gadamer reports sending Heidegger a copy of the work when it first came out and waiting for a response from Heidegger. None came. In spite of the fact that Gadamer had written the work, in part, to build a way for readers into Heidegger's later work, Heidegger seems to have found the work too dependent on concepts of which Heidegger was long critical, especially the concept of consciousness. Gadamer later defends his use of the concept of consciousness by pointing out that he has always sought to use ordinary language in his writing. He finds Heidegger's linguistic neologisms in the effort to avoid a philosophy of consciousness (like that of Husserl) to be too contrived. Further, Gadamer glosses the concept of consciousness, which literally in the German is "conscious-being" (*Bewusstsein*) with the statement that "consciousness is more Being than conscious" (*mehr Sein als Bewusst*), thus emphasizing the openness of consciousness to the world and to Being.[11] This, however, did not satisfy Heidegger. According to Gadamer, Heidegger praised Gadamer's little book on the poetry of Paul Celan as his favorite among Gadamer's writings. Further, Gadamer proudly, yet modestly, claims that his work on Plato had succeeded in persuading Heidegger, late in his life, that Heidegger's account of Plato had fallen short.[12]

THE PHENOMENOLOGICAL CHARACTER OF GADAMER'S PHILOSOPHICAL HERMENEUTICS

In a broad sense Gadamer's philosophical hermeneutics is phenomenological. Gadamer himself, in the foreword to the second edition of *Truth and Method*, explains that the work is "phenomenological in its method" (TM xxxvi). In a work that is critical of methodologism and whose usage of the term "method" in the title is ironic, Gadamer was careful in the first edition not to refer to his own "method." He comes to naming his own method in the foreword to the second edition in response to critics who are not clear about the nature of the work. By referring to his "method," Gadamer means, not a set of procedural rules, but rather the discipline of attending to things. By calling his method "phenomenological," he does not thereby subscribe to Husserl's account of the phenomenological method but rather indicates that the task of the enterprise is descriptive – in this case, descriptive of the human experience of understanding, i.e., of hermeneutical experience. In the same forward, Gadamer writes: "My real concern was and is philosophic: not what we do or what we ought to do, but what happens to us over and above our wanting and doing" (TM xxviii). One might wonder how the work is descriptive if it is not concerned with "what we do." The exclusion of "what we do" demarcates the properly philosophically over against the empirical. The enterprise is philosophical, not historical, anthropological, sociological, or psychological. This formulation also gives us a clue to the "transcendental" character of the enterprise. We cannot consider here the complicated and controverted history of transcendental philosophy, particularly in Kant, Husserl, and Heidegger – not to mention recent Anglo-American discussions of it. Gadamer, for the most part, avoids the expression, "the condition of the possibility of...," which marks much of transcendental philosophy. Nonetheless, Gadamer explicitly embraces the transcendental phenomenology of Heidegger's *Being and Time* as the relevant background and philosophical underpinning of his own account of understanding in *Truth and Method*. And Gadamer's important claim to the universality of hermeneutical experience means that he sees himself as providing an account of understanding as such. He embraces the paradox that his universal account of the understanding claims that all understanding is historical and partial.

In short, Gadamer's philosophical hermeneutic is transcendental and phenomenological in much the same sense as the fundamental ontology of Heidegger's *Being and Time*. This is a phenomenology that abjures the absolute, does not have a place for a transcendental ego, does not provide a treatment of philosophical method (*Methodenlehre*) except indirectly, and does not work toward a final foundation (*Letztbegründung*). These four characteristics importantly characterize the transcendental phenomenology of Edmund Husserl. Gadamer thereby avoids setting his project within a Husserlian frame. Yet, like Heidegger's early work, Gadamer's philosophical hermeneutics importantly and explicitly presupposes some of the accomplishments and concepts of Husserl's work. For Gadamer, Husserl overcame the priority that philosophy had come to give epistemology just as he overcame scientism and objectivism in philosophy. Husserl exhibited a sharpness of philosophical vision and intuition that Gadamer sought to emulate. And, further, Husserl established the philosophical concepts of "horizon" and the "life-world," which are significant for Gadamer's account of understanding in *Truth and Method*. Husserl also developed an account of the three-dimensional character of temporality (past, present, and future) in which the present moment is distended to include both retention and protention – aspects of the past and future. This account of temporality, which has roots in Augustine, is basic to Heidegger's *Being and Time* and Gadamer's *Truth and Method*. In summary, Husserl cleared the way for the hermeneutical ontology of Heidegger in *Being and Time*, which in turn provides the basis for the account of the understanding that Gadamer develops in *Truth and Method*.

Gadamer divides *Truth and Method* into three parts (Part I on truth in the experience of art, Part II on truth in the human sciences, and Part III on "the ontological shift of hermeneutics guided by language"), although the book divides neatly in half. The first half of the book, i.e., the Part I and the first section (of two) of Part II, provide a thematic and historical introduction to the account of understanding, which Gadamer provides in the last half of the book. The historical introduction, which takes the reader from Kant through Schleiermacher and Dilthey among others, leads us to Heidegger's treatment of the understanding in *Being and Time*. In the last paragraph of Part Two, Section 1, Gadamer writes:

Hence we too are beginning with the transcendental significance of Heidegger's problematic. The problem of hermeneutics gains a universal framework, even a new dimension, through his transcendental interpretation of understanding. . . .This existential structure of There-Being [*Dasein*] must find its expression in the understanding of historical tradition as well, and so we shall start by following Heidegger. (TM 264)

Thus, it is on the basis of Heidegger's treatment of understanding (*Verstehen*) in *Being and Time* that Gadamer develops his account of hermeneutical experience. We should also note, however, that there is much in Gadamer's account of hermeneutical experience that does not have Heidegger as its source, for example, the rehabilitation of authority and tradition, the reliance on the concepts of the hermeneutical circle (an age-old hermeneutical concept that Heidegger too takes up), play, effective-historical consciousness, the fusion of horizons, and the identification of the understanding with the Aristotelian virtue of *phronesis*, practical reason. Gadamer's often controverted rehabilitation of authority and tradition rests on the historical situatedness of any understanding that Heidegger treats as the "thrownness" (*Geworfenheit*) of *Dasein*. This historical situatedness of understanding represents one of the three dimensions of the temporality of understanding, i.e., the past.

At the very place in the text (end of section 1, Part 2), in which Gadamer clearly indicates that Heidegger's treatment of the understanding is the stepping off place for his own development of a philosophical hermeneutics, Gadamer indicates a serious failing of the Heideggerian account in *Being and Time*, namely, what Gadamer calls here the "problem of life" (TM 263). Put more precisely, this problem concerns how it is that human existence is "based on something that is outside history, i.e., on nature" (TM 263). Gadamer presents this failing as something that became clear to Heidegger and was one of the motivating grounds for Heidegger's "turn" away from the completion of the never finished project of *Being and Time*.

As we have noted, Gadamer hoped in *Truth and Method*, among other things, to assist the reader in following Heidegger in his later thought. Important themes for Heidegger after he abandons the project of *Being and Time* are the themes of language and art, especially poetry. The ontology of *Truth and Method* is an ontology of language. The fusion of horizons that takes place in the understanding is an accomplishment of language. Gadamer would have us see that the act of speaking and conversing is not so much us, using language, but language working its way with us such that truth happens. "Being that can be understood is language," writes Gadamer (TM 474), i.e., the understanding is linguistic. The kind of language that Gadamer would have us consider as he concludes the work is the beautiful language of poetry. *Truth and Method* begins with a consideration of art, i.e., with a critique of the aesthetization of art and its separation of beauty and truth. The work concludes and culminates in a discussion of beauty, because beauty, according to Gadamer, closes the gap of idea and appearance (TM 488). Beauty renders truth tangible.

The leading concept of the entire project is, of course, truth. When we understand something, we come to some truth about it. The full title of Part One is "The question of truth as it emerges in the experience of art," and the full title of Part Two reads: "The extension of the question of truth to understanding in the human sciences." Part Three provides an ontology according to which language is where truth happens. Here too, with regard to the question of truth, Gadamer situates himself within a Heideggerian framework. Truth is an event that happens in the encounter with the thing in language. Gadamer never provides a definition of truth in *Truth and Method*, but in several essays he makes clear his reliance on Heidegger's treatment of truth as unconcealedness (*Unverborgenheit*).[13] Truth is an event of revealing that, at the same time, conceals.

THE DIALOGICAL CHARACTER OF GADAMER'S PHILOSOPHICAL HERMENEUTICS: GADAMER'S DISTINCT PATH

If we pursue in greater detail Gadamer's consideration of truth, we come to see how Gadamer's treatment of this central theme, however much reliant on the Heideggerian definition, is significantly different than Heidegger's. Our examination of this difference will lead us to other important differences and to Gadamer's critique of Heidegger. Gadamer's account of truth differentiates itself from that of Heidegger in its temporality, in its exemplary occasion, and, above all, in the mediated character of the experience of truth, i.e., in its dialectical and dialogical character.

There are two ways in which Gadamer's treatment of the temporality of understanding and the event of truth distinguishes itself from Heidegger's account. We have noted above how Gadamer accepts the distended and three-dimensional account of temporality that Heidegger provides in *Being and Time*. Heidegger, however, gives a clear and distinct priority to the futural aspect of time. Whatever it is that we are about and hoping to accomplish shapes most importantly our temporality and our understanding. Ultimately, of course, in the account of *Being and Time* what lies ahead is our own death. *Dasein's* understanding of itself as Being-towards-death (*Sein-zum-Tode*) is the leading concept of the existential analyis of *Dasein* in this work. For Gadamer, the future does not have this predominate position. Although some have charged Gadamer with giving a priority to the past, this is also not the case. Rather, Gadamer's account shows a symmetry and mutual reciprocity of the three dimensions.

Secondly, and more specifically with regard to the question of truth, for Gadamer the event of truth takes time, while for Heidegger the event is almost always presented as sudden and abrupt. In *Being and Time*, it is momentary (*augenblicklich*). In the work after the "turn" the primary metaphor for the event of truth is lightning. In the lecture "The Turning" from 1949, for example, Heidegger writes: "The in-turning that is the lightning flash of the truth of Being is the entering, flashing glance – insight."[14] In this lecture Heidegger elaborates on its suddenness and explicitly insists that it happens "without mediation."[15] Another good example of the immediacy and abruptness of the truth-event for Heidegger can be found in the essay *Identity and Difference* (1957) in which Heidegger confronts Hegel's treatment of the title's concepts. Here, Heidegger treats truth as the belonging together of man and Being. Heidegger would have us see that we misunderstand "belonging together" if we consider it in terms of categories, mediation, and dialectic. It is rather an abrupt spring or leap; it is "without a bridge."[16] For Gadamer, by way of contrast, the truth-event takes time, requires language, and is the result of mediation, dialectic, and conversation.

In Gadamer's account of the mediated, dialectical, conversational truth-event, we can detect the voices of Plato, Aristotle, and Hegel. Gadamer takes up Hegel's dialectic to explicate the hermeneutical experience of understanding, even though he rejects the Hegelian absolute and endorses what Hegel calls the "bad infinity," because the conversation remains, for Gadamer, always open-ended. Aristotle is significant both for the concept of practical reason or *phronesis*, which is central to account of the understanding in *Truth and Method*, and for Gadamer's concept of "tarrying" (*Verweilen* – perhaps via Heidegger), which is central to the account Gadamer develops after *Truth and Method* both of theory and of the experience of the work of art. Tarrying, as the way of attending to art or to the world, is to be understood as a mode of comportment (to speak anglicized Heideggerian) or as a habit (to speak anglicized Aristotelian). "Tarrying" takes time, and in tarrying we lose ourselves in the thing and, thereby, lose track of time. Where Heidegger would have us await the sudden flash of insight, Gadamer would have us develop the habit of tarrying with things.

This tarrying is also a conversation – a conversation with oneself, with the thing at hand, and with others about whatever is at stake. Gadamer construes the understanding and the truth-event as linguistic – even the experience of the apparently nonlinguistic artwork, e.g., painting, sculpture, or music. As he writes in *Truth and Method*, "All understanding is interpretation, and all interpretation takes place in the medium of a language which would allow the object to come into words and yet at the same time the interpreter's own language" (TM 389). This bringing into words is not a matter of listening to the gods, as it is for Heidegger, but is, rather, a matter of joining a conversation. When we try to understand something, we are joining a conversation, entering a dialogue. This requires, as he said recently in an interview, not "hearing from" another but "listening to" another.[17] Conversation was an important concept for Heidegger, also, but, as we have just noted, his conversation was with the gods. Heidegger's treatment follows from a line in Hölderlin ("we have been a conversation"), which locates the conversation between the human and the divine.[18] His writing, accordingly, is meditative, I would suggest, and not dialogical. Although Heidegger, both in *Being and Time* with its concept of Being-with (*Mitsein*) and in his later work, provides a framework for the social and the dialogical, he never makes good on this aspect of the conversation that he says we are. The later Heidegger is not so much conversing as he is waiting and listening for the voice of the gods. We noted above how the truth-event for Heidegger is best characterized as the voice of the gods, comes like lightning – unmediated and "without a bridge." Gadamer, however, explicitly characterizes the conversation with the other as providing a "bridge."[19] Of the linguistic tradition, in which we participate when we join the conversation, Gadamer writes that its "lack of immediacy... is not a defect" (TM 389). Language is simply the necessary medium, for Gadamer, within which our conversation can come to understand something in a limited way. This coming to understand in language is, for Gadamer, necessarily dialectical. Unlike Heidegger, he defines understanding and philosophy as dialectical. In his writing Heidegger time and again attacks dialectical thinking as a conceptual sleight of hand or symptom of confusion.[20] Gadamer learns much about dialectic from Hegel, but ultimately it is Plato who shapes Gadamer's understanding of dialectic, for dialectic becomes defined by Gadamer as dialogue: "Philosophy is dialectic – the art of conducting a dialogue in which in the end nobody is conducting, but both partners are conducted, in such a way that the dialogue leads somewhere.[21]

THE GREEKS AND THE ANTINOMY
OF BEGINNINGS: THE CRITIQUE
OF HEIDEGGER

Heidegger's readings of the Western philosophical tradition clearly provoke much thought and consideration in Gadamer's own interpretation of the tradition. Gadamer is too good a philologian and scholar to be persuaded by the quirky etymologies and translations that Heidegger sometimes proposes, and he is too good a listener to the text to be persuaded by what Gadamer acknowledges are Heidegger's violent interpretations of classic philosophical texts.[22] Behind the quirky etymologies and the violent interpretations in Heidegger's work lies openly his thesis that the history of Western thought is a history of the forgetfulness of Being – which forgetfulness begins with Plato and culminates in the nihilism of Nietzsche. This nihilism has brought us the catastrophe of the past century's world wars and the dominance of our lives by technology. Heidegger awaits a new beginning that the god (or gods) might bring us. He goes back to the pre-Socratics to find this alternative. Gadamer accepts none of this.[23]

Gadamer often suggests that the first great service Heidegger provided in regard to Greek classical philosophy is that he freed the Greek from the tyranny of Latin, i.e., from the tyranny of Latin translation and the Latin tradition of interpreting the texts that dominated so much of the modern European appropriation of classical Greek philosophy. It is worth noting that many of Heidegger's early students came both to have an important impact on the revival of interest in Greek classical philosophy and to have been sharply critical of Heidegger's interpretations. These include Leo Strauss, Jakob Klein, Gerhard Krüger, Hannah Arendt, and Gadamer himself. Although Gadamer lectured and published on many Greek thinkers, he is most concerned with Plato. And it is Plato who, above all, represents for Heidegger the falling away from Being.

Two closely related theses are central to Heidegger's view of Plato: (1) that Being for Plato and the post-Platonic philosophers was Being-present-at-hand; and (2) that truth for Plato was correctness. In addition, Heidegger criticizes the Platonic notion of theory (*theoria*) for the priority it gives to sight. Gadamer rejects both these theses and gives an account of *theoria* as a way of being with something, i.e., tarrying, which is not merely a matter of sight.[24] Although Heidegger's critique is original, it embraces the Aristotelian critique that holds that Plato cannot make sense of the relation of his ideal forms to the world of experience. This follows from Plato's focus on unity and the One. In a number of his writings, Gadamer argues that the much discussed problem of the one and the many is, in the end, the problem of the "two," the indeterminate dyad.[25] On his account, the two is not reducible to the one. There are both "two" and "one." Both the soul and *logos* exhibit this structure. Both have a certain sort of unity, but both exhibit internal differentiation – twoness. Heidegger, however, finds here only unity, and in the *koinon* (commonality) of the *logos* he finds only the empty and abstract "most general."[26] Gadamer argues that the question of the one and the many is not be confused with the much discussed problem of participation (*methexis*), i.e., how it is that so many things can participate in one idea. This supposed problem is closely connected with the separation (*chorismos*) problem, i.e., that the ideas dwell somehow in some place beyond the heavens. Against the traditional and Heideggerian criticism, Gadamer insists that there is no separation problem in Plato, because Plato presupposes the participation of the individual thing in the idea.[27] Plato's dialogues show us how we too must make this presupposition.

The tension between the "one" and the "two" is closely related, for Gadamer, to the theme of finitude, which figures prominently in all his work on Plato as well as in his positive recovery of rhetoric and dialectic. In short, in opposition to Heidegger to whom he is indebted for the very theme of finitude, Gadamer shows us how for Plato knowledge is not reducible to "having" or "seeing" in the way that Heidegger claims it is for Plato. Heidegger reads Aristotelian divinity back into the human soul. For Heidegger, the human soul in Greek philosophy is a dim shadow of the nonerotic thought that thinks itself in its perfection and completeness. Gadamer, on the other hand, returns us to the erotic soul of Plato's *Symposium* and *Phaedrus*, in a way that acknowledges Aristotle's admonition to strive to be divine, yet recognizes our humanity, i.e., Gadamer emphasizes the erotic striving that marks our finitude. This supports his positive evaluation of conversation where rhetoric and opinion have their appropriate place.

Just as Gadamer resists Heidegger's critique of Plato and his reading of the whole of post-Platonic philosophy as Platonism, so too Gadamer resists Heidegger's reading of the pre-Socratics as providing a beginning of thinking that is not "metaphysical" and from whom Plato represents a falling away. For Heidegger, there is a great break between the pre-Socratics and Plato. Gadamer finds, rather, continuity. Gadamer at the beginning of his recently published lectures on the pre-Socratics made a methodological comment that decisively differentiates his approach from that of Heidegger:

The crucial thing in my lectures on the pre-Socratics is that I begin neither with Thales nor with Homer, nor do I begin with the Greek language in the second century before Christ; I begin instead with Plato and Aristotle. This, in my judgment, is the sole philosophical access to an interpretation of the pre-Socratics. Everything else is historicism without philosophy. (BP 10)

In his reading of the pre-Socratics, time and again, he shows how Plato and Aristotle take up pre-Socratic concepts in a positive way. Thus, he shows a certain continuity between the pre-Socratics and the Socratics, unlike Heidegger who sees an epochal break between them. Time and again Gadamer disagrees – sometimes implicitly, sometimes explicity – with Heidegger's readings. He disagrees, for example, with Heidegger's treatment of Anaximander's infinite (*apeiron*) (BP 88). And he takes issue with Heidegger's notion that the passage in Parmenides' *Proem* about the unshakeable heart of truth and opinions of mortals is about the miracle of self-differentiation (BP 124). As always very generous with regard to Heidegger, Gadamer in a number of instances suggests that Heidegger came to understand his own errors of interpretation (BP 111). Gadamer suggests further that Heidegger in part, here as elsewhere, was misled by his reliance on Nietzsche (BP 124).

Closely related to Heidegger's fascination with the pre-Socratics is Heidegger's notion that Western thought must begin again. He seeks a new beginning. For Gadamer, there has been no beginning as such, and it is a mistake to seek another one. We inevitably find ourselves in the middle of things with a past and future. So had Plato found himself and so had the pre-Socratics, even though their past is not much available to us. Gadamer suggests that, in a certain sense, it is appropriate to consider the Greek pre-Socratics as the beginning of Western philosophy and science, yet, at the same time, they too had a past with roots in Egypt and the East. The very concept of a beginning, according to Gadamer, is a dialectical one – very much in a Kantian sense: "I would like to suggest that, for existing things, the beginning consists in the fact that they have no beginning because what exists preserves itself in its continual periodicity" (BP 88).

Heidegger's hope for a new beginning was explicitly not a hope for a new beginning of philosophy, for philosophy means metaphysics for Heidegger. He looked for a kind of thinking that would be post-philosophical. Gadamer sees Heidegger's later work as extremely valuable and thought-provoking, a challenge and a provocation, but unsuccessful. Its lack of success was inevitable for Gadamer for a number of reasons. The very notion of stepping outside or overcoming or being done with the history of thought and making a new beginning make no sense. The attempt to leave philosophy behind cannot succeed, because for Gadamer philosophy is a natural disposition (RAS 139). And Heidegger's rejection of the language of metaphysics is unfounded according to Gadamer because there is no language of metaphysics.[28] The following three sentences by Gadamer reveal the deep affinity and indebtedness of Gadamer's thought to Heidegger's work and the deep divide: "I have made my own contribution to philosophy by linking up with this vision of the later Heidegger. To be sure, I did not follow him in his incessant and repeatedly frustrated effort to bypass the language of traditional metaphysics, its conceptual system and its talk of eidetic knowledge, and to exploit the evocative force of the poetic word for philosophic thought. To me this seems neither necessary nor possible."[29] Inevitably, the attempt to avoid the "language of metaphysics" leaves Heidegger suffering from a failing or lack of an appropriate language (*Sprachnot*). This, in part, for Gadamer, follows from the fact that Heidegger was too much struggling with Nietzsche. In a recent interview, Gadamer reports that shortly before his death Heidegger told his family that Nietzsche had ruined him.[30] Whereas Heidegger had largely oriented his hermeneutical effort around a confrontation with Nietzsche, Gadamer acknowledges that his hermeneutical orientation, whose impulse came in the first place from Heidegger, is a critical response to Dilthey.

It is clear that Gadamer's thought, like that of Heidegger, is motivated in large part by a consideration of our contemporary situation in a "modern" age in which science, especially the natural sciences, together with technology play such an important role and for which the intellectual legacy of the Enlightenment remains so decisive. And, like Heidegger, Gadamer can be counted among the critics of Enlightenment thought and the Enlightenment legacy. Unlike Heidegger, however, Gadamer does not paint a dark and apocalyptic picture of our age. He finds Heidegger's dismal view as overdramatized, dangerous, and hubristic. Gadamer writes, for example: "Don't we all run the risk of a terrible intellectual hubris if we equate Nietzsche's anticipations and the ideological confusion of the present with life as it is actually lived with its own forms of solidarity? Here, in fact, my divergence from Heidegger is fundamental."[31]

CONCLUSION

We have noted a number of significant divergences of Gadamer's views from those of Heidegger. It is important to recognize that Heidegger was a constant challenge and provocation for the development of Gadamer's thought – but he was more than that. In his lectures and in *Being and Time*, the young Heidegger provided the young doctor of philosophy both with a hermeneutical and phenomenological account of the understanding and with a fresh access to Greek classical philosophy. The account of the understanding importantly brought also powerful treatments of temporality and truth – both of which Gadamer would accept and modify. Heidegger's analysis of truth showed Gadamer how to escape the philosophical dead ends of subjectivism/objectivism and idealism/realism. Gadamer accepts Heidegger's critique of representational thinking, but he does not find the critique appropriate to Plato and Aristotle. Gadamer accommodates the Heideggerian critique of the classical tradition and its modern legacy but nonetheless sustains the work of Plato and Aristotle and the example of Socrates as a model of the good life. He shows us the relevance of their work to the philosophical questions and problems of our age.

It may be helpful to note Gadamer's own location of his work when he points to a place "between phenomenology and dialectic" – the title of a self-critique written in 1986 (GW 2, 3–26) much of which is incorporated in his "Reflections on My Philosophical Journey." We can take this location "between" as marking something important, even if it is a somewhat oversimplified demarcation. Gadamer places himself between the phenomenology of Husserl and, more importantly, Heidegger and the dialectic of Hegel and, more importantly, Plato. This philosophical location parallels for Gadamer the location of the human, which finds itself, in the language of classical Greek philosophy, between *nous* and *logos*. Both are constitutive of the human. Both are required for truth. There is, for us, no insight without speech, without conversation in language. And conversation is about something that often exceeds its grasp. In his work in a number of different contexts, Gadamer calls upon us to give ourselves to the conversation. This participation, *Teilhaben*, (another importantly Platonic concept) is an historical participation with others in the world – which participation presupposes a solidarity with others. Gadamer asks us both to recognize and to reaffirm this participatory solidarity in all the dimensions of human life.

NOTES

1 "Reflections on My Philosophical Journey," in *The Philosophy of Hans-Georg Gadamer*, edited by Lewis Hahn (Chicago and LaSalle: Open Court, 1997), pp. 46–7: "My own intention... was precisely to blaze a trail *to* the later Heidegger.... My philosophical hermeneutics seeks precisely to adhere to the line of questioning of this essay [Heidegger's "The Origin of the Artwork"] *and the later Heidegger* and to make it accessible in a new way.... I must leave it to others to decide whether the path I have followed can claim to have kept up, at least to some degree, with Heidegger's own ventures in thinking."

2 "Dem ältesten, treuen Schüler meines Vaters" in Martin Heidegger, *Reden und Andere Zeugnisse eines Lebensweges, Gesamtausgabe* vol. 16, edited by Hermann Heidegger (Frankfurt: Klostermann, 2000), p. v.

3 PA 36; also see Gadamer's contribution to memories of Husserl by his students in *Edmund Husserl und die Phänomenologische Bewegung: Zeugnisse in Text und Bild*, edited by Hans Rainer Sepp (Freiburg: Karl Alber, 1988), pp. 13–16.

4 For the habilitation's endorsement of the Heideggerian thesis, see *Plato's Dialectical Ethics* (PDE), p. 34. For the later rejection of the thesis see TM 413; also GW 2, 486, and *Hermeneutische Entwürfe* (Tübingen: Mohr Siebeck, 2000), 138, 142.

5 "Ich und Du," GW 4, 234–9.

6 *Anteile: Martin Heidegger zum 60. Geburtstag* (Frankfurt: Klostermann, 1950). For details on the complications of bringing out this Festschrift, see Grondin, pp. 302–3. Although Gadamer took responsibility for putting the Festschrift together, the volume appeared without listing an editor.

7 This essay has appeared twice in English translation under different titles: "Heidegger's Later Philosophy," translated by David Linge in *Philosophical Hermeneutics* and "The Truth of the Work of Art," translated by John Stanley in *Heidegger's Ways.*

8 Many of these are collected in *Heidegger's Ways* (German 1983, English translation 1994). An additional, as yet untranslated, seven articles are

collected in Volume 10 of his *Gesammelte Werke*. Another appears in *Hermeneutische Entwürfe* (2000).

9 "Reflections," p. 15.

10 In an interview with Alfons Greider in 1992 he said: "The most important Heideggerian text to have appeared posthumously is this earliest work of his, to which I have recently written an introduction." See "A Conversation with Hans-Georg Gadamer," *Journal of the British Society for Phenomenology* 26 (1995), p. 117. For Gadamer's introduction, see "Heideggers 'theologische' Jugendschrift," *Dilthey Jahrbuch für Philosophie und Geschichte der Geisteswissenschaften* 6 (1989), 228–34. For Gadamer's use of tarrying (*Verweilen*) to characterize the encounter with the work of art, see RB 45 and GW 2, 7.

11 "Reflections," pp. 27, 47; also PH 38; GW 2, 496; and *Hans-Georg Gadamer im Gespräch*, edited by Carsten Dutt (Heidelberg: C. Winter, 1995), p. 22.

12 "Reflections," pp. 48–9.

13 See "Truth in the Human Sciences," and "What is Truth?", both in *Hermeneutics and Truth*, edited by Brice Wachterhauser (Evanston: Northwestern University Press, 1994), pp. 25–46. See also "Von der Wahrheit des Wortes," (untranslated) in GW 8, 37–57, and "Selbstdarstellung Hans-Georg Gadamer," GW 2, pp. 479–508, especially p. 504.

14 Martin Heidegger, *The Question Concerning Technology*, translated by William Lovitt (New York: Harper & Row, 1977), p. 45.

15 *Ibid.*, 44.

16 "Brückenlos," *Identity and Difference*, translated by Joan Stambaugh (New York: Harper & Row, 1969), p. 33 (English), p. 96 (German).

17 *Hans-Georg Gadamer im Gespräch*, p. 13.

18 Martin Heidegger, *Existence and Being* (Chicago: Regnery, 1949), p. 279.

19 Admittedly the contexts for Heidegger's being without a bridge and Gadamer's bridge are quite different – the divine and the human. See "Text and Interpretation"(GDE 27).

20 See the following in the *Gesamtausgabe* (Frankfurt: Klostermann), volume 29/30, *Die Grundbegriffe der Metaphysik*, pp. 276, 306; 353; volume 32, *Hegels Phänomenologie des Geistes*, pp. 105, 162, 200; vol. 65, *Beiträge*, p. 412. See also *Identity and Difference*, pp. 32, 95.

21 "Phenomenology, Hermeneutics, Metaphysics," *Journal of the British Society for Phenomenology* 25 (1994), 109. In an interview in 1992 Gadamer states that "Later Heidegger too became monological. The early Heidegger was not like that at all, but was as I tried my life long to remain: ready to listen to the other, to respond to him or her." See

Journal of the British Society for Phenomenology 26 (1995), p. 118. In the same interview (p. 123), Gadamer characterizes his differences with Heidegger in the following way: "This was *my* way – that I told Heidegger that language is not the powerful word; language is reply."

22 In "Heidegger and the Greeks" (untranslated), for example, Gadamer states that he could never accept Heidegger's etymologies without resistance (GW 10, 36). He acknowledges further that one can find two dozen mistakes in Heidegger's translation of a choral song. He is presumably referring to the "Ode to Man" from Sophocle's *Antigone*, to which Heidegger returns frequently in his work (GW 10, 45). See also the interview with Carsten Dutt, *Hans-Georg Gadamer im Gespräch*, pp. 39–40.

23 See Gadamer's letter to Leo Strauss, in which he writes of the unreality of the assertion of the complete forgetfulness of Being, of the night of Being (*Seinsnacht*). "Correspondence concerning *Wahrheit und Methode*," (with Leo Strauss) *The Independent Journal of Philosophy* 2 (1978), p. 8.

24 TM, 455: "Within the horizon of [Heidegger's] temporal interpretation of being, classical metaphysics as a whole is an ontology of the present-at-hand, and modern science is, unbeknownst to itself, its heir. But in Greek theoria there was undoubtedly another element as well. Theoria grasps not so much the present-at-hand, as the thing itself (*die Sache selbst*), which still has the dignity of a 'thing'. . . . Thus we must keep the dignity of the thing (*Ding*) and the referentiality of language free from the prejudice originating in the ontology of the present-at-hand as well as in the concept of objectivity." See also PT 31.

25 "Plato's Unwritten Dialectic," in *Dialogue and Dialectic*, p. 132 (GW 6, 135).

26 Martin Heidegger, *Beiträge zur Philosophie, Gesamtausgabe* 65 (Frankfurt: Klostermann, 1989), pp. 206, 459. Gadamer writes: "What Plato is aiming at is rather that the talk of Being implies a differentiation which is not the distinction of various regions of Being but an inner structure of Being itself. To all talk of Being belongs just as much self-sameness and identity as also otherness and variety. And both these aspects are so little exclusive that they reciprocally determine one another." "Plato," GW 3, 343 (untranslated). We might call these reciprocal determinations of the one and the many in Being the dialectical structure of Being.

27 "Dialektik ist nicht Sophistik," GW 7, 343 (untranslated): "My thesis is that this is not at all a Platonic problem but rather a Platonic presupposition. Plato had always viewed the participation of the individual in the idea as self-evident and as that which makes the acceptance of ideas at all reasonable." See also "Reflections," p. 34.

28 See "Reflections," p. 48; and Gadamer's letter to Dallmayr: GDE 98.

29 "Phenomenology, Hermeneutics, Metaphysics," pp. 108–9.

30 "Heidegger und Nietzsche: Nietzsche hat mich kaputtgemacht!" *Aletheia* 5 (1994), 6–8.

31 "A Letter by Professor Hans-Georg Gadamer," in Richard Bernstein, *Beyond Objectivism and Relativism* (Philadelphia: University of Pennsylvania Press, 1983), pp. 261–5, especially 264.

12 The Constellation of Hermeneutics, Critical Theory and Deconstruction

"Hermeneutics," "critical theory," and "deconstruction" are the names of three intellectual orientations that have dominated continental philosophical debates during the latter part of the twentieth century. Although each of these orientations has its own complex lineage and affinities, they have nevertheless come to be associated with three outstanding thinkers: Hans-Georg Gadamer, Jürgen Habermas, and Jacques Derrida. At the most abstract level, all three exhibit what has come to be called the "linguistic turn." The concern with language is central to their philosophic investigations. Yet when we turn to what they mean by language, what they stress in their analyses, what consequences they draw from their reflections, their differences are initially much more striking than anything that they share in common. And even when one of these thinkers has addressed the concerns of the others, their encounters have often seemed more like nonencounters – like one of those surrealistic conversations where participants are speaking past each other. Yet there are not only striking differences among these three thinkers, there are also some important overlapping commonalities. It is best to look upon these three thinkers and their characteristic orientations as forming a tensed constellation – one in which their emphatic differences enable us to appreciate their strengths as well as their weaknesses. In this paper, my primary focus will be on Gadamer's philosophic hermeneutics, especially as it bears on questions of coming to grips with modernity and its discontents.

Although Gadamer, who was born in 1900, belongs to an older generation than Habermas and Derrida (who are contemporaries), his philosophical hermeneutics became known to a wider intellectual public primarily because of the critical attention that it received by the young Habermas. During the 1960s, Habermas wrote a now famous critical review of *Truth and Method*.[1] And when Habermas was first appointed as a professor at Frankfurt University in 1965, he dealt with hermeneutics in his inaugural lecture: "Knowledge and Human Interests."[2] It was these interventions that initiated what has come to be called the Gadamer-Habermas debate – a debate that has taken many twists and turns over the years, and has involved many other thinkers in addition to Gadamer and Habermas. I do not want to narrate the intricacies of this ongoing complex debate, but I do want to highlight some of the major issues that emerged from it.

During the 1960s, Habermas was engaged in a sharp critique of the positivist and behaviorist tendencies that were dominating the social sciences. In carrying out this critique, Habermas viewed Gadamer (and more generally, the German hermeneutic tradition) as an important ally. Both Gadamer and Habermas were relentlessly critical of the imperialistic tendencies of what they took to be a misguided positivist and scientistic epistemology – one that claimed that all *legitimate* knowledge had to satisfy the narrow criteria that the positivists set forth for empirical and analytic knowledge. Neither Gadamer nor Habermas were denigrating the achievements of the natural sciences. Their quarrel was a philosophic one. The positivists and their allies had an excessively narrow conception of what constituted knowledge (empirical and analytic), and they refused to recognize that there were any other valid conceptions of knowledge or understanding. The positivists, who prided themselves on being empirical and open-minded, were violently imposing their epistemic grid. Both Habermas and Gadamer argued that this epistemological restriction was not innocent. Rather, it was a manifestation of deeper forces at work in modern societies where instrumental or technological rationality was infiltrating and distorting the forms of everyday life – the very life forms that Gadamer claimed characteristic of our being-in-the-world. Although Gadamer and Habermas were attacking a common enemy, their standpoints were radically different.

In "Knowledge and Human Interests," Habermas distinguished three basic cognitive (or knowledge-constitutive) interests: the technical, practical, and emancipatory. These three cognitive interests are "rooted in the specific fundamental conditions of the production and self-constitution of the human species."[3] Each of these cognitive interests determines a distinctive domain and the appropriate *methodological* framework for ascertaining and warranting knowledge claims in these domains. Furthermore, there are three different types of sciences or disciplines that correspond to each of these over-arching cognitive interests. "The approach of the empirical-analytic sciences incorporates a technical cognitive interest; that of the historical-hermeneutic sciences incorporates a practical one; and the approach of the critically oriented sciences an emancipatory interest,"[4] In drawing a sharp distinction between the technical and practical cognitive interests, Habermas was appropriating a vital Gadamerian distinction that can be traced back to the distinction that Aristotle makes between *techne* and *praxis* in his *Nicomachean Ethics*. It is difficult today to recover this Aristotelian distinction because we frequently identify the "practical" with the "technical." But it is just this false identification of the practical with the technical (and the disastrous consequences that follow from it) that both Gadamer and Habermas wanted to expose. Both associate the "practical" with *praxis* and *phronesis*, the virtue of practical wisdom that Aristotle highlights in his *Ethics*. Habermas certainly agrees with Gadamer who writes: "The concept of 'praxis' which was developed in the last two centuries is a awful deformation of what practice really is."[5] And Gadamer would endorse what Habermas wrote in one of his early essays:

The real difficulty in the relation of theory and practice does not arise from this new function of science as a technological force, but rather from the fact that we are no longer able to distinguish between practical and technical power. Yet even a civilization that has been rendered scientific is not granted dispensation from practical questions. Therefore a peculiar danger arises when the process of scientification transgresses the limit of technical questions, without, however, departing from the level of rationality confined to the technological horizon. For then no attempt is made to attain a rational consensus on the part of citizens concerning the practical control of their destiny. Its place is taken by the attempt to attain technical control over history by perfecting the administration of society, an attempt that is just as impractical as it is unhistorical.[6]

For Habermas, it is the practical interest that governs the methodological framework of the "historic–hermeneutic" sciences.

The historic–hermeneutic sciences gain knowledge in a different methodological framework. Here the validity of propositions is not constituted in the frame of reference of technical control.... For theories are not constructed deductively and experience is not organized with regard to the success of operations. Access to the facts is provided by the understanding of meaning, not observation. The verification of law-like hypotheses in empirical-analytic sciences has its counterpart in the interpretation of texts. Thus the rules of hermeneutics determine the possible meaning of the validity of statements in the cultural sciences [*Geisteswissenschaften*].[7]

There is a third cognitive interest – the emancipatory interest. It is more accurate to say that the emancipatory interest is already implicit in both the technical and practical interests. Habermas (following the tradition of German idealism) explicitly identifies the emancipatory interest with the interest of Reason itself, the demand for self-reflection. "Reason ... means the will to reason. In self-reflection knowledge for the sake of knowledge attains congruence with the interest in autonomy and responsibility. The emancipatory cognitive interest aims at the pursuit of reflection as such."[8] It is here that some of the sharpest and the most consequential differences between Gadamer and Habermas begin to erupt. Consider how Habermas characterizes those *critical* social sciences that are governed by the emancipatory cognitive interest.

The systematic sciences of social action, that is economics, sociology, and political science, have the goal, as do the empirical–analytic sciences, of producing nomological knowledge. A critical social science, however, will not remain satisfied with this. It is concerned with going beyond this goal to determine when theoretical statements grasp invariant regularities of social action as such and when they express ideologically frozen relations of dependence that can be transformed.... The methodological framework that determines the meaning of validity of critical propositions of this category is established by the concept of *self-reflection*. The latter releases the subject from dependence on hypostatized powers. Self-reflection is determined by an emancipatory cognitive interest.[9]

In distinguishing the technical from the practical cognitive interest, and in claiming that the practical interest sets the methodological framework for the historic–hermeneutic disciplines, Habermas was attempting to situate the proper place of hermeneutics. But he also sought to specify the *limitations* of hermeneutics by stressing that there is an independent emancipatory interest. This enabled him to characterize the methodological framework of the critical social sciences that went beyond the achievements of hermeneutics.

Needless to say, this is not the way in which Gadamer understood the situation. Gadamer claimed that Habermas misunderstood and distorted the fundamental character and aim of philosophical hermeneutics. In the Foreword to the second German edition of *Truth and Method*, Gadamer (with Habermas clearly in mind) declared that he was not primarily concerned with epistemology or with distinguishing "methodological frameworks." He emphatically asserted: "My real concern was and is philosophic; not what we do or what we ought to do, but what happens to us over and above our wanting and doing."[10] To make his point as clear and firm as possible, Gadamer drew an analogy with Kant: "[Kant] asked a philosophical question; what are the conditions of our knowledge, by virtue of which modern science is possible, and how far does it extend? The following investigation also asks a philosophic question in the same sense. But it does not ask it only of the so-called human sciences . . . . It asks (to put it in Kantian terms) how is understanding possible" (TM xxix–xxx). Gadamer's project is ontological – not epistemological or methodological. Following Heidegger, Gadamer argues that the essential character of our being-in-the-world is to be individuals who understand the happening of truth through language. In this respect, philosophical hermeneutics is not only ontological and linguistic – it is also universal. For whatever we self-consciously do or want, the happening of understanding is always already taking place in our linguistic encounters with the world. Gadamer is skeptical about the very idea of distinguishing an *independent* emancipatory interest that provides the methodological framework for "the critique of ideology." He charges Habermas with succumbing to the worst utopian illusions of the Enlightenment in his attempt to delineate an independent domain of the "new" critical social sciences. Gadamer does not reject the idea of emancipation. He even agrees that it is implicit in Reason itself. But it is not an independent cognitive interest. Rather, it is already intrinsic in hermeneutic understanding. In an essay dealing with the legacy of Hegel, Gadamer writes:

The principle of freedom is unimpugnable and irrevocable. It is no longer possible for anyone still to affirm the unfreedom of humanity. The principle that all are free never again can be shaken. But does this mean that on account of this, history has come to an end? Are all human beings actually free? Has not history since then been a matter of just this, that the historical conduct of man has to translate the principle of freedom into reality? Obviously this points to the unending march of world history to the openness of its future tasks and gives no becalming assurance that everything is already in order. (RAS 37)

Habermas himself might have written this passage. But despite some of their common agreements, we should not underestimate the differences between them – even when their language sounds similar. Gadamer has always been critical of what he takes to be the *excesses* of the Enlightenment. In *Truth and Method*, he criticizes "the Enlightenment's prejudice against prejudice." All understanding requires prejudices or prejudgments – prejudgments that are inherited from tradition. Of course, Gadamer recognizes that there is a difference between blinding prejudices and enabling prejudices, but this is a distinction that emerges only through our dialogical encounters, and not by monological self-reflection. In the development of his philosophical hermeneutics, Gadamer emphasizes the role of the tradition in determining who we are. He also seeks to recover the type of world disclosing *truth* that is revealed through our encounters with history and works of art. Gadamer has always been concerned with ethical issues, and he sees philosophical hermeneutics as the heir to the Greek tradition of practical philosophy. Indeed, Gadamer claims that "if we relate Aristotle's description of the ethical phenomenon and especially of the virtue of moral knowledge to our own investigation, we find that Aristotle's analysis is in fact a kind of *model of the problems of hermeneutics*" (TM 324).

One way to grasp the significant differences between Gadamer and Habermas is to see how they respond to what they take to be the crisis situation of modernity and its discontents. As I have already indicated, both Gadamer and Habermas are deeply concerned about the ways in which the varieties of technological, means-end, or instrumental rationality are infiltrating and distorting the forms of everyday life. Both of them see that this tendency is one that undermines responsible political decision-making among citizens. Gadamer's characteristic response to this disturbing situation is primarily philosophical. "Relying on the tradition of practical philosophy helps to guard us against the technological self-understanding of the modern concept of science." Or again, he states "When Aristotle, in the sixth book of the *Nicomachean Ethics*, distinguishes the manner of 'practical' knowledge...from theoretical and technical knowledge, he expresses, in my opinion, one of the greatest truths by which the Greeks throw light upon the 'scientific' mystification of modern society of specialization."[11]

Gadamer is sometimes criticized for engaging in a sentimental nostalgia for past traditions and epochs. But such a criticism is unwarranted for it misses the primary intention of philosophical hermeneutics. Gadamer has always insisted that we cannot but help to approach past history, traditions, and alien cultures with the questions that arise from our *own* horizons. We never escape from our own linguistic horizon. It is an illusion to think that we can bracket or suspend *all* our current prejudgments. This is the basis for his quarrel with the Cartesian legacy that has influenced so much of modern thinking, a legacy that assumes we can achieve what Hilary Putnam has called a "God's eye" perspective on reality. The basic imperative of philosophical hermeneutics is to articulate and evaluate the claim to truth that traditions makes upon us, to seek for a *fusion* of horizons in which we expand and deepen our own horizon. In this sense, all hermeneutical understanding involves a *critical* appropriation. It is in this spirit that Gadamer appeals to the Aristotelian tradition of practical philosophy. It is not a nostalgic return that Gadamer advocates, but rather a critical appropriation for our current situation.

In my own eyes, the great merit of Aristotle was that he *anticipated* the impasse of our scientific culture by his description of the structure of practical reason as distinct from theoretical knowledge and technical skill. By philosophical arguments he refuted the claim of the professional lawmakers whose function at that time corresponded to the role of the expert in modern scientific theory. Of course, I do not mean to equate the modern expert with the professional sophist. In his own field he is a faithful and reliable investigator, and in general he is well aware of the particularity of his methodical assumptions and realizes that the results of his investigation have a limited relevance. Nevertheless, the problem of our society is that the longing of the citizenry for orientation and normative patterns invests the expert with an exaggerated authority. Modern society expects him to provide a substitute for past moral and political orientations. (my emphasis)[12]

But for Habermas, this appropriation of the classical tradition of practical philosophy is simply not sufficient to come to grips with an understanding of modernity and its discontents. If one is serious about meeting the challenges that confront us today, we cannot limit ourselves to seeking to recover the classical tradition of practical philosophy, or to appeal to classical ideas of friendship and solidarity. What is required is a much more concrete and systematic analysis of modern societies, their pathologies, and their distortions. Habermas argues that Gadamer is not sufficiently sensitive to the way in which the type of dialogue that he discusses and cherishes is systematically distorted by contemporary social forces and insidious forms of political power. Habermas deals with the complex issues of modern law, rights, constitutions, and political power in order to formulate an adequate normative theory of democracy. Furthermore, Habermas doesn't think that philosophical hermeneutics is sufficient to deal with the problems of legitimizing and justifying universal norms. It isn't sufficient in the modern world to appropriate *phronesis*. Even Aristotle claimed that *phronesis* as ethical and political virtue presupposes the existence of a well-ordered *polis*. Today, one must also address the question of how ethical and political universal norms are to be justified. The differences between Gadamer and Habermas are not limited to the questions of politics and political philosophy. Rather these differences are indicative of more basic differences that pervade their intellectual orientations, including their different conception of truth and validity. Gadamer believes in the distinctive independent character of philosophical reflection. But for Habermas, there is no longer a sharp boundary between philosophy and a social theory informed by the social sciences. Although Gadamer is eloquent in his characterization (and practice) of dialogue, Habermas argues that we need to develop a theory of communication and universal pragmatics in order to ground our understanding of the reciprocity and symmetry required for open dialogue. Hermeneutics may very well be universal in the sense that understanding is always already present in whatever we say or do. But it doesn't follow that philosophical hermeneutics is universal in the sense that it provides the conceptual resources analyzing the pathologies of modern societies that need to be addressed to develop a richly textured normative democratic theory.

Although I am sympathetic with Habermas insofar as he shows some of the limitations of Gadamer's philosophical hermeneutics, I also think that Gadamer provides a needed corrective to Habermas. At the heart of Gadamer's philosophical hermeneutics is a deep appreciation of human finitude. Whether we are dealing with morality, ethics, or politics, Gadamer advocates the necessity for cultivating hermeneutic sensitivity and *phronesis* in all dimensions of human life. He even speaks of the "*one-sidedness* of hermeneutic universalism": but he justifies this "one-sidedness" as having the "truth of a corrective."

It enlightens the modern viewpoint based on making, producing, and constructing concerning the necessary conditions to which that viewpoint is subject. In particular, it limits the position of the philosopher in the modern world . . . .
   What man needs is not just the persistent posing of ultimate questions, but the sense of what is feasible, possible, what is correct, here and now. The philosopher, of all people, must, I think, be aware of the tension between what he claims to achieve and the reality in which he finds himself. (TM xxxvii–xxxviii)

This is why I think that the metaphor of a constellation is the appropriate one in discerning the complex relationship between Habermas and Gadamer. Each serves as a corrective to the other. But each shines brighter when viewed together in a constellation.

* * *

When we turn to Gadamer and Derrida (and tensions between hermeneutics and deconstruction), we seem to be in an entirely different realm of discourse. The differences between Gadamer and Derrida – in temperament, vocabulary, style, and thematic concerns – seem so radical that one may despair of finding anything in common. And yet we can say that both are passionately concerned with the subtleties of language and the interpretation of texts. Both return over and over again to a reading of the canonical philosophic texts. Both display an impressive sensitivity to literary texts and the visual arts. Even when they take up issues of responsibility, justice, friendship, ethics, and politics, they typically focus on the interpretation of texts. In part, these commonalities are due to the profound influence of Heidegger on their thinking. But they read, appropriate, and even criticize Heidegger in such sharply divergent ways that it is sometimes difficult to realize that they are speaking about the "same" philosopher. In 1981, Gadamer accepted an invitation to participate in a conference held in Paris where Derrida was also a participant. It was clearly Gadamer's intention to explore the differences between hermeneutics and deconstruction in his face-to-face encounter with Derrida. But a serious intellectual encounter never really happened.[13] Since that time, Gadamer has taken up the question of deconstruction (and Heideggerian *Destruktion*) on several occasions, but his "conversation" with Derrida has been one-sided. A genuine dialogue between Gadamer and Derrida has never taken place. This is a shame because there are crucial and consequential issues that arise between hermeneutics and deconstruction. Once again, I believe that a constellation is the appropriate metaphor in appreciating the complex relationship between hermeneutics and deconstruction.

Because Gadamer and Derrida are so sensitive to language, I want to stress some of the differences in their linguistic styles. Gadamer derives his understanding of philosophical hermeneutics from Heidegger's hermeneutics of facticity that is so prominent in Part I of *Being and Time*. Gadamer does concede that "like many of my critics, Heidegger too would probably feel a lack of radicality in the conclusions I draw.... When science expands into total technocracy and thus brings on the 'cosmic night' of the 'forgetfulness of being,' the nihilism that Nietzsche prophesied, then may one not gaze at the last fading light of the sun setting in the evening sky, instead of turning around to look for the first shimmer of its return?" (TM xxvii). The figures that dominate Gadamer's writing are the metaphors of "fusion," "play," the "to-and fro" movement of conversation, In seeking to understand what is strange, alien and other, we expand and deepen our own finite horizon and historicity. In this process of *Bildung*, self-knowledge is achieved in and through a dialogical encounter with the other. And in this encounter (this happening), we seek a fusion of horizons. Gadamer sometimes characterizes himself as a Hegelian of the "bad infinite," and by this he means that there is no final *Aufhebung*. Experience is *always* open to further experience – without end. There is no finality in understanding and interpretation. For Gadamer, like

Hegel, when we confront what is alien, other, and different, we seek to appropriate the *truth* implicit in what we encounter. Gadamer is sensitive to the ruptures and breaks in our understanding. But these are challenges to be met; they set the task for hermeneutics. The metaphoric figures of Gadamer are marked by "fusion" – where we seek reconciliation and coherence through dialogical play.[14]

Initially, the contrast with Derrida could not be more dramatic. "Rupture," "break," "heterogeneity," "impossibilities" are terms that saturate his writing. When Derrida deconstructs a text, or as he would prefer to put it, when he shows how a text deconstructs itself, he attempts to show how underlying its surface unity and coherence, there are also sorts of crevices, abysses, and undecidable aporias. A favorite "formula" of his is to claim that something is both "necessary and impossible." Derrida does not "reduce" texts to absurdities or meaningless gibberish (as so many of his critics claim); he seeks to expose the irreducible undecidable internal tensions and aporias. His logic is a "both/and logic" where we uncover heterogeneities for which there is no satisfactory fusion. Like Hegel (whom Derrida also greatly admires), Derrida is a master in bringing forth internal conflicts and contradictions, and in showing how at the heart of what we take to be the same is already otherness and difference. But unlike Hegel (and Gadamer), Derrida is skeptical that we can reconcile these contradictions in an encompassing synthesis. Derrida's "world" is one in which we never quite achieve the moments of coherence and fusion that is the aim of hermeneutics. On the contrary, wherever we turn, we discover undecidables and aporias. Gadamer focuses on the dialogical *achievement* of understanding texts, traditions, and works of art, but Derrida is more preoccupied with the multifarious ways in which misunderstanding always threatens us. He decenters what we take to be unified, coherent, and structured. Our thinking and language are pervaded by apparent binary oppositions, which are always deconstructing themselves. Derrida acknowledges boundaries and limits – only to show the subversive ways in which they are called into question, and how what is taken to be marginal and supplementary becomes "central." This is true not only of language and metaphysics, but also true of ethics and politics. Like Levinas, Derrida claims that the dominant logic of the same and the other is deeply imperialistic. We are always on the verge of failing to do justice to the otherness of the other, and the otherness that lies at the heart of the same.

But although these differences in language (and temperament) are manifest, we must be careful not to slip into a simplified binary opposition. Hermeneutical understanding would not make sense unless we also had a profound experience of what is alien, different, and other. And even though Derrida stresses the pervasiveness of *differance*, the very force of his deconstructions depends on appreciating the power of the desire for coherence, unity, and harmony. Derrida has been a relentless critic of the "metaphysics of presence," (even accusing Heidegger of being tainted by it) but he is just as insistent that it is *impossible* to abandon or "escape" from metaphysics. Just as I have argued that holding Habermas and Gadamer together in a constellation enables us see how each can serve as a corrective to the other, I want to make a similar claim about Gadamer and Derrida.

Let me return to what stands at the core of Gadamer's philosophical hermeneutics – dialogue and conversation. A living dialogue always stands behind our dialogical understanding of texts, works of art, and traditions. *Überlieferung* (tradition) *is* this ongoing conversation. We come to understand a text by learning how to question it and how it poses questions to us. "The hermeneutic phenomenon...implies the primacy of dialogue and the structure of question and answer. That a historical text is made the object of interpretation means that it puts a question to the interpreter" (TM 369). The idea that a historical text or a work of art can "speak" to us, can pose a "question" to us, can make a "claim to truth" upon us is a crucial presupposition for Gadamer's philosophical hermeneutics. And yet, we must pause and insist that "strictly speaking," a text, work of art, or tradition does not literally *speak* to us. Unlike a living conversation, we are not confronting a dialogical partner who can speak for herself. Rather it is *we* as interpreters that speak on behalf of a mute text. It is *we* who interpret a text as posing a question to us. Unlike a real-life dialogue, the dialogue with texts is a "one-sided" monological dialogue in which we are *both* questioning a text and answering for it. When we face up to this disparity between a living dialogue and the dialogue with texts and traditions, then we open up all sorts of gaps and problems. And these are just the sorts of gaps that Derrida exploits. It is not quite accurate to say that when we have doubts about the interpretation of a text, we must return to the text itself, because this "return" is really a return to the text as *we* interpret it. This is a point that Nietzsche already effectively made when he questioned whether there is any "reality" or "text" beyond and below our interpretations. This is just the sort of gap (abyss) that Derrida delights in exposing. A deconstructive analysis of Gadamer might well point out the aporia that lies at the heart of hermeneutics. On the one hand, Gadamer insists that texts do *not* have meaning *in themselves*, meaning arises only in the happening of understanding. But at the same time, Gadamer also insists that a text is sufficiently resistant to arbitrary meanings so that it can "question" our interpretations. This is not a trivial or sophistical perplexity because it raises profound questions about the limitations of the very idea of a dialogue or conversation with texts, works of art, and traditions. How is one to decide whether or not one has properly answered for a text that we are seeking to understand? There is always something undecidable in the happening of understanding and interpretation.

We can further our understanding of the consequential differences between Gadamer and Derrida by seeing how undecidability operates in another context. In the past two decades, Derrida's writings have taken a much more explicit ethical turn, although a close reading of his early works shows that he has always been interested in (obsessed with) questions of response, responsibility, and ethics.[15] Derrida shares with Gadamer (and Habermas) a deep suspicion and criticism of the ways in which technological thinking and calculation have infiltrated our ethical and political lives. Like Gadamer, Derrida thinks that it is misleading to appeal to universal rules, algorithms, and strategic calculations to bring out what is distinctive about ethical decision. But their differences come to the fore when we see how they respond to this situation. Gadamer appeals to the tradition of practical philosophy and to the Aristotelian conceptions of praxis and *phronesis* as a corrective to the growing insidious pervasiveness of technological thinking. But Derrida has a very different response. *Phronesis* does not play any significant role in his thinking. On the contrary, he is always stressing the irreducible undecidability that is inescapable in any ethical decision. Undecidability, for Derrida is *not* to be confused with nihilistic indecision, or with a gratuitous decisionism. Undecidability is the very condition for the possibility (and impossibility) of deciding and acting. A decision is not an *ethical* decision if it can be calculated, programmed, or "deduced" from some universal rule. Ethical decision is a possibility that is sustained by its impossibility. Or to make the point in a less paradoxical manner, an ethical decision requires confronting its irreducible undecidability. In his essay, "The Force of Law: The Mystical Foundation of Authority," Derrida introduces a sharp distinction between justice and law, and even declares that "Deconstruction is Justice."[16] John Caputo succinctly summarizes Derrida's point:

> ...the opposite of "undecidability" is not "decisiveness" but programmability, calculability, computerizability, or formalizability. Decision-making, judgment, on the other hand, positively *depends* upon undecidability.... So a "just" decision, a "judgment" that is worthy of the name, one that responds to the demands of justice, one that is more than merely legal, goes eyeball to eyeball with undecidability, stares it in the face (literally), looks into that abyss, and then makes the leap, that is "gives itself up to the impossible decision."...That does not mean it is "decisionistic," for that would break the tension in the opposite direction, by dropping or ignoring the law altogether and substituting subjectivistic autonomy for responsibility to the other.[17]

The differences in the way in which Gadamer and Derrida think about ethical decision are emblematic of the differences that pervade their entire philosophic orientations (and are the source of so much misunderstanding between them). But we can also ask why it is fruitful to view them as forming a constellation. Both Gadamer and Derrida reject a conception of praxis and ethical decision that would subsume it under the rubric of technological or instrumental thinking. Both reject the idea that we can "deduce" specific decisions from universal principles alone. For Gadamer, this opens the space for *phronesis* (practical judgment), which cannot be assimilated to *episteme* or *techne*. But for Derrida, who never seems to be satisfied until he uncovers an aporia, this opens the space for undecidability. But in the constellation that I am proposing, they supplement each other. Derrida does not do "justice" to the type of practical judgment that Gadamer highlights. At the same time, Derrida makes us painfully aware of something that Gadamer does not sufficiently emphasize – that even in practical judgment at its best, there is an element of irreducible risk and undecidability. Gadamer's appeal to *phronesis* helps to avoid the type of gratuitous decisionism that Derrida desperately wants to avoid. And more generally we can read Gadamer and Derrida (hermeneutics and deconstruction) as requiring each other. In the fusion of horizons, there is a tendency to gloss over the heterogeneities and abysses that confront us. But there is also a danger of becoming so fascinated with impossibilities and undecidables that we lose any sense of coherence and unity in our lives.

In the heat of the polemical debates about hermeneutics, critical theory, and deconstruction, it is common to exaggerate differences and to structure these debates in an exclusionary disjunctive fashion: EITHER "Hermeneutics," OR "Critical Theory," OR "Deconstruction." Partisans of these different orientations have a tendency to claim exclusivity for their favored orientation. Although we should not play down the differences and conflicts among these orientations, nevertheless each of them takes on a more poignant significance when we view them as forming a new constellation with both affinities and differences, attractions, and repulsions.

NOTES

1 An English translation of this review, "A Review of Gadamer's *Truth and Method*," was published in *Understanding and Social Inquiry*, eds. Fred R. Dallmayr and Thomas A. McCarthy. (Notre Dame: University of Notre Dame Press, 1977).

2 An English translation of this lecture appears in *Knowledge and Human Interests*, trans. Jeremy J. Shapiro (Boston: Beacon Press, 1971).

3 *Knowledge and Human Interests*, p. 196.

4 *Knowledge and Human Interests*, p. 308.

5 "Hermeneutics and Social Science" in *Cultural Hermeneutics* 2 (1975), p. 312.

6 "Dogmatism, Reason, and Decision: On Theory and Praxis in Our Scientific Civilization," in *Theory and Practice*, translation by John Viertel. (Boston: Beacon Press, 1973), p. 255.

7 *Knowledge and Human Interests*, p. 309.

8 *Knowledge and Human Interests*, p. 314.

9 *Knowledge and Human Interests*, p. 310. It should be noted that Habermas's debate with Gadamer began before Habermas explicitly made his "linguistic turn." Habermas, in his own self critique, argued that the theory of cognitive interests was too closely associated with the philosophy of the subject. Furthermore, he also argued that "self-reflection" is a concept that needed to be clarified and explicated in a linguistic

communicative framework. Subsequently, Habermas reformulated his critique of Gadamer's hermeneutics from this communicative perspective. For a lucid and perceptive analysis of Habermas's critique of hermeneutics that places it in the context of the German tradition of hermeneutics, see Christina Lafont, *The Linguistic Turn in Hermeneutic Philosophy* (Cambridge, Mass.: MIT Press, 1999).

10 Hans-Georg Gadamer, *Truth and Method*, Second Revised Edition, trans. by Joel Weinsheimer and Donald G. Marshall (New York, Crossroad, 1989), p. xxviii. Already in the first edition of *Truth and Method*, Gadamer has emphatically stated: "The hermeneutics developed here is not, therefore, a methodology of the human sciences, but an attempt to understand what the human sciences truly are, beyond their methodological self-consciousness, and what connects them with the totality of our experience of the world." p. xxiii.

11 "The Problem of Historical Consciousness," in *Interpretive Social Science*, ed. Paul Rabinow and William Sullivan (Berkeley: University of California Press, 1979).

12 "Hermeneutics and Social Science," p. 312.

13 See *Dialogue & Deconstruction: The Gadamer-Derrida Encounter*, edited by Diane P. Michelfelder and Richard E. Palmer (Albany: SUNY Press, 1989). In addition to the papers by Gadamer and Derrida, this volume includes some subsequent reflections by Gadamer dealing with deconstruction, as well as a number of articles by other philosophers dealing with hermeneutics and deconstruction.

14 For a perceptive discussion of the relation of Gadamer to the Anglo-American tradition of epistemological holism, see Linda Alcoff, *Real Knowing: New Versions of the Coherence Theory* (New York: Cornell University Press, 1996).

15 See my essays "Serious Play: The Ethical-Political Horizon of Derrida" and "An Allegory of Modernity/Postmodernity: Habermas and Derrida" in *The New Constellation* (Cambridge, Mass.: MIT Press, 1991).

16 "The Force of Law: The Mystical Foundation of Authority" in *Deconstruction and the Possibility of Justice*, edited by Drucilla Cornell et al., (New York: Routledge, 1992).

17 John D. Caputo, *Deconstruction in a Nutshell* (New York: Fordham University Press, 1997), p. 137.

BIBLIOGRAPHY

I. Gadamer's Works
   A. In German
   B. In English Translation
   B.1. Books
   B.2. Articles
   B.3. Interviews
II. Secondary Works in English
   A. Books
   B. Articles

Gadamer has published extensively in many languages worldwide. Fortunately, he has gathered most of his work in a ten-volume *Collected Works* (*Gesammelte Werke*). The following bibliography restricts itself almost entirely to what is available in English and does not attempt to be complete. For the most complete bibliography of Gadamer's publications, see Etsuro Makita's *Gadamer-Bibliographie: 1922–1994* (New York: Peter Lang, 1994). Corrections and additions are available at his website: http://www.ms.kuki. sut.ac.jp/KMSLab/makita/gdmhp/gdmhp_d.html. A good bibliography is appended to Jean Grondin's biography of Gadamer: *Hans-Georg Gadamer: Eine Biographie* (Tübingen: Mohr Siebeck, 1999). In English, the best bibliography to date has been prepared by Richard Palmer and can be found in the Library of Living Philosophers volume dedicated to Gadamer: *The Philosophy of Hans-Georg Gadamer*, edited by Lewis Hahn (Chicago and LaSalle: Open Court, 1997), pp. 558–602.

I. GADAMER'S WORKS

A. In German

Gesammelte Werke. 10 vols. (Tübingen: Mohr Siebeck, 1986–1995).

Recent publications that are not included in the *Gesammelte Werke* include
the following books:
Der Anfang der Philosophie. Stuttgart: Reclam, 1996.
Das Erbe Europas: Beiträge. Frankfurt: Suhrkamp, 1989.
Über die Verborgenheit der Gesundheit. Frankfurt: Suhrkamp, 1993.
Hermeneutische Entwürfe. Tübingen: Mohr Siebeck, 2000.

B. In English Translation

B.1. BOOKS IN ENGLISH TRANSLATION
The Beginning of Philosophy. Translated by Rod Coltman (New York: Continuum, 1998).
Dialogue and Deconstruction: The Gadamer-Derrida Encounter. Edited and translated by Diane P. Michelfelder and Richard E. Palmer (Albany: SUNY Press, 1989). This includes:
  "Text and Interpretation"
  "Reply to Jacques Derrida"
  "Letter to Dallmayr"
  "*Destruktion* and Deconstruction"
  "Hermeneutics and Logocentrism"
Dialogue and Dialectic: Eight Hermeneutical Studies on Plato. Translated and edited by P. Christopher Smith (New Haven: Yale University Press, 1980). This includes:
  "*Logos* and *Ergon* in Plato's *Lysis*"
  "The Proofs of Immortality in Plato's *Phaedo*"
  "Plato and the Poets"
  "Plato's Educational State"
  "Dialectic and Sophism in Plato's *Seventh Letter*"
  "Plato's Unwritten Dialectic"
  "Idea and Reality in Plato's *Timaeus*"
  "*Amicus Plato Magis Amicia Veritas*"
The Enigma of Health: The Art of Healing in a Scientific Age. Translated by J. Gaiger and N. Walker (Stanford: Stanford University Press, 1996). This includes:
  "Theory, Technology, Praxis"
  "Apologia for the Art of Healing"
  "The Problem of Intelligence"
  "The Experience of Death"
  "Bodily Experience and the Limits of Objectification"
  "Between Nature and Art"
  "Philosophy and Practical Medicine"
  "On the Enigmatic Character of Health"

"Authority and Critical Freedom"
"Treatment and Dialogue"
"Life and Soul"
"Anxiety and Anxieties"
"Hermeneutics and Psychiatry"
Gadamer on Celan: "Who Am I and Who Are You?" and Other Essays.
Translated and edited by Richard Heinemann and Bruce Krajewski
(Albany: SUNY Press, 1997).
*Hans-Georg Gadamer on Education, Poetry, and History: Applied
Hermeneutics.* Edited by Dieter Misgeld and Graeme Nicholson. Trans-
lated by Lawrence Schmidt and Monica Reuss (Albany: SUNY Press,
1992). This includes:
    "Interview: The German University and German Politics. The Case
        of Heidegger"
    "On the Primordiality of Science: A Rectoral Address"
    "The University of Leipzig, 1409–1959: A Former Rector Commem-
        orates the 550th Anniversary of its Founding"
    "The University of Heidelberg and the Birth of Modern Science"
    "The Idea of the University – Yesterday, Today, Tomorrow"
    "Interview: Writing and the Living Voice"
    "Are the Poets Falling Silent?"
    "The Verse and the Whole"
    "Hölderlin and George"
    "Under the Shadow of Nihilism"
    "Interview: The 1920's, 1930's, and the Present: National Socialism,
        German History, and German Culture"
    "The Philosophy and the Religion of Judaism"
    "Notes on Planning for the Future"
    "The Limitations of the Expert"
    "The Future of the European Humanities"
    "Citizens of Two Worlds"
    "The Diversity of Europe: Inheritance and Future"
Hegel's Dialectic: Five Hermeneutical Studies. Translated by P. Christopher
Smith (New Haven: Yale University Press, 1976). This includes:
    "Hegel and the Dialectic of the Ancient Philosophers"
    "Hegel's Inverted World"
    "Hegel's Dialectic of Self-Consciousness"
    "The Idea of Hegel's Logic"
    "Hegel and Heidegger"
Heidegger's Ways. Translated by John W. Stanley (Albany: SUNY Press,
1994). This includes:
    "Existentialism and the Philosophy of Existence"

"Martin Heidegger – 75 Years"
"The Marburg Theology"
"What is Metaphysics?"
"Kant and the Hermeneutical Turn"
"The Thinker Martin Heidegger"
"The Language of Metaphysics"
"Plato"
"The Truth of the Work of Art"
"Martin Heidegger – 85 Years"
"The Way in the Turn"
"The Greeks"
"The History of Philosophy"
"The Religious Dimension"
"Being, Spirit, God"

Hermeneutics, Religion, and Ethics. Translated by Joel Weinsheimer (New Haven: Yale University Press, 1999). This includes:
"Kant and the Question of God"
"On the Possibility of a Philosophical Ethics"
"On the Divine in Early Greek Thought"
"The Ontological Problem of Value"
"Thinking as Redemption: Plotinus between Plato and Augustine"
"Myth in the Age of Science"
"The Ethics of Value and Practical Philosophy"
"Reflections on the Relation of Religion and Science"
"Friendship and Self-Knowledge: Reflections on the Role of Friendship in Greek Ethics"
"Aristotle and Imperative Ethics"

The Idea of the Good in Platonic-Aristotelian Philosophy. Translated by P. Christopher Smith (New Haven: Yale University Press, 1986).

Lectures on Philosophical Hermeneutics (Pretoria: Universiteit van Pretoria, 1982).

Literature and Philosophy in Dialogue: Essays in German Literary Theory. Edited by Dennis J. Schmidt. Translated by Robert H. Paslick (Albany: SUNY Press, 1994). This includes:
"Goethe and Philosophy"
"Goethe and the Moral World"
"On the Course of Human Spiritual Development: Studies of Goethe's Unfinished Writings"
"Hölderlin and Antiquity"
"Hölderlin and the Future"
"Bach and Weimar"
"The God of Most Intimate Feeling"

"Poetry and Punctuation"
"Rainer Maria Rilke's Interpretation of Existence: On the Book by
     Romano Guardini"
"Mythopoietic Reversal in Rilke's *Duino Elegies*"
Philosophical Apprenticeships. Translated by Robert R. Sullivan (Cambridge:
     MIT Press, 1985).
Philosophical Hermeneutics. Edited and translated by David E. Linge
     (Berkeley: University of California Press, 1976). This includes:
     "The Universality of the Hermeneutical Problem"
     "On the Scope and Function of Hermeneutical Reflection"
     "On the Problem of Self-Understanding"
     "Man and Language"
     "The Nature of Things and the Language of Things"
     "Semantics and Hermeneutics"
     "Aesthetics and Hermeneutics"
     "The Philosophical Foundations of the Twentieth Century"
     "The Phenomenological Movement"
     "The Science of the Life-World"
     "Martin Heidegger and Marburg Theology"
     "Heidegger's Later Philosophy"
     "Heidegger and the Language of Metaphysics"
*Plato's Dialectical Ethics: Phenomenological Interpretations Relating to the
     Philebus*, edited and translated by Robert M. Wallace (New Haven: Yale
     University Press, 1991).
Praise of Theory, translated by Chris Dawson (New Haven: Yale University
     Press, 1998). This includes:
     "Culture and the Word"
     "Praise of Theory"
     "The Power of Reason"
     "The Ideal of Practical Philosophy"
     "Science and the Public Sphere"
     "Science as the Instrument of the Enlightenment"
     "The Idea of Tolerance 1782–1982"
     "Isolation as a Symptom of Self-Alienation"
     "Man and His Hand in Modern Civilization: Philosophical Aspects"
     "The Expressive Force of Language: On the Function of Rhetoric in
        Gaining Knowledge"
Reason in the Age of Science. Translated by Frederick G. Lawrence
     (Cambridge: MIT Press. 1981). This includes:
     "On the Philosophic Element in the Sciences and the Scientific Char-
        acter of Philosophy"
     "Hegel's Philosophy and its Aftereffects until Today"

"The Heritage of Hegel"
"What is Practice?: The Conditions of Social Reason"
"Hermeneutics as Practical Philosophy"
"Hermeneutics as a Theoretical and Practical Task"
"On the Natural Inclination of Human Beings Toward Philosophy"
"Philosophy or Theory of Science?"

The Relevance of the Beautiful and Other Essays. Edited and introduced by Robert Bernasconi. Translated by Nicholas Walker (Cambridge: Cambridge University Press, 1986). This includes:
"The Relevance of the Beautiful"
"The Festive Character of Theater"
"Image and Gesture"
"The Speechless Image"
"Art and Imitation"
"On the Contribution of Poetry to the Search for Truth"
"Poetry and Mimesis"
"The Play of Art"
"Philosophy and Poetry"
"Aesthetic and Religious Experience"
"Intuition and Vividness"

Truth and Method. Translated by J. Weinsheimer and D. G. Marshall. 2nd Revised Edition (New York: Seabury Press, 1989).

B.2. ARTICLES IN ENGLISH TRANSLATION

"Aesthetic and Religious Experience," *Nederlands Theologisch Tijdschrift* 32 (1978), 218–30.

"Aristotle and the Ethic of Imperatives," translated by Joseph Knippenberg, in *Action and Contemplation*, edited by Robert Bartlett and Susan Collins (Albany: SUNY Press, 1999), pp. 53–67.

"Articulating Transcendence," in *The Beginning and the Beyond: Papers from the Gadamer and Voegelin Conferences*, edited by F. Lawrence (Chico: Scholars Press, 1984), pp. 1–12.

"Back from Syracuse?" *Critical Inquiry* 15 (1989), pp. 427–30.

"The Beginning and End of Philosophy," in *Martin Heidegger: Critical Assessments*, edited by C. Macann. (London: Routledge, 1989), pp. 16–28.

"Being, Spirit, God," translated by S. Davis, in *Heidegger Memorial Lectures*, edited by Werner Marx. (Pittsburgh: Duquesne University Press, 1982), pp. 55–74; also in *Heidegger's Ways*.

"Boundaries of Language," translated by Lawrence K. Schmidt, in *Language and Linguisticality in Gadamer's Hermeneutics*, edited by Lawrence K. Schmidt (Boston: Lexington Books, 2000), pp. 9–17.

"A Classic Text – A Hermeneutic Challenge," translated by Fred Lawrence, *Revue de l'Universite d'Ottawa* 50 (1980), pp. 637–2.

"Concerning Empty and Ful-filled Time," *The Southern Journal of Philosophy* 8 (1970), 341–53.

"The Conflict of Interpretations," and "Discussion [with Paul Ricoeur]," *Phenomenology*, edited by R. Bruzina and B. Wilshire (Albany: SUNY Press, 1982), pp. 213–30, 299–304.

"The Continuity of History and the Existential Moment," *Philosophy Today* 16 (1972), 230–40.

"Correspondence concerning *Wahrheit und Methode*," (with Leo Strauss) *The Independent Journal of Philosophy* 2 (1978), 5–12.

"Culture and Words," *Universitas* 24 (1982), 179–88.

"Culture and Media," translated by B. Fultner, in *Cultural–Political Interventions in the Unfinished Project of the Enlightenment*, edited by A. Honneth, T. McCarthy, C. Offe, and A. Wellmer (Cambridge: MIT Press, 1989), pp. 172–88.

"Dialogues in Capri," translated by Jason Gaiger, in *Religion*, edited by Jacques Derrida and Gianni Vattimo (Stanford: Stanford University Press, 1998), pp. 200–11.

"The Drama of Zarathustra," translated by T. Heilke, in *Nietzsche's New Seas*, edited by M. A. Gillespie and T. B. Strong (Chicago: University of Chicago Press, 1983), pp. 220–31.

"The Eminent Text and Its Truth," *Bulletin of the Midwest Modern Language Association* 13 (1980), 3–23.

"The Expressive Power of Language," translated by R. Heinemann and B. Krajewski, *PMLA* 107 (1992), 345–52.

"Gadamer on Gadamer," in *Gadamer and Hermeneutics: Science, Culture, Literature*, edited by H. J. Silverman (New York: Routledge, 1989), pp. 13–19.

"Heidegger and the History of Philosophy," *The Monist* 64 (1981), 434–44.

"Heidegger's Paths," translated by C. Kayser and G. Stark, *Philosophical Exchange* 2 (1979), 80–91.

"Hermeneutics and Social Science," *Cultural Hermeneutics* 2 (1975), 307–316; also "Summation," 329–30, and "Response," pp. 357.

"The Hermeneutics of Suspicion," *Man and World* 17 (1984), 313–23; also in *Hermeneutics: Questions and Prospects*, eds. G. Shapiro and A. Sica (Amherst: University of Massachusetts Press, 1984), pp. 54–65.

"Hilda Domin, Poet of Return," *The Denver Quarterly* 6 (1972), 7–17.

"Historical Transformations of Reason," in *Proceedings of the International Symposium one 'Rationality Today,'* ed. T. F. Geraets. Ottawa: The University of Ottawa Press, 1977, pp. 3–14.

"The History of Concepts and the Language of Philosophy," *International Studies in Philosophy* 18 (1986), 1–16.

"History of Science and Practical Philosophy," *Contemporary German Philosophy* 3 (1983), 307–13.

"The Ideal of Practical Philosophy," *Notes et documents: Pour une recherche personnaliste* 11 (1986), 40–5; also in *In Praise of Theory*.

"The Inverted World," translated by John F. Donovan, *The Review of Metaphysics* 28 (1975), 401–22; also in *Hegel's Dialectic*.

"Letter by Professor Hans–Georg Gadamer," in Richard Bernstein, *Beyond Objectivism and Relativism* (Philadelphia: University of Pennsylvania Press, 1983), pp. 261–5.

"Martin Heidegger's One Path," translated by P. C. Smith in *Reading Heidegger from the Start: Essays in His Earliest Thought*, edited by T. Kisiel and J. van Buren (Albany: SUNY Press, 1994), pp. 19–35.

"Mythopoetic Inversion in Rilke's *Duino Elegies*," in *Hermeneutics Versus Science: Three German Views*, edited and translated by John M. Connolly and Thomas Keutner (Notre Dame: Notre Dame University Press, 1988, pp. 79–101); also in *Literature and Philosophy in Dialogue*.

"Natural Science and Hermeneutics," translated by Kathleen Wright, *Proceedings of the Boston Area Colloquium in Ancient Philosophy*, edited by J. J. Cleary, vol. 1 (Lanham: University Press of America, 1986), pp. 39–52.

"A New Epoch in the History of the World Begins Here and Now," in *The Philosophy of Immanuel Kant*, ed. By J. Donovan and R. Kennington (Washington, D.C.: Catholic University Press, 1985), pp. 1–14.

"Notes on Planning for the Future," *Daedalus* (Spring 1966), pp. 572–89; also in *Hans-Georg Gadamer on Education, Poetry, and History*.

"On the Circle of Understanding," in *Hermeneutics Versus Science: Three German Views*, edited and translated by John M. Connolly and Thomas Keutner (Notre Dame: University of Notre Dame Press, 1988), pp. 68–78.

"On Man's Natural Inclination Toward Philosophy," *Universitas* 15 (1973), 31–40.

"On the Political Incompetence of Philosophy," *Diogenes* 46 (1998), 3–4; also in a different translation in *The Heidegger Case: On Philosophy and Politics*, edited by Tom Rockmore and Joseph Margolis (Philadelphia: Temple University Press, 1992), pp. 364–9.

"On the Problematic Character of Aesthetic Consciousness," translated by E. Kelley, *Graduate Faculty Philosophy Journal* 9 (1982), 31–40.

"On the Scope and Function of Hermeneutical Reflection," translated by G. B. Hess and R. E. Palmer, in *Hermeneutics and Modern Philosophy*, edited by Brice Wachterhauser (Albany: SUNY Press, 1986), pp. 277–99. Also in *Philosophical Hermenetics* (above), and under another title,

"Rhetoric, Hermeneutics, and Ideology-Critique," in *Rhetoric and Hermeneutics in Our Time* (below).

"On the Truth of the Word," translated by Lawrence K. Schmidt and Monika Reuss, in *The Specter of Relativism*, edited by Lawrence K. Schmidt (Evanston: Northwestern University Press, 1995), pp. 135–55.

"Phenomenology, Hermeneutics, Metaphysics," translated by A. Greider. *Journal of the British Society for Phenomenology* 25 (1994), 104–10.

"Philosophizing in Opposition: Strauss and Voegelin on Communication and Science," in *Faith and Political Philosophy: The Correspondence between Leo Strauss and Eric Voegelin 1934–1964*, edited and translated by P. Emberley and B. Cooper (University Park: Pennsylvania State University Press, 1993), pp. 249–59.

"Philosophy and Literature," *Man and World* 18 (1985), 241–59.

"Plato's *Parmenides* and Its Influence," translated by M. Kirby, *Dionysius* 7 (1983), 3–16.

"Plato and Heidegger," in *The Question of Being*, edited by Mervyn Sprung. University Park: Pennsylvania State Press, 1978, pp. 45–54; also in *Heidegger's Ways* under the title "Plato."

"Plato as Portraitist," translated by Jamey Findling and Snezhina Gabova, *Continental Philosophy Review* 33 (2000), 245–74.

"The Power of Reason," *Man and World* 3 (1970), 5–15; also in *Praise of Theory*.

"Practical Philosophy as a Model of the Human Sciences," *Research in Phenomenology* 9 (1979), 74–85.

"The Problem of Historical Consciousness," *Graduate Faculty Philosophy Journal* 5 (1975), 2–52. Also in *Interpretive Social Science*, edited by P. Rabinow and W. Sullivan (Los Angeles: University of California Press, 1979), pp. 103–60; 2nd edition (1987), pp. 82–140.

"The Problem of Language in Schleiermacher's Hermeneutic," translated by David Linge, *Journal for Theology and Church* 7 (1970), 68–84.

"Reflections on My Philosophical Journey," in *The Philosophy of Hans-Georg Gadamer*, edited by Lewis Hahn, volume 24 (The Library of Living Philosophers. Chicago and LaSalle: Open Court, 1997), pp. 2–63.

"The Relevance of Greek Philosophy for Modern Thought," *South African Journal of Philosophy* 6 (1987), 39–42.

"Religious and Poetical Speaking," in *Myth, Symbol, and Reality*, edited by A. M. Olson (Notre Dame: University of Notre Dame Press, 1980), pp. 86–98.

"Religion and Religiosity in Socrates," translated by R. Velkley, *Proceedings of the Boston Area Colloquium in Ancient Philosophy*, edited by J. J. Cleary, vol. 1 (Lanham, Md.: University Press of America, 1986), pp. 53–75.

"The Religious Dimension in Heidegger," in *Transcendence and the Sacred*, edited by Alan Olson (Notre Dame: University of Notre Dame Press, 1981), pp. 193–207; also in *Heidegger's Ways*.

"Reply to My Critics," in *The Hermeneutic Tradition*, edited by Gayle L. Ormiston and A. D. Schrift (Albany: SUNY Press, 1990), pp. 273–97.

"Reply to Nicholas P. White," in *Platonic Writings – Platonic Readings*, edited by C. Griswold (London: Routledge, 1988), pp. 258–66, 299–300.

"Rhetoric and Hermeneutics," in *Rhetoric and Hermeneutics in Our Time: A Reader*, edited by Walter Jost and Michael J. Hyde (New Haven: Yale University Press, 1997), pp. 45–59.

"Rhetoric, Hermeneutics, and Ideology-Critique," translated by G. B. Hess and R. E. Palmer, in *Rhetoric and Hermeneutics in Our Time: A Reader*, edited by Walter Jost and Michael J. Hyde (New Haven: Yale University Press, 1997, pp. 313–34). This is the same essay as "On the Scope and Function of Hermeneutical Reflection," see above.

"Science and the Public," *Universitas* 23 (1981), 161–8.

"Subjectivity and Intersubjectivity, Subject and Person," translated by Peter Adamson and David Vesey *Continental Philosophy Review* 33 (2000), 275–87.

"Theory, Technology, Practice: The Task of the Science of Man," translated by H. Brotz, *Social Research* 44 (1977) 529–61; also in *The Enigma of Health*.

"Thinking and Poetizing in Heidegger and in Hölderlin's *Andenken*" translated by R. E. Palmer, in *Heidegger Toward the Turn: Essays on the Work of the 1930's*, edited by J. Risser (Albany: SUNY Press, 1996), pp. 145–62.

"Towards a Phenomenology of Ritual and Language," translated by Lawrence K. Schmidt, in *Language and Linguisticality in Gadamer's Hermeneutics*, edited by Lawrence K. Schmidt (Boston: Lexington, 2000, pp. 19–50).

"Truth in the Human Sciences," in *Hermeneutics and Truth*, edited by Brice Wachterhauser (Evanston: Northwestern University Press, 1994), pp. 25–32.

"What is Truth?" in *Hermeneutics and Truth*, edited by Brice Wachterhauser (Evanston: Northwestern University Press, 1994), pp. 33–46.

"The Western View of the Inner Experience of Time and the Limits of Thought," in *Time and the Philosophers* (Paris: UNESCO, 1977), pp. 33–48.

B.3. INTERVIEWS

"A Conversation with Gadamer [by Michael Baur]," *Method* 8,1 (1990), 1–13.

"A Conversation with Hans-Georg Gadamer [by Alfons Grieder]," *Journal of the British Society for Phenomenology* 26 (1995), 116–26.

"Gadamer on Strauss – An Interview," *Interpretation* 12 (1984), 1–13.

"Hans-Georg Gadamer: Interview with Christiane Gehron and Jonathan Ree," *Radical Philosophy* (1995), 27–35.

"Hans-Georg Gadamer. Interview with Giacinto Di Pietrantonio," *Flash Art* 165 (1992), 143–44.

Hans-Georg Gadamer on Education, Poetry, and History (listed above) includes the following interviews:

> "Interview: The German University and German Politics. The Case of Heidegger"
>
> "Interview: Writing and the Living Voice"
>
> "Interview: Historicism and Romanticism"
>
> "Interview: The 1920's, 1930's, and the Present: National Socialism, German History, and German Culture

"Interview with Hans-Georg Gadamer [by Klaus Davi]," *Flash Art* 136 (1987), 78–80.

"Interview with Hans-Georg Gadamer [by Roy Boyne]," *Theory, Culture and Society* 5 (1988), 25–34.

II. SECONDARY WORKS IN ENGLISH

A. Books

Bernstein, Richard. *Beyond Objectivism and Relativism: Science, Hermeneutics, and Praxis* (Philadelphia: University of Pennsylvania Press, 1983).

Bullock, Jeffrey. *Preaching With a Cupped Ear: Hans-Georg Gadamer's Philosophical Hermeneutics as Postmodern Wor(l)d* (New York: Peter Lang, 1999).

Caputo, John. *Radical Hermeneutics: Repetition, Deconstruction, and the Hermeneutic Project* (Bloomington: Indiana University Press, 1987).

Coltman, Rod. *The Language of Hermeneutics: Gadamer and Heidegger in Dialogue* (Albany: SUNY Press, 1998).

Derksen, Louise Dorothea. *On Universal Hermeneutics: A Study in the Philosophy of Hans-Georg Gadamer* (Amsterdam: VU Boekhandel, 1983).

DiCenso, James. *Hermeneutics and the Disclosure of Truth: A Study in the Work of Heidegger, Gadamer, and Ricoeur* (Charlottesville: University Press of Virginia, 1990).

Foster, Matthew. *Gadamer and Practical Philosophy: The Hermeneutics of Moral Confidence* (Atlanta: Scholars Press: 1991).

Gallagher, Shaun. *Hermeneutics and Education* (Albany: SUNY Press, 1994).

Grondin, Jean. *Introduction to Philosophical Hermeneutics* (New Haven: Yale University Press, 1994).

Grondin, Jean. *Sources of Hermeneutics* (Albany: SUNY, 1995).

Hahn, Lewis Edwin, ed. *The Philosophy of Hans-Georg Gadamer*. The Library of Living Philosophers XXIV (Chicago and LaSalle: Open Court, 1997).

Hekman, Susan. *Hermeneutics and the Sociology of Knowledge* (Notre Dame: University of Notre Dame Press, 1986).

Hirsch, E. D. *Aims of Interpretation* (Chicago: University of Chicago Press, 1976).

Hirsch, E. D. *Validity in Interpretation* (New Haven: Yale University Press, 1967).

Hollinger, Robert, ed. *Hermeneutics and Praxis* (Notre Dame: University of Notre Dame Press, 1985).

How, Alan. *The Habermas-Gadamer Debate and the Nature of the Social* (Brookfield: Avebury, 1995).

Howard, Roy. *Three Faces of Hermeneutics: An Introduction to Current Theories of Understanding* (Berkeley: University of California Press, 1978).

Hoy, David Couzens. *The Critical Circle: Literature, History, and Philosophical Hermeneutics* (Berkeley: University of California Press, 1978).

Kögler, Hans Herbert. *The Power of Dialogue: Critical Hermeneutics after Gadamer and Foucault*. Translated by Paul Hendrickson (Cambridge, Mass.: MIT Press, 1996).

Kusch, Martin. *Language as Calculus vs. Language as Universal Medium: A Study in Husserl, Heidegger, And Gadamer* (Boston: Kluwer, 1989).

Lafont, Cristina. *The Linguistic Turn in Hermeneutic Philosophy*, translated by José Medina (Cambridge: MIT Press, 1999).

Llewelyn, John. *Beyond Metaphysics: The Hermeneutic Circle in Contemporary Continental Philosophy* (Atlantic Highlands: Humanities Press, 1985).

Madison, Gary B. *The Hermeneutics of Post-Modernity: Figures and Themes* (Bloomington: Indiana University Press, 1988).

Ormiston, Gayle and Schrift, Alan, ed. *The Hermeneutic Tradition* (Albany: State University of New York Press, 1990).

Palmer, Richard. *Hermeneutics: Interpretation Theory in Schleiermacher, Dilthey, Heidegger, and Gadamer* (Evanston: Northwestern University Press, 1969).

Rauch, Angelika. *The Hieroglyph of Tradition: Freud, Benjamin, Gadamer, Novalis, Kant*. (Farleigh Dickinson University Press, 2001).

Ringma, Charles Richard. *Gadamer's Dialogical Hermeneutic: The Hermeneutics of Bultmann, of the New Testament Sociologists, and of the Social Theologians in Dialogue with Gadamer's Hermeneutic*. (Heidelberg: Universitätsverlag C. Winter, 1999).

Risser, James. *Hermeneutics and the Voice of the Other: Re-reading Gadamer's Philosophical Hermeneutics* (Albany: SUNY Press, 1997).

Roberts, David. *Reconstructing Theory: Gadamer, Habermas, Luhmann* (Melbourne University Press, 1995).

Rosen, Stanley. *Hermeneutics as Politics* (Oxford: Oxford University Press, 1987).

Scheibler, Ingrid. *Gadamer: Between Heidegger and Habermas* (Lanham: Rowman & Littlefield, 2000).

Schmidt, Lawrence. *The Epistemology of Hans-Georg Gadamer* (Frankfurt: Peter Lang, 1985).

Schmidt, Lawrence, K., ed. *Language and Linguisticality in Gadamer's Hermeneutics* (Boston: Lexington Books, 2000).

Schmidt, Lawrence K., ed. *The Specter of Relativism: Truth, Dialogue, and Phronesis in Philosophical Hermeneutics* (Evanston: Northwestern University Press, 1995).

Shapiro, Gary and Sica, Alan, ed. *Hermeneutics: Questions and Prospects* (Amherst, Mass.: University of Massachusetts Press, 1984).

Silverman, Hugh J., ed. *Gadamer and Hermeneutics* (New York: Routledge, 1991).

Smith, Nicholas. *Strong Hermeneutics* (New York: Routledge, 1997).

Smith, P. Christopher. *Hermeneutics and Human Finitude: Toward a Theory of Ethical Understanding* (New York: Fordham Press, 1991).

Sullivan, Robert. *Political Hermeneutics: The Early Thinking of Hans-Georg Gadamer* (University Park: Pennsylvania State University Press, 1990).

Teigas, Demetrius. *Knowledge and Hermeneutic Understanding: A Study of the Habermas-Gadamer Debate* (Lewisburg: Bucknell University Press, 1995).

Thiselton, Anthony C. *The Two Horizons. New Testament Hermeneutics and Philosophical Description with Special Reference to Heidegger, Bultmann, Gadamer, and Wittgenstein* (Grand Rapids: W. B. Eerdmans, 1980).

Wachterhauser, Brice. *Beyond Being: Gadamer's Post-Platonic Hermeneutic Ontology* (Evanston: Northwestern University Press, 1999).

Wachterhauser, Brice, ed. *Hermeneutics and Modern Philosophy* (Albany, N. Y.: SUNY Press, 1986).

Wachterhauser, Brice, ed. *Hermeneutics and Truth* (Evanston: Northwestern University Press, 1994).

Wallulis, Jerald. *The Hermeneutics of Life History: Personal Achievement and History in Gadamer, Habermas, and Erikson* (Evanston: Northwestern University Press, 1990).

Warnke, Georgia. *Gadamer: Hermeneutics, Tradition, and Reason* (Stanford: Stanford University Press, 1987).

Weinsheimer, Joel. *Gadamer's Hermeneutics: A Reading of "Truth and Method"* (New Haven: Yale University Press, 1985).

Wolff, Janet. *Hermeneutic Philosophy and the Sociology of Art* (London: Routledge, 1975).

Wright, Kathleen, ed. *Festivals of Interpretation: Essays on Hans-Georg Gadamer's Work* (Albany: SUNY Press, 1990).

Zuckert, Catherine. *Postmodern Platos: Nietzsche, Heidegger, Gadamer, Strauss, Derrida* (Chicago: University of Chicago Press, 1996).

B. Articles

Agassi, Joseph. "Gadamer Without Tears," *Philosophy of Social Sciences* 24 (1994), 485–506.

Aiken, D. Wyatt. "Hermeneia: An Anatomy of History and *Ab-wesenheit*," in *The Philosophy of Hans-Georg Gadamer*, pp. 405–19.

Alexander, Thomas. "Eros and Understanding: Gadamer's Aesthetic Ontology of the Community," in *The Philosophy of Hans-Georg Gadamer*, pp. 323–45.

Ambrosio, Francis. "Caputo's Critique of Gadamer: Hermeneutics and the Metaphorics of the Person," in *The Specter of Relativism*, pp. 96–110.

Ambrosio, Francis. "Dawn and Dusk: Gadamer and Heidegger on Truth," *Man and World* 19 (1986), 21–53.

Ambrosio, F. J. "The Figure of Socrates in Gadamer's Philosophical Hermeneutics," in *The Philosophy of Hans-Georg Gadamer*, pp. 259–73.

Ambrosio, F. J. "Gadamer and the Ontology of Language: What Remains Unsaid," *Journal of the British Society for Phenomenology* 17 (1986), 124–42.

Ambrosio, Francis. "Gadamer: On Making Oneself at Home with Hegel," *Owl of Minerva* 19 (1987), 23–40.

Ambrosio, F. J. "Gadamer, Plato, and the Discipline of Dialogue," *International Philosophical Quarterly* 27 (1986), 1–32.

Apel, Karl Otto. "The Common Presuppositions of Hermeneutics and Ethics," *Research in Phenomenology* 9 (1979), 35–53.

Apel, Karl-Otto. "Regulative Ideas or Truth-Happening?: An Attempt to Answer the Question of the Conditions of the Possibility of Valid Understanding," in *The Philosophy of Hans-Georg Gadamer*, pp. 67–94.

Arthur, Christopher. "Gadamer and Hirsch: The Canonical Work and the Interpreter's Intention," *Cultural Hermeneutics* 4 (1977), 183–97.

Aylesworth, Gary. "Dialogue, Text, Narrative: Confronting Gadamer and Ricoeur," in *Gadamer and Hermeneutics*, pp. 63–81.

Behler, Ernst. "Deconstruction versus Hermeneutics: Derrida and Gadamer on Text and Interpretation" *Southern Humanities Review* 21 (1987), 201–23.

Beiner, Ronald. "Do We Need a Philosophical Ethics? Theory, Prudence, and the Primacy of *Ethos*," in *Action and Contemplation*, edited by Robert Bartlett and Susan Collins (Albany: SUNY Press, 1999), pp. 37–52.

Bernstein, Richard. "What is the Difference that Makes a Difference? Gadamer, Habermas, and Rorty," in *Hermeneutics and Modern Philosophy*, pp. 343–76.

Bernasconi, Robert. "Bridging the Abyss: Heidegger and Gadamer," *Research in Phenomenology* 16 (1986), 1–19.

Bernasconi, Robert. "Seeing Double: *Destruktion* and Deconstruction," in *Dialogue and Deconstruction*, pp. 233–50.

Bernasconi, Robert. " 'You Don't Know What I'm Talking About': Alterity and The Hermeneutic Ideal," in *The Specter of Relativism*, pp. 178–94.

Bertoldi, E. F. "Gadamer's Criticisms of Collingwood," *Idealistic Studies* 14 (1984), 213–28.

Biskowski, Lawrence. "Reason in Politics: Arendt and Gadamer on the Role of the Eide," *Polity* 31 (1998), 217–44.

Block, Ed. "Gadamer, Christian Tradition, and the Critic," *Renascence* 41 (1989), 211–32.

Bontekoe, Ron. "A Fusion of Horizons: Gadamer and Schleiermacher," *International Philosophical Quarterly* 27 (1987), 3–16.

Bouma-Prediger, Steve. "Rorty's Pragmatism and Gadamer's Hermeneutics," *Journal of the American Academy of Religion* 57 (1989), 313–24.

Bubner, Ruediger. "On the Ground of Understanding," in *Hermeneutics and Truth*, edited by Brice Wachterhauser (Evanston: Northwestern, 1994), pp. 68–82.

Buchman, Kenneth. "Gadamer on Art, Morality, and Authority," *Philosophy and Literature* 21 (1997), 144–50.

Cameron, W. S. K. "On Communicative Actors Talking Past One Another: The Gadamer-Habermas Debate," *Philosophy Today* 40 (1996), 160–8.

Caputo, John, "Hermeneutics as the Recovery of Man," *Man and World* 15 (1982), 343–67.

Caputo, John. "Gadamer's Closet Essentialism: A Derridean Critique," in *Dialogue and Deconstruction* pp. 258–64.

Carpenter, David. "Emanation, Incarnation, and the Truth-Event in Gadamer's *Truth and Method*," in *Hermeneutics and Truth*, pp. 98–122.

Carrington, Robert. "A Comparison of Royce's Key Notion of the Community of Interpretation with the Hermeneutics of Gadamer and Heidegger," *Transactions of the Charles S. Peirce Society* 20 (1984), 279–302.

Chan, Alan. "Philosophical Hermeneutics and the Analects: The Paradigm of 'Tradition'," Philosophy East & West 34 (1984), 421–36.

Chen, Juan-hsing. "Beyond Truth and Method: On Misreading Gadamer's Praxical Hermeneutics," The Quarterly Journal of Speech 73 (1987), 183–99.

Chen, Xun Wu. "A Hermeneutical Reading of Confucianism," Journal of Chinese Philosophy 27 (2000), 101–15.

Chessick, Richard. "Hermeneutics for Psychotherapists," American Journal of Psychotherapy 44 (1990), 256–73.

Chisholm, Roderick M. "Gadamer and Realism: Reaching an Understanding," in The Philosophy of Hans-Georg Gadamer pp. 99–108.

Cockhorn, Klaus. "Hans-Georg Gadamer's Truth and Method," Philosophy and Rhetoric 13 (1980), 160–80.

Colburn, Kenneth. "Critical Theory and the Hermeneutical Circle," Sociological Inquiry 56 (1986), 367–80.

Coltman, Rodney. "Gadamer, Hegel, and the Middle of Language," Philosophy Today 40 (1996), 151–9.

Connerton, Paul. "Gadamer's Hermeneutics," Comparative Criticism 5 (1983), 107–28.

Connolly, John. "Gadamer and the Author's Authority: A Language-Game Approach," The Journal of Aesthetics and Art Criticism 44 (1986), 271–78.

Cook, Deborah. "Reflections on Gadamer's Notion of Sprachlichkeit," Philosophy and Literature 10 (1986), 84–92.

Crowell, Steven J. "Dialogue and Text: Remarking the Difference," in The Interpretation of Dialogue, edited by Tullio Maranhao (Chicago: University of Chicago Press, 1990), pp. 338–60.

Crowley, Paul. "Technology, Truth, and Language: The Crisis of Theological Discourse," Heythrop Journal (1991), 323–39.

Dallmayr, Fred. "The Enigma of Health," in Language and Linguisticality in Gadamer's Hermeneutics, pp. 155–69.

Dallmayr, Fred. "Hermeneutics and Justice," in Festivals of Interpretation, pp. 90–110.

Davey, Nicholas. "Art, Religion, and the Hermeneutics of Authenticity," in Performance and Authenticity in the Arts, edited by Salim Kemal and Ivan Gaskell (New York: Cambridge University Press, 1999) pp. 66–93.

Davey, Nicholas. "Baumgarten's Aesthetics: A Post-Gadamerian Reflection," The British Journal of Aesthetics 29 (1989), 101–15.

Davey, Nicholas. "Hermeneutic Passions: Gadamer versus Nietzsche on the Subjectivity of Interpretation," International Journal of Philosophical Studies 2 (1994), 45–60.

Davey, Nicholas. "Hermeneutics, Language and Science: Gadamer's Distinction between Discursive and Propositional Language," *Journal of the British Society for Phenomenology* 24 (1993), 250–64.

Davey, Nicholas. "The Other Side of Writing: Thoughts on Gadamer's Notion of *Schriftlichkeit*," in *Language and Linguisticality in Gadamer's Hermeneutics*, pp. 77–111.

Davey, Nicholas. "Philosophical Hermeneutics and Literary Theory," *The British Journal of Aesthetics* 32 (1992), 279–82.

Davey, Nicholas. "A World of Hope and Optimism Despite Present Difficulties: Gadamer's Critique of Perspectivism," *Man and World* 23 (1990), 273–94.

Davidson, Donald. "Gadamer and Plato's *Philebus*," in *The Philosophy of Hans-Georg Gadamer*, pp. 421–32.

Deetz, Stanley. "Reclaiming the Subject Matter As a Guide to Mutual Understanding," *Communication Quarterly* 38 (1990), 226–43.

Detmer, David. "Gadamer's Critique of the Enlightenment," in *The Philosophy of Hans-Georg Gadamer*, pp. 275–86.

Detsch, Richard. "A Non-Subjectivist Concept of Play – Gadamer and Heidegger versus Rilke and Nietzsche," *Philosophy Today* 29 (1985), 156–72.

Devereaux, Mary. "Can Art Save Us? A Meditation on Gadamer," *Philosophy and Literature* 15 (1991), 59–73.

De Vries, Paul. "Godel, Gadamer, and Ethical Business Leadership," *Business and Professional Ethics Journal* 5 (1986), 136–49.

Diffey, T. J. "Some Thoughts on the Relationship between Gadamer and Collingwood," *Philosophical Inquiry* 20 (1998), 1–12.

DiTommaso, Tanya. "Play, Agreement, and Consensus," *Man and World* 29 (1996), 407–17.

Dostal, Robert J. "The Experience of Truth for Gadamer and Heidegger: Taking Time and Sudden Lightning," in *Hermeneutics and Truth*, pp. 47–67.

Dostal, Robert. "Gadamer's Continuous Challenge: Heidegger's Plato Interpretation," in *The Philosophy of Hans-Georg Gadamer*, pp. 289–307.

Dostal, Robert. "Philosophical Discourse and the Ethics of Hermeneutics," in *Festivals of Interpretation*, pp. 63–88.

Dostal, Robert. "The World Never Lost: The Hermeneutics of Trust," *Philosophy and Phenomenological Research* 47 (1987), 413–34.

Dow, Kathleen. "Art and the Symbolic Element of Truth: What Gadamer's Method Conveys," *International Philosophical Quarterly* 36 (1996), 173–82.

Dunne, Joseph. "Aristotle After Gadamer: An Analysis of the distinction Between the Concepts of Phronesis and Techne," *Irish Philosophical Journal* 2 (1985), 105–23.

Eisenstein, Gabe. "The Privilege of Sharing: Dead Ends and the Life of Language," in *Dialogue and Deconstruction*, pp. 269–83.

Ermath, Michael. "The Transformation of Hermeneutics," *The Monist* 64 (1981), 175–94.

Fairfield, Paul. "Truth without Methodologism: Gadamer and James," *American Catholic Quarterly* 67 (1993), 285–98.

Feher, Istvan. "On the Hermeneutic Understanding of Language: Word, Conversation and Subject Matter," translated by Lawrence K. Schmidt, in *Language and Linguisticality in Gadamer's Hermeneutics*, pp. 59–66.

Feldman, Leonard C. "Political Judgment with a Difference," *Polity* 32 (1999), 1–24.

Feldman, Stephen. "Made for Each Other: The Interdependence of Deconstruction and Philosophical Hermeneutics," *Philosophy and Social Criticism* 26 (2000), 51–70.

Figal, Günter. "*Phronesis* as Understanding: Situating Philosophical Hermeneutics," in *The Specter of Relativism*, pp. 236–47.

Figal, Günter. "The Practical Reason of the Good Life and the Freedom of Understanding – The Hermeneutic Vision of the Idea of that which is Good with Reference to Gadamer," *Antike und Abendland* 38 (1992), 67–81.

Figal, Günter. "The Region of Being in Word and Event," *Continental Philosophy Review* 33 (2000), 301–8.

Frank, Manfred. "Limits of the Human Control of Language: Dialogue as the Place of Difference between Neostructuralism and Hermeneutics," translated by Richard Palmer, in *Dialogue and Deconstruction*, pp. 150–61.

Forget, Philippe. "Argument(s)," translated by Diane Michelfelder, in *Dialogue and Deconstruction*, pp. 129–49.

Froman, Wayne. "*L'Ecriture* and Philosophical Hermeneutics," in *Gadamer and Hermeneutics*, pp. 136–48.

Garrett, Jan Edward. "Hans-Georg Gadamer on the 'Fusion of Horizons'," *Man and World* 11 (1978), 392–400.

Gilmour, John. "Dewey and Gadamer on the Ontology of Art," *Man and World* 20 (1987), 205–19.

Giurlanda, Paul. "Habermas' Critique of Gadamer: Does it Stand Up?" *International Philosophical Quarterly* 27 (1987), 33–41.

Gram, Moltke. "Gadamer on Hegel's Dialectic: A Review Article," *Thomist* 43 (1979), 322–30.

Griswold, C. L. "Gadamer and the Interpretation of Plato," *Ancient Philosophy* 2 (1981), 171–8.

Grondin, Jean. "Gadamer and Augustine," in *Hermeneutics and Truth*, pp. 137–47.

Grondin, Jean. "Gadamer on Humanism," in *The Philosophy of Hans-Georg Gadamer*, pp. 157–70.

Grondin, Jean. "Hermeneutics and Relativism," in *Festivals of Interpretation*, pp. 42–62.

Grondin, Jean. "On the Composition of *Truth and Method*," in *The Specter of Relativism*, pp. 23–38.

Grondin, Jean. "Play, Festival, and Ritual in Gadamer: On the Theme of the Immemorial in His Later Works," translated by Lawrence K. Schmidt, in *Language and Linguisticality in Gadamer's Hermeneutics*, pp. 51–7.

Gupta, Anoop. "Defending Metaphysical Realism from Putnam: Hermeneutics and the Argument from Analogy," *De-Philosophia* 14 (1998), 287–98.

Haase, Ullrich. "The Providence of Language in Gadamer's *Truth and Method*," *Journal of the British Society For Phenomenology* 22 (1991), 170–84.

Habermas, Jürgen. "The Hermeneutic Claim to Universality," in *The Hermeneutic Tradition*, pp. 245–72.

Habermas, Jürgen. "A Review of Gadamer's *Truth and Method*," in *Understanding and Social Inquiry*, eds. Fred Dallmayr and Thomas McCarthy (Notre Dame: University of Notre Dame Press, 1977), pp. 335–63. Also in *The Hermeneutic Tradition*, pp. 213–44.

Haidu, Peter. "The Semiotics of Alterity: A Comparison with Hermeneutics," *New Literary History* 21 (1990), 671–91.

Hammermeister, Kai. "*Heimat* in Heidegger and Gadamer," *Philosophy and Literature* 24 (2000), 312–326.

Hance, Allen. "The Hermeneutic Significance of the 'Sensus Communis'," *International Philosophical Quarterly* 37 (1997), 133–49.

Haney, David. "Aesthetics and Ethics in Gadamer, Levinas, and Romanticism: Problems of Phronesis and Techne," *PMLA* 114 (1999), 32–45.

Haney, D. P. "Viewing the Viewless-Wings-of-Poesy: Gadamer, Keats, and Historicity," *CLIO* 19 (1989), 103–22.

Hans, James. "Hans-Georg Gadamer and Hermeneutic Phenomenology," *Philosophy Today* 22 (1978), 3–19.

Harringon, Austin. "Some Problems with Gadamer's and Habermas' Dialogical Model of Sociological Understanding," *Journal for the Theory of Social Behaviour* 29 (1999), 371–84.

Healy, Paul. "Situated Rationality and Hermeneutic Understanding," *International Philosophical Quarterly* 36 (1996), 155–72.

Hekman, Susan. "Action as List: Gadamer's Hermeneutics and the Social Scientific Analysis of Action," *Journal for the Theory of Social Behavior* 14 (1984), 333–54.

Hekman, Susan. "Beyond Humanism: Gadamer, Althusser, and the Methodology of the Social Sciences," *The Western Political Quarterly* 36 (1983), 98–115.

Henley, Kenneth. "Protestant Hermeneutics and the Rule of Law: Gadamer and Dworkin," *Ratio-Juris* 3 (1990), 14–27.

Hinman, Lawrence. "Quid facti or quid juris?: The Fundamental Ambiguity of Gadamer's Understanding of Hermeneutics," *Philosophy and Phenomenological Research* 40 (1980), 512–35.

Hirsch, E. D. "Meaning and Significance Re-interpreted," *Critical Inquiry* 11 (1984), 202–25.

Hirsch, E. D. "Truth and Method in Interpretation," *Review of Metaphysics* 18 (1965), 488–507.

Hjort, Anne Meete. "The Conditions of Dialogue: Approaches to the Habermas-Gadamer Debate," *Eidos* 4 (1980), 512–35.

Hogan, John. "Gadamer and the Hermeneutical Experience," *Philosophy Today* 20 (1976), 3–12.

Hollinger, Robert. "Practical Reason and Hermeneutics," *Philosophy and Rhetoric* 18 (1985), 113–22.

How, Alan. "A Case of Misreading: Habermas's Evolution of Gadamer's Hermeneutics," *Journal of the British Society for Phenomenology* 16 (1985), 131–43.

How, Alan. "Dialogue as Productive Limitation in Social Theory: The Habermas-Gadamer Debate," *Journal of the British Society for Phenomenology* 11 (1980), 131–43.

How, Alan. "That's classic! A Gadamerian defense of the classic text in sociology," *The Sociological Review* 46 (1998), 828–48.

Hoy, David. "Legal Hermeneutics: Recent Debates," in *Festivals of Interpretation*, pp. 111–35.

Hoy, David. "Must We Say What We Mean? The Grammatological Critique of Hermeneutics," in *Hermeneutics and Modern Philosophy*, pp. 397–415.

Hoy, David. "Post-Cartesian Interpretation: Hans-Georg Gadamer and Donald Davidson," in *The Philosophy of Hans-Georg Gadamer*, pp. 111–28.

Hoy, David. "Taking History Seriously: Foucault, Gadamer, Habermas," *Union Seminary Quarterly Review* 34 (1979), 85–95.

Ibbet, John. "Gadamer, Application and the History of Ideas," *History of Political Thought* 8 (1987), 545–55.

Ihde, Don. "Recent Hermeneutics in Gadamer and Ricoeur," *Semiotica* 102 (1994), 157–62.

Ingram, David. "Hermeneutics and Truth," in *Hermeneutics and Praxis*, pp. 32–53.

Ingram, David. "The Historical Genesis of the Gadamer-Habermas Controversy," *Auslegung* 10 (1983), 86–151.

Ingram, David. "The Possibility of a Communication Ethic Reconsidered: Habermas, Gadamer, and Bourdieu on Discourse," *Man and World* 15 (1982), 149–61.

Innis, Robert. "Hans-Georg Gadamer's Truth and Method: A Review Article," *Thomist* 40 (1976), 311–21.

Johnson, Patricia. "The Task of the Philosopher: Kierkegaard/Heidegger/ Gadamer," *Philosophy Today* 28 (1984), 3–19.

Kelly, Michael. "Gadamer, Foucault, and Habermas on Ethical Critique," in *The Specter of Relativism*, pp. 224–35.

Kelly, Michael. "The Gadamer-Habermas Debate Revisited: The Question of Ethics," *Philosophy and Social Criticism* 14 (1988), 368–89.

Kelly, Michael. "On Hermeneutics and Science: Why Hermeneutics is Not Anti-Science," *Southern Journal of Philosophy* 25 (1987), 481–500.

Kepnes, Steven. "Buber as Hermeneut: Relations to Dilthey and Gadamer," *Harvard Theological Review* 81 (1988), 193–213.

Kerby, Anthony. "Gadamer's Concrete Universal," *Man and World* 24 (1991), 49–61.

Kestenbaum, Victor. "Meaning on the Model of Truth: Dewey and Gadamer on Habit and *Vorurteil*," *Journal of Speculative Philosophy* 6 (1992), 25–66.

Kidder, Paulette. "Gadamer and the Platonic *Eidos*," *Philosophy Today* 39 (1995), 83–92.

Kirkland, Frank. "Gadamer and Ricouer: The Paradigm of the Text," *Graduate Faculty Philosophy Journal* 6 (1977), 131–44.

Kiesel, Theodore. "The Happening of Tradition: The Hermeneutics of Gadamer and Heidegger," *Man And World* 2 (1969), 358–85.

Kiesel, Theodore. "Hegel and Heremeneutics," in *Beyond Epistemology*, edited by Frederick G. Weiss (The Hague: Nijhoff, 1974), pp. 197–220.

Kisiel, Theodore. "Repetition in Gadamer's Hermeneutics," *Analecta Husserliana* 2 (1972), 196–203.

Krell, David. "Ashes, Ashes, we all fall," in *Dialogue and Deconstruction*, pp. 222–31.

LaFountain, Marc. "Play and Ethics in *Culturus Interruptus*: Gadamer's Hermeneutics in Postmodernity," in *The Specter of Relativism*, pp. 206–23.

Lammi, Walter. "Hans-Georg Gadamer's Correction of Heidegger," *Journal of the History of Ideas* (1991), 487–507.

Lammi, Walter. "Hans-Georg Gadamer's Platonic 'Destruktion' of the Later Heidegger," *Philosophy Today* 41 (1997), 394–404.

Lampert, Jay. "Gadamer and Cross-Cultural Hermeneutics," *Philosophical Forum* 29 (1997), 35–68.

Larmore, Charles. "Tradition, Objectivity, and Hermeneutics," in *Hermeneutics and Modern Philosophy*, pp. 147–67.

Lawlor, Leonard. "The Dialectical Unity of Hermeneutics: On Ricouer and Gadamer," in *Gadamer and Hermeneutics*, pp. 82–90.

Lawn, Christophor. "Gadamer on Poetic and Everyday Language," *Philosophy and Literature* 25 (2001), 113–26.

Lawrence, Fred. "Gadamer and Lonergan: A Dialectical Comparison," *International Philosophical Quarterly* 20 (1980), 25–47.

Lawrence, Fred. "Self-Knowledge in History in Gadamer and Lonergan," in *Language, Truth and Meaning*, edited by Philip McShane (Notre Dame: University of Notre Dame Press, 1972), pp. 167–217.

Lawrence, Fred. "Truth and Method by Hans-Georg Gadamer," *Religious Studies Review* 3 (1977), 35–44.

Linge, David. "Dilthey and Gadamer: Two Theories of Historical Understanding," *Journal of the American Academy of Religion* 41 (1973), 536–53.

Lingiardi, Vittorio. "Hermeneutics and the Philosophy of Medicine: Hans-Georg Gadamer's Platonic Metaphor," *Theoretical Medicine and Bioethics* 20 (1999), 413–22.

Lucas, George. "Philosophy, Its History and Hermeneutics," in *The Philosophy of Hans-Georg Gadamer*, pp. 173–89.

MacKenzie, Ian. "Gadamer's Hermeneutics and the Uses of Forgery," *Journal for Aesthetics and Art Criticism* 45 (1986), 41–8.

McCormick, Peter. "Interpretation in Aesthetics: Theories and Practices," *The Monist* 73 (1990), 167–80.

McGillivray, Murray. "Creative Anachronism: Marx's Problems with Homer, Gadamer's Discussion of 'the Classical,' and Our Understanding of Later Literatures," *New Literary History* 25 (1994), 399–414.

Maddox, Randy. "Hermeneutic Circle-Vicious or Victorious?" *Philosophy Today* 27 (1983), 66–76.

Madison, Gary. "Beyond Seriousness and Frivolity: A Gadamerian Response to Deconstruction," in *Gadamer and Hermeneutics*, pp. 119–35.

Madison, Gary. "Coping with Nietzsche's Legacy: Rorty, Derrida, Gadamer," *Philosophy Today* 36 (1992), 3–19.

Madison, Gary. "Gadamer/Derrida: The Hermeneutics of Irony and Power," in *Dialogue and Deconstruction*, pp. 192–8.

Madison, Gary. "Hermeneutics' Claim to Universality," in *The Philosophy of Hans-Georg Gadamer*, pp. 349–65.

Maier, Donald. "Community and Alterity: A Gadamerian Approach," *Philosophy in the Contemporary World* 4 (1998), 26–33.

Marcus, Gyorgy. "Diogenes Laertius contra Gadamer: Universal or Historical Hermeneutics?" in *Life After Postmodernism: Essays on Value and Culture*, edited by John Fekete (New York: St. Martins Press, 1987), pp. 142–60.

Margolis, Joseph. "Three Puzzles for Gadamer's Hermeneutics," in *The Specter of Relativism*, pp. 84–95.

Marshall, Donald. "Dialogue and criture," in *Dialogue and Deconstruction*, pp. 206–14.

Martland, T. R. "Quine's Half-Entities and Gadamer's Too," *Man and World* 19 (1986), 361–73.

Mendelson, Jack. "The Habermas-Gadamer Debate," *New German Critique* 18 (1979), 44–73.

Michelfelder, Diane. "Gadamer on Heidegger on Art," in *The Philosophy of Hans-Georg Gadamer*, pp. 437–56.

Misgeld, Dieter. "Critical Theory and Hermeneutics: The Debate between Habermas and Gadamer," in *On Critical Theory*, edited by John O'Neill (New York: Seabury, 1976), pp. 164–83.

Misgeld, Dieter. "Discourse and Conversation: The Theory of Communicative Competence and Hermeneutics in Light of the Debate between Habermas and Gadamer," *Cultural Hermeneutics* 4 (1977), 321–44.

Misgeld, Dieter. "Modernity and Hermeneutics: A Critical-Theoretical Rejoinder," in *Gadamer and Hermeneutics*, pp. 163–77.

Misgeld, Dieter. "On Gadamer's Hermeneutics," *Philosophy of the Social Sciences* 9 (1979), 221–39.

Misgeld, Dieter. "Poetry, Dialogue, and Negotiation: Liberal Culture and Conservative Politics in Hans-Georg Gadamer's Thought," in *Festivals of Interpretation*, pp. 161–81.

Mitscherling, Jeff. "Hegelian Elements in Gadamer's Notions of Application and Play," *Man and World* 25 (1992), 61–7.

Mitscherling, Jeff. "Philosophical Hermeneutics and 'The Tradition'," *Man and World* 22 (1989), 247–50.

Mul, Jos de. "Dilthey's Narrative Model of Human-development: Necessary Reconsideration after the Philosophical Hermeneutics of Heidegger and Gadamer," *Man and World* 24 (1991), 409–26.

Murchadha, Felix. "Truth as a Problem for Hermeneutics: Towards a Hermeneutic Theory of Truth," *Philosophy Today* 36 (1992), 122–30.

Nagl-Docetal, Herta. "Towards a New Theory of the Historical Sciences: The Relevance of *Truth and Method*," in *The Philosophy of Hans-Georg Gadamer*, pp. 193–204.

Nenon, Tom. "Hermeneutical Truth and the Structure of Human Experience: Gadamer's Critique of Dilthey," in *The Specter of Relativism*, pp. 39–55.

Newton, K. M. "Hermeneutics and Modern Literary Criticism," *The British Journal of Aesthetics* 29 (1989), 116–27.

Nicholson, Graeme. "Answers to Critical Theory," in *Gadamer and Hermeneutics*, pp. 151–62.

Nicholson, Graeme. "Truth in Metaphysics and in Hermeneutics," in *The Philosophy of Hans-Georg Gadamer*, pp. 309–20.

Norenstam, Tore. "Wittgenstein vs. Gadamer," *International Wittgenstein Symposium* 8 (1983), 23–8.

Nyiro, Miklos. "On the Hermeneutic and Deconstructive Conceptions of Language," *Philosophical Writings* 7 (1998), 13–20.

Nuyen, A. T. "Interpretation and Understanding in Hermeneutics and Deconstruction," *Philosophy of the Social Sciences* 24 (1994), 485–506.

Nuyen, A. T. "Truth, Method and Objectivity: Husserl and Gadamer on Scientific Method," *Philosophy of the Social Sciences* 20 (1990), 437–52.

O'Collins, Gerald. "Hans-Georg Gadamer and Hans Kung: A Reflection," *Gregorianum* 58 (1977), 561–66.

Ommen, Thomas. "Bultmann and Gadamer: The Role of Faith in Theological Hermeneutics," *Thought* 59 (1984), 348–59.

Orozco, Theresa. "The Art of Allusion: Hans-Georg Gadamer's Philosophical Interventions Under National Socialism," *Radical Philosophy* 78 (1996), 17–26.

Outhwaite, William. "Hans-Georg Gadamer," in *The Return of Grand Theory in the Human Sciences*, edited by Quentin Skinner (Cambridge: Cambridge University Press, 1985).

Oxenhandler, Neal. "The Man with Shoes of Wind: The Derrida-Gadamer Encounter," in *Dialogue and Deconstruction*, pp. 265–68.

Page, Carl. "Axiomatics, Hermeneutics, and Practical Rationality," *International Philosophical Quarterly* 27 (1987), 81–100.

Page, Carl. "Historicistic Finitude and Philosophical Hermeneutics," in *The Philosophy of Hans-Georg Gadamer*, pp. 369–84.

Page, Carl. "Philosophical Hermeneutics and Its Meaning for Philosophy," *Philosophy Today* 35 (1991), 127–36.

Painter, Mark. "Phaedo 99D-101D: Socrates and Gadamer's 'Second Way'," *Southwestern Philosophical Review* 14 (1998), 179–86.

Palmer, L.M. "Gadamer and the Enlightenment's 'Prejudice' Against all Prejudices," *Clio* 22 (1993), 369–77.

Palmer, Richard. "Gadamer's Recent Work on Language and Philosophy: On "Zur Phänomenologie von Ritual und Sprache," *Continental Philosophy Review* 33 (2000), 381–93.

Palmer, Richard. "Ritual, Rightness, and Truth in Two Late Works of Hans-Georg Gadamer," in *The Philosophy of Hans-Georg Gadamer*, pp. 529–47.

Pannenberg, Wolfhart. "Hermeneutics and Universal History," in *Hermeneutics and Modern Philosophy*, pp. 111–46.

Paslick, Robert. "The Ontological Context of Gadamer's Fusion: Boehme, Heidegger, and Non-Duality," *Man and World* 18 (1985), 405–22.

Perez-Gomez, Alberto. "Hermeneutics as Discourse in Design," *Design Issues* 15 (1999), 71–9.

Pizer, John. "Aesthetic Consciousness and Aesthetic Non-differentiation: Gadamer, Schiller, and Lukacs," *Philosophy Today* 33 (1989), 63–72.

Pizer, John. "Gadamer's Reading of Goethe," *Philosophy and Literature* 15 (1991), 268–77.

Polet, Jeff. "Taking the Old Gods With Us: Gadamer and the Role of Verstehen in the Human Sciences," *The Social Science Journal* 31 (1994), 171–97.

Prufer, Thomas. "A Thought or Two on Gadamer's Plato," in *The Philosophy of Hans-Georg Gadamer*, pp. 549–51.

Ramberg, Bjorn. "The Source of the Subjective," in *The Philosophy of Hans-Georg Gadamer*, pp. 459–71.

Rapaport, Herman. "All Ears: Derrida's Response to Gadamer," in *Dialogue and Deconstruction*, pp. 199–205.

Risser, James. "From Concept to Word: On the Radicality of Philosophical Hermeneutics," *Continental Philosophy Review* 33 (2000), 309–25.

Risser, James. "Hermeneutics of the Possible: On Finitude and Truth in Philosophical Hermeneutics," in *The Specter of Relativism*, pp. 111–28.

Risser, James. "Philosophical Hermeneutics and the Question of Community," in *Interrogating the Tradition: Hermeneutics and the History of Philosophy*, edited by Charles Scott (Albany: SUNY Press, 2000), pp. 19–35.

Risser, James. "Poetic Dwelling in Gadamer's Hermeneutics," *Philosophy Today* 38 (1994), 369–79.

Risser, James. "Reading the Text," in *Gadamer and Hermeneutics*, pp. 93–105.

Risser, James. "The Remembrance of Truth: The Truth of Remembrance," in *Hermeneutics and Truth*, edited by Brice Wachterhauser (Evanston: Northwestern University, 1994), pp. 123–36.

Risser, James. "The Two Faces of Socrates: Gadamer/Derrida," in *Dialogue and Deconstruction*, pp. 176–85.

Risser, James. "The Voice of the Other in Gadamer's Hermeneutics," in *The Philosophy of Hans-Georg Gadamer*, pp. 389–402.

Rockmore, Tom. "Gadamer's Hermeneutics and the Overcoming of Epistemology," in *The Specter of Relativism*, pp. 56–71.

Rodi, Frithjof. "Dilthey, Gadamer and 'Traditional' Hermeneutics," *Reports on Philosophy* 7 (1983), 3–12.

Rorty, Richard. "On Hans-Georg Gadamer and the Philosophical Conversation," *London Review of Books* 22, no. 6 (2000), 23–25.

Rorty, Richard. "Questioning," *Bochumer Philosophisches Jahrbuch* 2 (1997), 243–52.

Rosen, Stanley. "Interpretation and the Fusion of Horizons: Remarks on Gadamer," in *Metaphysics and Ordinary Language* (New Haven: Yale University Press, 1999), pp. 182–201.

Rosen, Stanley. "Horizontverschmelzung," in *The Philosophy of Hans-Georg Gadamer*, pp. 207–18.

Rothberg, Donald. "Gadamer, Rorty, Hermeneutics, and Truth: A Response to G. Warnke's Hermeneutics and the Social Sciences," *Inquiry* 29 (1986), 355–61.

Rundell, John. "Gadamer and the Circles of Hermeneutics," in *Reconstructing Theory: Gadamer, Habermas, Luhmann*, edited by David Roberts (Melbourne: Melbourne University Press, 1995), pp. 10–38.

Sallis, John. "The Hermeneutics of Translation," in *Language and Linguisticality in Gadamer's Hermeneutics*, pp. 67–76.

Sallis, John. "Interruptions," in *Dialogue and Deconstruction*, pp. 251–7.

Sallis, John. "Rereading the *Timaeus*: The Memorial Power of Discourse," in *The Philosophy of Hans-Georg Gadamer*, pp. 475–81.

Schmidt, Dennis. "On the Dark Side of the Moon: Voice and the Event of the Word," *Continental Philosophy Review* 33 (2000), 289–99.

Schmidt, Dennis. "Poetry and the Political: Gadamer, Plato, and Heidegger on the Politics of Language," in *Festivals of Interpretation*, pp. 209–28.

Schmidt, Dennis. "Putting Oneself in Words…," in *The Philosophy of Hans-Georg Gadamer*, pp. 483–93.

Schmidt, Lawrence K. "Language in a Hermeneutic Ontology," in *Language and Linguisticality in Gadamer's Hermeneutics*, pp. 1–7.

Schmidt, Lawrence K. "Participation and Ritual: Dewey and Gadamer on Language," in *Language and Linguisticality in Gadamer's Hermeneutics*, pp. 127–42.

Schmidt, Lawrence. "Recalling the Hermeneutic Circle," *Philosophy Today* 40 (1996), 263–72.

Schmidt, Lawrence. "Respecting Others: The Hermeneutic Virtue," *Continental Philosophy Review* 33 (2000), 359–79.

Schmidt, Lawrence. "Uncovering Hermeneutic Truth," in *The Specter of Relativism*, pp. 72–83.

Schott, Robin. "Gender, Nazism, and Hermeneutics," in *The Philosophy of Hans-Georg Gadamer*, pp. 499–507.

Schott, Robin. "Whose Home Is It Anyway? A Feminist Response to Gadamer's Hermeneutics," in *Gadamer and Hermeneutics*, pp. 202–9.

Schuckman, Paul. "Aristotle's Phronesis and Gadamer's Hermeneutics," *Philosophy Today* 23 (1979), 41–50.

Schweiker, William. "Beyond Imitation: Mimetic Praxis in Gadamer, Ricoeur, and Derrida," *Journal of Religion* 68 (1988), 21–38.

Schweiker, William. "Sacrifice, Interpretation, and the Sacred: The Import of Gadamer and Girard for Religious Studies," *Journal of the American Academy of Religion* 55 (1987), 791–810.

Scott, Charles. "Gadamer's *Truth and Method*," *Anglican Theological Review* 59 (1977), 63–78.

Seebohm, Thomas. "Falsehood as the Prime Mover of Hermeneutics," *The Journal of Speculative Philosophy* 6 (1992), 1–24.

Seebohm, Thomas. "The New Hermeneutics, Other Trends, and the Human Sciences from the Standpoint of Transcendental Phenomenology," in *Continental Philosophy in America*, edited by H. Silverman, J. Sallis, and T. Seebohm (Pittsburgh: Duquesne University Press, 1983), pp. 64–89.

Seifert, Josef. "Texts and Things," *American Catholic Philosophical Quarterly* 72 (1998 Supplement), 41–68.

Serequeberhan, Tsenay. "Heidegger and Gadamer: Thinking as 'Meditative' and as 'Effective-Historical Consciousness'," *Man and World* 20 (1987), 41–64.

Shapiro, Gary. "Gadamer, Habermas, and the Death of Art," *British Journal of Aesthetics* 26 (1986), 39–47.

Shapiro, Susan. "Rhetoric as Ideology Critique: the Gadamer-Habermas Debate Reinvented," *Journal of the American Academy of Religion* 62 (1994), 123–50.

Shepherdson, Charles. "Imagining Understanding...," in *Dialogue and Deconstruction*, pp. 186–91.

Shusterman, Richard. "The Gadamer-Derrida Encounter: A Pragmatist Perspective," in *Dialogue and Deconstruction*, pp. 215–21.

Simon, Josef. "Good Will to Understand the the Will to Power: Remarks on an 'Improbable Debate,'" translated by Richard Palmer, in *Dialogue and Deconstruction*, pp. 162–75.

Smith, P. Christopher. "Between the Audible Word and the Envisionable Concept: Rereading Plato's *Theaetetus* after Gadamer," *Continental Philosophy Review* 33 (2000), 327–44.

Smith, P. Christopher. "The Ethical Dimension of Gadamer's Hermeneutical Theory," *Research in Phenomenology* 18 (1988), 75–92.

Smith, P. Christopher. "H-G Gadamer's Heideggerian Interpretation of Plato," *Journal of the British Society for Phenomenology* 12 (1981), 211–30.

Smith, P. Christopher. "Gadamer's Hermeneutics and Ordinary Language Philosophy," *Thomist* 43 (1979), 296–321.

Smith, P. Christopher. "Gadamer on Language and Method in Hegel's Dialectic," *Graduate Faculty Philosophy Journal* 5 (1975), 53–72.

Smith, P. Christopher. "The I-Thou Encounter (*Begegnung*) in Gadamer's Reception of Heidegger," in *The Philosophy of Hans-Georg Gadamer*, pp. 509–25.

Smith, P. Christopher. "Plato as Impulse and Obstacle in Gadamer's Development of a Hermeneutical Theory," in *Gadamer and Hermeneneutics*, pp. 23–41.

Smith, P. Christopher. "Plato's *Khora* as a Linguistic Index of Groundlessness," in *Language and Linguisticality in Gadamer's Hermeneutics*, pp. 113–26.

Smith, P. Christopher. "Toward a Discursive Logic: Gadamer and Toulmin on Inquiry and Argument," in *The Specter of Relativism*, pp. 159–77.

Soffer, Gail. "Gadamer, Hermeneutics, and Objectivity in Interpretation," *Praxis International* 12 (1992), 321–68.

Sokolowski, Robert. "Gadamer's Theory of Hermeneutics," in *The Philosophy of Hans-Georg Gadamer*, pp. 223–34.

Stambaugh, Joan. "Gadamer on the Beautiful," in *The Philosophy of Hans-Georg Gadamer*, pp. 131–4.

Stueber, Karsten. "Understanding Truth and Objectivity: A Dialogue between Donald Davidson and Hans-Georg Gadamer," in *Hermeneutics and Truth*, pp. 172–89.

Sullivan, Robert. "Gadamer's Early and Distinctively Political Hermeneutics," in *The Philosophy of Hans-Georg Gadamer*, pp. 237–55.

Tate, John. "The Hermeneutic Circle vs. the Enlightenment," *Telos*, Nr. 110 (1998), 9–38.

Templeton, A. "The Dream and the Dialogue: Rich's Feminist Poetics and Gadamer's Hermeneutics," *Tulsa Studies in Women's Literature* 7 (1988), 283–96.

Torrance, I. R. "Gadamer, Polanyi, and Ways of Being Closed," *Scottish Journal of Theology* 46 (1993), 497–505.

Tore, Nordenstam. "The Essence of Art – Wittgenstein Versus Gadamer," in *International Wittgenstein Symposium* 8 (1983), 23–8.

Tracy, David. "Is There Hope for the Public Realm? Conversation as Interpretation," *Social Research* 65 (1998), 597–609.

Tugendhat, Ernst. "The Fusion of Horizons," in Ernst Tugendhat, *Philosophische Aufsätze*. Frankfurt: Suhrkamp, 1992, pp. 426–32.

Vedder, Ben. "A Written History of Effects: From Concept to Application," in *Language and Linguisticality in Gadamer's Hermeneutics*, pp. 143–54.

Velkely, Richard. "Gadamer and Kant The Critique of Modern Aesthetic Consciousness in *Truth and Method*," *Interpretation* 9 (1981), 353–64.

Verram, V. "Gadamer's Hermeneutics in Italy," *Aut Aut* 242 (1991), 49–60.

Verene, Donald. "Gadamer and Vico on *Sensus Communis* and the Tradition of Human Knowledge," in *The Philosophy of Hans-Georg Gadamer*, pp. 137–53.

Vitkin, Marina. "The Fusion of Horizons on Knowledge and Alterity," *Philosophy and Social Criticism* 21 (1995), 57–76.

Vuyk, Kees. "Understanding and Willing," in *The Specter of Relativism*, pp. 195–205.

Wachterhauser, Brice. "Gadamer's Realism: The 'Belongingness' of Word and Reality," in *Hermeneutics and Truth*, pp. 148–71.

Wachterhauser, Brice. "Interpreting Texts: Objectivity or Participation," *Man and World* 19 (1986), 439–57.

Wachterhauser, Brice. "Prejudice, Reason and Force," *Philosophy* 63 (1988), 231–53.

Wachterhauser, Brice. "Must We Be What We Say? Gadamer on Truth in the Human Sciences," in *Hermeneutics and Modern Philosophy*, pp. 219–40.

Walsh, Robert. "When Love of Knowing Becomes Actual Knowing: Heidegger and Gadamer on Hegel's *die Sache selbst*," *Owl of Minerva* 17 (1986), pp. 163–4.

Warnke, Georgia. "Hermeneutics and the Social Sciences: A Gadamerian Critique of Rorty," *Inquiry* 28 (1985), 339–58.

Warnke, Georgia. "Hermeneutics, Tradition, and the Standpoint of Women," in *Hermeneutics and Truth*, pp. 206–26.

Warnke, Georgia. "Walzer, Rawls, and Gadamer: Hermeneutics and Political Theory," in *Festivals of Interpretation*, pp. 136–60.

Watson, Stephen. "Interpretation, Dialogue, and Friendship: On the Remainder of Community," *Research in Phenomenology* 26 (1996), 54–97.

Weberman, David. "A New Defense of Gadamer's Hermeneutics," *Philosophy and Phenomenological Research* 60 (2000), 45–65.

Weberman, David. "Reconciling Gadamer's Non-Intentionalism with Standard Conversational Goals," *The Philosophical Forum* 30 (1999), 317–28.

Weinsheimer, Joel. "Gadamer's Metaphorical Hermeneutics," in *Gadamer and Hermeneutics*, pp. 181–201.

Westphal, Merold. "Hegel and Gadamer," in *Hermeneutics and Modern Philosophy*, pp. 65–86.

Weiss, Gail. "Dilthey's Conception of Objectivity in the Human Studies: A Reply to Gadamer," *Man and World* 24 (1991), 471–86.

White, Nicholas. "Observations and Questions about H. G. Gadamer's Interpretation of Plato," in *Platonic Writings – Platonic Readings*, edited by C. Griswold (London: Routledge, 1988), pp. 247–57.

Wicks, Robert. "Understanding Gadamer," *Dialogue* 38 (1999), 827–34.

Wright, Kathleen. "The Fusion of Horizons: Hans-Georg Gadamer and Wang Fu-Chih," *Continental Philosophy Review* 33 (2000), 345–58.

Wright, Kathleen. "Literature and Philosophy at the Crossroads," in *Festivals of Interpretation*, pp. 229–48.

Wright, Kathleen. "The Speculative Structure of Language," in *Hermeneutics and Modern Philosophy*, pp. 193–218.

INDEX

Adorno, Theodor, 4, 24
aesthetic(s), 9, 10, 40, 79, 90, 143,
    145, 147, 150, 154–5, 157,
    162, 164
  aesthetic differentiation, 154
  aesthetic non-differentiation, 145,
    150, 152
agreement, 10, 32, 39, 40–2, 50
Albert, Hans, 6
Anaximander, 260
Apel, Karl-Otto, 49
Appiah, K. Anthony, 97
application, 3, 42–3, 46, 68–9, 84, 93, 98,
    110
  apply, 60, 68, 86
Aquinas, Thomas, 66
Arendt, Hannah, 17, 170, 258
Aristotle, 7–8, 16, 18, 24, 28, 38–9, 82–7,
    91, 100, 103, 110, 121–2, 130, 170–1,
    174–81, 192–3, 201–4, 207–14, 216,
    218–220, 226, 248, 250, 256, 258–9,
    262, 269, 272–3
  Aristotelian, 9, 79, 87, 98
  Aristotelianism, 99
art, 9–10, 15, 20, 31–2, 42, 45, 104,
    143–5, 148–50, 153–5, 157–8, 162–3,
    179, 183, 185, 188, 191, 213, 218,
    229, 253–4, 256, 272, 277–9
Augustine, 114, 167, 173–4, 253
Austin, John, 71
authority, 61, 64, 68, 79, 227, 240, 253

Bachelard, Gaston, 130
Bacon, Francis, 28
Barth, Karl, 167–9, 183, 192
Baumgarten, Alexander, 169
beauty (the beautiful), 8–9, 31–2, 145,
    158, 173, 218, 254
being, 1, 4, 29–30, 38, 66, 72, 77, 82, 103,
    105–6, 111, 115, 118, 120, 122–3,

    144, 160, 163, 170, 172, 175, 181,
    184, 202, 210, 213, 216, 235, 248,
    251, 254–5, 258
Betti, Emilio, 4, 6, 25, 179
Bismarck, Otto von, 15
Boeckh, August, 2
Böhlendorff, Casimir, 148
Bonhoeffer, Dietrich, 188
Bormann, Claus von, 44
Braig, Carl, 170
Brentano, Franz, 170
Brown, Peter, 135
Bultmann, Rudolf, 6, 16–7, 28, 168,
    189–90
Buren, John van, 171
Butler, Judith, 97

Caputo, John, 280
care (Sorge), 172, 174, 178
Cassirer, Ernst, 179
Cazalis, Henri, 156
Celan, Paul, 7, 26, 28, 162, 251
Chretien, Jean-Louis, 184
circle, 46–9, 80, 87
  circle, hermeneutic(al), 44, 47–9, 54–5,
    77–8(f), 80–1, 91, 93
Collingwood, R.G., 186
consciousness, 66, 170, 172, 225, 227,
    229, 231–4, 251
  consciousness, aesthetic, 9, 21,
    31, 183
  consciousness, hermeneutic, 184
  consciousness, historical, 25, 92–3,
    183, 205
  consciousness, historically effective,
    102–3, 183, 253
  consciousness, romantic, 183
  consciousness, self-, 172, 183, 188,
    225–6, 229–30, 233–5

conversation, 32, 41, 55–6, 64, 102,
    106–9, 116–7, 127, 134, 182, 184,
    186–8, 203, 228–9, 249, 256–7, 259,
    262–3, 267, 276, 278–9
Cook, Albert, 157
critical theory, 4, 185, 267, 281
Curtius, Ernst, 16

Danto, Arthur, 163
Dasein, 38, 109, 171–2, 178–80, 183,
    185, 204, 229, 253, 255
Davidson, Donald, 75–6, 137–8
de Man, Paul, 146, 151, 162
deconstruction(ism), 4, 151–2, 267,
    276, 281
Democritus, 7
Derrida, Jacques, 4–5, 11, 27–8, 56, 146,
    166(f), 184, 267, 275–81
Descartes, Rene, 62, 168, 176–7
dialectic, 8, 18, 29–31, 95, 108, 111, 117,
    146, 160, 163, 181–3, 186, 188, 202,
    204, 206, 213–4, 216–8, 226, 228,
    230–1, 235, 249, 256–7, 262
dialogue, 8, 27, 41, 45, 63, 74–5, 95, 108,
    184, 187, 202, 204, 206, 231, 247,
    249, 257, 274, 278–9
Dilthey, Wilhelm, 2, 7, 24, 28, 36–8,
    40–1, 149, 172–3, 179, 253, 261
Domin, Hilde, 7
Dostoyevsky, Fyodor, 15
Dworkin, Ronald, 96

Ebeling, Hans, 6
Eliot, T. S., 146, 162
Enlightenment, the, 5, 61, 167, 261,
    271–2
Ernesti, Johann August, 37
epistemology (ical), 10, 36–7, 39–40, 47,
    49, 58, 69–70, 76, 136–7, 167, 171,
    176, 180, 192, 252, 268, 271
ethics, 10, 31–2, 39, 79, 82, 85, 88, 96,
    98, 103–4, 275, 277, 279
Euclid, 41

fallibilism, 70
Farrer, Austin, 185
Fichte, J. G., 105, 169, 233–4, 240–1
finitude, 45, 56–8, 61, 64, 69, 73, 121,
    129, 179, 230, 238, 259, 275
foundationalism, 68–70, 180
Foucault, Michel, 4, 184
Frank, Erich, 20
Frank, Manfred, 6
freedom, 59–63, 68–9, 89–90, 233,
    271–2

Freud, Sigmund, 167
Friedländer, Paul, 17–18
Fuchs, Ernst, 6

Gadamer, Frida, 22
Gadamer, Johannes, 14–15
Galileo, 207
game(s), 67, 111, 185–6, 189, 190(f), 226,
    239, 241
Gehlen, Arnold, 19
George, Stefan, 7, 16, 21
Gibbon, Edward, 135
Gilson, Étienne, 55
Gleispach, Wenzel, 20
Goedeler, Carl, 21–22
Goethe, J. S. von, 7
good, the, 39, 55, 82–3, 87, 103, 177,
    180–3, 193, 204, 211–8
Grondin, Jean, 17

Habermas, Jürgen, 4–5, 11, 26–7,
    66, 87–90, 94, 267–72, 274–5,
    278–9
Hamann, Richard, 15
Harnack, Adolf von, 168
Hartmann, Nicolai, 16
Hegel, G. W. F., 7–8, 11, 19, 26, 28, 77,
    81, 100, 104–5, 109, 122, 128, 146–7,
    151, 153–5, 157–8, 161–5, 168, 179,
    225–246, 256, 262, 277
Heidegger, Hermann, 247
Heidegger, Martin, 1–4, 7–8, 11, 15–19,
    22–25, 27–30, 36–39, 41, 46–50, 56,
    79, 106, 109, 122, 148, 162–3, 166(f),
    167–184, 187, 189, 192, 201–3,
    205–6, 218, 225–7, 230–1, 237,
    239–40, 247–62, 276, 278
Heisenberg, Werner, 20
Henry, Michel, 184
Heraclitus, 7, 123
Herder, Johann Gottfried, 7, 19, 21, 226,
    249
Hermann, Wilhelm, 168
Hirsch, E. D., 4
historicism, 4, 25, 205, 225
historicity, 58, 65, 80, 92, 104, 173
history, effective (Wirkungsgeschichte),
    3, 49–50, 65, 80, 121, 142, 237
Hitler, Adolf, 18–9, 21–22, 40
Hölderlin, Friedrich, 7, 29, 106, 147–8,
    151–2, 159, 162–4
Homer, 260
horizon(s), 3, 97, 103, 112, 118–20,
    133–6, 138, 153, 184, 188, 190,
    205–6, 218, 229, 236, 252, 273, 276

horizons, fusion of
 (*Horizontverschmelzung*), 3, 134–6,
 138–142, 206, 229, 254, 273,
 276, 281
Horkheimer, Max, 4, 24
humanism, 21, 23–4
Hume, David, 76
Husserl, Edmund, 3–4, 16, 18, 27,
 29, 151–2, 168–72, 201, 237,
 248–53, 262

idealism, 10, 31, 237–8, 262
idealism, aesthetic, 146
Idealism, German, 19, 225, 233
idealism, linguistic, 4, 75
Immerman, Karl, 7
incarnation, 114, 119, 122, 192
intentionality, 170

Jaeger, Werner, 212
Jaspers, Karl, 18, 24, 28
Jauss, Hans-Robert, 5
John Paul II, Pope, 6, 30
Jonas, Hans, 17

Kant, Immanuel, 28, 62, 91, 99–100,
 105, 162, 168–9, 176, 229, 232–3,
 240–1, 252–3, 260, 271
Kierkegaard, Søren, 15, 168, 173,
 179, 230
Kiesel, Theodore, 171
Klein, Jakob, 17, 222(f), 258
Krauss, Werner, 22
Krebs, Engelbert, 171
Kristeva, Julia, 156
Kroner, Richard, 20, 28
Krüger, Gerhard, 17, 25, 28, 170, 258
Kuhn, Helmut, 24, 190
Kuhn, Thomas, 6, 54, 130, 238

Lask, Emil, 170
Lehmann, Karl, 170
Leibniz, G. W., 169
Lekebusch, Katie, 22
Lessing, Gotthold, 167
Lessing, Theodor, 15
Levinas, Emmanuel, 184, 277
life-philosophy (*Lebensphilosophie*), 2,
 171, 227
lifeworld (*Lebenswelt*), 123, 238, 252
linguisticality, 2, 28, 41–2, 102, 106,
 111, 128–9, 155
Lipps, Hans, 28
listen (listening), 107, 128, 257
Locke, John, 168, 232

logos, 8, 114, 178, 180, 201, 203, 207,
 209, 211, 214, 259, 262
Lotze, Hermann, 170
Löwith, Karl, 17, 25, 28, 170,
 179–80, 249
Luther, Martin, 147, 152, 173–4, 191
Lyotard, Jean-Francois, 4

Mallarmè, Stephane, 146–7, 150–1,
 153–60, 162–4
Marion, Jean Luc, 184
Marquard, Odo, 48
Marx, Karl, 167
Melanchthon, Phillip, 16, 47
McDowell, John, 59–61, 75–76
meaning(s), 4, 11, 28, 41, 43, 61, 76–7,
 99–100, 104, 108, 112–3, 116–23,
 130, 132, 149, 152–3, 170, 172–3,
 189, 205–6, 210, 228, 230, 232,
 236–7, 239, 279
metaphysics, 9–10, 30, 76, 169, 171, 173,
 183–4, 229, 260–1, 277–8
method, 2, 7, 10, 231, 251–2
methodologism, 2
methodology, 2, 38, 45, 227, 229, 236
mimesis, 9, 117, 149–50
modernity, 5, 11, 154, 231, 267, 272
Morus, Samuel, 37

Nagel, Thomas, 52
National Socialism (Nazism), 2, 19–24,
 33–4(f), 249–50
Natorp, Paul, 15–6, 28, 248, 250
neo-Kantianism, 15–16, 168–72, 175–6,
 181, 225, 227, 237
Nietzsche, Friedrich, 24, 27–8, 56, 167,
 179–80, 239, 258, 260–1, 276, 279
Nussbaum, Martha, 97–8

objectivity, 23, 44, 52, 92, 126, 170
Ockham, William, 177
ontology (ical), 1, 3, 16, 31, 46, 50, 76,
 102–5, 118, 122–3, 138, 145–7, 156,
 159, 169, 176, 183, 204, 209, 212,
 214, 219, 252–4, 271
Orozco, Teresa, 33(f), 221(f)
Ott, Hugo, 170
Overbeck, Franz, 190

Parmenides, 7, 220, 231, 260
Paul, Jean, 16
Paul, 17, 173–4, 190
phenomenology (ical), 3, 8, 16, 31,
 47–49, 146, 169–70, 172, 186, 206,
 237, 250–2, 262

phronesis, 8, 31, 38, 178–82, 192, 212, 214–5, 253, 256, 274–5, 279–80
Plato, 7–9, 11, 15, 18–20, 26, 28–31, 38–40, 43–4, 47, 77, 82–3, 95, 116–7, 130, 144, 177–8, 181–3, 186, 193, 201–20, 226–7, 231, 248–9, 251, 256–9, 262, 265(f)
play, 104, 119, 132, 185–6, 189, 200(f), 239, 277
Plotinus, 7
poetry, 9–10, 20, 26, 31, 145–65, 191, 254
Pöggeler, Otto, 170
politics, 10, 14–5, 19–20, 31–2, 33(f), 79, 82, 88, 98, 126, 131, 181, 205, 238, 250, 274–5, 277
postmodernism, 4, 130
poststructuralism, 146–7, 156
practice (*praxis*), 10, 31, 39, 83–4, 86, 100, 104, 176, 180, 205, 214, 220, 269, 279–80
pragmatics, 82
prejudice(s), 3, 27, 44–5, 50, 72, 79, 82, 92, 95, 132, 146, 184, 225, 236, 272
pre-Socratics, 8, 201, 258–60
Protagoras, 116
Protarchus, 217
psychoanalysis, 27, 270
Putnam, Hilary, 52–4, 273

question(s), 8, 58, 81, 86, 91, 94, 102, 108–12, 116–7, 121, 135, 138, 141, 171, 184, 186–8, 203, 207, 212–4, 218, 220, 230–2, 271, 279
Quine, W. V. O., 238

Rabinow, Paul, 5
realism, 10, 52, 66
  realist, 66, 75, 77
reason, 14, 55, 57, 64, 73, 79, 82, 90, 185, 203, 214, 240, 270–1
  reason, practical, 8, 82, 180, 226, 253, 256, 273
reduction, eidetic, 151
reduction, phenomenological, 152
reduction, transcendental, 172
reflection, 56, 59–61, 88, 90, 105, 119, 154–5, 209, 231–5, 234–5, 238, 241, 270, 272, 274
Reinhardt, Karl, 28
relativism, 1, 4, 10, 25, 42, 44, 52–3, 71–2, 99, 126, 130, 134, 144, 227
Richardson, William, 170
Rickert, Heinrich, 170
Ricoeur, Paul, 6, 184

Rilke, Rainer Maria, 7, 29, 40–41, 147, 150, 158–61, 163–4, 175
Ritschl, Albrecht, 168
romanticism, 21, 147, 157, 164
Rorty, Richard, 5, 54, 56
Rousseau, Jean-Jacques, 238

Sartre, Jean-Paul, 146
Scheler, Max, 16, 28, 237
Schelling, Friedrich, 19, 122, 168, 230
Schleiermacher, Friedrich, 7, 37, 80, 100, 172, 253
Schmitt, Carl, 179
Schweitzer, Albert, 168
Schubert, Franz, 43
science(s), 2, 6–7, 9, 14, 22–23, 30–1, 52, 91, 127–31, 134, 141–2, 154, 172, 174, 178, 203, 214–5, 250, 260–1, 271, 273
  natural science(s), 14, 52, 130–1, 220, 225, 261, 268
  historical-hermeneutical sciences, 27, 269–70
  human science(s) (*Geisteswissenschaften*), 2–3, 5–6, 11, 21, 31, 36–9, 127, 130, 140–1, 184, 236–7, 241, 253, 270–1
  nomothetical science, 135
  social science(s), 5, 26, 31, 39, 92, 126, 139, 268, 270–1, 274
scientism, 1, 180, 252
Scotus, Duns, 169–70, 177
Seebohm, Thomas, 4, 6
Sellars, Wilfrid, 59–60, 241
Shakespeare, William, 14, 230
Sheehan, Thomas, 170, 194(f)
skepticism, 58, 69–70, 72
Socrates, 31–2, 83, 95, 204, 208–9, 211–3, 215, 217–20
sophists, the, 116, 212–3
Sophocles, 40–1
Spinoza, Baruch, 167
Stenzel, Julius, 208, 231
Strauss, Leo, 4, 17, 25, 27, 170, 181, 221(f), 258
Strauss, David Friedrich, 168
Suarez, Francisco, 169–70
subjectivism, 31, 42, 168, 189, 229, 262
subjectivity, 105, 157, 183, 226, 228–9, 231, 237–9
Sullivan, William, 5

Taminiaux, Jacques, 170–1
tarry, tarrying, 250, 256

technique (*techne*), 10, 108, 177, 212–4, 218, 269
  technical, 83–5, 213, 268
technology, 9, 30–1, 45, 258, 261
temporality, 81, 92, 98, 252–3, 255
  temporal distance, 45–6
text(s), 2, 10, 28, 38–40, 80–1, 95, 110–3, 119, 121, 123, 126, 132, 134, 143–4, 148, 152–3, 155, 162, 169, 179, 187–9, 191, 206, 216, 219, 228, 232, 236, 258, 270, 275, 277–9
  text, eminent, 191–2
Taylor, Charles, 162, 166(f)
Thales, 260
theory, 8, 10, 31, 43, 53, 81–2, 104, 181, 214, 220, 229, 233, 235, 250, 258, 269–70, 273–4
Tillich, Paul, 24
time, 45, 64–5
Tracy, David, 184
tradition(s), 3, 5, 27, 30, 37, 40, 54, 58, 60–5, 67–8, 73, 79, 81, 87–8, 91–3, 95, 121, 136, 202, 205–6, 219, 228, 235, 253, 257, 262, 272–3, 277–9

transcendental philosophy, 58, 252
Troeltsch, Ernst, 168
truth, 2, 5, 8–10, 31, 52–3, 55, 88, 95, 126, 128, 132, 134–5, 145, 147, 149, 153, 176, 180, 183–5, 203, 211, 220, 228, 253–5, 262, 271, 275, 277–8
truthfulness, 150

Ulbricht, Walter, 23

Valery, Paul, 43
Vattimo, Gianni, 6, 184
Vorhandenheit, 49, 176–7, 193, 248, 258

Walzer, Michael, 88–91
Wartenburg, Graf Yorck von, 173
Weinsheimer, Joel, 145
Wiehl, Reiner, 154
Williams, Bernard, 52
Williams, Rowan, 188
Wittgenstein, Ludwig, 123, 188
Wolff, Christian, 169
Wolin, Richard, 33–4(f)

Zeno, 230